Internet Pricing

European University Studies
Europäische Hochschulschriften
Publications Universitaires Européennes

Series V
Economics and Management

Reihe V Série V
Volks- und Betriebswirtschaft
Sciences économiques

Vol./Band 3137

PETER LANG
Bern · Berlin · Bruxelles · Frankfurt am Main · New York · Oxford · Wien

Andrea Graber

Internet Pricing

Economic Approaches to Transport Services and Infrastructure

PETER LANG
Bern · Berlin · Bruxelles · Frankfurt am Main · New York · Oxford · Wien

Bibliographic information published by Die Deutsche Bibliothek
Die Deutsche Bibliothek lists this publication in the Deutsche Nationalbibliografie; detailed bibliographic data is available on the Internet at ‹http://dnb.ddb.de›.

British Library and Library of Congress Cataloguing-in-Publication Data: A catalogue record for this book is available from *The British Library*, Great Britain, and from *The Library of Congress*, USA.

The Faculty of Economics and Social Sciences at the University of Freiburg neither approves nor disapproves the opinions expressed in a doctoral dissertation. They are to be considered those of the author (decision of the Faculty Council of 23 January 1990).

ISSN 0531-7339
ISBN 3-03910-670-8
US-ISBN 0-8204-7550-5

To my parents
and Basile

Foreword

This book is my Ph.D. thesis which I wrote at the chair of Microeconomics and Empirical Economic Research, Faculty of Economics and Social Sciences, University of Freiburg, Switzerland. In December 2003, the thesis was completed in content. State-of-the-art statements in this work refer to this date. Since Internet technologies and pricing practices can change rapidly, some of these statements may no longer be up-to-date when this book is published.

I would like to take the opportunity to thank the persons who have, in one way or the other, made this thesis possible. Special gratitude goes to my Ph.D. supervisor, Professor Reiner Wolff, for his detailed and constructive comments and for his important support throughout this work, to my second referee, Professor Wolfgang Eichhorn, for his straightforwardness as well as for his valuable and encouraging advice, and to Professor Stephanie Teufel, for taking part in the doctoral examination commission and bringing in her vast technical and practical knowledge about the Internet economy.

Members of the Department of Quantitative Economics, especially Dr. J.-F. Emmenegger, Michael Beer, and Yavuz Karagoek, are thanked for numerous stimulating discussions as well as for their help with mathematical and Latex problems. In particular, I wish to thank Yavuz for being a congenial office colleague.

Many thanks to Dr. Adrian Turtschi for all the competent answers to my questions concerning Internet technology and practice. Also, I am very grateful to Clare O'Dea for revising the English of my manuscript. A big thank you goes to Dr. Peter Mantsch for his support, general advice, and encouragement.

Above all, I would like to express my deep gratitude to my 'backbone' – my family and my friends for their endless support, care, and cheering up, and Basile for his understanding, patience, and encouragement when it was most required.

Contents

List of Figures

List of Tables

1. The Internet Pricing Debate

> There should be pricing – pricing in markets that have choice and competition. It's not that I think only one particular pricing structure will work. I'm saying the current structure is inadequate because it's either free or flat. It does not approximate cost or value or competition anywhere near close enough to be a viable economic model [...] I think the marketplace will tolerate a wide variety of pricing mechanisms. My prediction is – and my advice is – that we should welcome experiments which attempt to approximate cost and value in the prices.
>
> Bob Metcalfe ([117], p. 17)

The Internet is a worldwide network of computers and computer networks that transports digital data. It has evolved from a research network to a commercial and integrated network, a network that simultaneously supports voice, video, and data services, with heterogeneous user demand. For successful delivery of data, interconnection between the different networks is critical. Interconnection creates positive network externalities. Positive network externalities arise if the utility of a subscriber to a network increases with additional subscribers. These positive network externalities have led to a high growth in the number of Internet users. Due to this process of growth and to the introduction of bandwidth-hungry applications such as video on demand or Peer-to-Peer (P2P) file sharing, demand is likely to exceed supply of bandwidth[1] resulting in network congestion.

The problem of network overload can be approached both from the supply and from the demand side of the market. On the supply side, capacity can be increased, the method adopted so far. This approach to handling congestion was named 'fat dumb pipe model.'[2] The problem with this approach is that somewhere in the Internet there will

1 Bandwidth refers to the amount of data units a network can transmit in a given time period. It is usually expressed in the number of bits transferred per second. We will use the term bandwidth loosely and let it designate transmission and router capacity.

2 Odlyzko ([181], p. 2).

always be bottlenecks where congestion occurs. On the demand side of the market, network capacity may either be rationed or appropriate pricing may be introduced. Appropriate prices are efficient prices that allocate resources to users who value them the highest.

While network engineers generally consider user behavior as fixed and focus on the supply side of the market, economists tend to view technology and capacity as given and investigate the design of a resource allocation mechanism that provides appropriate incentives such that demand matches supply. These two approaches are complementary. Nevertheless, we will concentrate on the second approach, i.e., we will consider pricing to be the primary instrument to manage data traffic, while having in mind technical solutions to the congestion problem.

In practice, pricing of network services is often done heuristically. Popular flat rates lack incentives to limit usage of scarce bandwidth. Instead, they induce users to overuse the network. This overuse triggers congestion and congestion externalities. Congestion externalities are the costs in the form of waiting times and unrealized data transmissions that a single user may impose on other users without having to pay for the inconveniences caused. This constellation results in the so-called tragedy of the commons, where a common resource is overused due to wrong price incentives.[3] Evidence of this tragedy is given by the fact that the introduction of unlimited Internet access for a one-off payment of £50 by Breathe, an Internet Service Provider (ISP) based in Great Britain, resulted in a demand explosion the provider could not cope with. At first, the lack of capacity forced the ISP to skim off the heaviest 1% of Internet users and, finally, to close the service.[4] Similarly, when America Online (AOL) switched from a time-based to a flat-rated pricing scheme in 1996, it initially could not handle the surge in demand. In consequence, AOL was forced to pay extensive compensation to unsatisfied users.[5]

We can conclude that popular flat rates lead to an inefficient allocation of resources: Capacity is often allocated to users with the

---

3 See Hardin [105].

4 See McIntosh [167].

5 See Stiller et al. ([231], p. 21).

lowest opportunity costs of time instead of being allocated to users with the highest valuations for some service.

The solution to the allocation problem is to find a price mechanism that internalizes negative congestion externalities. With the implementation of such a pricing system the network is used as long as the value of an additional unit of network usage, e.g., the transmission of an extra data packet, exceeds the marginal costs of this network use. In other words, network usage is increased until marginal costs of data transfer correspond to the price. Since physical marginal costs of data transport are negligible as long as the network is not overloaded, marginal transport costs are determined by negative congestion externalities.

Note that the aim is not to totally eliminate congestion. Total elimination of congestion would require large amounts of excess capacity to accommodate peak Internet usage demands. Since Internet traffic is bursty, as will be explained in Section 2.2.2, this would result in large amounts of unused capacity during long time periods, i.e., in excess capacity installed.

The migration from a flat rate to a usage-based pricing[6] scheme may be beneficial to both users and ISPs. On the one hand, users who generate less than average traffic demand, which is used to calculate the flat rate, subsidize users who generate more than average traffic demand when being priced at that flat rate.[7] Light users would thus gain by switching to a usage-based pricing plan. On the other hand, ISPs that mainly attract heavy users, also called power users, may completely fail to recover costs, incur losses, and drop out of the market.

Apart from the network load, the offered Quality of Service (QoS) also has to be integrated into the pricing mechanism. Not all applications have the same demands regarding timely delivery and loss tolerance, i.e., concerning QoS. While delay is not a serious problem

---

6 The expression 'usage-based pricing' refers to both volume-based pricing and time-based pricing. In this work usage-based pricing usually refers to volume-based pricing.

7 Henceforth, for the purpose of simplification, we will call users who generate less (more) than average traffic demand 'light users' ('heavy users').

for email, for example, real-time applications such as video on demand are worthless in the event of delay. Today, the Internet offers a best-effort data transmission service which means that bandwidth is allocated among users as well as possible and as soon as possible, without giving any quality guarantees. The only service differentiation that can be found in today's Internet are different access bandwidths providing different transmission rates, priced at a flat rate that depends on the maximal capacity. Users who only occasionally need high bandwidths must either lease overprovisioned dedicated lines or accept best-effort quality.

Overprovisioning is widely used as a method to provide QoS in private networks that, in consequence, show low utilization rates.[8] This highlights the existence of demand for QoS. Further evidence of the existing demand for QoS is given by the emergence of streaming providers such as Akamai, Digital Islands, or Abovenet. Streaming providers offer services for fast transmission of multimedia applications over their own networks, called overnets. They install servers at networks of important ISPs and supply these servers with information over their own networks. That way, streaming providers avoid potential congestion at interconnection points. This technique allows the delivery of multimedia, audio and video files, as well as Television (TV) and radio services over the Internet.[9]

With the commercialization and the growth of the Internet, user preferences have become more heterogeneous with respect to tolerance of performance degradation. As a consequence, users' willingnesses to pay may vary widely. Moreover, the development of e-commerce makes QoS a critical factor. For all these reasons we claim that in the Internet market there is room for ISPs in a higher price segment if they can offer faster navigation and different service qualities.

By offering different service qualities, network resources can be assigned to applications that are most performance sensitive, such as real-time applications like voice or video on demand that do not

8 See Odlyzko ([185], p. 356).
9 See Borchers ([28], p. 60).

tolerate delay. Prices for different QoS levels must differ in order to induce an appropriate use of multiple service classes.

We will distinguish between relative and guaranteed QoS. Relative QoS can be implemented with the current version of the Internet Protocol, Internet Protocol version 4 (IPv4), without major modifications: Relative QoS requires priority numbers to be included in each packet header, for example in the precedence field that is currently unused. Routers must be programmed such that packets with higher priorities are forwarded faster than packets with lower priorities. Relative QoS does not allow for guaranteed QoS. But higher priority packets encounter relatively smaller delay since routers forward these packets first if congestion occurs.

When offering guaranteed QoS, ISPs make explicit and quantified promises on the QoS provided. Therefore, resources must be reserved along the entire transmission path from the sender to the receiver. Moreover, an admission control is necessary that checks the availability of the required resources. An application request is only admitted if indeed enough resources are available.

There is a diversity of opinions concerning the question of whether scarcity of Internet resources is a temporary or a permanent phenomenon: It is argued that there will be a bandwidth glut due to considerable investments in capacity in the core network, the backbones, coupled with advances in optical networking and routing technologies such as Dense Wavelength Division Multiplexing (DWDM). Evidence of supply exceeding demand in backbone networks is given by the rapid decline in prices for backbone links in recent years. In consequence, attempts to internalize congestion externalities and to differentiate quality would be superfluous. Nevertheless, carriers are continuing to expand Internet backbone capacity, albeit at a lower growth rate. Growth of capacity in Internet backbones was estimated to be 74% in 2003. Bleich, Kuri, and Vogt ([25], p. 185) argue that if providers abstain from expanding capacity, in 2005 bottlenecks will appear in the Internet.

The experience of past years shows that higher bandwidth in particular generates bandwidth-intensive applications such as video transmissions in real-time. These applications are generally only rendered possible by the higher supply of capacity. Correspondingly, Say's Law states that supply creates demand. In other words, Say's Law claims that any installed capacity will finally be saturated. Say's Law goes back to the French economist Jean-Baptiste Say (1767–1832). According to Say's Law there can be no bandwidth glut in the long run. In this work we start from the hypothesis that Say's Law holds.

Let us give some motivations to support this hypothesis: First, excess capacity cannot be observed everywhere in the Internet. Bandwidth-intensive applications such as video often require more capacity than available. A sports video or a video in Digital Video Disk (DVD) quality, for example, require transmission speeds in ranges from 500 kilobits per second[10] (Kbps) to 1.5 megabits per second (Mbps) and from 6 to 8 Mbps, respectively.[11] In comparison, ADSL (Asymmetric Digital Subscriber Line) technology typically provides retail customers with a downstream speed of 256 or 512 Kbps and an upstream speed of 64 or 128 Kbps.

Even though currently capacity is generally available in excess in the core of the Internet, it is limited at the borders. However, this may not hold true for some particular cases. Not either does it have to apply permanently. So far, the Internet has experienced many changes in technology, user behavior, utilization, and applications and it is very likely that this will continue to be the case. In particular, even though capacity is currently available in excess in the core network there are less and less carriers willing to manage this capacity given the price decline for backbone links. If one backbone carrier goes bankrupt as a consequence of this price decline the core network will shrink. Unsatisfactory profitability in the core network due to low prices will discourage new carriers from getting into the business.

10 In the metric system, a kilobit equals 1000 (10^3) bits while in binary terms one kilobit equals 1024 (2^{10}) bits. To alleviate this ambiguity, in 1998, prefixes for binary multiples such as kibi (=2^{10}), mebi (=2^{20}), or gibi (=2^{30}) have been adopted by the International Electrotechnical Commission (IEC). The decimal version is always used to measure the bit rate. Hence, a kilobit per second means 1000 bits per second. See http://www.e-paranoids.com/b/bi/binary_prefix.html (15.01.05).

11 See Huerlimann ([110], p. B7).

Accordingly, there will be less or even insufficient bandwidth supplied. Then, prices for backbone links as well as profitability will be likely to rise again which in turn will render market entry attractive.

We can conclude that bottlenecks may change. Here, we do not try to localize existing bottlenecks in the Internet. Instead, it is argued that the location of bottlenecks can change over time and that it depends on the technical and economic environment.[12]

Second, data traffic is characterized by arbitrarily long bursts of traffic that occur at random. These bursts may trigger sudden congestion anywhere in the Internet.

Third, broadband Internet access technologies priced at flat rates incite users to generate huge volumes of data traffic.[13] An example of popular bandwidth-hungry applications are P2P file sharing services such as Napster and KaZaA that lead to congestion and profit problems faced by many ISPs.[14] Recent studies point out that about 60% of traffic on any given ISP network is generated by file sharing activities.[15] Given that bandwidth is a scarce resource and given the growth of Internet demand and the emergence of bandwidth-hungry and delay-sensitive applications, such as remote consultations for surgeries as well as audio and video on demand, we consider bandwidth to be a costly and congestible resource.

It was already mentioned that the Internet is all about connectivity. Any two computers on the Internet can only communicate with each other provided that there are thousands of connectivity agreements, called Service Level Agreements (SLAs), between networks owned by different entities. To ensure interconnection of various networks, each ISP must be compensated for its investments in infrastructure and for conveyed data. There may be many ISPs involved in the delivery of data to an end-user who purchases the

12 According to Nelson ([174], pp. 464–466) main sources of congestion are routers, server capacity at destination, switches of the PSTN (Public Switched Telephone Network), PSTN lines, and the modem pools.

13 Note that, initially, heavy users were constrained in their bandwidth consumption by analog dial-up Internet access allowing transmission speeds of up to 56 Kbps.

14 See Maitland [154].

15 See Sandvine ([205], p. 2).

service from one ISP only, namely from her Internet Access Provider (IAP). Therefore, inter-provider financial settlements[16] become necessary. However, well-defined settlement schemes do not exist in today's Internet. Often, there are either no settlements made or flat rate settlement agreements based on the capacity of the onward link are set up.

A consequence of this settlement policy is the absence of accurate price signals indicating where to expand capacity. This might be a reason why Internet Backbone Providers (IBPs) have installed excess fiber optic capacity in core long-haul networks, while, at the same time, congestion occurs at interconnection and access points as well as at downstream links from the backbones to smaller ISPs, specifically those aggregating modem traffic.[17] Therefore, as Internet traffic generally transits several networks from the sender to the receiver, users encounter quality degradations due to congestion, despite excess capacity in the core network.

Note that wholesale interconnection pricing agreements are closely related to retail pricing models: An ISP that pays volume-based interconnection fees incurs a financial risk when offering flat rates to its end-users. Hence, not only retail prices but also interconnection charges should reflect network usage. Both interconnection fees and retail pricing schemes have to be compatible in order to transmit appropriate incentives. This implies that a multi-service network requires interconnection charges to be differentiated with respect to the QoS offered.

As already noted above, the current Internet lacks well-defined pricing models and cost recovery schemes, both between ISPs and their retail clients and between interconnected ISPs. One might argue that established retail and interconnection pricing models designed for voice networks should be applied to the Internet. However, two reasons refute this proposition: First, technical characteristics of the traditional telecommunications network and the Internet are

16 Settlements are also called interconnection, access, or termination charges. They are financial transfers between ISPs to receive interconnection and interoperability.

17 See Semret ([210], p. 5) and Odlyzko ([185], p. 346).

distinct, leading to different cost drivers.[18] Second, while retail and interconnection pricing schemes applied in traditional telecommunications networks have been subject to regulation, or at least subject to close regulatory supervision, there is no global authority which regulates the Internet.[19]

To summarize, with the development of the Internet from a research network to a commercial and integrated network with heterogeneous user demand, appropriate pricing is a requisite for the following reasons: First, pricing is a tool to control congestion and to realize an efficient allocation of scarce resources. Second, differentiated prices can accommodate both applications with different requirements on QoS and heterogeneous user demand. Third, it is essential to account and charge users for network usage in order to allow ISPs to recover costs.

This work deals with pricing related to resource allocation and will, except in Sections 4.2.2 and 4.2.3, not focus on pricing strategies emerging from competition for subscribers among different networks, i.e., we do not concentrate on strategic interaction between firms. Also, throughout the analysis, the focus is on pricing data transport services. Content pricing and billing[20] issues will be left aside. At least, the final chapter provides a primer on bundling data transport and information services.

The aim and the contribution of this work are to give an overview of Internet pricing proposals, to classify, investigate, and evaluate pricing schemes as well as to elaborate on relations between them. Our evaluations of the pricing proposals are based on normative criteria for Internet pricing mechanisms we establish in Section 2.2.3. There is a large variety of proposed Internet pricing schemes in both the technical and economic research literature. Not every pricing approach can be treated. However, both classical and central pricing schemes are analyzed while references are made to and general in-

---

18 As will be further explained in Section 2.1.2 the Internet is a packet-switched network while the traditional telecommunications network is circuit-switched.

19 See Laffont et al. ([135], p. 288).

20 Billing 'involves collecting charge information over a given period and communicating this to the customer in the form of a bill'. Songhurst ([223], p. 2).

formation is given on related pricing approaches. While some pricing proposals are explicitly designed for the Internet environment, other pricing proposals, such as nonlinear outlay schedules and peak-load pricing, presented in Sections 3.1.2 and 3.1.3, respectively, have been adapted to fit the Internet environment. In the framework of nonlinear pricing analyzed in Section 3.1.2, we propose to allocate fixed costs according to usage while charging an additional variable price component for each unit of data traffic demanded that equals marginal costs of data transport. We call the resulting pricing scheme ex-post weighted-average Coase tariff. Section 3.5 provides an evaluation synopsis of the pricing models presented in Chapter 3. We will find that none of the presented pricing proposals meets all normative criteria for Internet pricing set up in Section 2.2.3 at best. However, we will examine how different pricing proposals can be combined in order to satisfy these criteria as well as possible. Furthermore, wholesale interconnection pricing agreements will be analyzed in Chapter 4. Also, the compatibility of the different retail pricing schemes, introduced in Chapter 3, with the interconnection pricing models, presented in Chapter 4, will be determined. Moreover, we will show that congestion pricing for interconnected networks exhibits the same desirable characteristics as congestion pricing for retail customers presented in Section 3.3.1, namely that appropriate settlements make the decentralized private optimum correspond to the social optimum.

The structure of this work is as follows: First, the basics of the Internet economy will be introduced, starting with the architectural and technical framework that includes Internet history and that comments on different Internet access technologies. To determine prices for Internet data transmission, network costs must be known. Network costs and network externalities, the latter of which may be positive and negative, will be the focus of Section 2.2.1. Moreover, the design of acceptable pricing models requires the analysis of user demand characteristics. These are investigated in the subsequent section. User demand experiments suggest that users are willing to pay a premium price to be offered a flat rate and, at the same time, endorse the possibility of obtaining higher QoS on demand. The final section of Chapter 2 introduces normative criteria for Internet pricing mechanisms. We will distinguish between desired characteristics from the welfare theoretic point of view and from the individual perspectives of ISPs as well as Internet users.

Chapter 3 gives an overview of proposed pricing mechanisms for Internet transport services. The pricing proposals presented are classified according to the QoS offered. The first section covers pricing proposals for a single service network with best-effort service. Then, pricing proposals designed for relative priorities will be presented. Many pricing schemes fall into this category. Therefore, a distinction is made between load-insensitive and load-sensitive pricing proposals. While the former pricing proposals are independent of network loads, the latter approaches include network externalities in the pricing structure. Finally, Section 3.4 introduces pricing proposals for network environments with guaranteed QoS. Each section of Chapter 3 evaluates the proposed pricing scheme according to the normative criteria formulated in Section 2.2.3. A synopsis of the evaluations of all pricing models presented is given in Section 3.5.

We already pointed out that retail pricing models and wholesale interconnection arrangements between ISPs are closely related. Some of the retail pricing proposals, namely dynamic priority pricing, expected capacity pricing, dynamic volume pricing, effective bandwidth pricing, and resource-based pricing, already include a solution on how to price traffic exchanged between different ISPs. This bottom-up approach, where, given the proposed retail pricing model, a compatible interconnection pricing solution is presented, will be complemented with a top-down approach in Chapter 4 that focuses on interconnection settlements and analyzes which retail pricing structures match the proposed interconnection pricing models. In Section 4.1, a positive economic analysis of interconnection pricing will be made, suggesting that the interconnection market is inefficient due to the absence of accurate price signals and a lack of both price transparency and dynamics. Section 4.2 discusses optimal interconnection models. Both Sections 4.1 and 4.2 on positive and normative economic analysis of interconnection pricing, respectively, focus on network environments with one service class. Section 4.3, which is also based on normative economics, introduces QoS requirements into the analysis of interconnection pricing. In this context, two auction mechanisms for electronic market places are presented: The double auction and the progressive second price auction. The latter has already been implemented in the framework of Merkato, a software platform which creates electronic market places and which is used commercially to automate buying, selling, and allocating bandwidth dynamically in real-time. The advantage of using auctions as a pricing method is that appropriate auction rules allow the achievement of an efficient allocation of resources with a minimum of informational requirements. Auctions become especially attractive when the seller has major difficulties in obtaining information on demand valuations, as is the case in the Internet. A summary of Chapter 4 can be found in Section 4.4. The final chapter concludes and provides a primer on bundling strategies.

In this work, we will analyze several optimization problems which require conditions of second order to be checked. Generally, we will not explicitly specify sufficient conditions for relative extrema but content ourselves with considering in which cases these conditions are satisfied. However, in Appendix A, on the basis of a utility maximization problem, we exemplarily illustrate how to test whether conditions of second order are met.

The reader will find that it has become customary to use acronyms in the Internet and in the telecommunications industry. Such acronyms used in this work can be found in Appendix B. Appendix C explains specific expressions of the Internet and the telecommunications industry.

2. Basics of the Internet Economy

Technology changes. Economic laws do not.

Shapiro and Varian ([218], p. 2)

2.1 Architectural and Technical Framework

2.1.1 Internet History and Architecture

The Internet started its development in 1969 when the Advanced Research Projects Agency (ARPA), a division of the U.S. Department of Defense, created the first packet-switched network,[1] named ARPANET, which allowed single data packets to be independently transmitted between two computers. In 1985 the success of ARPANET prompted the National Science Foundation (NSF) to found and fund the NSFNET, the first Internet backbone.

In the beginning, the Internet was structured hierarchically with three layers: At the top, the NSFNET operated as the single backbone. Several mid-level or regional networks, consisting of ten to thirty universities each, were connected to the backbone. The bottom layer comprised Local Area Networks (LANs) such as campus networks connecting to a mid-level network. With this structure, full connectivity prevailed.

Gradually, commercial backbones emerged to meet the needs of the commercial user community. But the Acceptable Use Policy (AUP) restricted commercial traffic on the NSFNET. The need to meet the emerging demand of commercial traffic exchange led to the formation of a Network Access Point (NAP) called Commercial Internet

1 Technical elements of the Internet will be explained in the next section.

Exchange (CIX) in August 1991, founded by three commercial backbones, CERFNet, Performance Systems International (PSI), and AlterNet. Each member of the CIX was charged an annual membership fee. In a multilateral agreement, the exchange of traffic was agreed to be free of settlement charges. The creation of the CIX was followed by the Metropolitan Area Exchange-East (MAE-East), the MAE-West, and the U.S. Federal Internet Exchanges (FIX-East and West). Unlike the CIX, all other NAPs in the United States were predominantly based on bilateral agreements where an interconnecting network pays the operator of the NAP to place a router at the NAP and for interconnection with the exchange architecture. Without obligation, each Internet provider may thereafter conclude bilateral agreements with other operators connected to the exchange point. The advantage of this model is its flexibility as not each Internet provider connecting to the exchange point has to interconnect with every other carrier.

Until 1995, each Internet provider had to connect directly or via another provider to the NSFNET backbone. In April 1995 the NSF stopped funding NSFNET operation, judging the technology mature enough to be provided more efficiently by the private market. To ease the transition towards a predominantly privately managed Internet, the NSF created and funded several NAPs.[2] Concretely, the purpose was to promote interconnection and to prevent a balkanization of the Internet since Internet providers were not required to interconnect. By August 1996, NAPS also existed in Europe including the London Internet Exchange (LINX) and MAE-Paris.[3]

In the terminology of Bailey ([9], pp. 163–165), NAPs in the United States predominantly rely on the third-party administrator model where the exchange is run by an independent profit-oriented firm not operating a network. In Europe, NAPs are mostly based on

2 Precisely, the four NAPs founded were the New York NAP operated by Sprint, the San Francisco NAP managed by Bellcore and Pacific Bell, the Chicago NAP run by Bellcore and Ameritech, and the Washington D.C. NAP conducted by Metropolitan Fiber Systems (MFS Corporation). See Farnon and Huddle ([71], p. 379).

3 See Farnon and Huddle ([71], pp. 378–381). Consider as well Huston ([114], Chapter 1) for comments on the history of the Internet.

a cooperative agreement. The exchange is run by a non-profit committee composed of the interconnecting firms with the objective to recover costs.

While Internet Backbone Providers (IBPs), also called core providers, exchanged traffic at NAPs under so-called public peering agreements, smaller companies, ISPs, accessed the Internet via backbones. With increasing utilization of the Internet these public NAPs became susceptible to congestion, resulting in delays and dropped packets. In consequence, large backbones began to directly interconnect with each other through so-called private peering arrangements and started to charge transit fees[4] for providing interconnection to smaller providers.[5] Usually, private peering partners share interconnection costs equally and exchange traffic free of charge. Today, private peering is the predominant form of interconnection between backbones.[6] In comparison with private peering, public peering has the theoretical and practical advantage of providing good aggregation of traffic. Hence, it is appropriate and cost effective whenever low traffic volumes are exchanged between many peers.[7]

Today, the Internet industry essentially still has a vertical structure: On the one hand, the upstream industry consists of over 40 IBPs comprising five top-tier backbones, also named Tier-1 providers.[8] MCI's UUNET, Level3, AT&T, Sprint, and Cable & Wireless are classified as top-tiered backbones. The so-called Big Five control about 80% of backbone data traffic. This concentration illustrates their market and bargaining power. On the other hand, the downstream industry currently includes over 10'000 ISPs.[9] Downstream providers serve residential users, businesses, and even smaller providers. Downstream providers serving end-users, i.e., companies, organizations, and in-

4 Section 4.1.2 will focus on interconnection fees payed between providers in practice. We will see that transit fees, i.e., interconnection charges paid to upstream providers, are usually not based on actual usage, but take the form of a flat rate depending on the overall traffic pattern.
5 See Lehr and McKnight ([141], p. 5).
6 See Manenti ([156], pp. 4 f.).
7 See Bartholomew ([17], p. 38).
8 See Weiss and Shin ([254], p. 2).
9 See Weinberg [253].

dividuals, are called Internet Access Providers (IAPs). Downstream providers collect monies at the edge of the Internet and buy connectivity from upstream ISPs or from backbones.

Many writers express their concern about concentration and market power in the core network. The problem has its source in 1997 when, starting with UUNET, top-tiered IBPs began to refuse to peer with smaller backbone providers and to exclusively peer among each other under so-called non-disclosure agreements which means that peering conditions are kept secret.

However, Milgrom, Mitchell, and Srinagesh ([168], pp. 183–192) counter these concerns by arguing that a hierarchically built Internet with a small number of core providers is cost effective since it minimizes both routing and transaction costs.[10] The authors justify their first statement with the argument that the costs of core routing are likely to be subadditive.[11] Transaction costs are lower when there is only a small group of core providers since coordination and compatibility are obtained more easily in smaller groups. Moreover, incentives for backbone free-riding[12] vanish.

The actual Internet structure is not purely hierarchical. Downstream providers also interconnect directly with each other, called secondary peering, to exchange local traffic in order to economize on expensive transit fees charged by backbones. That way, local traffic is not inefficiently sent through several hierarchies. Meshed horizontal bilateral peering can be simplified through the introduction of a

10 Core providers operate and manage core routers capable of default-free or full routing: In contrast to edge routers, core routers do not forward packets with unknown destination addresses to a default router, but discard the packet and send an error message to the sender. Routing tables provide routers with the necessary information on how to forward incoming packets. See Milgrom, Mitchell, and Srinagesh ([168], pp. 178–182).

11 Costs of core routing are subadditive in case it costs less if one backbone maintains global routing tables to produce full routing capability as compared to many backbones maintaining global routing tables. See Tirole ([239], pp. 19 f.).

12 Backbone free-riding occurs if smaller providers pass their traffic as soon as possible onto larger transmission networks without being charged for the transport services obtained. This phenomenon will be further studied in Section 4.1.2.

local exchange where several local ISPs interconnect. The difference between local exchanges and NAPs is that the latter also allow for vertical interconnection.[13] Weiss and Shin ([254], p. 17) argue that peering in the downstream industry may help to mitigate the feared market power of core providers.

Besides backbones and downstream ISPs, Telegeography ([237], pp. 29–32) identifies two further classes of providers, namely online service providers and ISPs specializing in web hosting. Online service providers like AOL sell Internet access together with content. In particular, further revenues are collected by selling advertising space. Online service providers buy connectivity to the Internet from backbones or from other upstream providers. Web hosting providers such as Exodus host websites. Their traffic pattern is roughly unidirectional since small user requests trigger large data transfers. Since web hosting providers send large volumes of data over the Internet they have to buy connectivity from upstream providers.

2.1.2 *Technical Basics*

The Internet consists of links which connect pairs of nodes, i.e., computers. A user who connects to the Internet needs a physical and a software connection. Software for browsing the World Wide Web (WWW) such as Microsoft Explorer, Netscape, or Mosaic is called browser. The network hardware of the Internet is composed of communication lines and computers called routers. On the backbone and on the regional level of the Internet, communication lines are mostly fiber optic lines. The speed[14] of lines started out with 56 Kbps to 1.5 Mbps, known as T-1 lines, in the late 1980s. In the early 1990s, T-3 lines came up with a speed of 45 Mbps. Major progress in optical fiber technology in the late 1990s allowed the achievement of a speed of up

13 See Huston ([114], pp. 542–554).

14 Faster in this context refers to the possibility of sending more bits of data within the same time period and, thus, delivering bits faster. A single bit has about the same speed in all networks. See MacKie-Mason and Varian ([150], p. 35).

to 40 gigabits per second (Gbps) in backbones.[15] To get an idea, T-3 45 Mbps lines in thirty seconds can transport an encyclopedia including twenty volumes from U.S. coast to U.S. coast.[16]

In order to communicate with each other computers use a standard or a set of rules called protocol. The protocol makes different networks using distinct physical supports for data transport, such as copper lines, fiber optic cables, or wireless communications, interoperable. The current communication protocol emerged in the 1980s and is called Transmission Control Protocol/Internet Protocol (TCP/IP). TCP is responsible for the breaking up of data into small pieces, called packets, at the source and the reassembly of the packets at the destination. Packets vary in size. Typically, they contain between 20 and 4000 bytes.[17] According to TCP each packet obtains a header that indicates the source and the destination IP addresses[18] of a packet as well as the sequence number of the packet that allows for packet reassembly at the destination. IP gives instructions to the routers on how to move packets from their origin to their destination. IP is connectionless which signifies that no end-to-end connection is set up for packet delivery. Instead, packets are forwarded independently. In principle, the packets of a certain data stream can follow different paths to the destination.

Routers process arriving packets in order of arrival, i.e., they apply the First-In, First-Out (FIFO) principle. Routers inspect the packet header and consult their routing tables that keep track of routes and provide the necessary information to determine the next router the

---

15 See Bleich and Kuri ([24], p. 74).

16 See MacKie-Mason and Varian ([150], pp. 35 f.).

17 See Carpenter and Nichols ([37], p. 1479).

18 Each computer in the Internet can be identified by at least one globally unique address, called IP address. The current version of the Internet Protocol, IPv4, has an address number consisting of 32 bits. The number of IP addresses will be increased with the introduction of IP version 6 (IPv6), also called IP next generation (IPng). Address numbers of IPv6 will be composed of 128 bits. The Internet Architecture Board (IAB) that belongs to the Internet Society, a non governmental voluntary organization, regulates issues concerning the determination, access, and use of Internet addresses. See http://www.iab.org/iab/ (26.11.03).

packet is sent to. The packets may vary in size during their travels as they can be broken up into smaller packets or reassembled into bigger ones.[19] If the incoming packet rate at a router exceeds the outgoing packet rate, the router becomes congested. Packets are queued which causes delays. Once buffer space at a router is full, packets are discarded. Packet losses are detected by TCP at the destination. For each successfully delivered packet a so-called Acknowledgment (ACK) is sent back from the destination computer to the source. Dropped packets are not confirmed with an ACK. In consequence, TCP orders the data transmission rate to be slowed down and attempts to retransmit the lost data. Gradually, the sending rate is increased again until congestion occurs anew.

The network can make no commitment concerning packet delivery. Instead, the network offers a best-effort service. Hence, the bandwidth allocated to each user depends on the network utilization of all other users at a given time. Users can end up not getting any bandwidth at all.[20] Experience suggests that TCP works well when the network load, defined as average data rate divided by the link capacity, remains at or below 70%.[21]

In the Internet, the network load may change very quickly since Internet data traffic generated by a single user is generally very bursty, i.e., Internet data traffic fluctuates heavily over short time periods. Often, short periods of high utilization are separated by long periods where little or no traffic is transferred. Consider, for example, a user browsing the web. Infrequent traffic burst occur each time she visits a new web page.[22]

Packet transmission technology where packets are routed independently based on a best-effort service and where network resources are shared between users is called packet-switching. The advantage of packet-switching is that it allows for statistical sharing, also called statistical multiplexing, which means that limited bandwidth is shared by the packets from multiple sources. Thus, it enables an efficient

19 See MacKie-Mason and Varian ([150], pp. 33–35).
20 See Dolan ([63], pp. 38 f.).
21 See Apostolopoulos et al. ([5], p. 603).
22 See Clark ([44], p. 171).

use of scarce bandwidth. In contrast to the packet-switched Internet, telephone networks partially use a circuit-switching technology for their transport service.[23] Circuit-switching technology needs an end-to-end connection, called circuit, set up before the actual call can take place. A fixed amount of network bandwidth has to be reserved for the call which cannot be used by other customers until the connection has been closed. Bandwidth is kept reserved irrespective of whether conversation is taking place. An advantage of the circuit-switching technology is the possibility to give QoS guarantees like guaranteed maximum delay, which is critical for real-time applications such as voice telephony.[24]

With the best-effort service model no such guarantees may be given. Instead, all applications like, e.g., electronic mail (email), File Transfer Protocol (FTP), Voice over IP (VoIP), video on demand, or interactive gaming are offered the same service quality, i.e., best-effort service. This is not efficient since not all applications have the same demands regarding timely delivery and loss tolerance.

According to their service demands applications are divided into real-time and non-real-time applications. Non-real-time applications, also called elastic applications, such as email and FTP are delay-insensitive. In contrast, real-time applications, also called inelastic applications, such as VoIP, video on demand, or interactive gaming may become worthless or are of significantly lower value if data transmission is delayed. Inelastic applications are further categorized as being tolerant or intolerant with respect to occasional packet loss such as VoIP and interactive gaming, respectively.[25] Hence, scarce resources should be allocated to applications that are most performance-sensitive. Therefore, multiple service qualities must be introduced.

QoS in packet-switched networks can be expressed and measured using the following QoS parameters: Packet latency which is the de-

23 To be precise, modern telephone networks only apply circuit-switching on the last mile from the central office to the home. Central offices are connected by fiber optic lines where calls are multiplexed. However, traditionally, telephone networks were entirely circuit-switched.

24 See MacKie-Mason and Varian ([150], pp. 33 f.).

25 See Peterson and Davie ([192], pp. 496–498).

lay of packet delivery incurred between the sender and the receiver, packet jitter[26] that refers to the variation in the delay of packets belonging to the same application, time transparency that corresponds to the maximum delay between arriving packets, the amount of bandwidth provided which is the maximal capacity provided measured in bits per second, throughput which is the amount of bits actually transmitted per second, and packet loss referring to the loss rate, i.e., the proportion of lost packets relative to delivered packets, due to packet discarding.[27] QoS measures are especially important in times of network congestion.

One way to implement QoS in today's best-effort Internet is by overprovisioning. However, this is an expensive way to introduce and to maintain network quality. Alternatively, monetary incentives may be given to encourage users to select the appropriate service class. If prices are used to signal scarcity of bandwidth, packets generated by users who are ready to pay relatively more for packet transmission compared to other users can be given preferential treatment. This may be achieved by introducing relative priorities combined with priority pricing. The packet header of IPv4, the current version of IP, contains an eight-bit Type Of Service (TOS) field which is itself composed of a three-bit precedence field that is momentarily unused. A priority number can be assigned to that field to identify the priority class of the packet. Routers then have to be programmed such that packets of a higher priority are forwarded preferentially. However, rather than guarantees only relative priorities can be given by today's best-effort service model.

Research within the Internet Engineering Task Force (IETF) has focused on the question of how to introduce guaranteed QoS into today's best-effort service model. Guaranteed QoS require the network to make explicit and quantitative service commitments. Therefore, resources must be reserved along the path from the sender to the receiver. For this purpose, the Resource Reservation Protocol (RSVP) has been developed. Moreover, admission control becomes necessary

26 Jitter mainly affects real-time applications.

27 See Tektronix ([236], pp. 2 f.).

that only admits an application if enough network resources are available.

The work within the IETF led to the development of the Integrated Services Architecture (IntServ). The integration of bandwidth reservation into the network connection has given IntServ its name. IntServ offers two classes of service for which Internet standards have been specified, namely the controlled-load service class and the guaranteed QoS service class. While the guaranteed QoS service class offers a deterministically guaranteed bound on delay without packet loss, the controlled-load service emulates the QoS obtained in a lightly loaded best-effort network even if the network is actually heavily utilized. This can be done with the implementation of a queuing mechanism, that demarcates controlled-load data traffic from other data traffic, and with admission control. Admission control restricts controlled-load traffic on a connection such that the network load remains on an adequate level. The controlled-load service class does not offer an absolute service guarantee, but a statistical service guarantee.

By providing absolute and statistical service guarantees IntServ allows very demanding application requirements to be satisfied. However, it does not scale well, i.e., it is both too complex and too resource hungry since admission control and end-to-end reservations have to be done for millions of individual data flows.

These scalability problems led to a new technology standard defined by the IETF, the Differentiated Services Architecture (DiffServ). This concept was named DiffServ since it differentiates between packets. The DiffServ concept standardizes the use of the TOS byte in both IPv4 and IPv6 packet headers. Instead of allocating resources to individual flows like IntServ, DiffServ allocates network resources to different packet classes. Moreover, DiffServ preserves the attribute of statistical multiplexing of today's Internet. However, the higher scalability compared to IntServ is associated with coarser quality differentiation.

In DiffServ environments IP packets are classified at the edge of the network by a mark in their header according the traffic profile of a customer. Traffic profiles specify how many packets belong to a certain service class, i.e., they indicate the contracted QoS parameters such as average packet rate, peak packet rate, and burst size of the customer. Traffic profiles are declared in Service Level Agreements (SLAs) between ISPs and customers that specify the service delivered in terms of the expected bandwidth demands, certain QoS parameters, and the corresponding price. SLAs are concluded both between retail customers and IAPs and between different operators. In case a provider fails to meet these performance guarantees some compensation for damages must be given. If, instead, the customer sends more packets than contracted, excess packets are marked as being out of profile. Out-of-profile packets do not obtain the contracted QoS, but only best-effort service.

Packets belonging to distinct classes are forwarded differently in the network. Different forwarding treatments in the DiffServ framework are known as Per-Hop Behaviors (PHBs). DiffServ defines three standardized PHBs: Expedited Forwarding (EF), formerly known as Premium Service, Assured Forwarding (AF), and best-effort forwarding. EF is a low latency, low jitter, low loss, assured bandwidth, and end-to-end service. The EF service appears to end-users like a virtual leased line.[28] AF provides a low loss service where packets are forwarded by priority according to four specified traffic classes with three levels of drop precedences in each class. Compared to the EF service, the AF service has the advantage that it can handle bursts.

In the context of DiffServ, SLAs between different providers may be static and negotiated between humans. Alternatively, SLA's may be automated. In the latter case, each network has a so-called bandwidth broker that exchanges SLA information automatically with bandwidth brokers of adjacent networks. Bandwidth brokers are also responsible for admission control.[29]

Neither IntServ nor DiffServ has taken over the Internet so far. However, it is conceivable that in the future both IntServ and DiffServ will be implemented, with IntServ being used for on-net traffic, i.e.,

28 A virtual leased line emulates a leased line.

29 See Carpenter and Nichols [37], Fankhauser ([66], pp. 40–45 and pp. 59 f.), Flury et al. ([77], p. 7), Parameswaran, Stallaert, and Whinston ([190], p. 353), and Peterson and Davie ([192], pp. 492–517).

for traffic that is originated and terminated on the same network, and DiffServ being used for off-net traffic, i.e., for traffic that is originated and terminated on distinct networks.[30]

Apart from the efforts undertaken by the IETF to develop standards that support QoS, two projects, Next Generation Internet (NGI) and Internet2 (I2), intend to establish high-speed Internet connectivity which can support high-performance applications such as multimedia learning, interactivity, and real-time collaboration. While NGI is a U.S. government project I2 is sponsored by universities, high-tech companies, and the U.S. government.

Within the next years, IP version 6 (IPv6), also called IP next generation (IPng), will be introduced Internet-wide. IPv6 is the successor of IPv4.[31] Implementation of IPv6 is eased by its backward compatibility with IPv4. Hence, IPv6 can be gradually introduced in the Internet. As with IPv4, IPv6 allows the classification of packets according to the QoS required. Besides other improvements, such as more efficient routing and security functions, for example, IPv6 provides an increase in the maximal admissible number of IP addresses, the dominant driver for the introduction of IPv6.[32]

NTT Communications Corporation (NTT Com) was the first operator to offer IPv6 services.[33] It is estimated that by 2006 about 50% of ISPs will offer IPv6 services.[34] The U.S. Department of Defense is planning to switch to IPv6 in about 2008. In Japan the use of IPv6 will even become mandatory already by 2005.[35]

---

30 See Rupp ([202], p. 7).

31 IP version 5 (IPv5) is not the successor of IPv4 since the former was assigned to Internet Stream Protocol Version 2 (ST2), a protocol created as an adjunct to IP for the support of real-time transmission of multimedia data. See Newton ([175], p. 429).

32 See Dolan ([63], pp. 39 f.).

33 See Ermert ([65], p. 71).

34 See Hagen ([103], p. B23).

35 See Reardon [196].

2.1.3 Internet Access Technologies

Internet access can be provided by telephone operators over twisted-pair copper telephone lines or over fiber optic links, by wireless operators such as satellite systems or cellular communications operators, by cable service operators over coax cables, and by power providers over power supply lines. These operators provide a network connection and transport data from the residential or business customer to the Point Of Presence (POP), i.e., the Internet access node, of the Internet Access Provider (IAP).

Traditionally, residential customers access the Internet via an analog modem over the copper telephone line, that is, over the Public Switched Telephone Network (PSTN). Each time a user wishes to access the Internet she calls the telephone number used by the IAP for dial-up access. Modems convert the digital information of computers into analog waves transmitted by the telephone lines to the POP of the IAP. Dial-up access is also provided via the Integrated Services Digital Network (ISDN). ISDN digitizes the last mile from the local switching office to end-users and upgrades the bandwidth offered by analog dial-up Internet access from up to 56 Kbps to a maximum of 64 Kbps. By bundling two or several channels ISDN offers a speed of 128 Kbps or more.[36]

Dial-up Internet access over the PSTN is priced per minute.[37] Hence, users have incentives to disconnect to the Internet when no traffic is being transmitted and again dial up their ISP each time they wish to access the Internet. Note that dial-up Internet access is circuit-switched. Also, recall that circuit-switching does not allow for statistical multiplexing. Therefore, for circuit-switching, time-based pricing rather than volume-based pricing satisfies the causer pays principle.

Business users and large organizations access the Internet via a dedicated leased line that connects the Local Area Network (LAN) of the institution with the IAP. Predominantly, very high-speed Internet access is offered to large customers by fiber optic links that allow

36 See Vahldiek ([242], p. 111).

37 In Section 3.1.1 pricing practices will be presented in detail.

the transmission of data at a speed of several Gbps. To offer the same service to residential users, i.e., to bring fiber to the home of residential customers, would be very costly.

Pricing practices for leased lines are not time-based, but either flat-rated, volume-based, or a hybrid thereof. Hence, no usage costs occur as long as no data traffic is generated. This allows users to always be connected to the Internet which is called 'always on'.

There are several broadband Internet access technologies that are not priced per minute of access and therefore allow users to connect to the Internet on an always-on basis. Broadband access technologies provide high-speed Internet access. According to the Organization for Economic Co-operation and Development (OECD), broadband is a service that provides a minimum downstream speed from the provider to the customer of 256 Kbps and a minimum upstream speed from the customer to the IAP of 64 Kbps.[38] Broadband Internet access can be obtained via Digital Subscriber Line (DSL), via cable TV, via powerline or wireless via satellite, via mobile phone, via Wireless Local Loop (WLL), and via Wireless Local Area Network (WLAN).

DSL provides Internet access over the regular telephone copper line. Under optimal conditions, DSL can transmit up to 8 Mbps. However, such speeds can only be achieved if the last mile is shorter than 1.5 kilometers. Hence, in practice, much slower speeds are offered.[39] Each DSL subscriber has a dedicated line that connects the DSL modem at home and a device, named Digital Subscriber Line Access Multiplexer (DSLAM), at the central office. The DSLAM modulates data transfer on the last mile from the central office to the home and multiplexes multiple DSL lines together before data packets are sent to the Internet. The most important variants of DSL are Symmetric Digital Subscriber Line (SDSL), Asymmetric Digital Subscriber Line (ADSL), and Rate-Adaptive Digital Subscriber Line (RADSL). While SDSL provides the same speeds for both upstream and downstream data transmission, ADSL offers a faster transmission speed downstream. Hence, users who download much informa-

38 See Bundesministerium für Wirtschaft und Technologie ([35], p. 110).
39 See Mansmann ([157], p. 156).

tion from the Internet while sending mainly information requests that consist of only a few bits subscribe to ADSL. Users who provide information themselves and wish to send much data traffic upstream opt for SDSL.[40] RADSL supports both symmetric and asymmetric applications. Depending on the application requirements, transmission speed is adapted accordingly, i.e., adaptive data rates are allowed for.[41]

Internet access over cable TV necessitates a cable modem. Moreover, the TV system must be upgraded with an upload link so that data can also be sent. The cable network is technically able to offer very high data transmission rates. In practice, this is yet impossible since a share of the bandwidth is already allocated to TV and radio transmission services. As well as this, all households on a cable run have to share the capacity of the cable. Hence, in practice, users can expect data transmission rates from 0.5 Mbps up to 2 Mbps.

Not only the TV cable, but also the power supply line, called powerline, can become a broadband Internet access medium. Powerline has the advantage that every household is already connected. Transfer rates up to 2 Mbps are offered. However, users must share bandwidth with all other users connected to the same power provision line.[42]

Internet access over satellite allows downstream speeds from 2 Mbps to 4 Mbps. Generally, retail customers are offered a hybrid Internet satellite access: While data is downloaded via satellite, data traffic upload is done over any other Internet access medium, but usually via dial-up Internet access. Hybrid Internet access is offered since hardware installations for upstream traffic are rather expensive.

Internet access via mobile phones over a cellular phone network has become increasingly popular. The standard of the cellular phone network of the so-called third generation (3G) is the Universal Mobile Telecommunications System (UMTS). UMTS allows the transmission of data at a maximal speed of 2 Mbps, while the circuit-switched Global System for Mobile Communications (GSM) technology, the standard of the cellular phone network of the second generation (2G)

---

40 See Vahldiek ([242], p. 110).

41 See Newton ([175], p. 657).

42 See Bleich and Mansmann ([26], pp. 140–143).

that predominated in the early 1990s, only allows data to be transmitted at a speed of 9.6 Kbps. Modern successors of GSM technology including the connection-oriented High-Speed Circuit-Switched Data (HSCSD) service, the packet-switched Generalized Packet Radio Service (GPRS), and Enhanced Data for GSM Evolution (EDGE) theoretically reach maximal transmission rates of 57.6 Kbps, 53.6 Kbps, and 384 Kbps, respectively.

In Europe, in 2000, some of the spectrum licenses for UMTS were granted through auctions. Converted into U.S. dollars, billions of dollars were payed in some countries including Great Britain, the Netherlands, and Germany. It was conjectured that the winners of the auctions may have overestimated the value of the spectrum, resulting in heavy overpays. This problem is known in economic literature as 'Winner's Curse'. The Winner's Curse occurs if the auctioned object has an unknown common value for all bidders. In this case, the most optimistic bidders are likely to systematically overestimate the common value. In consequence, the winner of the auction obtains less profit than expected or even incurs a loss.[43]

The setup of the UMTS network is done cautiously and is lagged. It was not until spring 2003 that UMTS was first introduced in Great Britain, Austria, and Italy.[44] One of the reasons for the late introduction of UMTS is that UMTS capable cellular phones have only recently become available. UMTS capable cellular phones must be compatible with GSM networks. Otherwise, UMTS pioneer users would need two cellular phones, one for each technology. Further reasons for the delayed introduction of UMTS are insufficient battery capacity and the lack of so-called killer applications which are popular applications justifying the need for faster and more expensive data transmission. Further obstacles for a rapid introduction of UMTS are unknown factors such as the measurement and calculation of limit values of electromagnetic radiation set by regulatory authorities and the opposition of the population against the setup of new antennas.[45]

43 For an introduction to common-value auctions and the Winner's Curse consider Wolfstetter ([257], pp. 225–229).

44 See Holzer [108].

45 See NZZ ([178], p. 45).

Users may also access the Internet via Wireless Local Loop (WLL). WLL allows data to be transmitted at a speed of 10 Mbps and more.[46] The WLL concept has not achieved the desired popularity. Even though the tender for the frequencies of the radio link system started in 1999, one cannot yet observe many WLL Internet access offers.[47] The reasons are its high investment costs and that WLL is being replaced by alternative technologies such as DSL and GPRS.

Alternatively, Internet may be accessed via Wireless Local Area Networks (WLANs). WLAN, also known as Wireless Fidelity (Wi-Fi) or IEEE 802.11, refers to the wireless data transmission between computers over short distances using the 802.11 radio technology standard developed by the Institute of Electrical and Electronics Engineers (IEEE). The radio technology standard 802.11 exists, for example, in versions a, b, and g. While the b-standard theoretically allows data to be transmitted at a speed of up to 11 Mbps over distances up to 300 meters, the a-standard permits transmission at a speed of up to 54 Mbps over distances up to 600 meters.[48] In practice, the b-standard achieves a speed of up to 4 Mbps over a distance of a few dozen meters. The g-standard permits a speed of up to 54 Mbps. In contrast to the a-standard, the g-standard is compatible with the b-standard.[49] Wireless technology is available at frequented public places such as hotel lobbys, restaurants, conference centers, coffee shops, airports, bus stops, train stations, and gas stations. In 2004 Lufthansa is planning to introduce WLAN in its long haul aircrafts.[50] Such Public WLANs (PWLANs) are called hotspots. They allow the public to access the Internet equipped with either a laptop or a handheld Personal Computer (PC).

In practice, WLAN achieves higher transmission speeds, i.e., up to 2 Mbps, compared to other wireless Internet access mediums such as GPRS or UMTS that allow data to be transmitted at a speed of 30 to 50 Kbps and 300 Kbps, respectively. However, about 1000 WLAN

46 See Staubli ([229], p. B25).
47 See Vahldiek ([242], pp. 110 f.).
48 See Bundesministerium für Wirtschaft und Technologie ([35], pp. 135 f.).
49 See c't magazin für computer technik [56].
50 See Settele ([215], p. 87).

fixed parts would be necessary to replace one UMTS antenna. While WLAN allows faster data transmission, but is only available punctiform, UMTS can be received area-wide. Hence, WLAN is an attractive Internet access medium complementary to UMTS and GPRS.[51] For this reason, Swisscom, the Swiss incumbent, is planning to introduce UMTS bundled[52] with GPRS and WLAN for its business customers. Users equipped with either a laptop or a handheld PC obtain access to all technologies: At hotspots the WLAN technology will be applied. In areas outside hotspots UMTS or GPRS will perform data conveyance depending on the respective availability. The three technologies are complements in the sense that every technology covers a distinct area such that area-wide access to the Internet can be offered.[53]

Last, we provide some statistics on the popularity of the various Internet access technologies presented in this section: At the end of June 2003 the top three DSL countries by market penetration were South Korea with 29.7%, Taiwan with 16.54%, and Hong Kong with 16.08%. Belgium figures at rank 4 with 12.65% while Germany occupies rank 10 with 9.5% market penetration.[54]

In Switzerland, in January 2003, 53% of residential users still accessed the Internet via an analog modem while 21% logged on via an ISDN connection, 12% over ADSL, and 10% over cable TV.[55]

In 2002 the number of U.S. broadband connections increased by 55% to 19.9 million. In December 2002 6.5 million users thereof accessed the Internet via ADSL while 11.4 million users opted for Internet access via TV cable.[56] Impressive double digit growth rates in the broadband access market, especially in the DSL access market, cannot only be observed in the United States, but are a general phenomenon.[57]

51 See NZZ ([177], p. 81).
52 Bundling strategies will be the focus of the final chapter.
53 See NZZ ([180], p. 25).
54 See Le Maistre [153].
55 See NZZ ([179], p. 77).
56 See Matsumoto [163].
57 See Le Maistre [152, 153].

The consulting company Arthur D. Little finds that at the end of 2003 penetration of broadband Internet access, including DSL, cable modem lines, and other high-speed network infrastructure (not including mobile Internet access), is highest in Korea with about 80%, followed by Hong Kong and Taiwan with roughly 55% and 50%, respectively. Only in these Asian countries does broadband penetration rates exceed the 50% mark. Switzerland, for example, displays a penetration rate of approximately 26% and the United States one of about 25%.[58]

Forecasts state that in the long run ISDN and analog Internet access will be replaced by ADSL. It is estimated that DSL will be the most popular broadband Internet access technology in Europe while in the United States, due to the strong cable industry, Internet access via cable modem will dominate.[59]

2.2 Economics of Network Management

2.2.1 Network Costs and Network Externalities

To determine cost-based prices for Internet data transmission, network costs must be known. Typically, the setting up of a network involves large fixed costs. These fixed costs are often sunk, i.e., irrecoverable. Once the infrastructure is set up, marginal costs of network operation are very low. In the context of the Internet, marginal costs of data transport are roughly zero if the network is not congested.

Economic efficiency, or, Pareto efficiency,[60] is achieved when prices reflect marginal costs. But in the presence of large fixed or sunk costs,

---

58 See George et al. ([83], p. 5).

59 See Bundesministerium für Wirtschaft und Technologie ([35], p. 123 and p. 125).

60 An allocation is said to be Pareto efficient 'if it is impossible to make some individuals better off without making some other individuals worse off'. Mas-Colell, Whinston, and Green ([160], p. 307).

marginal cost pricing does not allow network providers to break even. To avoid losses, providers need either to include a markup on marginal costs if they wish to offer a uniform price or they must recover the fixed costs in the form of a flat fee, or rental price, which is charged in addition to the usage price. Given that marginal costs of data transport are negligible as long as the network is free of congestion, one could argue that prices should match the willingness to pay of Internet users rather than marginal costs. However, in a competitive environment, the implementation of such pricing strategies is difficult, if not impossible. Moreover, as will be discussed below, marginal costs of data transport often cannot be ignored.

MacKie-Mason and Varian ([151], pp. 288–292) identify the following cost categories in the Internet: There are the fixed costs of providing the network infrastructure including the costs of laying cable or buying bandwidth, rent for communication lines, the costs of modems and routers, as well as the salary for the support staff.[61] Moreover, there are incremental costs of connecting a new subscriber to the network consisting of the costs for access lines, switching equipment, connecting a new subscriber to the modem pool at a POP, as well as adding server capacity for email and personal web pages. Moreover, with the growth of the customer base and increasing demand for data traffic, capacity must be periodically expanded. This means that investment in network infrastructure increases in a sequence of steps. The costs of expanding network capacity are determined by the costs of additional routers, new lines, and new staff. As a further cost category, one should add interconnection costs such as the costs of accessing a Network Access Point (NAP), for example. Interconnection costs may either be fixed or variable, depending on the interconnection agreement. Transit fees, i.e., interconnection charges paid to upstream providers, are a significant cost burden to ISPs. In the case of variable transit charges, i.e., volume-based transit pricing, ISPs that offer a flat rate to their customers for unlimited Internet access may run into serious profitability problems. Popular P2P file

61 Procurement prices for transmission lines have been decreasing continuously. This is due to overprovisioning, that results in excess capacity, and to technological changes, that lead to cost reductions.

sharing, for example, which consumes a large amount of bandwidth, has triggered increased transit charges and unplanned network expenditures for many providers.[62]

In addition to those resource costs, MacKie-Mason and Varian ([151], p. 288) identify marginal costs of sending extra packets. Those costs are essentially zero when the network is only lightly loaded, but may be considerable in times of network congestion. In the latter case, an additionally sent packet generates social costs borne by other Internet users in the form of delayed and dropped packets, i.e., in the form of declined QoS.[63] Those social costs are negative externalities called congestion externalities. Such externalities appear when the behavior of one market participant affects others without any pecuniary compensation being made. Network resources affected by network overuse are bandwidth, routers, and computer capacity, for example.

The consequence of negative congestion externalities is a so-called tragedy of the commons. This term goes back to Harding [105] and refers to a community property, called the commons, which may be used by all peasants of the community to graze their animals. Each peasant maximizes her individual gain by increasing her flock while ignoring the associated social costs which results in an overuse of the commons.

In the case of the Internet, the tragedy of the commons would become manifest in heavy congestion and significant delays. Hence, in order to achieve an efficient allocation of resources, these negative congestion externalities have to be accounted for. One way to deal with negative congestion externalities is to internalize them. Conges-

62 See Sandvine ([205], pp. 8 f.).

63 According to Clark ([44], p. 171, p. 176, and p. 180), network performance should not be measured in the delay of individual packets, but rather in the reduced throughput of typical data units of current applications, such as the size of a typical web page, the typical size of an email message, or a file in FTP. Clark justifies his claim with the statement that the rate adaptation of TCP rather than individual packet delay is responsible for reduced throughput of data traffic. However, discarded packets are the origin of a rate adjustment of TCP. Therefore, we will assume that delay of packets provides a reasonable criterion to evaluate network performance.

tion pricing is an instrument to internalize negative network effects. Section 3.3.1 will analyze congestion pricing in detail. Here, we give a short introduction to the idea of congestion pricing. Consider Figure 2.1. Assume for the purpose of illustration that all Internet users are identical. While the horizontal axis measures the amount of Mbps

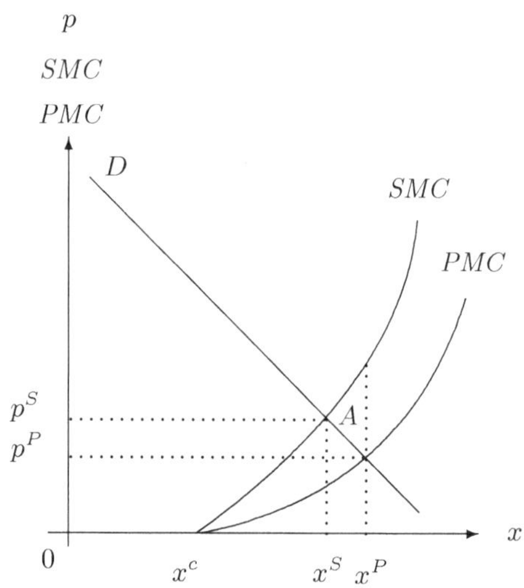

Figure 2.1: Congestion pricing
Source: See Dahl [57].

of data traffic conveyed, depicted by x, the vertical axis measures the price p per Mbps of data traffic transported as well as the social and the private marginal congestion costs of data transmission, denoted by *SMC* and *PMC*, respectively. Suppose the values p, *SMC*, and *PMC* to be expressed in units of waiting time rather than in monetary units. The inverse demand curve for Internet usage D is assumed to be linearly downward sloping. It reflects the marginal benefits of Internet usage at each level of x.

Up to a critical value of Internet usage, x^c, no congestion occurs. Both social and private marginal congestion costs of data transfer equal zero. As the amount of Internet traffic exceeds x^c, congestion occurs. As congestion increases, both private and social marginal congestion costs rise. However, social marginal congestion costs increase faster than private marginal congestion costs since the former include the costs each Internet user imposes on all other users.

If Internet usage is not priced, as with the currently popular flat rates, each Internet user generates additional data traffic up to the point where her private marginal cost function intersects the inverse demand function, i.e., where private marginal costs equal marginal benefits of Internet usage. Hence, each user demands x^P Mbps of data traffic transfer and incurs private marginal costs equal to p^P. However, at x^P Internet usage is underpriced: If the price shall internalize negative congestion externalities it has to equal social marginal costs of congestion. Therefore, Internet users should pay p^S, the price that also includes the congestion costs imposed on all other users. Confronted with p^S, each user would demand less, namely x^S Mbps of data transfer.

Note that congestion pricing enhances welfare: While the area under the inverse demand curve between x^S and x^P depicts the welfare loss from the reduction in Internet usage, the larger area under the social marginal cost curve between x^S and x^P reflects the gain in welfare resulting from reduced congestion. Hence, congestion pricing increases welfare by the triangle A.

Also, we find that the solution characterized by the price p^S and the usage level x^S does not totally eliminate congestion. However, congestion can only occur as long as private marginal benefits of Internet usage exceed social marginal costs.[64] Finally, note that congestion pricing should be applied to both retail customers and to ISPs since the latter may be customers of upstream providers.

One could argue that rather than internalizing congestion externalities via pricing, congestion shall be alleviated by capacity expansion. However, lower congestion increases the marginal benefits of Internet usage due to better QoS and triggers an increase in demand

64 See Dahl [57].

for Internet usage.[65] Hence, increasing capacity may not help to alleviate congestion. Recall that in the fist chapter we suggested that Say's Law is likely to apply to the Internet. Say's Law states that supply generates its own demand.

The cost structure of ISPs may vary considerably depending on whether they are Internet Access Providers (IAPs), upstream ISPs, or Internet Backbone Providers (IBPs). While IBPs such as Sprint, for example, have high sunk costs but, due to excess capacity, face negligible marginal costs of data transport, IAPs are often only resellers of capacity.[66] In consequence, they experience negligible sunk costs but may incur considerable congestion costs since, for profitability reasons, they will abstain from buying capacity in excess.

Apart from negative network externalities, one can also identify positive network externalities. Positive network externalities arise when the value or the utility of a network increases with the number of users connected to the network: The more people that can be reached via email, the more valuable the service. Hence, the willingness of a potential Internet user to pay for network subscription is likely to increase with the number of other subscribers.

Positive network externalities provide the background of Metcalfe's Law, named after the inventor of Ethernet, Bob Metcalfe. Metcalfe's Law roughly states that the value (loosely defined) of a network increases proportionally with the square of the number of its subscribers.[67] One has to keep in mind that Metcalfe's Law may only be valid in the absence of negative congestion externalities.

The emergence of positive network externalities requires the network to have achieved a so-called critical mass. In other words, the size of a network must reach a certain threshold in order for the network to thrive. After the critical mass has been reached high growth can be observed, since then the network is able to offer the necessary value of participation to a broad set of potential users. Thus, the growth pattern of networks with positive externalities is typically characterized by long lead times followed by a sharp increase in subscriptions, a re-

65 See Gibson ([88], p. 84).

66 See Gupta et al. ([92], p. 44).

67 See Shapiro and Varian ([218], pp. 183 f.).

sult of positive feedback: With the growth of the installed subscriber base, the network becomes more valuable, attracting more and more subscribers.

This growth pattern can also be observed in the Internet. The Internet was only being utilized by early adopters in the early 1970s until the critical mass was finally reached in the late 1980s.[68] Since that point, Internet usage has roughly doubled each year.[69]

The need to achieve a critical mass could be one justification for cheap and unmetered Internet access. However, with the high growth of Internet subscribers in past years, one must admit that 'the need of providing a free lunch to promote the Internet is over.'[70]

Besides these so-called direct positive network externalities associated with the growth of the network, Katz and Shapiro [125] identify indirect positive network externalities. Indirect positive network externalities increase the demand for complementary goods or services, such as Internet access modems, mobile phones, or Internet content.

The pricing proposals presented in this work do not explicitly take positive network externalities into account. Instead, it is assumed that all positive externalities are already included in the utility functions of Internet users. Note that if the number of Internet users and Internet traffic demand grow large, positive network externalities are outweighed by negative congestion externalities.

2.2.2 *Internet User Demand*

The design of acceptable pricing models requires an analysis of user demand characteristics which will be the focus of this section. In 1998, the Internet Demand Experiment (INDEX) project started.[71] INDEX is a market experiment that measured demand for Internet access

68 See Shapiro and Varian ([218], pp. 13 f.).

69 Growth rates underlying this statements are measured in the amount of bytes of data transported on the Internet. See Coffman and Odlyzko [50].

70 Dolan ([63], p. 37).

71 The following remarks on the INDEX project and its findings are drawn from the contributions of Altmann and Chu [3], Edell and Varaiya [64], Rupp [202], and Varian [246].

depending on QoS in terms of the amount of bandwidth provided and on the pricing structure. Within the INDEX framework, subjects (members of the University of California at Berkeley) were offered a menu of different quality-price choices. Usage prices varied with the QoS chosen.

Concretely, subjects could choose between different bandwidth levels in a range of 8 Kbps to 128 Kbps for different prices. The service class offering 8 Kbps could be obtained free of charge at any time. Subjects had the option to momentarily require higher QoS in return for an additional usage-based charge.

Different experiments have been conducted within INDEX. Each experiment was preceded by a free trial week such that subjects could adapt to the pricing structure. As expected, usage during these periods significantly exceeded usage during priced periods. During priced periods, both total expenditures and the volume of traffic heavily increased under a flat-rate pricing scheme compared with a measured pricing model. However, revenues generated per megabyte (MB) of data transferred nevertheless turned out to be lower with unmetered access pricing.[72]

Time-based pricing led to higher network utilization rates and to lower connect times compared to volume-based pricing. Having a choice between volume-based pricing and time-based pricing, subjects preferred the former. This preference might be explained by the convenience of volume-based pricing to being always on without having to pay the minutes of Internet connection.[73]

INDEX data also show that demand heavily increases with quality. The reason for this quality-sensitivity may be twofold: First, certain applications such as real-time applications may provide better user satisfaction at higher speeds. Hence, with increasing transmis-

72 The same change in user demand was observed when in December 1996 AOL modified its pricing practice from a time-based pricing scheme to a flat rate: While the average monthly connect time to the Internet increased from 6.4 to 22.1 hours in 1998, both revenues per hour of connect time and the operating margin of AOL decreased. See Edell and Varaiya ([64], p. 23).

73 However, as will be mentioned below, when having the choice between volume-based pricing and flat-rated pricing subjects tend to prefer the latter.

sion speed, the demand for such applications rises. Second, apart from the monetary costs of usage, Internet users face costs in the form of waiting time. Thus, total costs consisting of monetary and delay costs might be higher at lower speeds compared to higher speeds.[74]

INDEX findings further suggest high negative own-price effects and high positive cross-price effects to the next higher and lower QoS.[75] The latter result indicates that different service qualities are considered as substitutes.

Generally, INDEX findings indicate that Internet user demand is sensitive to both price and quality: Subjects responded to price signals and made wide use of different service qualities illustrating that demand for network service varies over time. However, subjects appeared to prefer flat-rate pricing schemes over measured pricing models. Evidence is given by the fact that subjects were willing to pay a premium to obtain unlimited access to the Internet for a certain price. Nevertheless, subjects chose higher usage-priced QoS after having subscribed to a flat-rate pricing scheme for lower bandwidth. Moreover, subjects did not seem to care much about the level of bandwidth available under the flat-rate option. Therefore, Altmann and Chu ([3], p. 529) propose that ISPs offer flat-rated Internet access for basic service with the possibility of momentary service upgrades for peak bandwidth usage at a usage-based charge. Such a pricing scheme can mitigate or even prevent over-usage of network resources, especially if basic service is only provided in the absence of congestion.

Furthermore, INDEX findings show that flat-rate pricing indeed leads to cross-subsidies from light to heavy users. This cross-subsidy increases in the variation of demand among users. INDEX data suggest a large variation in user demand.[76] Independently of the pricing model applied, 30% of the subjects generated 70% of data traffic.[77]

---

74 See Edell and Varaiya ([64], pp. 22 f.).

75 This result is supported by a demand analysis of Kridel, Rappaport, and Taylor ([133], p. 21) who find that the cross-price elasiticity of high-speed residential Internet access over cable modem with respect to the price of dial-up Internet access is positive.

76 This discrepancy in user behavior is likely to increase with the introduction of new Internet applications.

77 See Rupp ([202], pp. 82 f.).

Accordingly, in the presence of a flat rate, about 70% of the subjects financed the traffic generated by the 30% of high-volume users. A majority of Internet users, namely 70%, would have been better off under usage-based pricing.

One can conclude that users particularly value the flexibility in choosing different service qualities on demand as well as unmetered Internet access. Without the possibility of requesting different service qualities on demand, users who only occasionally would like a better QoS will not find it worthwhile to subscribe to a higher level of bandwidth at a flat rate. Hence, they will be excluded from the use of such higher quality services. However, results also highlight that users are willing to pay a premium for simple, transparent, and predictable prices, i.e., for flat rates.[78]

Fishburn, Odlyzko, and Siders ([76], p. 172) identify three reasons for the preference for flat rates. First, there is an insurance effect since predictable fees reduce financial risks for users. Second, customers typically overestimate their own usage. Third, there exists a hassle factor in terms of mental transaction costs or decision-making costs incurred by Internet users each time they have to decide whether their use of the Internet is worth the associated costs.

Further evidence on user preferences is given by a simulated experiment conducted at the University of Texas at Austin. A flat-rate pricing scheme, such as the one offered by AOL, was compared to dynamic priority pricing with respect to profits of ISPs, customer satisfaction, and the level of congestion. Dynamic priority pricing is a volume-based and load-sensitive pricing scheme which will be introduced in Section 3.3.3. In the experiment, subjects could choose between two identical subnetworks applying the two different pricing schemes: One, named AOL, charged a flat rate and the other

78 The same conclusion has been drawn within two further projects, i.e., within CATI (Charging and Accounting Technology for the Internet) and M3I (Market-Managed Multiservice Internet), founded by the Swiss National Science Foundation and the EU Fifth Framework programme, respectively. Both projects pursue the aim to design and to implement charging and accounting mechanisms that permit different pricing for multiple service qualities in the Internet. See Foukia et al. ([78], pp. 1–7) and http://www.m3i.org (26.11.03).

adopted dynamic priority pricing. While the subjects were always allowed to switch to the dynamic priority pricing scheme, they could only periodically decide whether or not to subscribe to AOL. The experiment showed that only heavy users, who have a low value of time, subscribed to AOL. The experiment also demonstrated that dynamic priority pricing yields higher profits, better customer satisfaction, and lower levels of congestion compared to flat-rate pricing.[79]

One can conclude that users accept volume-based and load-sensitive prices for Internet usage provided that congestion eases. With the introduction of bandwidth-hungry real-time applications such as video on demand, the acceptance of volume-based pricing or even of dynamic priority pricing will be further enhanced.

When introducing usage-based tariffs, ISPs have to convince users that they gain compared to a flat-rate pricing model. Therefore, ISPs must consider the insurance factor, try to minimize the hassle factor, and convince users that they overestimate their demand. To minimize the hassle factor, one can imagine software agents acting on behalf of users. These software agents would automate the decision-making process to provide the required simplicity to users. This way, subscribers would not be directly confronted with relatively complicated tariff tables. The introduction of micropayments, e.g., payments below a cent, will further increase the acceptability of usage-based pricing schemes. Micropayments are aggregated and only charged if the accumulated prices reach a certain threshold.

Users who pay a flat rate could be confronted with their overestimation of demand if they received a hypothetical usage-based (electronic) bill showing potential savings. Light users might then choose ISPs with an exact, i.e., usage-based, pricing scheme. ISPs that offer flat rates would be left with heavy users that no longer obtain cross-subsidies from light users. Flat rates would have to rise in order to recover costs. As a consequence, further subscribers would switch to an ISP charging usage-based prices until only heavy users remain with providers offering flat rates.[80]

---

79 See Stahl [226].
80 See Rubner ([200], p. B32).

So far, Internet user demand has been analyzed based on demand information given by experiments. Alternatively, actually observed traffic patterns in the Internet is evidence of user demand. We first have a look at symmetry characteristics of Internet traffic at the edge of the network and then focus on traffic demand patterns.

At the edge of the network, the traffic pattern of inbound and outbound traffic of an Internet user is asymmetric: While portal sites or web hosting providers generate predominantly outbound traffic, individual users mainly produce inbound traffic. According to Huston ([114], p. 571) about 80% of all Internet traffic is initiated by receiver requests such as requests to download files.

Empirical studies on the distribution of demand or on the existence of general demand patterns show ambiguous results. While some authors such as Hwang ([115], p. 77) argue aggregate traffic intensity to be relatively predictable and stationary in the peak period, others claim data traffic to be unpredictable and to exhibit self-similar characteristics. Let us look at the two points of view in turn.

Traditionally, bursty individual data traffic has been assumed to smooth out on the aggregate level. Moreover, it has been supposed that packets arrive independently and at random at routers and that the probability of a new packet arrival in any time interval is independent of the number of packets in the queue at a router. These assumptions allow the arrival rate of packets to be modeled as a so-called Poisson (random) process.[81] Aggregate traffic following a Poisson process becomes smoother, i.e., less bursty, the more traffic sources are aggregated. Poisson processes are successfully applied to conventional telephone traffic.[82]

---

81 A Poisson process is a discrete stochastic process in continuous time which describes the total number of occurrences in an arbitrary time interval of a certain length t. A Poisson process satisfies the following properties: First, the numbers of occurrences in disjunct time intervals are independent for all time intervals. Second, the probability for any particular number of occurrences is the same for all time intervals of an equal duration t. Third, the probability of two or more events occurring in a sufficiently small time interval is essentially zero. Consider Gut ([101], pp. 195–251) for a detailed description of the Poisson process.

82 See Newton ([175], p. 621) and Rupp ([201], pp. 30 f.).

This point of view has been criticized with the argument that Internet data traffic is self-similar. Self-similar or fractal data traffic is characterized by the absence of any natural lengths of bursts. Independently of whether one observes time scales of milliseconds, minutes, or hours, traffic bursts look similar. Aggregating such self-similar data traffic does not smooth out fluctuations.[83]

Recognizing the self-similar characteristic of data traffic, Odlyzko ([182], pp. 19–22) argues data traffic still smoothes out to a certain degree, resulting in a high predictability of data traffic. Besides a regular growth of data traffic, Odlyzko identifies a regular time-of-day and day-of-week variation of data traffic. Regular variation of data traffic provides a good foundation for peak-load pricing presented in Section 3.1.3.

2.2.3 Normative Criteria for Internet Pricing

In order to evaluate the pricing proposals presented in the next chapter we first have to state normatively which characteristics we want an Internet pricing mechanism to have. We will distinguish between demands on Internet pricing schemes from the welfare theoretic point of view and from the individual perspectives of both ISPs and Internet users.[84]

Each pricing proposal of Chapter 3, at the end of the corresponding section, will be evaluated according to the criteria introduced and discussed below. To judge to which extent the adopted criteria are met we introduce the following rating: Very good, good, satisfactory, adequate, and inadequate. At the end of each section these ratings are summarized in a table.

To remain systematic, the pricing proposals will always be evaluated in the same order as the criteria are presented below: First,

83 See Rupp ([201], pp. 30 f.).

84 Some of the normative criteria for Internet pricing mechanisms established below can be found in Gerpott and Böhm ([84], p. 236), in Gupta, Stahl, and Whinston ([100], pp. 59 f.), in Kilkki, Kalervo, and Ruutu ([132], p. 1), in MacKie-Mason and Varian ([151], p. 292), and in Nagel ([171], pp. 3 f.).

the pricing proposals will be analyzed from a welfare theoretic point of view. From this perspective, a pricing mechanism should lead to allocative efficiency, to efficient capacity expansion, and to incentive compatibility. Second, we will evaluate the pricing proposals from the point of view of ISPs. They also want pricing mechanisms to bring about an efficient allocation of resources, efficient capacity expansion, as well as incentive compatibility. Apart from having these criteria in common with the welfare theoretic perspective, ISPs moreover intend a pricing plan to be profit generating which includes cost-orientation and the possibility to price discriminate. But practical criteria like feasibility and accounting efficiency are also important to ISPs. Finally, from the point of view of Internet users, a pricing scheme shall be utility-orientated and transparent. We will now explain how these criteria are to be understood.

From a welfare theoretic point of view, a pricing mechanism should have the following characteristics:

- *Allocative efficiency*
  Maximization of social welfare, defined as the sum of consumer and provider surplus,[85] presupposes an efficient allocation of available resources, i.e., of network capacity. Thereto, prices must reflect scarcity of capacity. Such prices should account for social costs of congestion which can be done by internalizing congestion externalities. Consequently, the price for sending a packet should be close to zero when the network is not congested and should have a positive markup on private marginal costs in times of congestion, where the markup is determined by the social marginal costs of congestion. Hence, efficient allocation of resources requires prices to discourage network usage in times of congestion and to encourage network usage during off-peak periods. In short, an efficient allocation of available resources ensures that Internet users

85 Consumer surplus is defined as the amount of money that results from the difference between the willingness and obligation of a consumer to pay in a particular market. Provider surplus is defined as the difference between revenues and variable costs of a carrier in a particular market. Both consumer and provider surplus are measured in monetary terms. See Brown and Sibley ([32], pp. 8–16).

are charged according to the real costs of data transport. Then, there are no cross-subsidies between different user groups.

Not all pricing proposals presented in the next chapter rely on a welfare analysis. In this case, we must content ourselves with using reasonable economic intuition to judge whether the criterion of allocative efficiency is likely to be satisfied.

- *Capacity expansion*
  Prices should give correct monetary incentives to expand capacity in bottlenecks. For this, sufficient revenues have to be generated to fund the necessary capacity expansion. We will see below that, generally, prices need to vary with the load of the network in order to indeed generate these revenues.
- *Incentive compatibility*
  In order for a pricing scheme to be incentive compatible, on the one hand, prices should induce Internet users to reveal their true willingness to pay for capacity or for different service qualities. ISPs, on the other hand, should be given the right incentives to adopt the pricing scheme and to provide the required QoS based on the profits they derive from it.

  Not all pricing proposals studied in the next chapter are explicitly derived by means of profit maximization. In this case, we cannot judge whether the pricing scheme is incentive compatible for ISPs. But, prices that are incentive compatible for users are a prerequisite for profit maximization. Therefore, we will also judge a pricing proposal to be incentive compatible if we cannot make a statement about incentives of ISPs.

By analogy with the criteria established from the welfare theoretic point of view, profit maximizing ISPs require a pricing mechanism to lead to an efficient allocation of resources, to give correct monetary incentives to expand capacity in bottlenecks, and to be incentive compatible. To avoid duplications, when evaluating the different pricing proposals below, the three desirable characteristics allocative efficiency, capacity expansion, and incentive compatibility will only be discussed from the welfare theoretic perspective.

Apart from the criteria common with the welfare theoretic point of view, ISPs would like a pricing mechanism to have the following attributes:

- *Cost-orientation*
  The pricing scheme should match the cost structure of ISPs. Thereto, prices must appropriately reflect congestion costs such that, as will be explained in Sections 3.1.3 and 3.3.1, the revenues necessary to expand capacity in bottlenecks are generated. In other words, the pricing mechanism should focus on the short-run costs of congestion as well as on the long-run marginal costs of bandwidth. As already pointed out in Section 2.2.1, costs of ISPs are to a large extent fixed or even sunk costs. To ensure that these costs are indeed covered, ISPs would like to receive a flat rate up-front.
  Accordingly, in our evaluations of the pricing proposals presented in the next chapter, we will downgrade the rating of cost-orientation if the recovery of fixed costs is not ensured and if prices are load-insensitive since, then, as will be explained in Sections 3.1.3 and 3.3.1, no revenues for capacity expansion are generated.
- *Price discrimination*
  Profits of ISPs are not only determined by costs, but also by revenues. In order to increase their revenues ISPs try to exploit differences in willingnesses to pay which can be achieved by price discrimination.[86] Price discrimination means that ISPs charge a customer, or several customers, different prices for multiple units of the same good or service.[87] Apart from discrimination among subscribers with respect to volume, ISPs can differen-

86 One can distinguish between first, second, and third degree price discrimination. First degree price discrimination prevails if the seller can charge each consumer a different price. Thereto, the seller has to know each consumer's reservation price. If information about individual preferences is incomplete the seller can still extract some consumer surplus with the use of self-selecting devices like, e.g., different price-quantity choices or two-part tariffs introduced in Section 3.1.2. This is known as second degree price discrimination. Third degree price discrimination prices identifiable user groups differently. See Tirole ([239], p. 135).

87 See Tirole ([239], p. 133).

tiate their prices according to the QoS offered, called quality discrimination,[88] and according to the network load.

Below, in our evaluations of pricing proposals, we will downgrade the rating of the possibility to price discriminate if the pricing scheme in question is not load-sensitive. But, our rating will not be demoted if a pricing proposal for a single service Internet does not differentiate with respect to service qualities since the lack of quality differentiation is a feature of the network technology, but not of the pricing plan.

- *Feasibility*
  While focusing their profits, ISPs also have to carefully consider whether a pricing scheme is indeed feasible: In order for a pricing mechanism to be feasible its implementation should be simple. Thereto, on the one hand, technical implementation should be realizable with moderate effort. On the other hand, the information necessary to calculate the prices should be easily obtainable. Feasibility furthermore includes that the pricing scheme can be implemented in a decentralized way. A centralized pricing scheme would not be viable in a commercialized and competitive Internet. Independent ISPs should be able to locally determine the appropriate and desired pricing scheme.

  Below, in our evaluations of pricing plans, our assessment of feasibility is downgraded if a system-wide configuration of routers is necessary to provide relative priorities or guarantees on QoS. In the latter case our feasibility rating is even considerably downgraded.
- *Accounting efficiency*
  A practical pricing scheme also includes accounting[89] efficiency, which implies that the amount of information necessary for price calculation must be moderate and that transaction costs have to be low. In other words, the overhead costs involved in calculating the prices should be low. Accounting efficiency possibly includes

88 See Tirole ([239], pp. 149–152).

89 Accounting 'involves gathering the information necessary so that total charges can be itemized against tariffs and usage measurements'. Songhurst ([223], p. 2).

accounting units to be coarser than packets, like, e.g., MB or units of reserved bandwidth, so that the pricing mechanism is easier and less costly to implement.

Finally, from the perspective of utility maximizing Internet users, a pricing scheme should have the following characteristics:

- *Utility-orientation*
  Below, we will analyze utility maximization problems of Internet users and welfare maximization problems, where welfare is defined as the sum of consumer and producer surplus. We call those prices utility-oriented which at the same time maximize individual utilities or consumer surplus, as well as social welfare. Hence, utility-oriented prices imply allocative efficiency. We shall see that in times of network congestion, a utility-oriented pricing scheme only serves users with a relatively high willingness to pay. In other words, utility-oriented prices are considerate of heterogeneous user preferences. In consequence, such prices do not allow for cross-subsidies between Internet users since light users, who are subsidizing heavy users, would be better off with a pricing scheme which eliminates such cross-subsidies.

  Also, heterogeneous user preferences concerning the willingness to pay for bandwidth triggers the necessity for quality differentiation, i.e., for the supply of multiple service qualities. Quality differentiation should be followed by price differentiation to avoid cross-subsidies between user groups and to make the pricing scheme incentive compatible.

  Not all pricing proposals introduced in the next chapter rely on a consumer welfare analysis. Then, by analogy with our remark concerning allocative efficiency, we must content ourselves with using reasonable economic intuition to judge whether the criterion of utility-orientation is likely to be satisfied.

  Below, when evaluating pricing proposals, we will downgrade our rating of utility-orientation if the concerned pricing scheme is not load-sensitive. But, just as when judging the possibility of price discrimination, our rating will not be demoted if a pricing proposal for a single service Internet does not differentiate with respect to QoS since the lack of quality differentiation is a characteristic of the network technology, but not of the pricing scheme.

- *Price transparency*
  Together with utility-orientation Internet users favor price transparency. Price transparency is achieved if prices are either known before a data transport service is claimed or if expenditures are predictable. At least, users should be able to roughly estimate expenditures in a simple way. To accommodate the demand for price transparency, complicated tariff tables should be avoided.

In our analysis below we will see that some criteria mentioned above are complementary while there exists a trade-off between other desirable characteristics of a pricing scheme. In the next chapter each pricing proposal will be evaluated according to the mentioned criteria. A synopsis of these evaluations can be found in Tables 3.16 to 3.19 in Section 3.5.

3. Pricing Internet Access and Usage

> An iron law of economics states that demand always expands beyond the supply of free goods to cause congestion and queues.
>
> Gary Becker ([20], p. 26)

3.1 Pricing Proposals for a Single Service Internet

3.1.1 State of the Art: Pricing Models in Practice

Today, a variety of pricing structures can be found in the Internet including flat rates, time-dependent and volume-based charging. Tariff tables of ISPs can be rather complex in order to avoid direct price comparisons with competing providers.

One can distinguish between pricing plans for residential users and business customers who connect to the Internet via a permanent connection. In North America, residential customers often pay a flat rate for a defined time period for both dial-up and broadband Internet access. In Europe, flat-rated broadband Internet access is also popular while dial-up users are charged based on the minutes of Internet usage in addition to a flat subscription fee.[1]

Time-based charging makes sense for the use of the circuit-switched telephone network to the Point Of Presence (POP) of the Internet Access Provider (IAP) since, as explained in Section 2.1.2, a connection must be built up that does not allow for statistical multiplexing gains. In the narrower sense, this time-dependent charge is not a fee for Internet access, but for the use of the Public Switched Telephone Network (PSTN). Time-based pricing does not make sense in a packet-switched network where resources are not reserved because

1 See Ismail and Wu ([119], p. 11).

capacity is only scarce, i.e., marginal transport costs are only positive, during peak periods. However, time-based pricing potentially leads to a better allocation of scarce resources than flat-rate charges. In the same line of argumentation, time-based pricing does not make sense for broadband Internet access since broadband Internet access is not based on circuit-switching.[2]

For residential users, free unlimited Internet access can also be observed. However, subscribers still have to pay the local telecommunication bill. Providers offering free Internet access generate revenues from advertisers. Furthermore, these providers obtain a slice of the call revenue collected from local telephone operators. Note that call revenue redistribution would not be possible if the call prices reflected costs. Instead, as will be discussed in Section 4.1.1, there is a rent to be distributed. However, as Antoniadis ([4], p. 7) points out, many providers that offered free access have gone out of business or given incentives to their free subscribers to change to a charged premium access service.

An alternative common retail pricing practice is flat-rate pricing with limited access based on the time spent online, on the amount of megabytes transferred, or on both. After the specified ceiling on hours or megabytes has been reached the customer is charged a casual rate for additional hours connected or/and volume transferred. Limited access flat-rate pricing is an example of nonlinear tariffs studied in detail in the next section.

An alternative nonlinear tariff is volume-based pricing, usually associated with a recurring flat access fee based on access capacity and with volume discounts. Volume-based charging has been successfully introduced in New Zealand to recover costs on specific bottleneck links such as the trans-oceanic connections and in Great Britain's research network, named JANET. Both New Zealand and Great Britain introduced volume-based pricing combined with peak-load pricing, studied in the Section 3.1.3. Internet pricing in New Zealand was furthermore characterized by volume and low-priority traffic discounts. The pric-

2 In packet-switched networks per-minute pricing may be appropriate if network utilization per minute was roughly the same. However, as already noted in Section 2.1.2, Internet traffic is characterized by infrequent bursts.

ing model of New Zealand was abandoned in 1996 as the Internet became commercial.[3]

Business customers and institutions usually require a permanent high bandwidth connection to the Internet. They may access the Internet via a leased line priced at a flat rate, depending on the capacity of their connection to the ISP. Sometimes, in addition to the recurring flat rate a usage fee per megabyte of data transferred, mostly with volume discounts, is levied. The flat price component generally includes a certain amount of volume transmitted free of charge.[4] The use of volume-based charging indicates that the measurement of bytes is not too expensive.

If business customers do not require to use the full line, tiered bandwidth and burstable dedicated lines are alternative options. If, for example, a T-1 line is tiered, the customer is allocated a full T-1 line, but is only charged for the contracted utilization of the bandwidth. The advantage is that if the user's traffic pattern changes, upgrades can be made easily.

If the user subscribes to a burstable connection, she is also allocated a full T-1 line.[5] The pricing scheme applied is percentile pricing. With the popular 95% percentile pricing plan, for example, average bandwidth usage is sampled every five minutes. At the end of the accounting period, e.g., after a month, the top 5% peak traffic are discarded and the 95th percentile is used to bill the customer. Percentile pricing is a popular method to charge customers for web hosting and server colocation services. Percentile pricing is either applied to the sum of inbound and outbound traffic or, more commonly, to the maximum of inbound and outbound traffic, i.e., to whichever of the two is the larger.[6]

From the point of view of customers, the percentile pricing method has the advantage of disposing of uncapped bandwidth. However, it penalizes users who have bursty traffic since they pay high charges

3 See Brownlee [33] and Rogerson [198] for a description of Internet pricing in New Zealand and for JANET, respectively.
4 See Stiller, Reichl, and Leinen ([233], pp. 150 f.).
5 See Crémer and Hariton ([54], pp. 287–289).
6 See Leber [140].

set by their peak traffic while their overall bandwidth usage may be substantially lower. The advantage to ISPs is that they can derive revenues based on the 95th percentile while their costs are calculated based on the 50th percentile. In the future, percentile pricing might not only be used for dedicated Internet access lines, but also for broadband service.[7]

We will not rate all of the above pricing practices with respect to the criteria established in Section 2.2.3, but content ourselves with an evaluation of flat-rate pricing. Here, we only consider flat-rate pricing since volume-based pricing will be discussed in detail in the next section. Percentile pricing is a compromise between flat-rate pricing and volume pricing and will therefore not be treated separately. Note that the introduced pricing practices neither allow for congestion-based pricing nor for quality differentiation. For this reason, a variety of alternative pricing methods will be presented in the following sections.

Briefly stated, flat-rate pricing does not meet any of the criteria established in Section 2.2.3 with the exceptions of customer satisfaction due to high price predictability and transparency, accounting efficiency, as well as feasibility. The subsequent more detailed evaluation is shown in Table 3.1.

- *Allocative efficiency*
  Allocation of network resources is not efficient given that prices do not reflect true costs of Internet usage. The lack of price incentives induces a wasteful handling of network resources and leads to a degradation of average service quality, the tragedy of the commons. Here, the fact that users are not charged according to the real costs of data transport makes light users subsidize heavy users.
- *Capacity expansion*
  Flat rates do not provide monetary signals for network planning and network expansion.

7 See Massey [162] and Semret ([211], p. 3).

Table 3.1: Evaluation of flat-rate pricing

ISP/Welfare	*Allocative efficiency*	▼
	Capacity expansion	▼
	Incentive compatibility	▼
ISP	*Cost-orientation*	▽
	Price discrimination	▼
	Feasibility	▲
	Accounting efficiency	▲
User	*Utility-orientation*	▼
	Price transparency	▲

▲ = very good, △ = good

◊ = satisfactory, ▽ = adequate, ▼ = inadequate

– *Incentive compatibility*

Flat-rate pricing schemes lack incentive compatibility: Generally, flat-rate offers attract predominantly heavy users. At the same time, ISPs have an incentive to degrade service quality, for example, by excessive oversubscription of bandwidth, and to deter subscribers from network utilization, for example, by contractual Internet access limits. Service degradation may be limited by the threat of losing subscribers to competitors. However, this threat can be mitigated if ISPs increase provider switching costs.[8] Moreover, flat rates may incite abusive resale of access capacity. This phenomenon is observed in the DSL and the cable access market

8 See Edell and Varaiya ([64], pp. 23 f.).

where several neighbors can agree to share one broadband Internet access connection by setting up a wireless network.[9]

From the point of view of providers flat-rate pricing is judged as follows:

- *Cost-orientation*
  One can imagine ISPs to favor flat rates since they promise calculable monthly revenues which can reduce financial risks of ISPs. Moreover, if there were no congestion externalities, flat rates would match the cost structure well since, as already noted in Section 2.2.1, provider costs predominantly consist of fixed and sunk costs while marginal costs of data transport are essentially zero when the network is not congested. However, in practice, flat rates do not allow for cost recovery if subscribers are mainly heavy users, generating considerable congestion externalities, and if ISPs face variable transit costs. The reason for the difficulties with recovering costs is as follows: Flat-rate pricing provides users with no incentives for rational use of network resources given that Internet clients do not have to bear higher costs when increasing network usage. Typically, when charging a flat rate, network usage of a given ISP will increase without any corresponding change in the revenues. This either leads to a decrease in service quality on a given carriage infrastructure or, if the ISP decides to expand its capacity to match the increased demand, to higher expenditures of the ISP. In the case that the ISP has to pay volume-based transit charges, the mismatch between revenues and costs is even aggravated. One way to avoid reduced, or even negative, profits is to increase the flat rate. One can argue that high enough flat rates always allow to recover costs. Indeed, if Internet subscribers were willing to pay flat fees high enough to recover costs, they could persist. However, in practice, the majority of users expects Internet services to be cheep or, even, free. Therefore, in a competitive ISP industry, Internet users are likely to subscribe to an ISP offering a low flat rate. For this reason, we favor the intro-

9 See Maitland [155].

duction of a usage-based pricing scheme in order to match higher traffic levels with increases in revenues.

- *Price discrimination*
  The possibility to price discriminate between users is inadequate since flat rates render the exploitation of different willingnesses to pay impossible.
- *Feasibility*
  We judge the feasibility of flat rates to be very good: They are simple to implement, since they eliminate the need for traffic measurement, and allow for a decentralized implementation.
- *Accounting efficiency*
  Accounting efficiency is very good: The traffic generated by each user does not have to be measured and billing can even be done in advance of service delivery.

One could support the idea of flat-rate pricing for start-up ISPs as an instrument to rapidly penetrate the market or when introducing new access technologies. T-Mobile USA, for example, currently charges its existing customers a monthly flat fee of $19.99 for unlimited use of its hotspots. Note that flat-rate pricing is a form of bundling, i.e., the sale of unlimited data transport at a single price, which will be discussed in the final chapter. There, we will show that bundling potentially increases providers' revenues. However, this is only possible in the absence of negative congestion externalities.

From the point of view of consumers, flat-rate pricing is appreciated as follows:

- *Utility-orientation*
  Flat rates are not utility-oriented since they are neither cost-based nor do they allow for for discrimination between high and low-value users in times of network congestion. In particular, light users cross-subsidize heavy users.
- *Price transparency*
  A major argument in favor of flat-rate pricing is its predictability. Remember the evidence gained from the INDEX experiment showing that users are willing to pay more for simple tariffs.

To mitigate the drawbacks of flat-rate pricing, Flury et al. ([77], pp. 14–16) propose an adaptive flat rate. The idea is to make the flat rate volume-sensitive without the loss of price predictability. The authors propose periodically adapting the flat rate according to the volume of traffic generated during several past billing periods. The advantage of adaptive flat-rate pricing is its user acceptance, due to its predictability, and its simple implementation while providing users with small incentives not to overuse the network.

3.1.2 Nonlinear Outlay Schedules

In Section 2.2.1 we pointed out that the ISP industry is characterized by large fixed costs and that marginal costs of data transport approach zero in the absence of congestion. Pareto efficiency requires that prices equal marginal costs of data transport. Hence, in the ISP industry, a uniform price would have to exceed marginal costs of data transport in order to avoid losses. Uniform prices found in the Internet pricing practice take the form of volume prices: Tiscali, for example, in July 2003, has offered DSL Internet access by call, i.e., without a monthly flat rate, for 1.19 cents per MB of data conveyed.[10]

Following Willig ([255], pp. 61–65), it will be shown below that any uniform price that does not reflect marginal costs of data transport can be Pareto dominated by a nonlinear outlay schedule.[11] That is, for any uniform price diverging from marginal costs, there is a nonlinear tariff that makes all consumers and a representative provider at least as well off compared to the uniform price. In consequence, welfare, defined as the sum of consumer and provider surplus, increases. We will see below that detailed personalized information about individuals is not a prerequisite of the proposed nonlinear tariff. Indeed, we will show that this tariff is superior to uniform prices, which do not reflect marginal costs, even if information is asymmetric, i.e., even

10 See Mansmann and Hüskes ([159], p. 120).

11 In the subsequent analysis the expressions 'nonlinear outlay schedule,' 'nonuniform outlay schedule,' 'nonlinear prices,' and 'nonlinear tariffs' will be used as synonyms.

if ISPs do not have perfect information about the preferences of their subscribers.

With a nonuniform outlay schedule expenditures of Internet users do not rise proportionally with the amount of data generated;[12] there can be quantity discounts and quantity premia. Since the price varies with the amount of data generated, nonlinear tariffs are a form of second degree price discrimination.

Nonlinear prices can frequently be found in the provider industry. Manet, for example, a provider that offers powerline Internet access in Mannheim, Germany, in July 2003, has charged Internet access for 3.3 cents per MB of data generated in addition to a monthly rental of 14.90 euros. An alternative example is Primacom, an ISP that offers Internet access over cable TV in Germany. Primacom, in July 2003, has charged 9 cents per MB of data generated in addition to a monthly flat rate of 5.95 euros.[13] A further example is mobile Internet access with GPRS technology currently offered by Swisscom for 0.19 CHF per 10 kilobytes (KB) for the first MB of data traffic conveyed per month. Traffic quantities exceeding this threshold are priced at 0.10 CHF per KB.[14]

In this section we focus on outlay schedules which are not uniform. After having introduced the idea of nonlinear outlay schedules, the argument of Willig ([255], pp. 61–65) will be analyzed. Then, we will have a look at optimal nonlinear tariffs. This section is based on classical literature in the field of public utility pricing. If not indicated otherwise, the analysis rests upon Braeutigam ([29], pp. 1327–1337) and upon Brown and Sibley ([32], Chapters 4 and 5).

Two-part tariffs are the simplest form of nonlinear outlay schedules. As illustrated in Figure 3.1, two-part tariffs consist of an access charge, or rental, r and a constant variable price component p per unit of data traffic generated. Total outlay E of an Internet user under a two-part tariff would be

$$E(x) := r + px,$$

12 This means that affine linear outlay schedules are not called linear.

13 See Mansmann and Hüskes ([159], p. 118).

14 See http://www.swisscom-mobile.ch/gprs (26.11.03).

where x depicts the amount of data traffic generated. Note that a uniform price is a special case of a two-part tariff with $r = 0$.

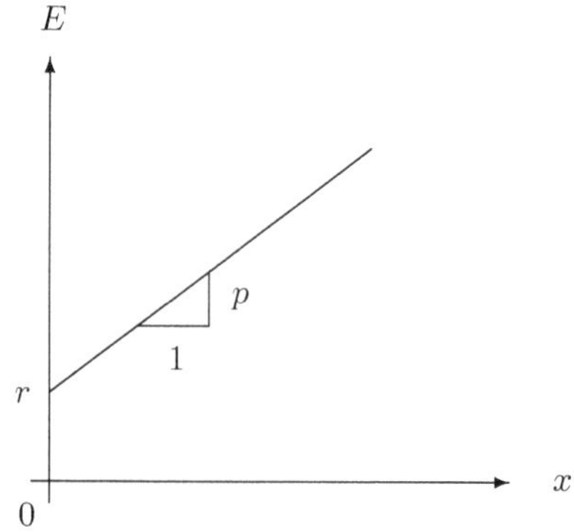

Figure 3.1: Two-part tariff
Source: Braeutigam ([29], p. 1328).

One can imagine a nonlinear outlay schedule with multiple parts, a so-called multi-part tariff or n-part tariff. An n-part tariff is a nonlinear price schedule that consists of a fixed access charge r and $(n-1)$ variable components $p_1, \ldots, p_{n-1}$. Total outlay can then be written as

$$E(x) := \begin{cases} r, & x = 0 \\ r + p_1 x, & 0 < x \leq x_1 \\ r + p_1 x_1 + p_2(x - x_1), & x_1 < x \leq x_2 \\ \vdots & \\ r + \sum_{i=1}^{n-2} p_i x_i + p_{n-1}(x - x_{n-2}), & x_{n-2} < x. \end{cases}$$

In the limit, as n approaches infinity and the corresponding intervals Δx tend to zero and if quantity discounts are provided, i.e., if $p_1 \geq p_2 \geq \ldots \geq p_{n-1}$, a nonlinear price schedule can take the form of a smooth outlay function as illustrated in Figure 3.2. Here, the

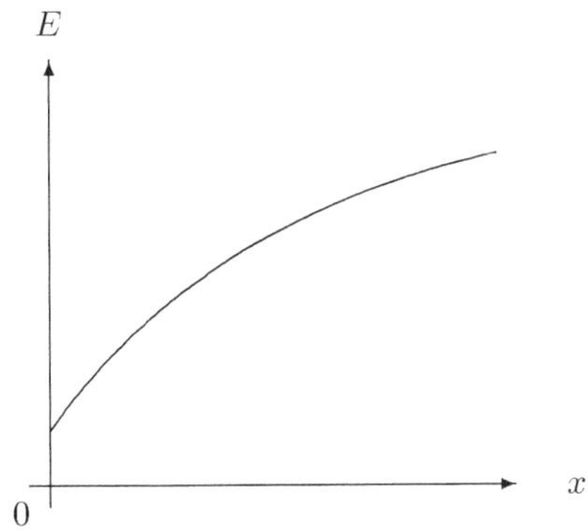

Figure 3.2: Smooth outlay function
Source: See Brown and Sibley ([32], p. 64).

slope of the outlay function, representing the marginal outlay, is continuously changing as the amount of data traffic increases. Marginal outlay equal the price $p(x)$ charged for a certain amount x of data traffic. The usage price

$$p(x) := E'(x) \tag{3.1}$$

is called the marginal price at x.

We now analyze the statement of Willig ([255], pp. 61–65). In a first step, we want to confirm the intuitive argument that welfare, defined as the sum of consumer and provider surplus, can be enhanced if ISPs set a two-part tariff instead of a uniform price. However, it will be illustrated that this argument only holds in the aggregate: Some consumers can be worse off with the two-part tariff compared to a uniform price. In a second step, we will demonstrate that this problem can be eliminated by offering consumers an optional tariff. In consequence, we will be able to conclude that an optional tariff Pareto dominates any uniform pricing schedule.

Suppose that there are two Internet user types in the market, a light-user and a heavy-user type, respectively. The demand for Internet data traffic transport of the heavy-user type, $x_H(p)$, shall exceed the demand of the light-user type, $x_L(p)$, at each price p. Suppose that a representative ISP[15] incurs marginal costs of data transport equal to c and fixed costs equal to F. Then, the uniform price

$$\overline{p} := \frac{F}{x_L(\overline{p}) + x_H(\overline{p})} + c$$

equals average costs and, therefore, allows the ISP to break even.[16]

In Figure 3.3 the inverse demand schedules of the light-user and the heavy-user type are depicted by D_L and D_H, respectively. Suppose that the two inverse demand schedules do not cross each other.[17] Given $\overline{p}$ the light-user type generates $x_L(\overline{p})$ units of data traffic. Her consumer surplus, defined as the amount of money that results from the difference between the willingness and the obligation to pay of a consumer, is given by the area a. The heavy-user type consumes $x_H(\overline{p})$ units of data traffic. Her consumer surplus is depicted by the area w. The area $(b+y)$ reflects provider surplus, defined as the difference between revenues and variable costs. With marginal cost pricing, traffic demands would amount to $x_L(c)$ and $x_H(c)$, generating additional surplus equal to the area $(d+z)$. Thus, the uniform price leads to deadweight losses represented by the area $(d+z)$ in Figure 3.3.

Ronald Coase [48] suggested a special variant of two-part tariffs where the fixed costs are divided equally among all n users. Then, the fixed access fee equals $\frac{F}{n}$. The suggested two-part tariff encompasses an additional variable price component for each unit of data traffic demanded that equals marginal costs of data transport.

In our example of two users, the Coase tariff would be given by $r = \frac{F}{2}$ and $p = c$. With this tariff structure, both types of Internet

15 In a competitive environment it is always possible to interpret an ISP as a representative provider since 'the aggregate profit obtained by each [... ISP] maximizing profit separately taking prices as given is the same as that which would be obtained if they were to coordinate their actions [...] in a joint profit maximizing decision'. Mas-Colell, Whinston, and Green ([160], p. 148).

16 Note that in the Internet industry the assumption of globally constant marginal costs of data transport is not very plausible since they approach zero when the network is not congested and are positive otherwise. One would expect increasing marginal costs of data transport when congestion externalities are taken into account. This issue will be addressed below in our critical evaluation of nonlinear tariffs.

17 This assumption will be formalized below.

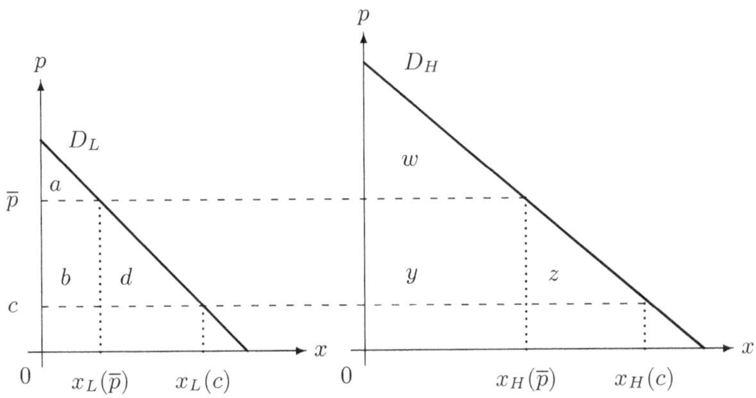

Figure 3.3: Deadweight loss with uniform pricing
Source: Brown and Sibley ([32], p. 66).

users subscribe provided that $(a+b+d) \geq \frac{F}{2}$. If this inequality did not hold the low-user type would earn negative consumer surplus when subscribing. Then, the low-user type could do better by refraining from subscription. Furthermore, the high-user type always subscribes if the low-user type decides to do. To see this, note that, by assumption, the inverse demand schedule of the heavy-user type always lies to the right of the inverse demand schedule of the light-user type. Therefore, the triangle $(w+y+z)$ exceeds the area $(a+b+d)$, which itself may not be smaller than $\frac{F}{2}$ to ensure that the light-user type remains in the market. With both types of consumers remaining in the market the proposed two-part tariff leads to a first-best solution where the ISP just breaks even and where deadweight losses $(d+z)$ are eliminated since demands increase from $x_L(\overline{p})$ and $x_H(\overline{p})$ to $x_L(c)$ and $x_H(c)$, respectively.

Note that the light-user type may be worse off with the two-part tariff compared to the uniform price. This is the case if $\frac{F}{2} > (b+d)$, which implies that some of the original consumer surplus a is eliminated. At the limit, one can imagine that $(a+b+d) < \frac{F}{2}$. Then, as already noted above, the light-user type is better off by refusing subscription. In consequence, the first-best solution, where deadweight losses are entirely eliminated, can no longer be realized.

A possible remedy to the problem would be to split fixed costs among the two user types in a way which ensures that the light-user type will subscribe. The light-user type would be charged a low rental $r_L \leq (a+b+d)$ and the heavy-user type would have to pay a high rental $r_H \leq (w+y+z)$, where $r_L + r_H = F$.[18] One may imagine fixed costs being split according to usage. Then, the low-type user faces a rental price, r_L, smaller than $\frac{F}{2}$ while the rental price of the high-user type, r_H, exceeds $\frac{F}{2}$. Concretely, provided that the participation constraints $r_L \leq (a+b+d)$ and $r_H \leq (w+y+z)$ can be met, the fixed price component could be a weighted average of fixed costs:

$$r_L := \left(\frac{x_L(c)}{x_L(c)+x_H(c)}\right) F \quad \text{and} \quad r_H := \left(\frac{x_H(c)}{x_L(c)+x_H(c)}\right) F,$$

where the weights are determined by the traffic demand of each user type relative to total usage, and where $r_L \leq (a+b+d)$ and $r_H \leq (w+y+z)$.

An outlay scheme where the rental discriminates between user types can be implemented if a representative ISP has perfect information about the type of Internet users. If this is not the case we say that information is asymmetric. Then, the heavy-user type has an incentive to claim to be the light-user type in the hope to pay the lower rental r_L, which would impede the ISP from breaking even. This problem can be solved if ISPs offer multiple tariffs that truthfully sort different user types through self-selection. If users do not reveal their type truthfully through an appropriate tariff choice, we say that the tariff options are not incentive compatible.

The fact that light users are potentially worse off with the two-part tariff compared to the uniform price does not only apply to the Coase tariff, but is a general result. To see this consider Figure 3.4

18 If the fixed costs F are so large that no such pair of entry fees (r_L, r_H) can be found the ISP should cease operation since, then, the costs of the ISP exceed the willingness to pay of consumers.

and imagine that a representative ISP shifts from offering a uniform price p_1 to the outlay schedule

$$E(x) := \begin{cases} 0 & \text{if} \quad x = 0 \\ r + p_2 x & \text{if} \quad x > 0, \end{cases}$$

where $p_1 > p_2$. The move from a uniform price to the two-part tariff

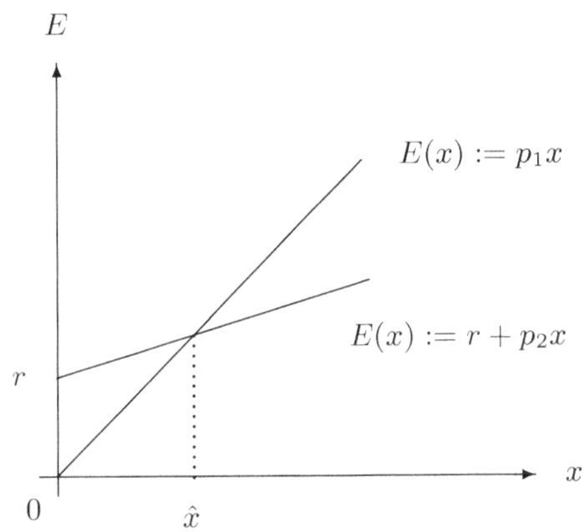

Figure 3.4: Uniform price versus two-part tariff
Source: Willig ([255], p. 61).

benefits heavy Internet users since total outlay decreases for $x > \hat{x}$. Light users are worse off with the two-part tariff since, when $x < \hat{x}$, total outlay with the two-part tariff exceeds the outlay resulting from uniform pricing. If there is a positive correlation between user income and the quantity of data transport demanded, two-part tariffs harm low-income users. We will show below that such distributional effects can be avoided if Internet users can choose between the two outlay schedules.

We have seen that a move from a uniform price to a two-part tariff can harm certain user groups. At the limit, a user group may even refrain from subscribing. If the fixed rental price causes some types of Internet users to drop out of the market, a Coase tariff no longer ensures deadweight losses to be entirely eliminated. A solution that consists in charging different user types different rentals is not feasible due to incentive compatibility problems. Note that the Coase tariff, where the allocation of fixed costs is done according to usage, would not contain an incentive compatibility problem if pricing occurred ex post. In this case, ISPs would measure the data generated by each Internet user and determine the level of the fixed fee to be paid at the end of each accounting and billing period. We call this pricing scheme ex-post weighted-average Coase tariff. The disadvantage of this pricing mechanism is its lack of price transparency.

An alternative solution to the incentive compatibility problem, that also prevents the welfare loss of light users, is provided by Willig ([255], pp. 61–65). He shows that an optional tariff, that sorts different users onto different tariffs, Pareto dominates any uniform pricing schedule. To see this, consider Figure 3.5. Suppose that a represen-

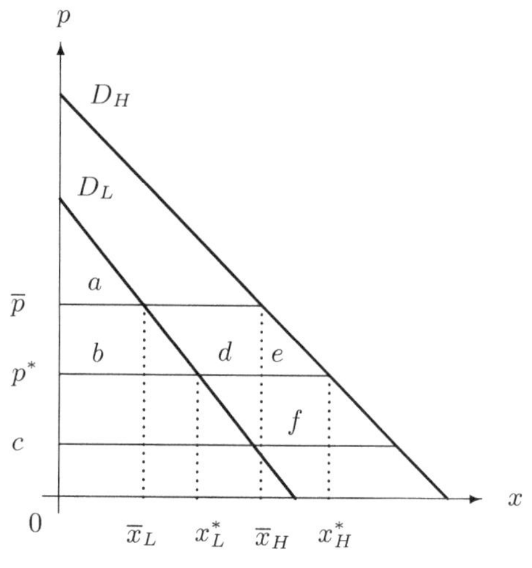

Figure 3.5: Pareto superior nonlinear outlay schedule
Source: Brown and Sibley ([32], p. 69).

tative ISP offers the following two-part tariff as an alternative to the uniform price $\overline{p}$:

$$E(x) := r + p^* x$$

where

$$r := x_H(\overline{p})(\overline{p} - p^*),$$

and $c \leq p^* < \overline{p}$.

Which tariff option is chosen by each user type? The light-user type obtains a surplus represented by the area a if she chooses the uniform price $\overline{p}$. If she chose the two-part tariff her demand for data transport would rise from $\overline{x}_L$ to x_L^* which increases her potential consumer surplus by the trapezoid b. However, this rise in consumer surplus is more than offset by the access fee reflected by the area $(b + d)$. Therefore, a utility maximizing light-user type chooses the uniform price schedule.

With the two-part tariff, potential surplus of the heavy-user type rises by an amount reflected by the area $(b + d + e)$ as her demand rises from $\overline{x}_H$ to x_H^*. Subtracting the fixed fee illustrated by the area $(b + d)$ the heavy-user type gains a net consumer surplus equal to the triangle e when moving from a uniform price schedule to the two-part tariff. Therefore, she chooses the two-part tariff.

A representative ISP is also better off when offering an optional tariff: While the ISP gains the same profits from the light-user type as under uniform pricing the profits derived from the heavy-user type increase by the square f in Figure 3.5.

Figure 3.6 depicts total outlay under the uniform price, chosen by the light-user type, and under the two-part tariff, chosen by the heavy-user type. The lower envelope of the two outlay schedules indicates the minimal outlay under the two different schedules.

We have shown that the optional tariff Pareto dominates the uniform price since, given the optional tariff, the heavy-user type and a representative ISP are better off while the welfare of the light-user type remains unchanged. The light-user type could be made strictly better off, if some of the additional profits of the ISP are rebated to the light-user type. This is a plausible scenario in a competitive ISP industry that is characterized by zero profits.

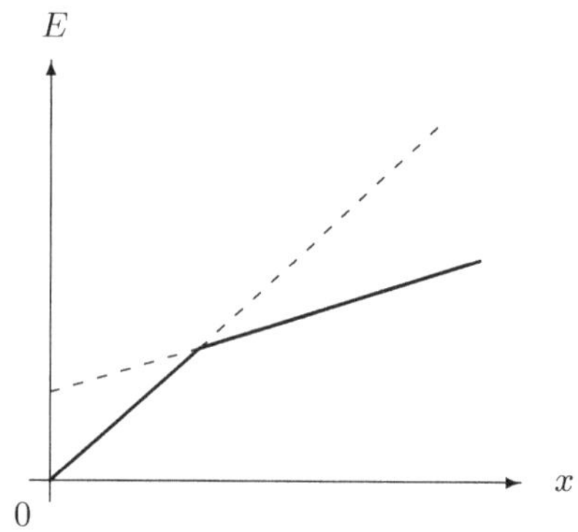

Figure 3.6: Optional tariff
Source: Willig ([255], p. 62).

Pareto improvements can be achieved by optional tariffs since they induce users to sort themselves according to their preferences with respect to Internet usage. Multi-part tariffs introduce an even finer sorting of user preferences compared to a two-part tariff. Faulhaber and Panzar [72] point out that a multi-part tariff can be interpreted as a collection of several two-part tariffs that serve as devices to sort Internet users according to their preferences. To see that, consider the outlay curve $r_1M_1M_2M_3$ of a five-part tariff as depicted in Figure 3.7. The outlay curve $r_1M_1M_2M_3$ can be decomposed into the undominated parts, i.e., into the lower envelope, of the four two-part tariffs

$$(r_1, p_1), (r_2, p_2), (r_3, p_3), (r_4, p_4),$$

where

$$r_1 < r_2 < r_3 < r_4,$$
$$p_1 > p_2 > p_3 > p_4.$$

A two-part tariff with a higher access charge than another one must have a lower variable price in order to be selected by some type of Internet user. Since rational Internet users seek to minimize outlay for any amount of data traffic demanded they only select tariff options

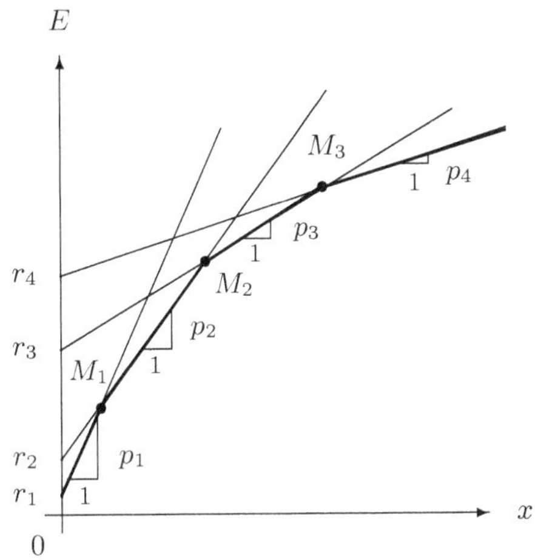

Figure 3.7: Self-selecting set of two-part tariffs
Source: See Brown and Sibley ([32], p. 82).

on the lower envelope of the juxtaposed two-part tariffs, represented by $r_1M_1M_2M_3$. Therefore, a multi-part tariff with quantity discounts can be interpreted as the lower envelope of a collection of two-part tariffs from which Internet users pick their preferred tariff option. This is why the menu of the different two-part tariffs offered is called a 'self-selecting set'[19] of two-part tariffs. Finer sorting can be achieved with the introduction of an n-part outlay schedule with a fixed access charge and $(n-1)$ variable price components.

Table 3.2 depicts an example of a self-selecting set of two-part tariffs offered by Schott, an ISP that provides Internet access over satellite in Germany. Since ISPs that offer Internet via satellite usually do not provide an uplink, upload traffic runs over the telephone line which generates additional telephone costs.

19 Brown and Sibley ([32], p. 81).

Table 3.2: Tariff table of the provider Schott for Internet access via satellite

Maximal upload/ download speed	*Monthly flat rate*	*Free volume per month*	*Price per extra MB/min*
64/2000 Kbps	38 euros	512 MB	5.4 cents/MB
64/2000 Kbps	56 euros	1 GB	5.3 cents/MB
64/2000 Kbps	103 euros	2 GB	5.2 cents/MB
64/2000 Kbps	150 euros	3 GB	4.7 cents/MB
64/2000 Kbps	194 euros	4 GB	4.4 cents/MB

Source: Mansmann and Endres ([158], p. 111).

For a moment, we will focus on a nonlinear outlay schedule with quantity premia in order to illustrate that it cannot be the result of a self-selecting set of two-part tariffs. To see this, consider the following nonlinear outlay schedule for Internet transport services with quantity premia:

$$\begin{aligned} r &= 4.99, & \\ p_1 &= 0.0255, & x \leq 500 \\ p_2 &= 0.03, & x > 500, \end{aligned}$$

where x depicts the amount of MB transferred per month. The corresponding set of two-part tariffs is the following:[20]

$$\begin{aligned} r_1 &= 4.99, & p_1 &= 0.0255 \\ r_2 &= 2.74, & p_2 &= 0.03. \end{aligned}$$

If Internet users can pick their preferred tariff, users who generate more traffic than 500 MB per month choose the first tariff option. Those users who demand no more traffic than 500 MB per month choose the second tariff option. This behavior turns quantity premia

20 The rental r_2 is calculated as follows: $r_2 = 4.99 - 500(0.03 - 0.0255) = 2.74$.

into quantity discounts. Therefore, quantity premia can only be successfully implemented if ISPs have perfect information about the type of Internet users or if tariffs, depending on observed usage patterns, are determined ex post. For that reason, from now on, we will focus on nonlinear outlay schedules with quantity discounts.

We now restate the above argument of Willig [255] on the Pareto dominance of optional tariffs over uniform prices for the more general case with multiple types of Internet users. Imagine that there are j, $j = 1, \ldots, J$, different user types who can choose from n optional tariffs i, $i = 1, \ldots, n$, and $J = n$. Let an Internet user of type j generate $x_j(p_i)$ data units when confronted with the outlay schedule (r_i, p_i).[21] Suppose that Internet users can be ordered according to the quantity of transport services demanded and assume strong monotonicity of demands in j:

$$x_1(p_i) < x_2(p_i) < \ldots < x_J(p_i) \quad \forall \quad p_i. \tag{3.2}$$

This assumption rules out that demand schedules of any two user types cross each other at some variable price component p_i. Imagine n two-part tariffs

$$(r_1, p_1), (r_2, p_2), \ldots, (r_n, p_n),$$

where

$$\begin{aligned} 0 = r_1 < r_2 < \ldots < r_n, \\ p_1 > p_2 > \ldots > p_n \geq c, \\ r_i := x_j(p_1)(p_1 - p_i), \end{aligned}$$

and where $i = 1, \ldots, n$. With the same argumentation as above, we can show that user type j can enhance her consumer surplus by selecting the tariff option (r_i, p_i) tailored for her instead of choosing the

21 In order to simplify our exposition we assume demands for data transport solely to depend on p_i rather than on p_i and r_i. Thereby, we ignore the fact that some Internet users may drop out of the market when being charged a rental. Consider Wilson ([256], Sections 4.4, 6.7, and 7.4) for an analysis of nonlinear tariffs where rentals are explicitly considered.

uniform price p_1. Other user types remain unaffected by her move and profits of the ISP rise.

However, there is an additional problem arising in the case of multiple user types and with multiple tariff options: How can we be sure that user type j does not choose a tariff option l, $l < i$, that was designed for a smaller user type? The construction of the two-part tariff (r_i, p_i) only assures that type j prefers that tariff over the uniform price, but there is no guarantee that she will not prefer another tariff option over (r_i, p_i). If type j were to choose (r_l, p_l), the profits of the ISP might decrease relative to the scenario where it charges type j and all other users the uniform price p_1. Therefore, the collection of tariffs offered must be incentive compatible with each other. In this context, incentive compatibility means that no Internet user type has an incentive to mimic another type. Otherwise, one can no longer be sure that all parties gain from the new tariff.

In a moment, we will explain how the problem of incentive compatibility can be accounted for by the choice of an appropriate tariff structure. At present, suppose that the J different user types initially face n incentive-compatible two-part tariffs, where $p_n > c$ and $J > n$. Willig ([255], pp. 65–68) shows that by finer sorting through the introduction of an additional incentive-compatible tariff option

$$(r_{n+1}, p_{n+1})$$

with

$$c \leq p_{n+1} < p_n$$

and

$$r_{n+1} := x_J(p_n)(p_n - p_{n+1}), \tag{3.3}$$

a Pareto improvement can be achieved as long as the number of user types exceeds the amount of tariffs offered, i.e., if $J > n$.

The line of reasoning is as follows: Consider the heaviest Internet user type J who has chosen the tariff (r_n, p_n) under the n-part tariff outlay schedule. Consequently, her demand amounts to $x_J(p_n)$ and her expenditures equal $r_n + p_n x_J(p_n)$. Type J user switches to the $(n+1)$th tariff structure provided that

$$r_{n+1} + p_{n+1} x_J(p_n) \leq r_n + p_n x_J(p_n).$$

Through the introduction of the $(n+1)$th tariff the consumer surplus of type J user increases by the amount of the surplus on the additional data units $(x_J(p_{n+1})-x_J(p_n))$ she generates given the outlay schedule (r_{n+1}, p_{n+1}). Note that type J user does not gain any surplus from the $x_J(p_n)$ units of data generated since her savings from a lower variable price are offset by a larger fixed access charge r_{n+1}.

A representative ISP is also better off through the move to the $(n+1)$-part tariff since its profits increase by the revenues above marginal costs on the additional data units $(x_J(p_{n+1})-x_J(p_n))$ conveyed. Smaller consumer types remain unaffected by the introduction of the $(n+1)$-part tariff. They also have the option of choosing the tariff (r_{n+1}, p_{n+1}). If they choose to do so they must pay the rental r_{n+1}. This rental is designed such that a representative ISP obtains at least the revenues from user type J it would realize under the n-part tariff. Strong monotonicity of demands assures that under the n-part tariff the outlay of smaller user types is smaller than the one of type J users. Hence, if smaller user types select the tariff (r_{n+1}, p_{n+1}) a representative ISP can increase its surplus compared to the case where smaller users stay with their original tariff choice under the n-part tariff. We can conclude that the $(n+1)$-part tariff Pareto dominates the n-part tariff. Moreover, the $(n+1)$-part tariff is incentive compatible with the n-part tariff since only the Internet user type for which the $(n+1)$th tariff option was designed for, i.e. user type J, has an incentive to indeed select that tariff option.

The argumentation above can be applied over and over again until the variable price component charged to the heaviest user type equals marginal costs. We can conclude that an optimal outlay schedule requires the variable price of the largest consumer to equal marginal costs of data transport. This intuitive result will be analytically shown below.

By complete induction we can now justify our temporary assumption about the incentive compatibility of the n-part tariff: The property of incentive compatibility between the tariff options (r_n, p_n) and (r_{n+1}, p_{n+1}) holds for all n. Hence, we can start our analysis with $n = 1$ and, by applying the argument of Willig over and over again, can ensure that every additional two-part tariff introduced fulfills the requirement of incentive compatibility.

So far, we were concerned with Pareto dominating outlay schedules. We now turn our attention to optimal nonlinear tariffs that maximize total surplus, defined as the sum of consumer and provider surplus, subject to the break-even constraint of a representative ISP. Markets are assumed to be contestable such that there are no positive profits in the industry.[22] The above analysis was independent of the distribution of user types. We only needed to know that different user types exist. We will see below that if we want to determine the exact values of the parameters of an optimal nonlinear outlay schedule, the distribution of user types must be known, i.e., we must know the number of Internet users of each type.

Consider the case of a continuum of user types. Let θ be a continuous taste variable to reflect the user type, where $\underline{\theta} \leq \theta \leq \overline{\theta}$. The inverse demand, or the willingness to pay schedule, of a user of type θ is given by a differentiable function $\rho(x, \theta)$. Assume that

$$\begin{aligned} \frac{\partial \rho(x,\theta)}{\partial x} &< 0, \\ \frac{\partial \rho(x,\theta)}{\partial \theta} &> 0. \end{aligned} \tag{3.4}$$

Moreover, suppose that the integral of $\rho(x, \theta)$ has an upper bound. The assumption that demand increases in θ reflects strong monotonic preferences in θ. Strong monotonicity ensures that the inverse demand curve of a high-θ type of user is always situated to the right of the inverse demand curve of a low-θ type of user. Thus, demand curves of different user types cannot intersect. For this reason, (3.4) is usually called non-crossing assumption about demands. It is equivalent to the assumption made above in expression (3.2).

Let $g(\theta)$ be the continuous density function of θ. This function can be integrated to obtain the probability that the taste variable θ takes a value in a given interval. The resulting cumulative distribution

22 Due to the threat of potential competition there is no profit opportunity in contestable markets. See Tirole ([239], pp. 308–311) for an introduction into the theory of contestable markets.

function of θ shall be reflected by $G(\theta)$. This function describes the probability that the taste variable θ takes on a value less than or equal to a given value θ. As above, a representative ISP shall incur marginal transport costs equal to c and fixed costs in the amount of F. The tariff schedule is given by $p(x)$ which shall be non-increasing. Let $\hat{\theta}$ be the marginal user type, i.e., the critical value of θ such that a user of type $\hat{\theta}$ would just have an incentive to generate the xth (marginal) unit of data traffic when confronted with the tariff schedule $p(x)$. Thus, intuitively, the marginal Internet user type $\hat{\theta}$ at x is defined by the incentive compatibility constraint

$$p(x) = \rho(x, \hat{\theta}). \tag{3.5}$$

Users of a lower type would not generate the xth (marginal) data unit while users of a higher type $\theta > \hat{\theta}$ would do so. Note that x^* which satisfies the constraint (3.5) is determined by a function of $\hat{\theta}$: $x^* = x(\hat{\theta})$. To simplify notation this dependency will not always be shown explicitly in our analysis. Assume x^* to be uniquely determined by $\hat{\theta}$ such that $x^{-1}(x^*) = \hat{\theta}$.[23]

To understand the incentive compatibility constraint[24] (3.5), note that x^* depicts the optimal amount of data transport services demanded by type θ that maximizes her quasilinear (monetary) utility function[25]

$$U(x, b, \theta) := u(x, \theta) + b \tag{3.6}$$

23 Our assumption (3.4) guarantees that $x(\hat{\theta})$ is weakly monotonically increasing in $\hat{\theta}$. To see this, suppose that $x(\hat{\theta})$ is not weakly monotonically increasing in θ. Then, consumer surplus of a user type $\theta_2 > \theta_1$ must decrease if she increases her consumption from $x(\theta_2)$ to $x(\theta_1)$ while the surplus of a user type θ_1 increases over that interval. This implies that the demand schedule of type θ_2 lies below the demand schedule of type θ_1 which contradicts assumption (3.4). To simplify the analysis, suppose that $x(\hat{\theta})$ is strictly monotonically increasing. Then, $x(\hat{\theta})$ is invertible.

24 The subsequent derivation of the incentive compatibility constraint is drawn from Varian ([243], pp. 614 f.).

25 Given a quasilinear utility function, demand for data transfer is independent of the level of income. The choice of this utility function can be motivated by the fact that each consumer spends only a small portion of her overall budget on data transfer.

subject to the budget constraint $E(x) + b = m$, where m denotes the exogenous income and where the consumption of the numeraire good is depicted by b.[26] This good can be interpreted as the money Internet users spend on goods other than Internet usage. Solving the budget constraint for the numeraire b and substituting the result for b in the utility function (3.6) yields the unconstrained maximization problem

$$\max_x \quad u(x, \theta) + m - E(x). \tag{3.7}$$

The point where the function (3.7) reaches its maximum does not depend on the budget m. Hence, to find the utility maximizing value x^*, rather than maximizing (3.7), we can as well maximize

$$\max_x \quad u(x, \theta) - E(x). \tag{3.8}$$

We go on working with (3.8).

To guarantee incentive compatibility, self-selection constraints have to be set up ensuring that a user of type $\hat{\theta}$ prefers $x(\hat{\theta})$ to $x(\tilde{\theta})$, whenever $\tilde{\theta} \neq \hat{\theta}$:

$$u(x(\hat{\theta}), \hat{\theta}) - E(x(\hat{\theta})) \geq u(x(\tilde{\theta}), \hat{\theta}) - E(x(\tilde{\theta})) \quad \text{for all} \quad \tilde{\theta} \neq \hat{\theta}.$$

Define

$$g(\tilde{\theta}) := u(x(\hat{\theta}), \hat{\theta}) - E(x(\hat{\theta})) - u(x(\tilde{\theta}), \hat{\theta}) + E(x(\tilde{\theta})),$$

where $g(\tilde{\theta}) \geq 0$ and $g(\hat{\theta}) = 0$. Therefore, the function $g(\tilde{\theta})$ reaches its minimum at $\tilde{\theta} = \hat{\theta}$. Hence,

$$\left.\frac{dg(\tilde{\theta})}{d\tilde{\theta}}\right|_{\tilde{\theta}=\hat{\theta}} = -\left[\frac{\partial u(x(\hat{\theta}), \hat{\theta})}{\partial x} - \frac{\partial E(x(\hat{\theta}))}{\partial x}\right] \left.\frac{dx(\hat{\theta})}{d\tilde{\theta}}\right|_{\tilde{\theta}=\hat{\theta}} = 0.$$

This implies that

$$\left[\frac{\partial u(x(\hat{\theta}), \hat{\theta})}{\partial x} - \frac{\partial E(x(\hat{\theta}))}{\partial x}\right] = 0.$$

26 We assume the consumer to exhaust her budget.

Since

$$\rho(x,\hat{\theta}) := \frac{\partial u(x(\hat{\theta}),\hat{\theta})}{\partial x} \tag{3.9}$$

and, according to (3.1),

$$p(x) := \frac{\partial E(x(\hat{\theta}))}{\partial x}, \tag{3.10}$$

we obtain the incentive compatibility constraint (3.5).

In order to define the social welfare function below, we first introduce aggregate consumer surplus. Therefore, consider an interval dx located at a certain quantity x. Aggregate consumer surplus over the interval dx resulting from all Internet users who generate the traffic demand x or more is defined as

$$CS := \int_{\hat{\theta}}^{\overline{\theta}} [\rho(x,\theta) - p(x)]g(\theta)d\theta,$$

where $\hat{\theta}$ is the least type served. The model predicts, by condition (3.5), that the consumer surplus of the marginal user of type $\hat{\theta}$ is zero. Provider surplus over the interval dx is defined as follows:

$$PS := \int_{\hat{\theta}}^{\overline{\theta}} [p(x) - c]g(\theta)d\theta = [1 - G(\hat{\theta})][p(x) - c].$$

We define social welfare to be total consumer and provider surplus over all quantities x:

$$W(p(x)) := \int_0^{\infty} \left\{ \int_{\hat{\theta}}^{\overline{\theta}} [\rho(x,\theta) - p(x)]g(\theta)d\theta + [1 - G(\hat{\theta})][p(x) - c] \right\} dx.$$

Formally, given that the integral of $\rho(x,\theta)$ is bounded from above and that the tariff schedule $p(x)$ is non-increasing, the addends of the social welfare function, i.e. consumer and the provider surplus over the interval dx, become smaller the higher the value of x. We assume these increments to approach zero such that the integral converges.

The social welfare function shall be maximized subject to the break-even constraint of a representative ISP

$$\Pi(p(x)) := \int_0^{\infty} \left\{[1 - G(\hat{\theta})][p(x) - c]\right\} dx - F \geq 0.$$

We can set up the Lagrangian that takes the form

$$L(p(x), \lambda) := \int_0^{\infty} \left\{\int_{\hat{\theta}}^{\overline{\theta}} [\rho(x, \theta) - p(x)]g(\theta)d\theta + [1 - G(\hat{\theta})][p(x) - c]\right\} dx$$
$$+ \lambda \left\{\int_0^{\infty} [1 - G(\hat{\theta})][p(x) - c]dx\right\} - \lambda F.$$

Optimal functions such as $p(x)$ are usually derived by means of the calculus of variations. However, since our welfare function does not depend on the partial derivative of $p(x)$ with respect to x our optimization problem is a degenerate problem in the calculus of variations. In this case, the Euler equation,[27] which is a first-order condition for an optimum in the calculus of variations, is not a differential equation, but is reduced to a standard calculus condition of first order. Then, for our example, the optimal solution can be obtained by optimizing the integrand of the objective function with respect to $p(x)$ for all x.

Also, in order to derive the optimal nonlinear tariff note that, when considering the effect of a variation in the price on consumer surplus, we study the effect of such a price variation on the consumer surplus of the marginal consumer type $\hat{\theta}$. This allows us to fix the willingness to pay schedule of type θ at $\rho(x, \hat{\theta})$. Hence, in order to simplify calculation, we can also express aggregate consumer surplus as

$$[1 - G(\hat{\theta})][\rho(x, \hat{\theta}) - p(x)]$$

when studying the effect of a small variation in $p(x)$ on aggregate consumer surplus. Also, when differentiating the Lagrangian with respect to $p(x)$, one has to keep in mind that $\hat{\theta}$ depends on $p(x)$ since

27 See Kamien and Schwartz ([124], pp. 14-19) for an explanation of the Euler equation.

$\hat{\theta} = x^{-1}(x^*, p)$, where $x^* = x(\hat{\theta}, p)$ maximizes (3.8). Assuming an interior solution, a necessary condition for optimality[28] is given by

$$\frac{\partial L(p(x), \lambda)}{\partial p} = \int_0^\infty \left\{ [p(x) - \rho(x, \hat{\theta})] g(\hat{\theta}) \frac{\partial \hat{\theta}}{\partial p} - [1 - G(\hat{\theta})] + [1 - G(\hat{\theta})] \right.$$
$$\left. - g(\hat{\theta}) \frac{\partial \hat{\theta}}{\partial p} [p(x) - c] \right\} dx$$
$$+ \lambda \int_0^\infty \left\{ -g(\hat{\theta}) \frac{\partial \hat{\theta}}{\partial p} [p(x) - c] + [1 - G(\hat{\theta})] \right\} dx = 0. \tag{3.11}$$

With $\rho(x, \hat{\theta}) = p(x)$, condition (3.11) reduces to

$$\frac{\partial L(p(x), \lambda)}{\partial p} = \int_0^\infty \left\{ -(1 + \lambda)[p(x) - c] g(\hat{\theta}) \frac{\partial \hat{\theta}}{\partial p} + \lambda [1 - G(\hat{\theta})] \right\} dx = 0.$$

In the optimum, the derivative of the integrand must vanish at each x:

$$-(1 + \lambda)[p(x) - c] g(\hat{\theta}) \frac{\partial \hat{\theta}}{\partial p} + \lambda [1 - G(\hat{\theta})] = 0.$$

Division by $p(x) \neq 0$ and rearranging terms yields

$$\frac{p(x) - c}{p(x)} = \frac{\lambda}{1 + \lambda} \frac{1 - G(\hat{\theta})}{p(x) g(\hat{\theta}) \frac{\partial \hat{\theta}}{\partial p}}. \tag{3.12}$$

---

28 We assume second-order conditions for a maximum of welfare and for consumer self-selection to be satisfied. Second-order conditions of incentive compatibility require the second derivative of (3.8) with respect to x to be non-positive. Hence, by (3.9) and (3.10), we must have $\frac{\partial \rho(x, \hat{\theta})}{\partial x} - \frac{dp(x)}{dx} \leq 0$ if type $\hat{\theta}$ purchases the xth unit. This says that the marginal price curve $p(x)$ must intersect the willingness to pay curve $\rho(x, \hat{\theta})$ from below for all $\hat{\theta}$. Then, $p(x)$ is said to be single-crossing for all x. See Goldman, Leland and Sibley ([90], pp. 306–316). One has to keep in mind that these assumptions about second-order conditions are not innocuous. Consider Brown and Sibley ([32], pp. 208–215) for a discussion of cases where these assumptions fail to hold.

To understand the above equation note that $G(\hat{\theta})$ reflects the number of Internet users having θ values less than or equal to a given value $\hat{\theta}$. The number 1 reflects the normalized total number of Internet users. The aggregate demand for an increase of data traffic transport from x to $(x + dx)$ is generated by Internet users having a θ value $\theta \geq \hat{\theta}$, where $\hat{\theta}$ is the marginal consumer type who just has an incentive to generate the xth unit of data traffic when confronted with the marginal price $p(x)$. In contrary, the willingness to pay of Internet users of a type $\theta < \hat{\theta}$ is less that $p(x)$. Thus, they do not demand any data to be transferred in the increment market dx. Hence, we may express the aggregate demand for data traffic transport in the dx increment market at x as $[1 - G(\hat{\theta})]$. Stated differently, we decompose the willingness to pay schedule into independent demands for marginal units of traffic transport. Then, for a given quantity x, we consider the demand for the marginal unit of data traffic, given the price $p(x)$. Demand for this marginal unit equals $[1 - G(\hat{\theta})]$.

Now, consider the price elasticity of demand for data transport in an increment market dx at x. This price elasticity is to be read as the percentage of users who, at x, drop out of that increment market dx if the price increases by one percent. In order to better explain how to formally express this price elasticity we discretize our analysis: Interpreted discretely, the number of consumers who drop out of a particular increment market Δx due to an incremental increase in price $p(x)$ by Δp is given by the change in $\hat{\theta}$ due to a small increase in $p(x)$, multiplied by the number of users that have a θ value of $\hat{\theta}$. The number of users that have a θ value of $\hat{\theta}$ is the density function of θ evaluated at $\hat{\theta}$ if θ is a discrete variable.

With this explanation in mind we can define the price elasticity of demand in the concerned increment market dx as

$$\epsilon(x, p(x)) := \frac{p(x)}{1 - G(\hat{\theta})} \left(\frac{\partial \hat{\theta}}{\partial p(x)} \right) g(\hat{\theta}).$$

We are now ready to rewrite the optimal nonlinear tariff (3.12) as

$$\frac{p(x)-c}{p(x)} = \frac{\lambda}{1+\lambda}\frac{1-G(\hat{\theta})}{p(x)g(\hat{\theta})\frac{\partial\hat{\theta}}{\partial p}} = \frac{\lambda}{1+\lambda}\frac{1}{\epsilon(x,p(x))}. \tag{3.13}$$

The optimal outlay schedule given in (3.13) shows that marginal cost pricing is optimal for the heaviest type of Internet users since then, $G(\hat{\theta}) = 1$. In order to give an alternative interpretation of (3.13) note that the price elasticity of the final market increment is infinite since only users of type $\bar{\theta}$ are in that market. By equation (3.13), price must equal marginal costs in the market for the final data increment generated by the heaviest user type. This reinforces our argument made above.

The optimal outlay schedule in (3.13) is interesting for one more reason: It can be interpreted as a Ramsey pricing rule. Ramsey prices are linear prices that are second-best optimal. These prices are called second-best optimal because they maximize welfare while allowing ISPs to recover costs. Ramsey prices determine the distribution of fixed costs among different users such that allocative deviations from the first-best solution, characterized by marginal cost pricing, are minimized. Ramsey prices are relevant in markets where firms offer multiple products or services. In our context, ISPs can offer multiple services by selling different service qualities.

In the literature on Ramsey pricing it is assumed that demands for, in our case, the different service qualities have distinct price elasticities of demand at a given price. Provided that demands for different service qualities are independent, which implies that cross-price elasticities of demands are zero,[29] Ramsey prices take the following form:

$$\frac{p_i - c_i}{p_i} = \frac{\lambda}{1+\lambda}\frac{1}{|\epsilon_i|},$$

where p_i denotes the price per unit of data transport of service quality i, where c_i depicts marginal costs of data transport of quality i, where

29 This is a simplifying assumption. The more general case with cross-price elasticities of demand not equal to zero does not change the nature of Ramsey prices in any fundamental way. See Baumol and Bradford ([19], p. 270).

λ reflects the non-negative Lagrange multiplier associated with the break-even constraint, and where $|\epsilon_i|$ is the price elasticity of demand for data transport with service quality i in absolute terms.

The Ramsey rule states that the markup over marginal costs of data transport of quality i to recover fixed costs must be inversely proportional to the price elasticity of demand for that quality. This is the so-called inverse elasticity rule. The larger the price elasticity of demand, ϵ_i, the lower the markup. Relatively inelastic demand would then be priced relatively high and vice versa.

Ramsey pricing could be a further proposal for load-insensitive priority pricing if we assumed demand for data traffic with high QoS to be relatively inelastic. Then, data transport services with a high quality would also be higher priced. However, there is no apparent reason why demand for data traffic with high QoS should be more inelastic than demand for data traffic with low QoS. Without empirical evidence this would be a rather speculative assumption.[30] Moreover, if Ramsey pricing were used to price different service qualities, in order to avoid market entry, the price for the QoS with the most inelastic demand might not exceed the separate price for the same service of a specialized ISP offering only this single service. Market entry would render Ramsey pricing structure impossible and lead to losses.[31] Therefore, this pricing approach will not be further investigated in Section 3.2 on load-insensitive priority pricing.[32]

Let us summarize our considerations on nonlinear outlay schedules: Nonuniform prices enhance welfare in the Paretianian sense if ISPs cannot break even with marginal cost pricing. Such Pareto improvements are obtained if each user type is offered the outlay tariff

30 Rupp ([201], p. 38) brings up a further argument against applying Ramsey pricing in the Internet by saying that a correct estimation of demand elasticities is hardly possible in a complex system such as the Internet. Laffont and Tirole ([137], pp. 131 f.), on the contrary, claim that in practice, in competitive markets where price structure has to be adjusted to demand, these elasticities of demand can indeed be assessed.

31 See Braeutigam ([29], pp. 1340–1342) and Laffont and Tirole ([137], p. 104).

32 See Baumol and Bradford [19], Braeutigam ([29], pp. 1320–1327), Brown and Sibley ([32], pp. 39–44), Laffont and Tirole ([137], pp. 60–84), or Ramsey [194] for further information on Ramsey prices.

that fits her preferences. Generally, the user type is unknown to ISPs. Therefore, ISPs offer a menu of different nonlinear tariffs that induce users to reveal their true demand for data transport services. Providers are said to screen their users through self-selecting tariffs. We have shown that as long as the number of user types exceeds the number of two-part options within a tariff structure offered, welfare can be improved through the introduction of an additional two-part tariff designed for the heaviest user type. An optimal nonlinear outlay schedule covers total costs of data transport where the marginal cost pricing principle applies for the heaviest type of Internet users.

We close our analysis on nonlinear tariffs with an evaluation thereof. Table 3.3 summarizes our subsequent evaluation.[33]

Table 3.3: Evaluation of nonlinear outlay schedules

ISP/Welfare	*Allocative efficiency*	▽
	Capacity expansion	▼
	Incentive compatibility	▲
ISP	*Cost-orientation*	△
	Price discrimination	△
	Feasibility	△
	Accounting efficiency	△
User	*Utility-orientation*	△
	Price transparency	△

▲ = very good, △ = good

◊ = satisfactory, ▽ = adequate, ▼ = inadequate

33 Our evaluation is partially based on Gerpott and Böhm ([84], p. 238).

- *Allocative efficiency*
  From the point of view of social welfare, with the introduction of nonlinear tariffs aggregate welfare is improved relative to the scenario with a uniform pricing scheme. However, nonlinear tariffs do not vary with the load of the network. Instead, if marginal costs of data transport are interpreted as marginal congestion costs, marginal congestion costs are assumed to be constant. Thus, congestion externalities cannot be internalized appropriately. In particular, in the presence of network externalities, volume discounts may further enhance congestion. One could argue that nonlinear outlay schedules with quantity premia provide a solution to that problem. However, such tariffs would penalize heavy users who generate huge volumes of data traffic during off-peak periods in an unjustified way. Additionally, as explained above, nonlinear tariffs with quantity premia cannot be the result of a self-selecting set of two-part tariffs.

  We can conclude that nonlinear outlay schedules fail to guarantee an efficient use of capacity, but, in comparison with flat-rate pricing, resources are allocated more efficiently. Furthermore, monetary incentives are missing to shift peak demands into off-peak periods. However, Brown and Sibley ([32], pp. 121–128) extend the theory of nonlinear pricing to the multi-commodity case that can be interpreted as a scenario where ISPs price peak and off-peak demand differently. The theory of peak-load pricing will be introduced in the next section.
- *Capacity expansion*
  Nonlinear prices give no monetary incentives to expand capacity in bottlenecks. The reason is that nonlinear prices are load-insensitive. This argument will become clearer in the next section, where an additional pricing instrument is introduced such that expenditures for Internet services do not only vary with the amount of traffic generated, but also with the load of the network.
- *Incentive compatibility*
  Nonlinear outlay schedules, when designed appropriately, are incentive compatible in the sense that through the choice of a tariff option every user type truly reveals her preferences. Moreover,

ISPs can increase their profits by offering additional tariff choices until the variable price component charged to the heaviest user type equals marginal costs.

- *Cost-orientation*
  Only in the case of constant marginal costs of congestion, which is a rather unrealistic scenario, do nonlinear tariffs allow ISPs to fully recover their costs. Nevertheless, we still judge cost-orientation of nonlinear tariffs to be good.
- *Price discrimination*
  Different willingnesses to pay can be exploited in the form of second degree price discrimination. Thereby, compared to the case where a uniform price is offered, nonlinear tariffs allow ISPs to increase their profits. For this purpose, ISPs do not necessitate detailed consumer information since consumers reveal their type by selecting the appropriate tariff designed for them. However, further extraction of consumer surplus would be possible by making the usage-based price components load-sensitive.
- *Feasibility*
  The feasibility of nonlinear tariffs depends upon the amount of different tariff choices offered. In reality, it is not essential to offer users a continuum of tariffs. But, appropriate tariffs should be designed for principal consumer types. Thus, provided that information on the distribution of user types necessary to determine optimal tariffs can be obtained or estimated easily, implementation of nonlinear tariffs is rather simple. Moreover, implementation of nonlinear tariffs can be done in a decentralized manner: ISPs can offer the tariff choices which best fit the preferences of their clientele.
- *Accounting efficiency*
  Accounting efficiency is lower compared to flat-rate pricing, but is still good: Only the amount of traffic generated has to be measured, a widely adopted task in practice.
- *Utility-orientation*
  From the perspective of end-users, nonlinear tariffs increase individual user utilities compared to a uniform price. These tariffs are utility-oriented in the sense that different user types are

considered in the pricing structure. Users have the possibility to select their most preferred tariff option. The introduction of load-sensitive prices would further enhance utility-orientation.

- *Price transparency*
  Price transparency is obtained since nonlinear price tariff tables are not complicated and are known ex ante. However, compared to flat-rate pricing price transparency decreases.

Nonlinear prices in the form of ex-post weighted-average Coase tariffs, where the rental is a weighted average of total fixed costs, have the same desirable characteristics as optimal nonlinear tariffs, with the exception of price transparency. Price transparency would decrease as rentals would only be known ex post. But, at the same time, no information would be necessary concerning the distribution of different user types which simplifies implementation.

3.1.3 Peak-Load Pricing

Peak-load pricing, i.e., price discrimination according to the time of day, may be applied if demand exceeds the supply of capacity of one or several providers during peaks and if there is idle capacity in off-peak periods. Peak-load prices are used to smooth such fluctuations in demand over time such that existing physical capacities are more efficiently utilized: Internet users who generate data traffic during peak hours should have to pay a higher price compared to those using the Internet during off-peak periods.

In practice, phone calls during business hours in the telecommunications sector, day power in the energy sector, or principal traffic hours in the transport sector are priced at peak-load prices. Recall from Section 3.1.1 that both New Zealand and Great Britain applied peak-load pricing in the Internet environment. Moreover, in July 2003, T-Online offered ADSL Internet access for 1.59 cents per MB of data generated between 7 p.m. to 7 a.m., while data traffic conveyance was free of charge from 7 a.m. to 7 p.m. Additionally, a flat rate that amounted to 24.95 euros was charged per month.[34] The subsequent analysis of peak-load pricing is based on the contributions of Steiner [230] and Braeutigam ([29], pp. 1316–1320).

Assume that there are two periods i, $i = 1, 2$, of equal length.[35] Let x_i denote the quantity of data units conveyed in period i. Marginal costs of data transport are depicted by c. These costs approach zero if the network is not congested. Marginal costs of capacity are reflected by β. It is assumed that c and β are constant.[36] If there is excess capacity marginal costs of data transport equal c. If capacity should be expanded marginal costs shall equal $(c + \beta)$.[37]

Inverse demand curves for data transport of the two periods are assumed to be negatively sloped and to be independent of each other which implies that cross-price elasticities between periods equal zero. Moreover, we suppose that at a given price demand in period 1 always exceeds demand in period 2. Prices for data transport in period i are denoted by p_i, $i = 1, 2$. They are set ex ante, i.e., ahead of the accounting period. Network utilization shall vary systematically with the respective period.

Our aim in this section is to find a price schedule which, in both periods, incites consumers to generate such amounts of data transport which maximize social welfare, defined as the sum of consumer and provider surplus. We will see below that maximization of social welfare requires prices to reflect marginal costs. Moreover, the price schedule we search for should ensure cost recovery. Such prices that at once maximize social welfare and allow to recover costs lead to a social and to a private optimum. In the subsequent analysis we

---

34 See Mansmann and Hüskes ([159], p. 121).

35 The assumption of periods of equal length is not necessary, but simplifies the distribution of costs of capacity among the different periods.

36 The assumption of constant marginal costs of data transport is not very plausible in the Internet industry since they approach zero when the network is not congested and are positive otherwise. When congestion externalities are taken into account one would expect increasing marginal costs of data transport. To include congestion externalities into the analysis we will in a future step introduce increasing marginal costs of data transport.

37 By splitting up marginal costs into marginal costs of data transport and capacity we implicitly assume a Leontief technology.

will distinguish between two cases, the so-called firm peak and the so-called shifting peak.

We first consider the firm peak case illustrated in Figure 3.8. Marginal costs of data transport c have been subtracted from the

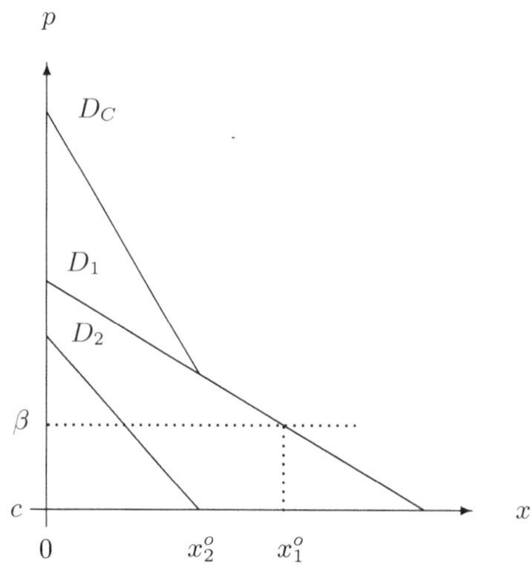

Figure 3.8: Firm peak case
Source: See Steiner ([230], p. 588).

inverse demand curves D_1 and D_2. Therefore, these curves depict the demands for capacity. Vertical addition of the inverse demand curves D_1 and D_2 yields D_C.[38] To simplify, inverse demand schedules are drawn linearly. In Figure 3.8 multiple price-quantity combinations can be identified. If we ask for prices that maximize total surplus, reflected in Figure 3.8 by the area between marginal costs and the inverse demand schedules, prices have to reflect marginal costs.

38 Demands are added vertically since the amount of capacity financed in one period is also available in the second period. Hence, to obtain the total willingness to pay for capacity the demand, or the willingness to pay, for capacity in each period must be added. In other words, users fund capacity jointly. The extent of joint funding depends on the positions and the shapes of the inverse demand curves.

In period 1 demand for capacity matches marginal costs of capacity at x_1^o. Marginal capacity demand is only generated by users of period 1. Hence, the appropriate price in period 1 equals

$$p_1 = c + \beta \tag{3.14}$$

for each unit of data transport. The capacity to accommodate the traffic volume x_1^o would also be installed if there was no demand in period 2. Since capacity already exists, off-peak users should only have to pay marginal costs of data transport, i.e.,

$$p_2 = c. \tag{3.15}$$

Confronted with this price off-peak users demand the quantity x_2^o of data transports. Even though only peak users bear the costs of capacity peak demand continues to occur in period 1, the peak period. Therefore, this case is the so-called firm peak case.

We now analyze important properties of the prices p_1 and p_2. First, they cover total costs: Costs of capacity and of data transport equal βx_1^o and $c(x_1^o + x_2^o)$, respectively. Second, these prices maximize welfare since they reflect marginal costs. Third, p_1 and p_2 are non-discriminatory since the difference in prices is based on distinct costs: Costs of capacity expansion are carried by peak users who cause the scarcity of capacity in the first place.

We now turn our attention to the shifting peak case. If we apply the price schedule derived for the firm peak case to a changed demand schedule, as illustrated in Figure 3.9, peak demand moves from period 1 to period 2: With the prices (3.14) and (3.15) the traffic quantities x_1^o and x_2^o are demanded in the two periods. The peak price p_1 has to be paid for the x_1^o traffic units generated in period 1 even though the maximal demand is generated in period 2. The peak price is paid by off-peak users and peak-users pay the off-peak price. This phenomenon explains why this case is the so-called shifting peak case.

The off-peak price (3.15) charged for x_2^o data units that make the peak demand upon capacity does not allow for cost recovery. Costs are only recovered up to x_1^o. For each further unit of data traffic only marginal costs of data transport may be recovered.

Neither does an average price

$$\overline{p} = c + \frac{\beta}{2}$$

allow for cost recovery. With an average price $\overline{p}$ the quantities demanded in the two periods are $\overline{x}_1$ and $\overline{x}_2$. Then, revenues of an ISP equal

$$(\overline{x}_1 + \overline{x}_2)\left(c + \frac{\beta}{2}\right).$$

These revenues recover transport costs $(\overline{x}_1 + \overline{x}_2)c$ but not total costs of capacity. Costs of capacity are only covered up to the quantity

$$\frac{(\overline{x}_1 + \overline{x}_2)}{2}.$$

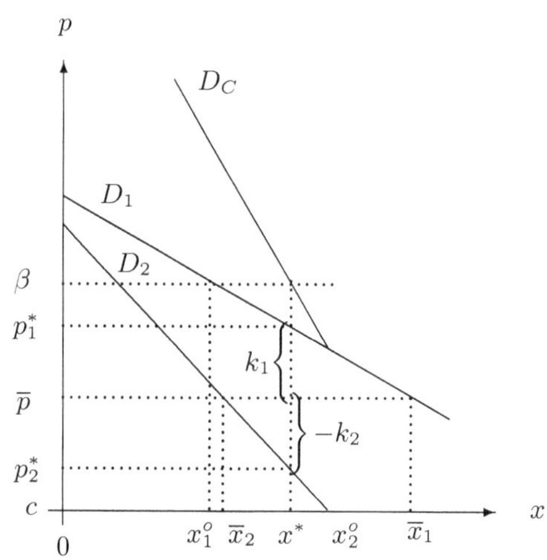

Figure 3.9: Shifting peak case
Source: See Steiner ([230], p. 588).

The solution is obtained if the aggregate inverse demand curve D_C is used to determine the prices. The intersection of marginal costs

$(c+\beta)$ and the D_C curve determines the total amount of capacity, justified by the added demands, to accommodate the traffic volume x^*. The amount of data traffic transported in each period should be increased up to this capacity since in both periods the willingness to pay exceeds the marginal costs of data transport up to x^*. Hence, the socially optimal quantities in both periods are given by x^*. In our example, the corresponding socially optimal prices that equilibrate supply and demand can be written as

$$\begin{aligned} p_1^* &= c+\frac{\beta}{2}+k_1, \quad k_1>0, \\ p_2^* &= c+\frac{\beta}{2}+k_2, \quad k_2<0, \end{aligned}$$

where $k_1+k_2=0$. These prices recover total costs: Transport costs and costs of capacity equal $2cx^*$ and βx^*, respectively. Hence, total costs equal $(2cx^*+\beta x^*)$. Revenues in period 1 and in period 2 equal

$$p_1^* x^* = x^* \left(c+\frac{\beta}{2}+k_1\right)$$

and

$$p_2^* x^* = x^* \left(c+\frac{\beta}{2}+k_2\right),$$

respectively. Total revenues are given by

$$x^*(2c+\beta)$$

which equal total costs.

Apart from cost-covering, the prices p_1^* and p_2^* are discriminatory, more precisely, discriminatory of the third degree, since different prices are paid for the same amount of data traffic demanded. Users who bring about a major demand for capacity pay a higher price compared to users with a low demand.

We can generalize our results of the shifting peak case as follows: While in the firm peak case only peak users bear the costs of capacity in the shifting peak case both periods bear a part of these costs. In the shifting peak case the division of these costs depends on the intensity of demand. Moreover, capacity is fully used in both periods:

$$D_1^{-1}(p_1^*) = D_2^{-1}(p_2^*) = x^*.$$

The same amount of data units are transported in both periods while differences in demand are only visible through different prices which satisfy

$$\beta + c > p_1^* > p_2^* > c,$$

where

$$(p_1^* - c) + (p_2^* - c) = \beta.$$

Generally speaking, a unit of capacity is justified if and only if it is justified by the demand of a single period or if and only if it is justified by the combination of two or several periods. Costs of capacity are borne by users of the unique peak period or by users of different periods whose aggregate demand justifies an additional unit of capacity. In the latter case costs of capacity are distributed among the periods in proportion to their demand for capacity. Therefore, costs of capacity are allocated according to demand on a discriminatory basis.

The above results may be generalized to more than two periods where one can imagine mixed cases, in the sense that among a certain subset of periods shifting peak cases prevail, while between this subset and the other subsets a firm peak relationship applies. This mixed case is illustrated in Figure 3.10 for a three-period example. Periods 1 and 2 are peak periods. Together they generate the peak demand upon capacity. Their combined demands justify a further unit of capacity. While the shifting peak case prevails between periods 1 and 2 the relationship between this group of periods and period 3 depicts the firm peak case. Hence, in our example, socially optimal prices are

$$\begin{aligned} p_1 &= c + \frac{\beta}{2} + k_1, \quad k_1 > 0, \\ p_2 &= c + \frac{\beta}{2} + k_2, \quad k_2 < 0, \\ p_3 &= c, \end{aligned}$$

where $k_1 + k_2 = 0$.

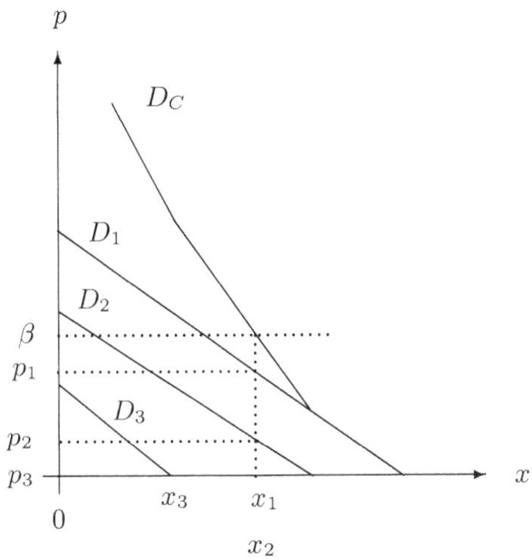

Figure 3.10: Mixed case
Source: See Steiner ([230], p. 591).

The generalization to n periods i, $i = 1, \ldots, n$, for the case of constant marginal costs of data transport can be found in the appendix of Steiner ([230], pp. 604–608). Below, when introducing increasing marginal costs of data transport, we will consider n periods.

The position and the slope of the inverse demand curves determine whether the firm peak or the shifting peak case prevails. If peak demand is situated significantly higher than off-peak demand, the firm peak case is more plausible. In contrast, the shifting peak case typically occurs if demand schedules are situated more closely to each other. Moreover, a large ratio of marginal costs between the peak and off-peak period, i.e., a large value of β, makes the shifting peak case more plausible.

In the Internet, one can imagine the firm peak case prevailing if the Internet is predominantly used during business hours while people spend most of their spare time off-line. If this is not the case the shifting peak case could also occur where heavy users demand applications such as video on demand or video conferences after work and on week-ends. In this case, peak and off-peak demand would lie close together.

Above, the assumption of constant marginal costs of data transport has been criticized since one would expect increasing marginal costs of data transport if these marginal costs are interpreted as marginal congestion costs. Therefore, we now analyze peak-load pricing in the context of increasing marginal costs of data transport.[39] There are n periods i, $i = 1, \ldots, n$. Consider a representative ISP and assume this ISP to have a variable cost function $C(x_i, K)$ of data transport in period i. This variable cost function shall depend on the amount of data traffic transported in period i, x_i, and on the transport capacity K. Suppose the capacity K to be fixed across all time periods. The variable cost function $C(x_i, K)$ in period i is assumed to be increasing and convex in x_i, to equal zero at $x_i = 0$, and to be decreasing[40] in K whenever $x_i > 0$. Furthermore, the inverse demand function in period i shall be reflected by $p_i := f_i(x_i)$ and the area below the inverse demand function in period i between 0 and x_i shall be given by $F_i(x_i) := \int_0^{x_i} f_i(z)dz$.

Consumer surplus $CS(\cdot)$, provider surplus $PS(\cdot)$, and the social welfare function $W(\cdot)$, defined as sum of consumer and producer surplus, are given by

$$CS(x_1, \ldots, x_n) := \sum_{i=1}^{n} F_i(x_i) - \sum_{i=1}^{n} p_i x_i, \tag{3.16}$$

$$PS(x_1, \ldots, x_n, K) := \sum_{i=1}^{n} p_i x_i - \sum_{i=1}^{n} C(x_i, K) - \beta K, \tag{3.17}$$

$$W(x_1, \ldots, x_n, K) := \sum_{i=1}^{n} F_i(x_i) - \sum_{i=1}^{n} C(x_i, K) - \beta K. \tag{3.18}$$

39 The subsequent analysis is partly based on the contributions of Braeutigam ([29], pp. 1318 f.) and Schnellhaaß ([208], p. 467).

40 This means that x_i and K are substitutes in production. Given a substitutional production function marginal costs of data transport and marginal costs of capacity cannot be separated.

The functions (3.16) to (3.18) must be maximized to determine optimal prices in the social and in the private optimum for each period.

Setting the derivatives of definition (3.16) equal to zero and rearranging terms yields[41]

$$p_i = f_i(x_i), \quad \forall \quad i. \tag{3.19}$$

The above expression shows that in each period i Internet users generate additional data traffic until the price per unit of data traffic matches the marginal utility thereof, or equivalently, the willingness to pay for a marginal unit of data traffic.

A representative ISP maximizes its provider surplus with respect to x_i and K. Setting the derivatives of provider surplus (3.17) equal to zero and rearranging terms gives[42]

$$p_i = \frac{\partial C(x_i, K)}{\partial x_i}, \quad \forall \quad i, \tag{3.20}$$

$$\beta = -\sum_{i=1}^{n} \frac{\partial C(x_i, K)}{\partial K}. \tag{3.21}$$

Condition (3.21) shows that capacity should be added until total savings in variable costs through a capacity increment are just offset by the costs of an incremental unit of capacity.

Maximizing $W(\cdot)$ with respect to x_i and K, setting the derivatives equal to zero, and rearranging terms yields[43]

$$f_i(x_i) = \frac{\partial C(x_i, K)}{\partial x_i}, \quad \forall \quad i \tag{3.22}$$

41 Definition (3.16) is additively separable in $x_1, \ldots, x_n$. In this case, consumer surplus reaches its maximum if all its addends are maximal. Hence, a sufficient condition for a global maximum is that $f_i(x_i)$ is decreasing in x_i in every period i. We assume this condition to be satisfied.

42 We assume the Hessian matrices of the variable cost function in each period i to be positive semidefinite which requires these cost functions to be convex. Then, each function $-C(x_i, K)$ is concave. Also, revenues generated in each period i are linear and, thus, (weakly) concave functions of x_i while costs of capacity are linear and, thus, (weakly) convex in K. Hence, provider surplus – the sum of concave functions – is concave. Thus, conditions (3.20) and (3.21) indeed identify a local maximum.

43 By our assumptions, the first sum in the definition of social welfare (3.18) consists of concave addends while the second sum is taken over convex func-

and (3.21). Conditions (3.22) require each x_i to be determined such that in the respective period marginal utility per unit of data traffic equals marginal costs. Note that marginal costs of data transport now depend on the amount of data traffic generated.

In order for the private and social optimum to coincide, by equations (3.19), (3.20), and (3.22), the price per unit of data traffic must reflect marginal costs:

$$p_i = \frac{\partial C(x_i, K)}{\partial x_i}, \quad \forall \quad i. \tag{3.23}$$

We now graphically illustrate peak-load prices in the case of increasing marginal costs of data transport. Assume there are two periods i, $i = 1, 2$, and suppose that demand for data transport is higher in period 1, i.e., $x_1 > x_2$. According to expression (3.23) optimal prices are given by

$$\begin{aligned} p_1 &= \frac{\partial C(x_1, K)}{\partial x_1}, \\ p_2 &= \frac{\partial C(x_2, K)}{\partial x_2}. \end{aligned}$$

Since the variable cost function $C(x_i, K)$ is increasing and convex in x_i and since $x_1 > x_2$ we conclude that $p_2 < p_1$. Prices thus always differ if demands for data traffic are distinct in the two periods. The distinction between the firm and the shifting peak case becomes redundant. Each period contributes to cover costs of capacity. This situation is illustrated in Figure 3.11. To simplify, inverse demand schedules D_1 and D_2 are drawn linearly. Marginal costs of data transport are denoted by MC. In the off-peak period demand for data transports amounts to x_2 at the price p_2. In the peak period the quantity-price combination is given by x_1 and p_1. Due to increasing

tions. Therefore, $-\sum_{i=1}^{n} C(x_i, K)$ is concave. Moreover, costs of capacity are linear and, thus, (weakly) convex in K. Hence, social surplus – the sum of concave functions – is concave. We can conclude that conditions (3.22) and (3.21) indeed identify a local maximum.

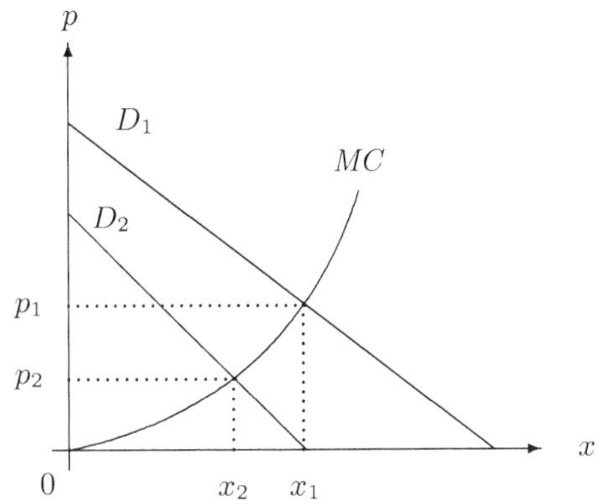

Figure 3.11: Peak-load prices with increasing marginal costs of data transport

Source: See Schnellhaaß ([208], p. 467).

marginal costs of data transport, users in each period contribute to cover the costs of capacity. The more intensive the demand in a certain period, the higher the utilization of the capacity which results in a higher price and a larger contribution of the users in the respective period to recover costs.

At this point, recall that in the Internet marginal costs of data transport approach zero if the network is not congested. Therefore, increasing marginal costs of data transport can be interpreted as increasing marginal congestion costs: The more units of data generated, the larger the queues at routers and the more packets dropped, resulting in increased delay. It seems reasonable to suppose that the costs of delay are increasing and convex.

We close our analysis with an evaluation of peak-load prices which is resumed in Table 3.4.[44]

44 Our evaluation is partially based on Gerpott and Böhm ([84], pp. 238 f.).

Table 3.4: Evaluation of peak-load pricing

ISP/Welfare	*Allocative efficiency*	△
	Capacity expansion	△
	Incentive compatibility	▲
ISP	*Cost-orientation*	△
	Price discrimination	▲
	Feasibility	△
	Accounting efficiency	◇
User	*Utility-orientation*	▲
	Price transparency	△

▲ = very good, △ = good
◇ = satisfactory, ▽ = adequate, ▼ = inadequate

- *Allocative efficiency*
  As already pointed out in Section 2.2.2, opinions on whether demand patterns in the Internet can be anticipated are controversial. If it is difficult to correctly anticipate and estimate demand, the determination of peak-load prices becomes a subtle task. If demand is not anticipated correctly an apparent off-peak period can in reality become a peak period as we have seen in the shifting peak case. According to Gerpott and Böhm ([84], pp. 238 f.) periodic usage patterns can be identified empirically in local access networks and on national transmission links, but hardly on international transit links where traffic demands from locations all over the world are aggregated. Therefore, the authors suggest that peak-load prices should only be applied at a national

level. However, European Internet users usually suffer congestion on international transit links in the afternoon.[45] This fact validates peak-load prices also for the use at the international level. Moreover, remember that Odlyzko ([182], pp. 20–22) finds a regular time-of-day and day-of-week variation of data traffic. In brief, further research on the predictability of usage patterns should be done in order to give satisfactory answers to the problem of correct demand anticipation. In this evaluation, we assume that demand patterns in the Internet can be correctly anticipated. If traffic patterns were unpredictable, peak-load pricing would be unsatisfactory for all parties involved.

Provided that demand can be anticipated correctly, peak-load prices approximately lead to an efficient allocation of resources. Efficient resource allocation can only be approximated since peak-load prices are based on average, not on actual network utilization. Approximation of efficient resource allocation is enhanced if increasing marginal costs of data transport are assumed. In this case, congestion externalities are about internalized.

- *Capacity expansion*
  Peak-load prices do give monetary incentives for capacity expansion. Since peak-load prices are based on average rather than on actual network utilization, peak-load prices only roughly provide the necessary revenues to expand capacity.
- *Incentive compatibility*
  Peak-load prices are incentive compatible: On the one hand, they induce users to reveal their true willingness to pay. Users continue to generate Internet traffic as long as their marginal utility of data conveyance exceeds the associated price. ISPs, on the other hand, transport additional data units until the price matches marginal costs of data conveyance.

45 From this perspective, at first sight, the peak-load tariff offered by T-Online introduced on page 86 does not seem to be reasonable since this tariff only charges users for Internet services in an apparent off-peak period, namely between 7 p.m. to 7 a.m. However, the local access network of T-Online may be used to full capacity in this period if many heavy retail customers spend their spare time online.

- *Cost-orientation*
  From the point of view of ISPs, peak-load prices have the advantage of recovering both usage costs and the costs of capacity expansion. However, there is no flat rate paid ex ante to recover fixed costs.
- *Price discrimination*
  The possibility to price discriminate is very good given that third degree price discrimination can be applied.
- *Feasibility*
  The feasibility of peak-load prices depends on the possibility of correctly anticipating demand. The more reliable demand anticipation is, the easier the implementation of peak-load pricing will be. Feasibility is enhanced by the fact that peak-load prices can be implemented in a decentralized manner.
- *Accounting efficiency*
  Accounting overhead is moderate provided that there are not too many differentiated time periods: Packets or bytes must be counted while the price per unit of data transport depends on the time of day. However, accounting efficiency is lower compared to nonlinear tariffs since volume prices additionally depend on the time of day.
- *Utility-orientation*
  From the perspective of Internet users, peak-load prices are utility-oriented since they maximize consumer surplus as well as social welfare. In peak periods only users with a relatively high willingness to pay are served. In other words, peak-load prices take the willingness of users to pay in different time periods into account. In consequence, peak-load prices do not allow for cross-subsidies between Internet users.
- *Price transparency*
  Furthermore, peak-load prices are transparent to users provided that there are not too many prices differentiated over time. However, price transparency is lower compared to flat-rate pricing since, with peak-load pricing, expenditures for Internet services vary with both the quantity of data traffic generated and the load of the network.

3.2 Load-Insensitive Priority Pricing

3.2.1 Voluntary User Declarations

The pricing approaches proposed in this section are designed for ISPs that offer relative priority services while ignoring network loads. Relative priority services do not allow for service guarantees. But higher priority packets encounter relatively smaller delay compared to lower priority packets since routers forward the former packets first if congestion occurs. Recall from Section 2.1.2 that, without major modifications, relative QoS can be implemented with the current version of the Internet Protocol, IPv4. Priority values are indicated in the packet header, for example, in the three-bit precedence field that is currently unused. The potential number of priority classes would then be restricted to 8 ($= 2^3$). Routers must be programmed such that they do not apply simple First-In, First-Out (FIFO), but, in periods of congestion, forward packets with higher priorities faster than packets with lower priorities.

In a classical paper in the field Bohn et al. [27] propose the offering of multiple service levels at a flat rate coupled with voluntary user declarations and the introduction of quotas. We will see below that the major drawback of this proposal is that it lacks incentive compatibility. It will be argued below that this problem can be eliminated if quotas are priced appropriately.

Concretely, Bohn et al. suggest that software developers assign default priority levels to applications or services based on some general guidelines such as latency-sensitivity.[46] Depending on the application, a default priority number from 0 to 7 is indicated in the precedence field of each packet header. Users are left with the opportunity to modify the priority of the application. The modification may be done either on a per session basis or permanently.

---

46 Delay-sensitive applications such as IP telephony would be assigned a high priority level while FTP bulk transfer and email would be treated as low priority traffic.

Bandwidth allocation is done via a quota system. Each Internet user, who can be a retail user, an organization, or a downstream ISP, receives a quota Q from her ISP. The quota scheme proposed is intended for both the retail and the interconnection level. The quota equals the weighted sum of the packets generated by a user per time unit, where the weights are determined by the selected priorities:

$$Q := \sum_{i=2}^{6} x_i \alpha^{i-2}.$$

The number of packets with priority i, generated during the metered period, is reflected by x_i and α is a parameter greater than 1. Concretely, the authors suggest to set $\alpha = 2$. Note that the priority values 0, 1, and 7 are not considered in the quota. Zero weights are given to the two lowest priority classes, i.e., to priority 0 and to priority 1 such that they do not use up any of the quota. The lowest priority class would be appropriate for applications that tolerate delay well such as email. Higher priorities would have progressively higher weights using up greater amounts of the quota. The authors propose that the precedence value 7 should be reserved for traffic surrounding issues of network management, routing, or other traffic considered critical.

The proposed quota scheme only improves the efficiency of bandwidth utilization if each user always selects the correct category for each application. However, prices do not vary with the chosen priority class. Hence, users have clear incentives to always choose the highest priority class.

Recognizing this incentive compatibility problem, Bohn et al. ([27], p. 7) propose that ISPs monitor traffic and enforce compliance with quotas. Enforcement of compliance can consist of a monetary penalty, more careful traffic monitoring, or, if the abuse persists, ISPs might refuse service to the abusive customer. Choi, Stahl, and Whinston ([42], p. 122) criticize the monitoring and enforcement system with respect to its implementation and effectiveness.

The question remains how the quota for each Internet user is determined. Bohn et al. ([27], p. 7) leave it up to ISPs to appoint the quota allocated to each consumer and suggest to base the quota either on past usage patterns or on the bandwidth of the access link. However, the dependency of the quota on past usage patterns gives incentives to exceed the quota in order to get a higher quota in the subsequent period. The authors do not tie the quota to pricing, but propose that extra quota could be pre-purchased.

We proceed with an evaluation of flat-rate pricing coupled with voluntary user declarations and the introduction of quotas. The resumed evaluation can be found in Table 3.5.

Table 3.5: Evaluation of voluntary user declarations

ISP/Welfare	*Allocative efficiency*	▼
	Capacity expansion	▼
	Incentive compatibility	▼
ISP	*Cost-orientation*	▽
	Price discrimination	▼
	Feasibility	△
	Accounting efficiency	▲
User	*Utility-orientation*	▼
	Price transparency	▲

▲ = very good, △ = good
◇ = satisfactory, ▽ = adequate, ▼ = inadequate

- *Allocative efficiency*
  Allocation of network resources is not efficient as the proposed quota system is not tied to pricing. As with pure flat-rate pricing, the lack of price incentives induces a wasteful handling of network

resources and leads to a degradation of average service quality, the tragedy of the commons. Users are not charged according to the real costs of data transport. In particular, light users and low-priority users subsidize heavy users and high-priority users, respectively.

- *Capacity expansion*
  As already mentioned in Section 3.1.1, flat rates, even if they are coupled with voluntary user declarations and the introduction of quotas, do not provide monetary signals for network planning and network expansion.
- *Incentive compatibility*
  Recall that the proposed quota system is not tied to pricing. The absence of both efficient enforcement of quotas and monetary incentives lead to a lack of incentive compatibility. Users have clear incentives to always choose the highest priority. Suggesting voluntary compliance in the anonymous Internet is illusive. ISPs are not given incentives to provide multiple service classes either since they are not appropriately rewarded to do so. The problem of missing incentive compatibility on the subscriber side might be mitigated if different quotas were related to different prices, i.e., different flat rates. The proposal of Bohn at al. would then resemble both the adaptive flat rate proposed in Section 3.1.1 and the cumulus pricing scheme that will be mentioned later on in Section 3.3.4.

  It should be noted that the authors consider flat-rate pricing coupled with voluntary user declarations and a quota system to be an interim solution to Internet congestion. Over time they expect multiple service qualities to be tied to monetary incentives like a 'pay per priority scheme'[47] such that incentive compatibility is achieved.
- *Cost-orientation*
  Flat-rate pricing coupled with voluntary user declarations and a quota system may hinder ISPs in recovering costs in the same way as pure flat-rate pricing: Recall from Section 3.1.1 that, in

47 Bohn et al. ([27], p. 7).

practice, flat rates do not allow for cost recovery if subscribers are mainly heavy users, generating considerable congestion externalities, and if ISPs face variable transit costs.

- *Price discrimination*
  The possibility to price discriminate between users is inadequate since ISPs are withheld from exploiting different willingnesses to pay.
- *Feasibility*
  An advantage, however, of the proposal made by Bohn et al. is its feasibility: Quotas can be handled in a decentralized way where providers can set, measure, and enforce quotas as they desire. Hence, the proposed quota system can be implemented gradually and in a decentralized manner. As is the case for all pricing proposals made in Sections 3.2 and 3.3, implementation requires router and user software to be modified in the entire Internet to support multiple queues and priority forwarding and to set precedence levels, respectively. Once these technical requirements are installed, associated flat rates are easy to implement.
- *Accounting efficiency*
  A further argument in favor of the approach by Bohn et al. is its accounting efficiency since traffic generated by each user does not have to be measured.
- *Utility-orientation*
  Quality differentiation is not followed by price differentiation which leads to cross-subsidies between user groups, a lack of incentive compatibility and hence, to very inadequate utility-orientation.
- *Price transparency*
  In return for the inadequate utility-orientation, price transparency of flat-rate pricing coupled with voluntary user declarations and the introduction of quotas is very good since flat rates are charged ex ante.

3.2.2 Static Priority Pricing

In a classical paper Cocchi et al. [49] propose a usage-sensitive priority model with price discrimination called static priority pricing. The proposed priority prices are static in the sense that they do not vary with the load of the network. Even if this approach does not solve the congestion problem, the pricing proposal ensures, in case of network congestion, that scarce network resources are allocated to users with a high willingness to pay. As will be explained below, static priority prices guarantee that Internet users select the socially optimal priority class.

We first introduce some notation: The are n Internet users i, $i = 1, \ldots, n$. The QoS received by user i is denoted by s_i which is associated with expenditures e_i. The utility that user i derives from s_i is reflected by $u_i(s_i)$. Let σ_i denote the QoS required by user i. We assume σ_i to belong to the space $\mathcal{S}$ of possible service quality requests. The vector of required QoS of all users is given by $\boldsymbol{\sigma} \in \mathcal{S}^n$. The QoS received by user i, s_i, shall be a function of $\boldsymbol{\sigma}$. Moreover, expenditures e_i shall be determined by the vector of requests $\boldsymbol{\sigma}$. We assume $s_i(\boldsymbol{\sigma})$ and $e_i(\boldsymbol{\sigma})$ to be non-decreasing in $\boldsymbol{\sigma}$.

We can now define the (monetary) utility function of user i. This utility function is assumed to be quasilinear:

$$U_i(\boldsymbol{\sigma}, b_i) := u_i(s_i(\boldsymbol{\sigma})) + b_i, \tag{3.24}$$

where b_i designates the consumption of the numeraire good of user i. Solving the budget constraint

$$e_i(\boldsymbol{\sigma}) + b_i = m_i,$$

where m_i denotes the exogenous income of user i, for b_i and substituting the result for b_i in the utility function (3.24) yields

$$U_i(\boldsymbol{\sigma}) := u_i(s_i(\boldsymbol{\sigma})) + m_i - e_i(\boldsymbol{\sigma}),$$

or, since m_i does not influence utility maximization of user i,

$$U_i(\boldsymbol{\sigma}) := u_i(s_i(\boldsymbol{\sigma})) - e_i(\boldsymbol{\sigma}).$$

Utility maximizing behavior of Internet users shall result in a request vector $\boldsymbol{\sigma}^*$ where no individual i has an incentive to unilaterally deviate from her choice σ_i^*. In other words, utility maximizing behavior of Internet users results in a Nash equilibrium $\boldsymbol{\sigma}^*$ which we will assume to exist and to be unique. The request vector $\boldsymbol{\sigma}^*$ is a Nash equilibrium provided that

$$U_i(\boldsymbol{\sigma}^*) \geq U_i(\boldsymbol{\sigma}^*|^{\mathbf{i}}\boldsymbol{\sigma}) \quad \forall \quad i, \quad \forall \quad \sigma_i \in \mathcal{S},$$

where $\boldsymbol{\sigma}^*|^{\mathbf{i}}\boldsymbol{\sigma}$ denotes the vector where the ith component is given by σ_i and where all other components j are determined by σ_j^*. In other words, the vectors $\boldsymbol{\sigma}^*$ and $\boldsymbol{\sigma}^*|^{\mathbf{i}}\boldsymbol{\sigma}$ differ only in the ith component.

Cocchi et al. ([49], p. 618) introduce two normative criteria that static priority prices have to comply with, namely adoptability and acceptability. A pricing system is called adoptable if, for every Internet user, it generates a Pareto superior allocation in comparison to the status quo allocation. Expressed differently, the adoptability condition requires individual rationality relative to the status quo pricing scheme.

A price system is called acceptable if its unique Nash equilibrium is given by the request vector $\boldsymbol{\sigma}^*$ which maximizes the sum $\sum_{i=1}^{n} u_i(s_i(\boldsymbol{\sigma}))$:[48]

$$\sum_{i=1}^{n} u_i(s_i(\boldsymbol{\sigma}^*)) \geq \sum_{i=1}^{n} u_i(s_i(\boldsymbol{\sigma})) \quad \forall \quad \boldsymbol{\sigma} \in \mathcal{S}^n.$$

Given an acceptable price system, utility maximizing behavior leads to efficient use of network resources in the sense that multiple service classes allow the network to focus on performance-sensitive applications in case of congestion. In game theoretic language the acceptability condition is called Nash implementation of maximal efficiency. In Nash implementations individual and collective rationality coincide.

48 We assume that such a maximum exists which is the case if the mappings $u_i(s_i(\boldsymbol{\sigma}))$ are continuous and the space $\mathcal{S}$ is compact, i.e., bounded and closed. There could be multiple utility maximizing vectors, however. We assume the solution $\boldsymbol{\sigma}^*$ to be unique.

Cocchi et al. ([49], pp. 618–624) illustrate their abstract model with an example in view of finding an adoptable and acceptable pricing system by simulation. For this purpose, the authors introduce two priority classes; i.e., a service class with high and another service class with low priority. Routers form packet queues where packets with a high priority are ordered at the head of the queue according to the arrival time. After the high priority packets low priority packets are queued up according to their arrival time of these packets. Packets are forwarded beginning with the first packet in the queue. If necessary, packets at the tail are dropped.

Furthermore, the authors consider two different price systems. While in the first price system a uniform price is charged per unit of data traffic, in the second price system there are two different unit prices, $\overline{p}$ and $\underline{p}$, for high and low priority service, respectively, where $\overline{p} \geq \underline{p}$. In order to facilitate a comparison between these two pricing schemes, in their simulation, the authors suppose that in equilibrium both price systems yield the same revenues $\sum_{i=1}^{n} e_i(\boldsymbol{\sigma}^*)$.

Moreover, data traffic generated by an Internet user is assumed to be independent of the price. Stated differently, data traffic demand is supposed to be price inelastic. Only the choice of priority classes is modeled. In the example given by the authors the requests σ_i consist of the priority settings on the packets.

In their example, the authors measure user satisfaction with utility functions specified for different application types such as email, FTP, Telnet, and VoIP. These utility functions describe how the perceived performances of these application types depend on the QoS received. Telnet and voice VoIP are both real-time applications that are highly delay-sensitive. FTP and email, on the contrary, are delay tolerant. Delay-sensitivity increases from email through FTP and Telnet to VoIP. It is assumed that all Internet users demand the same QoS for the same applications.

By simulation, the authors show that for a wide range of network conditions static priority prices, $\overline{p}$ and $\underline{p}$, may be found that comply with the adoptability and the acceptability criteria: When revenues under the two pricing schemes are held constant, prices lead to a Pareto improvement compared to a uniform price given that, with uniform pricing, all users request high priority service for each application. Moreover, static priority prices induce users to select the correct priority class for each application such that the sum of utilities and network efficiency are maximized in the following sense: While multiple service classes allow the network, in case of congestion, to focus on performance-sensitive applications, static priority pricing permits the benefits of multiple service classes to be spread also to users of performance-insensitive applications in the form of a price discount. Users who request high priority service receive a QoS that more than offsets higher expenditures. Likewise, the savings of users who demand low priority outweigh the decrease in service quality.[49]

We now get to an evaluation of static priority pricing.[50] The summary of our evaluation can be found in Table 3.6.

- *Allocative efficiency*
  From the point of view of social welfare, static priority prices lead to an efficient use of network resources in the sense that these prices incite users to select their QoS requirements such that, in case of congestion, the network can focus on performance-sensitive applications. In other words, static priority prices incite users to voluntarily select the socially optimal priority. Thereby, in times of congestion, network resources are allocated to higher-valued uses. However, the fact that prices do not vary with network utilization results in high priority prices that are too low during times of congestion. In the opposite case, if the network is lightly loaded, high-priority users pay a premium that cannot be justified from the welfare theoretic point of view. There is a lack of monetary incentives to shift peak demands into off-peak periods. But, as already noted, even if network externalities are not included in the pricing scheme, static priority prices allocate network resources

49 Similar to the seminal paper of Cocchi et al. [49], Orda and Shimkin [188] propose prices that give users incentives to choose the appropriate service class for different types of data traffic. Then, Orda and Shimkin ([188], pp. 251–255) propose an algorithm to compute these prices. Furthermore, Orda and Shimkin ([188], pp. 255–260) extend their pricing model by incorporating congestion effects.

50 Our evaluation is partially based on Gerpott and Böhm ([84], pp. 239 f.).

Table 3.6: Evaluation of static priority pricing

ISP/Welfare	*Allocative efficiency*	◊
	Capacity expansion	▼
	Incentive compatibility	▲
ISP	*Cost-orientation*	◊
	Price discrimination	△
	Feasibility	▼
	Accounting efficiency	◊
User	*Utility-orientation*	△
	Price transparency	△

▲ = very good, △ = good
◊ = satisfactory, ▽ = adequate, ▼ = inadequate

to higher-valued uses in times of congestion. In short, static priority prices meet the criterion of allocative efficiency only in a satisfactory way.

- *Capacity expansion*
  Also, static priority prices do not provide monetary signals for network planning and network expansion. The reason is that static priority prices, just as nonlinear tariffs, are load-insensitive.
- *Incentive compatibility*
  One advantage of static priority pricing from the welfare theoretic perspective is its incentive compatibility. Outlay of users vary with both the amount of traffic generated and with the QoS required. Hence, users are given monetary incentives to select those service classes that best fit their requirements on QoS. At the same time,

these QoS demands, in case of congestion, enable the network to focus on performance-sensitive applications. Hence, as already noted above, static priority prices incite users to voluntarily select the socially optimal priority.

- *Cost-orientation*
  From the perspective of ISPs, a relation between the average use of capacity of an application and its price is established which enhances cost-orientation. However, it is difficult to correctly anticipate traffic volumes demanded. Therefore, an additional flat rate may be necessary to recover fixed costs and to enhance the predictability of revenues. Moreover, there are no revenues generated through congestion fees. One may doubt if the necessary revenues can be generated to expand capacity in bottlenecks given that static priority prices ignore the network load.
- *Price discrimination*
  Static priority prices allow the exploitation of different willingnesses to pay. However, further price discrimination would be possible if the pricing scheme considered different network loads.
- *Feasibility*
  Feasibility of static priority pricing is inadequate: Cocchi et al. [49] do not introduce a computational algorithm to determine static priority prices. To determine these prices the values users attach to each class of service should be known; a proprietary information which is difficult to obtain.[51] Moreover, static priority prices, that fulfill both the criteria on adoptability and acceptability, must be implemented system-wide. Hence, implementation of static priority pricing is rather difficult.
- *Accounting efficiency*
  We judge accounting efficiency to be satisfactory: Traffic volumes differentiated according to the respective QoS must be counted.
- *Utility-orientation*
  From the point of view of end-users, static priority prices are utility-oriented since they are adoptable and acceptable at once. These prices increase individual user utilities compared to a uni-

51 See Choi, Stahl, and Whinston ([42], p. 117).

form price while ensuring an efficient use of network resources in the sense that, in times of congestion, the network can focus on performance-sensitive applications. Moreover, a relation between the average use of capacity of an application and its price is established. Quality differentiation is followed by price differentiation. There are no cross-subsidies between user groups. However, utility-orientation could be enhanced if static priority prices varied with the load on the network.

- *Price transparency*
  If there is a manageable number of prices differentiated with respect to quality, static priority prices satisfy the criterion of price transparency well even if there is no flat rate to be paid ex ante.

3.2.3 Paris Metro Pricing

Another Internet pricing proposal designed for networks that distinguish between different service qualities, but which gives no guarantees for the service quality offered, is Paris Metro Pricing (PMP). PMP was introduced by Odlyzko [181]. He named his pricing proposal after the subway of Paris which, until about 1994, had identical cars that were differentiated in price, resulting in first and second class carriages. As prices for first class cars were higher than those for second class, first class cars were less congested. Therefore, it was more likely to find a seat in first class cars than in second class cars. The interesting feature about the Paris Metro system was its self-regulating character: Users sorted themselves according to their preferences concerning congestion and the prices set for the two transport classes. In cases where first class carriages became too crowded, people often were not prepared to pay an extra charge for first class and moved to second class cars, reducing congestion in first class and maintaining the difference in QoS between first and second class cars.

Odlyzko [181] proposes that the same scheme should be applied to the Internet. His idea consists in partitioning the Internet into logically separate channels where each logical channel obtains a fixed fraction of the capacity of the entire network. In other words, on each link a fixed share of the bandwidth is allocated to each traffic class. In order to create different service qualities the price per unit of data conveyed has to be differentiated according to the channel used for the data transport. On average, it is to be expected that a more expensive channel experiences less congestion and can therefore deliver a higher service quality compared to channels with lower usage prices. Users choose the channel they wish to send their packets on and pay accordingly. Those users with the highest willingness to pay will choose first class service.

Odlyzko ([181], p. 3) argues that the number of channels should be small in order to minimize losses of the advantages from statistical multiplexing of sources with varying and unpredictable bandwidth demands and also to fit consumers' preferences for simple and transparent pricing schemes. Concretely, Odlyzko proposes either two, three, or four channels.

Odlyzko ([181], p. 8) does not give a formal framework to determine prices and capacities of the separate channels. Instead, he proposes that these decisions be based on customer surveys and on the data from time-of-day variations in traffic patterns. He suggests maintaining prices and capacities of the separate channels constant for extended time periods to provide transparent prices and predictable service qualities to users.

When first introducing PMP, one can imagine the price per unit of data conveyance to be zero for the cheapest service class. This eases transition. In the long run, prices for the lowest service channel should be zero only during idle periods. Odlyzko ([181], p. 8) points at the possibility of designing paris metro prices in the form of peak-load prices. This would allow PMP to take network load into consideration.

The implementation of PMP is relatively simple and can be done by using the three-bit precedence field in packets headers. Such as other usage-based pricing schemes, PMP requires the installation of a device to count the data traffic generated by each user. Moreover, routers have to be programmed to give appropriate priority to packets from different logical channels.

The question remains how ISPs that have adopted PMP interact with ISPs that have not done so. Odlyzko ([183], p. 142) proposes conveying data traffic delivered by ISPs that have not adopted PMP, i.e., packets without a priority indication, at lowest costs on the lowest priority channel.

To motivate PMP, Odlyzko ([181], Appendix 1) analyzes the gains that can be obtained by having logically separate networks which operate at different utilization levels. Therefore, he introduces two types of users, namely delay-sensitive and delay-insensitive user types. Odlyzko assumes a competitive market environment with zero profits in the provider industry. His numerical results suggest that PMP Pareto dominates the status quo where heterogeneous user types all use the same network and pay a single price for best-effort service. Concretely, the PMP system only slightly increases the benefits of the delay-insensitive user type while the delay-sensitive user type experiences a large increase in benefits. ISPs obtain zero profits in both scenarios as the provider industry is assumed to be competitive.

Two contributions criticize PMP. We will consider the critical voices in turn. Gibbens, Mason, and Steinberg [87] point out a possible problem of PMP in a market with competing ISPs. They analyze a simplified version of PMP where, in the presence of negative congestion externalities, two competing ISPs can choose to offer data transports either with a single service quality or with multiple service qualities. Quality differentiation is generated by logically separate channels that are characterized by distinct congestion levels. The congestion level of a channel depends upon the fraction of the capacity of a network allocated to this channel and upon the number of users of this channel. The authors show that both a social planner, who maximizes welfare, and a monopolist would choose to offer multiple service qualities, but duopolists would abstain from doing so.

The intuition that neither of the duopolists wants to subdivide its bandwidth into separate channels is the following: The decision of ISPs about how many different service classes they wish to offer is influenced by two opposite effects. On the one hand, competing providers would like to discriminate between users with heterogeneous valuations for data transport through different prices on distinct channels. This is the so-called 'segmentation effect.'[52] But quality differentiation leads to more intensive competition since, then, duopolists compete with each other over a broader range of service qualities. This effect is the so-called 'competition effect.'[53] Gibbens, Mason, and Steinberg [87] show that due to the interaction of these two opposite effects, under competition, there will be either no equilibrium outcome or there will be an equilibrium where the competition effect always offsets the segmentation effect. Consequently, the duopolists earn higher profits by only offering a single service class compared to the case where multiple services classes are supplied. However, the conclusion of Gibbens, Mason, and Steinberg [87] relies on several assumptions such as a uniform distribution of user preferences regarding congestion, a linear congestion function, and a determined number of providers in the industry.[54] One can conjecture that in a competitive ISP industry with free entry, i.e., if the number of ISPs in the market may vary, the segmentation effect is likely to offset the competition effect.[55]

Further critique on PMP is made by Cao and Shen [36] who propose studying the Internet pricing problem with the theory of cooperative games. A game is called cooperative if players, in our case represented by an ISP and a user, can enter binding commitments. This requires that players can communicate, negotiate a fair outcome, and that the agreement can be enforced by exogenous mechanisms. The cooperative solution depends on the chosen concept of fairness that both parties agreed upon and that may be specified by a set of axioms. Cao and Shen ([36], p. 2) adopt the Nash bargaining solution for their analysis.[56] The authors compare the Nash bargaining

52 Gibbens, Mason, and Steinberg ([87], p. 2491).
53 Shaked and Sutton ([217], p. 47).
54 Further information on the competition of multiproduct duopolists can be found in Champsaur and Rochet [40] as well as in Shaked and Sutton [217].
55 Confronted with the critique of Gibbens, Mason, and Steinberg, Odlyzko ([184], p. 160) replies 'whether this analysis poses serious problems for PMP is not settled. [...] Also, it has not been shown yet how any other QoS scheme can be realistically implemented in the Internet, which consists of many heterogeneous subnetworks.'
56 The Nash bargaining solution will be presented in Section 4.1.3.

solution of a cooperative game, where a single service class is offered and a unique price is charged per unit of data transferred, with the Nash bargaining solution of a cooperative game, where the pricing scheme implemented is PMP, assuming two different service classes. The authors find that PMP lowers the gains attainable in the Nash bargaining solution. Cao and Shen ([36], p. 5) motivate their result with the loss of some advantages of statistical multiplexing incurred with PMP. However, one also has to mention that Cao and Shen do not consider congestion externalities in their analysis which might lead to the unsatisfactory performance of PMP. To sum up, the critiques of PMP base on a number of assumptions which may fail to hold in the Internet. We will resume this argument in the subsequent evaluation.

We now get to our evaluation of the PMP proposal, summarized in Table 3.7.

- *Allocative efficiency*
  The numerical example given by Odlyzko ([181], Appendix 1) suggests that PMP enhances social welfare compared to a single network with a single volume price. However, Cao and Shen [36] provide a counterexample where they argue that, within the framework of the theory of cooperative games, a single unit price leads to a higher social welfare compared to the PMP approach. But, it is not obvious why players should act cooperatively in an anonymous, commercialized, and competitive environment such as the Internet. Nevertheless, with PMP advantages of statistical multiplexing decrease through the subdivision of the network into several channels even if the subdivision concerns the logical and not the physical level. This reduces efficiency of resource allocation which is furthermore deteriorated by the fact that paris metro prices do not depend on the network load. This latter drawback may be mitigated by the self-regulating character of PMP. Recall that PMP encourages users to separate themselves into different service classes. Alternatively, this drawback in question may be offset with the introduction of paris metro prices in the form of peak-load prices. But, the decrease in advantages of statis-

Table 3.7: Evaluation of Paris Metro Pricing

ISP/Welfare	*Allocative efficiency*	◊
	Capacity expansion	▼
	Incentive compatibility	▲
ISP	*Cost-orientation*	◊
	Price discrimination	△
	Feasibility	△
	Accounting efficiency	◊
User	*Utility-orientation*	△
	Price transparency	△

▲ = very good, △ = good
◊ = satisfactory, ▽ = adequate, ▼ = inadequate

tical multiplexing with PMP remains a factor that vitiates social welfare and, hence, allocative efficiency.

- *Capacity expansion*
  Since congestion externalities are ignored by paris metro prices there is a lack of correct monetary incentives to expand capacity in bottlenecks. The introduction of paris metro prices in the form of peak-load prices may mitigate or even offset this drawback.
- *Incentive compatibility*
  PMP has the desirable characteristic of being incentive compatible since higher traffic volumes result in more expenditures and since better service qualities are more expensive. Thereby, Internet users are induced to reveal their true willingness to pay for capacity and for different service qualities.

- *Cost-orientation*
  From the perspective of ISPs, as with static priority pricing, a relation between the average use of capacity and the price is established which enhances cost-orientation. However, it is difficult to correctly anticipate traffic volumes demanded. Therefore, an additional flat rate may be necessary to recover fixed costs and to enhance predictability of revenues. The necessary revenues to expand capacity in bottlenecks cannot be generated given that PMP does not consider the load of the network.
- *Price discrimination*
  ISPs have the possibility of price discriminating between users, both with respect to volume and service quality, to exploit different willingnesses to pay. If paris metro prices additionally varied with the time of day the potential of price discrimination would be further enhanced.
- *Feasibility*
  Feasibility of PMP is good: Pricing can be done at the edges of the network. Incoming traffic from ISPs that have not adopted PMP can be forwarded with lowest priority. Implementation of PMP is quite simple: Apart from the usual technical efforts common to all relative priority pricing proposals, e.g., the indication of priority numbers in packet headers and the programming of routers to forward packets accordingly, the network has to be divided into logically separate channels. In the future, PMP might be implemented within Next Generation Internet (NGI) or Internet2 (I2), two projects that intend to establish a high-speed Internet which, in the framework of PMP, can be seen as a first-class network.
- *Accounting efficiency*
  Accounting only has to be done at the edge of the network. At the edge, traffic volumes differentiated according to the chosen channel must be counted. There is no need for any detailed accounting or pricing in the core of the network where speed of operations is of major importance. Hence, just as in the case of static priority pricing, accounting efficiency is satisfactory. It could be simplified through sampling, i.e., through only accounting a certain percentage of traffic volumes in order to determine entire traffic volumes.

- *Utility-orientation*
  We judge PMP to be utility-oriented for the following reasons: First, numerical results obtained by Odlyzko [181] indicate that all users are better off with PMP compared to a pricing plan where a single price is paid per traffic unit transported with best-effort service. Second, PMP is considerate of heterogeneous user preferences: Internet users on average obtain their requested service that corresponds to their willingness to pay. Moreover, no user is forced to participate in PMP. Users who do not indicate a priority number in the header of their packets obtain the lowest QoS, possibly free of charge. Utility-orientation could be further enhanced by making prices dependent on the load of the network.
- *Price transparency*
  Given that prices and capacity of the separate logical channels are maintained constant over extended time periods, price transparency is good. Recognizing the preference of Internet users for flat rates, Odlyzko ([184], p. 160) argues that PMP can partially accommodate flat-rate pricing by selling large blocks of transmission capacity. Concretely, an ISP would sell the right to send or to receive a certain amount of data traffic within a particular time period with a specified priority. In this case, PMP takes the form of a prepaid price plan. Alternatively, Odlyzko ([183], p. 143) proposes the implementation of PMP in the form of a flat rate where users commit themselves to using a fixed channel for a given time period. This would avoid the costs of packet or byte counting. However, then, the data traffic would no longer be separated according to the tolerance of congestion.

So far, we have been looking at pricing proposals that take different demands on QoS into account, but ignore the existence of network externalities which implies that prices do not vary with the load on the network. The next section introduces pricing models that consider both different service qualities and the network load. The section starts with the analysis of congestion pricing.

3.3 Load-Sensitive Priority Pricing

3.3.1 Pricing Congestion Externalities

The idea of congestion pricing goes back to Pigou [193]. As already mentioned, congestion is a negative externality that leads to a gap between private and social valuations of resource utilization. Pigou [193] proposed closing this gap by pricing the resource based on usage. On the one hand, the usage price should ensure an efficient level of resource consumption and, on the other hand, should provide correct monetary incentives for efficient capacity expansion. The two objectives can be achieved if the price a user faces includes the sum of marginal costs that her additional unit of usage imposes on all other users of the resource. By charging each user the full costs of her usage the price is said to internalize the congestion externality.

The idea of congestion pricing was brought up later by Gale and Koenker [82] in connection with interactive computer services. They argue that prices for the use of interactive computer services should reflect social marginal costs in terms of the expected delay imposed on other users. To reduce administrative complexity, the authors suggest that prices should not vary over time. Instead, they define a set of fixed time periods with constant congestion prices. If one interprets marginal costs within the paradigm of peak-load prices as congestion externalities the approach becomes similar to peak-load pricing.

MacKie-Mason and Varian [148, 149, 151] apply the idea of congestion pricing to the Internet. Their contributions will be the focus of this section. We will first consider the setup of the congestion model. In a second step, we will analyze optimal congestion pricing and capacity expansion. Then, it will be shown that congestion pricing and capacity expansion in a competitive market correspond to a social optimum. Finally, we will investigate the equilibrium outcome when there are no congestion prices within two scenarios, namely, in a scenario where the number of Internet users is fixed and in a scenario where it can vary. It will be shown that with a fixed number of Internet users and in the absence of congestion pricing, equilibrium capacity is higher compared to equilibrium capacity with congestion pricing. Moreover, we will find that there is higher equilibrium congestion in the absence of congestion pricing. Without congestion pricing and if we allow the number of Internet users to vary, we will end up in a so-called 'Yogi Berra equilibrium'[57] where only few intensive and delay-tolerant users with a small willingness to pay for capacity expansion use the Internet. Finally, congestion pricing will be evaluated.

We first introduce some notation. The number of packets generated by user i is depicted by x_i. The aggregate traffic over all users j, $j = 1, \ldots, n$, is given by $X := \sum_{j=1}^{n} x_j$. The capacity of the network is denoted by K (> 0). Total utilization or, in other words, the level of congestion of the network is reflected by $Y := X/K$, where $X \leq K$. Packets may be dropped in order for the condition $X \leq K$ to hold. Finally, let $C(K)$ depict the costs of capacity provision. At the moment, we do not consider the shape of this curve. However, a detailed discussion will follow below.

The (monetary) utility function of a representative user[58] i is assumed to be quasilinear and is given by

$$U_i(x_i, Y, b_i) := u_i(x_i, Y) + b_i,$$

where b_i denotes the money that user i has at her disposal to spend on all other goods except Internet traffic transport. The utility function is assumed to be differentiable, to be an increasing concave function of x_i,[59] and to be a decreasing concave function of Y. That is, we assume marginal utility of data transport to be decreasing in x_j while the marginal disutility of congestion shall be increasing in Y. We now consider the optimal congestion price and optimal capacity expansion.

57 MacKie-Mason and Varian ([148] p. 1146). The reason for this naming will be explained below.

58 According to Mas-Colell, Whinston, and Green ([160], p. 116) a representative user is 'a fictional individual whose utility maximization problem when facing society's budget set [...] would generate the economy's aggregate demand function,' whereas the aggregate demand function is independent of the distribution of wealth.

59 This assumption implies diminishing marginal utility of data transport. The concept of diminishing marginal utility is known in economic literature as 'Gossen's First Law,' named after H. H. Gossen (1810–1858).

We first study efficient usage given a certain level of capacity K. By definition, efficient use of the network maximizes total benefits minus total costs, i.e., social surplus:[60]

$$W(K) := \max_{x_1,\dots,x_n} \sum_{j=1}^{n} u_j(x_j, Y) - C(K), \tag{3.25}$$

where

$$Y := \frac{X}{K} \quad \text{and} \quad X := \sum_{j=1}^{n} x_j.$$

Suppose an interior solution. Differentiating definition (3.25) with respect to each x_i, setting the derivative equal to zero, and rearranging terms yields[61]

$$\frac{\partial u_i(x_i, Y)}{\partial x_i} = -\frac{1}{K} \sum_{j=1}^{n} \frac{\partial u_j(x_j, Y)}{\partial Y}. \tag{3.26}$$

Condition (3.26) states that user i should generate additional data traffic until her marginal utility from data traffic transfer equals the sum of her own, or direct, marginal costs of usage and total marginal external costs she imposes on all other Internet users.

As will be shown below, the optimal solution can be decentralized with the introduction of the shadow price, or, efficiency price

$$p^* := -\frac{1}{K} \sum_{j=1}^{n} \frac{\partial u_j(x_j, Y)}{\partial Y} \tag{3.27}$$

60 Here, we do not consider lump-sum transfer payments between the agents since such payments would not alter the form of the solution to our welfare maximization problem. Neither does the money $\sum_{j=1}^{n} b_j$ Internet users have to spend on all other goods except Internet usage modify the form of the solution. Therefore, we omit the sum $\sum_{j=1}^{n} b_j$ in our welfare analysis.

61 We assume all $u_j(x_j, Y)$ to be sufficiently concave in Y such that social surplus (3.25) has a maximum. In other words, for small quantities of x_j we suppose the direct effect of x_j on utility to dominate while the indirect effect of x_j over Y on utility shall dominate for large quantities of x_j. That is, we suppose marginal utility of data transport to be decreasing in x_j and marginal disutility of network utilization to be increasing in Y.

which equals total marginal congestion costs imposed on all users by an increase in x_i. By making each user face both direct costs and external costs of usage, imposed on all other users, the shadow price p^* internalizes congestion externalities. To see this, consider consumer i who, confronted with p^*, maximizes[62]

$$\max_{x_i} \quad u_i(x_i, Y) - p^* x_i, \quad \text{where} \quad Y := \frac{\sum_{j=1}^{n} x_j}{K}.$$

Differentiating the above function with respect to x_i, setting the derivative equal to zero, and rearranging terms yields[63]

$$\frac{\partial u_i(x_i, Y)}{\partial x_i} + \frac{1}{K}\frac{\partial u_i(x_i, Y)}{\partial Y} = p^*. \tag{3.28}$$

Refer to the definition of p^* in (3.27) to note that for a large number n of Internet users the second expression on the left-hand side of (3.28) is negligible relative to the right-hand side of the equation. For a large n, expression (3.28) essentially corresponds to condition (3.26), necessary to determine the social optimum. Hence, the decentralized solution coincides with the social optimum.

We now analyze when capacity expansion is socially desirable. We defined maximal social welfare for an arbitrary level of capacity K as $W(K)$. The change in maximal social welfare due to an incremental increase in capacity is given by (3.29). Note that due to the envelope theorem indirect effects of K on maximal social welfare over the variable x_j can be ignored.[64] In other words, terms that comprise the partial derivative $\partial x_j / \partial K$ vanish due to condition (3.26).[65] Hence, we have

$$W'(K) = -\sum_{j=1}^{n} \frac{\partial u_j(x_j, Y)}{\partial Y}\frac{X}{K^2} - C'(K). \tag{3.29}$$

62 The unconstrained maximization problem of consumer i is obtained as explained on page 76 in Section 3.1.2.

63 By our assumption in footnote 61 a sufficient condition for utility maximization is satisfied.

64 The envelope theorem is explained in Mas-Colell, Whinston, and Green ([160], pp. 964–966).

65 The demand for data traffic x_j depends on K since K is a parameter of the maximization problem (3.25).

Substituting the shadow price (3.27) into expression (3.29) yields

$$W'(K) = p^* \frac{X}{K} - C'(K). \tag{3.30}$$

Supposing an interior solution, at the welfare maximizing level of capacity, expression (3.30) equals zero.[66] Then, the congestion price p^* is characterized by

$$p^* = C'(K)\frac{K}{X}, \quad \text{where} \quad X \leq K. \tag{3.31}$$

This result provides an important insight: In equilibrium, the optimal congestion price can be calculated without direct knowledge of the utility functions of individual subscribers.

Furthermore, given that marginal costs of capacity are non-decreasing such that a sufficient condition for a maximum is satisfied, whenever expression (3.30) is positive, revenues p^*X derived from congestion fees exceed the value of capacity $C'(K)K$ measured in terms of marginal costs of capacity:

$$W'(K) > 0 \Leftrightarrow p^*X - C'(K)K > 0. \tag{3.32}$$

Therefore, given that marginal costs of capacity are non-decreasing, capacity expansion improves welfare if and only if congestion revenues p^*X exceed the value of capacity measured in terms of marginal costs of capacity. In other words, if an optimally priced network generates the necessary revenues to cover the costs of new capacity, then this capacity should be added.

Note the dual role of the shadow price p^*: On the one hand, it reflects congestion externalities or social marginal costs of increased

66 We assume such a maximum to exist which is the case if the mapping $W(K)$ is continuous and if the domain of K is compact, i.e., bounded and closed, where the lower bound is at $K = X$. Furthermore, we assume the social welfare function $W(K)$ to be concave in K, which is the case if

$$-p^* \frac{X}{K^2} < C''(K).$$

This inequality, which is a sufficient condition for a maximum, always holds if marginal costs of capacity are non-decreasing.

network usage for a given level of capacity. On the other hand, the shadow price determines the social value that results from a change in capacity.

Moreover, note that only in the presence of constant returns to scale are optimal revenues p^*X, derived from congestion fees, just high enough to cover the costs of capacity $C(K)$ since then we have $C(K) = C'(K)K$ for $K > 0$. With increasing returns to scale and, hence, with decreasing marginal costs of capacity, a deficit results since then we have $C(K) > C'(K)K$ for $K > 0$. Finally, in the presence of decreasing returns to scale a surplus occurs. In this case, $C(K) < C'(K)K$ for $K > 0$.

We want to consider the more critical case with increasing returns to scale where $C(K)$ is concave in K. Then, costs of capacity would not fully be recovered by marginal cost pricing.[67] In this case,

$$p^*X - C'(K)K > 0$$

is a necessary, but not a sufficient condition for capacity expansion.

Recognizing this theoretical problem, MacKie-Mason and Varian ([149] studied whether it is indeed relevant in practice: From their examination of the cost structure of the Internet they conclude that 'constant returns to scale is not a bad approximation, at least for small changes in scale.'[68] Hence, in practice, optimal prices should send the correct signals for capacity expansion. Therefore, we assume marginal costs of capacity to be non-decreasing.

If, nevertheless, marginal costs of capacity were decreasing and, consequently, the costs of optimal capacity expansion would not be covered by congestion revenues, the question arises how to finance the deficit. One could think of welfare maximizing tariffs subject to the break-even constraint of ISPs. These are so called second-best tariffs such as the optimal nonlinear tariff and Ramsey prices discussed in Section 3.1.2.

We now analyze whether congestion pricing and capacity expansion in a competitive market lead to the social optimum derived

67 See Shenker et al. ([219], p. 185).

68 MacKie-Mason and Varian ([149], p. 130).

above. The analysis below is based on the following assumptions: Each ISP is supposed to own a network with capacity K and to carry X packets, where the price per packet transferred is p. Each provider charges user i a two-part tariff

$$T_i = r + px_i, \tag{3.33}$$

where r denotes the monthly rental or subscription fee. Profits of a representative provider amount to

$$\Pi(X, K) = pX + nr - C(K).$$

Different ISPs may have different utilization levels Y. In this case, they offer different levels of QoS. The price offering $(p(Y), r(Y))$, where $p'(Y), r'(Y) < 0$, of a representative ISP that faces utilization Y is determined by the competitive market and is therefore outside of the control of the individual ISPs.

For simplicity, suppose that each provider offers only one class of service, i.e., one level of Y. Moreover, Internet users shall be both price and quality takers. This means that the amount of traffic generated by one user does not influence the price offering.

We now consider the maximization problem of consumers in a competitive market. Consumers must decide which provider to subscribe to and how much traffic to generate. The utility maximization problem, expressed in monetary terms, for a representative consumer i is given by

$$\max_{x_i, Y} \quad u_i(x_i, Y) - p(Y)x_i - r(Y).$$

Given our assumption about Internet users being quality takers we can ignore the effect of x_i on Y when solving the utility maximization problem. Differentiating the utility function of user i with respect to x_i and Y and setting the derivatives equal to zero yields[69]

$$\begin{aligned} \frac{\partial u_i(x_i, Y)}{\partial x_i} - p(Y) &= 0, & (3.34)\\ \frac{\partial u_i(x_i, Y)}{\partial Y} - p'(Y)x_i - r'(Y) &= 0. & (3.35) \end{aligned}$$

Condition (3.34) shows that each user generates additional data traffic until the marginal utility of packet transfer equals the price. Condition (3.35) shows that consumers choose an ISP which ensures that their marginal disutility of increased network utilization is just offset by a reduction in expenditures, expressed by

$$p'(Y)x_i + r'(Y).$$

Adding up condition (3.35) with respect to Y over the n users and rearranging terms yields

$$\sum_{j=1}^{n} \frac{\partial u_j(x_j, Y)}{\partial Y} = p'(Y)X + nr'(Y). \qquad (3.36)$$

We now turn our attention to the maximization problem of profit maximizing ISPs that choose both the capacity K of their network and how much traffic X to carry over their network. The profit maximization problem[70] of a representative provider is given by

$$\max_{X,K} \quad p(Y)X + nr(Y) - C(K), \quad \text{where} \quad Y := \frac{X}{K}.$$

First-order conditions with respect to X and K are

$$\begin{aligned} p(Y) + p'(Y)\frac{X}{K} + n\frac{r'(Y)}{K} &= 0,\\ -p'(Y)\left(\frac{X}{K}\right)^2 - nr'(Y)\frac{X}{K^2} - C'(K) &= 0. \end{aligned}$$

69 The Hessian matrix of the utility function of user i is assumed to be negative semidefinite. For the purpose of illustration, this Hessian matrix is calculated and discussed in Appendix A.

70 We assume the Hessian matrix of the profit function to be negative semidefinite. In particular, this requires marginal profits to be non-increasing in both X and K.

By factoring out and rearranging terms we obtain

$$p(Y) + \left(p'(Y)X + nr'(Y)\right)\frac{1}{K} = 0, \tag{3.37}$$

$$-\left(p'(Y)X + nr'(Y)\right)\frac{X}{K^2} = C'(K). \tag{3.38}$$

Having in mind that $Y := X/K$, by using condition (3.34), substituting the left-hand side of expression (3.36) for $(p'(Y)X + nr'(Y))$ in equations (3.37) and (3.38), and rearranging terms, we obtain

$$p(Y) = \frac{\partial u_i(x_i, Y)}{\partial x_i} = -\frac{1}{K}\sum_{j=1}^{n}\frac{\partial u_j(x_j, Y)}{\partial Y}, \tag{3.39}$$

$$-Y\sum_{j=1}^{n}\frac{\partial u_j(x_j, Y)}{\partial Y} = C'(K)K. \tag{3.40}$$

By comparing equation (3.39) to condition (3.26) we find that the competitive price results in the optimal degree of congestion, i.e., that the competitive price equals the optimal price.

Combining expressions (3.39) and (3.40), by definition of Y, yields

$$p(Y)X = C'(K)K. \tag{3.41}$$

Contrast equation (3.41) with expression (3.30) to see that the competitive price engenders the optimal level of capacity. Moreover, compare expression (3.41) to formula (3.31) to find that in equilibrium the optimal congestion price can be calculated without direct knowledge of the utility functions of the individual subscribers.

What is the intuition of the fact that the competitive price equals the socially optimal price for the QoS offered or, in other words, equals the sum of marginal congestion costs? First of all, note that for a large number of Internet users the marginal disutility of user i due to an increase in x_i, $\frac{1}{K}\frac{\partial u_i(x_i,Y)}{\partial Y}$, is negligible relative to the right-hand side of equation (3.39). Hence, we can interpret the term $\left[-\frac{1}{K}\sum_{j=1}^{n}\frac{\partial u_j(x_j,Y)}{\partial Y}\right]$ essentially as the willingness to pay of all other subscribers to convince the ISP to refrain from transferring additional data packets from user i. If the willingness to pay for additional packet transfer of user i exceeds $\left[-\frac{1}{K}\sum_{j=1}^{n}\frac{\partial u_j(x_j,Y)}{\partial Y}\right]$ the competitive ISP conveys the additional load generated by user i. The ISP transfers additional data traffic until the price that user i is willing to pay for the conveyance of an additional packet equals the willingness to pay for a reduction in total usage of all other users.

We can conclude that in a competitive market, where a two-part tariff is charged for Internet access and usage, both the equilibrium price and the equilibrium capacity maximize social surplus. Since the competitive price engenders the socially optimal level of capacity this price must give correct monetary incentives for capacity expansion. To make this statement more explicit, we will consider two different scenarios where a competitive ISP has to decide whether to add capacity.

In the first scenario, assume that a competitive ISP, which has to decide whether to invest in additional capacity, has already maximized its profits with respect to X and, therefore, takes X as given. Then, the only choice variable of the ISP is K. If the ISP increases capacity, network utilization decreases and, in consequence, the ISP can charge a higher price. By the two-part tariff (3.33) and by definition of Y, the extra amount the ISP can charge subscriber j by a marginal increase in K is

$$\frac{dT_j(\cdot)}{dK} = -\left(r'(Y) + p'(Y)x_j\right)\frac{X}{K^2}.$$

Using equation (3.35), which is a necessary condition for utility maximization with respect to Y, yields

$$\frac{dT_j(\cdot)}{dK} = -\frac{1}{K}\frac{\partial u_j(x_j,Y)}{\partial Y}\frac{X}{K}.$$

Summing over all subscribers and using equation (3.39), which is a necessary condition for profit maximization with respect to X, yields additional revenues from capacity expansion that amount to

$$p(Y)\frac{X}{K}.$$

These revenues cover marginal costs of expanding capacity if

$$p(Y)\frac{X}{K} - C'(K) \geq 0.$$

Comparing this expression to equation (3.30) and bearing in mind that, according to (3.39) and (3.27), we have $p(Y) = p^*$, we see that a competitive provider expands its capacity if and only if it is socially optimal to do so. Profits increase if and only if social surplus increases.

In the second scenario, the competitive ISP keeps its price offering $(p(Y), r(Y))$ at a fixed level and expands its capacity by ΔK (> 0). In a competitive market environment the price offering can only be kept fixed if Y remains constant. Given X^* and K^* as optimal values of an initial equilibrium, by definition of Y, we have

$$Y^* := \frac{X^*}{K^*}.$$

In order to keep Y fixed at $Y = Y^*$ and, therefore, to keep the two-part tariff fixed, additional number of packets must satisfy

$$\Delta X = Y^* \Delta K.$$

Profits increase by

$$p(Y)\Delta X - C'(K)\Delta K = \left(p(Y)\frac{X}{K} - C'(K)\right)\Delta K.$$

Once again, we can see that capacity expansion is optimal if and only if it increases profits. We can conclude that a competitive ISP invests in capacity expansion if and only if it is socially optimal to do so. Hence, efficient congestion prices of the competitive market give correct monetary incentives for capacity expansion.[71]

We now examine how marginal costs of capacity influence the role the components of the two-part tariff play in total cost coverage. To begin with, note that, without any barriers to entry, new ISPs will enter the market until profits equal zero:

$$\Pi(X, K) = p(Y)X + nr(Y) - C(K) = 0.$$

71 Mason and Valletti ([161], pp. 409 f.) provide a numerical example of optimal congestion pricing and capacity expansion.

By equation (3.41), we substitute $C'(K)K$ for $p(Y)X$ in the zero-profit condition and rearrange terms to obtain

$$nr(Y) = C(K) - C'(K)K.$$

Dividing the above expression by $C(K)$ (> 0) gives

$$\frac{nr(Y)}{C(K)} = 1 - C'(K)\frac{K}{C(K)}.$$

This result provides the following insights: If marginal costs of capacity are small relative to average costs $C(K)/K$ the subscription fee $r(Y)$ covers most of the costs of Internet service. In the opposite case, revenues derived from congestion fees contribute most to recover total costs.

After having analyzed the outcome with congestion pricing we now investigate, in a first step, the equilibrium in the absence of usage or congestion fees that characterizes the pricing practice of many providers nowadays. In a second step, we will compare the equilibrium without congestion pricing with the efficient equilibrium where congestion externalities are internalized.

We assume that ISPs only charge a flat subscription fee $r(Y)$. For the moment, we abandon our assumption that the utility of user i is always increasing in x_i. Instead, we suppose that subscriber i satiates at some quantity x_i^s, where the superscript s stands for 'satiation'. Total data traffic at the satiation quantity of all users amounts to $X^s := \sum_{j=1}^{n} x_j^s$. To simplify the exposition we introduce an additively separable utility function for a representative user i:

$$u_i(x_i, Y) := z_i(x_i) - D(Y),$$

where $D(Y)$ is identical for all consumers and depicts the total delay experienced by each user, where $D'(Y) > 0$ and $D''(Y) > 0$. For the additively separable utility function, by conditions (3.39) and (3.40), the equilibrium values x_i^*, K^*, and Y^* with congestion pricing are given by:[72]

$$\begin{aligned} z_i'(x_i^*) &= \frac{n}{K^*} D'(Y^*), \\ nD'(Y^*)Y^* &= C'(K^*)K^*. \end{aligned} \tag{3.42}$$

If there are no congestion prices each user i ignores the effect her data traffic has on Y, i.e., her congestion externalities created, and thus generates data traffic up to her satiation point x_i^s. Consequently, each user i maximizes utility only with respect to Y:

$$\max_Y \quad z_i(x_i^s) - D(Y) - r(Y).$$

Differentiating this utility function with respect to Y, setting the derivative equal to zero, and rearranging terms yields

$$-D'(Y) = r'(Y).$$

This condition states that each user chooses an ISP which ensures that her marginal disutility of increased network utilization is just offset by a reduction in expenditures.[73] By adding up the above equation across all subscribers we obtain

$$-nD'(Y) = nr'(Y). \tag{3.43}$$

We now consider the profit maximization problem of ISPs in the absence of congestion prices.[74] In the absence of congestion prices

72 We introduce the asterisks to be able to distinguish the equilibria with and without congestion pricing below as well as for the purpose of geometrical illustration.

73 As long as $r''(Y)$ is not too negative, i.e., as long as $-D''(Y) < r''(Y)$ holds, a sufficient condition for a maximum is satisfied, which we assume to be the case. In other words, a second-order condition for a utility maximum requires the variation of marginal expenditures to exceed the decrease in marginal utility due to higher network utilization.

74 Note that in the absence of congestion prices maximal profits have to be lower than maximal profits with congestion prices. Otherwise, we would have obtained a profit maximizing p^* equal to zero in the above analysis with congestion prices.

ISPs cannot control the level of X. Their sole choice variable is K. Hence, the profit maximization problem of a representative ISP for a given level of X can be written as

$$\max_{K} \quad nr(Y) - C(K), \quad \text{where} \quad Y := \frac{X}{K}.$$

A first-order condition is

$$-nr'(Y)\frac{X}{K^2} = C'(K). \tag{3.44}$$

This condition states that a profit-maximizing ISP should increase capacity until marginal revenues equal marginal costs of capacity.[75] By substituting the left-hand side of condition (3.43) for $nr'(Y)$ in (3.44), observing that $Y := X/K$, and by rearranging we can determine the equilibrium condition in the absence of usage fees:

$$nD'(Y^s)Y^s = C'(K^s)K^s, \tag{3.45}$$

where Y^s and K^s denote equilibrium values of network utilization and capacity without congestion pricing.

By comparing equation (3.45) to equation (3.42) we can conclude that both equations, that determine equilibrium utilization and equilibrium capacity, have an identical form. However, even if the form of the equations is identical in both cases, the equilibrium values of the relevant variables X^*, K^*, and Y^* may be distinct from X^s, K^s, and Y^s. Particularly, the number of users may vary with and without congestion prices. In turn, we will consider both the equilibrium capacity and the equilibrium congestion in the absence of congestion pricing when the number of users is fixed and when the number of users varies. The results will then be compared to the equilibrium values of these variables in the presence of congestion prices.

75 A second-order condition requires the second derivative of the profit function to be negative, i.e., the variation in marginal revenues must not exceed the variation in marginal costs due to increased capacity. We assume this second-order condition to be satisfied.

Provided that the number of users is fixed, the equilibrium capacity for a given level of X is determined by

$$nD'\left(\frac{X}{K}\right)\frac{X}{K} = C'(K)K. \tag{3.46}$$

This equilibrium is illustrated in Figure 3.12. Since $D'(Y) > 0$, the

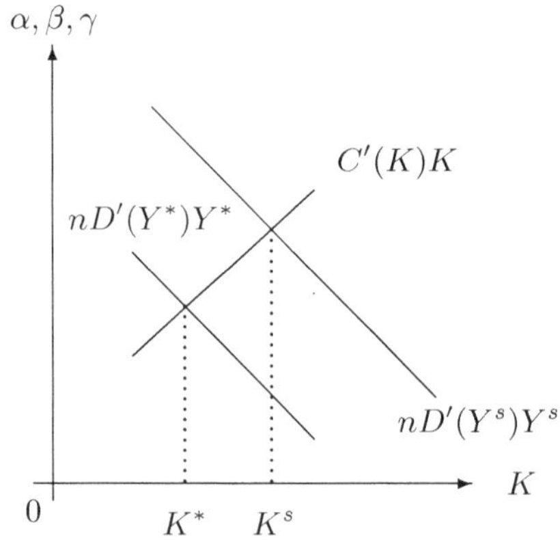

$\alpha := nD'(Y^*)Y^*, \quad \beta := nD'(Y^s)Y^s, \quad \gamma := C'(K)K$

Figure 3.12: Equilibrium capacity with a fixed number of Internet users

Source: See MacKie-Mason and Varian ([148], p. 1146).

left-hand side of equation (3.46) is decreasing in K while $C'(K)K$ is increasing K as long as $C''(K)$ is not too negative. Consider the equilibrium with optimal congestion prices. The use of the Internet is higher without congestion pricing than with usage fees, i.e., $X^s > X^*$. Therefore, the curve $nD'(Y^*)Y^*$ must lie below the curve $nD'(Y^s)Y^s$. Hence, equilibrium capacity without congestion pricing, K^s, exceeds equilibrium capacity with congestion pricing, K^*.

How does equilibrium congestion change with the suppression of congestion prices? We have seen, on the one hand, that a zero congestion price leads to a higher use of the network. But, on the other hand, equilibrium capacity is higher. A priori, it is not clear whether network congestion decreases or increases in the absence of congestion fees. Consider Figure 3.13. Note that by definition of Y we have $K = X/Y$. The curve $nD'(Y)Y$ is increasing in Y and the curve

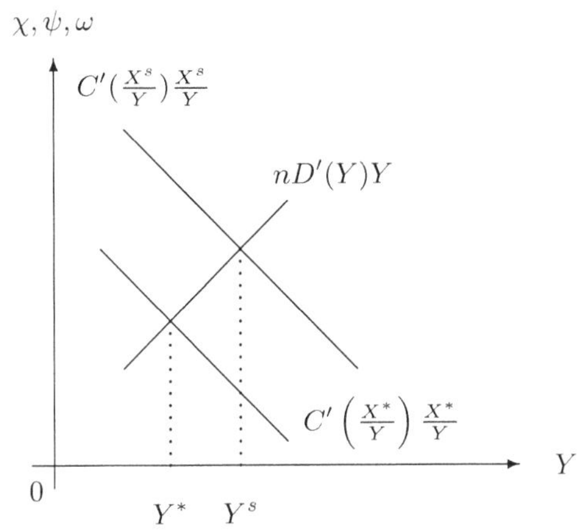

$\chi := C'\left(\frac{X^*}{Y}\right)\frac{X^*}{Y}, \quad \psi := C'\left(\frac{X^s}{Y}\right)\frac{X^s}{Y}, \quad \omega := nD'(Y)Y$

Figure 3.13: Equilibrium congestion
Source: See MacKie-Mason and Varian ([148], p. 1146).

$C'(X/Y)X/Y$ is decreasing in Y as long as $C(K)$ is convex. The $C'(X^s/Y)X^s/Y$ curve lies above the $C'(X^*/Y)X^*/Y$ curve since $X^s > X^*$. This results in a higher equilibrium congestion Y^s in the absence of congestion pricing compared to the equilibrium congestion Y^* with congestion pricing.[76]

76 The same result is derived by Shy ([220], pp. 177 f.). He demonstrates that in the absence of congestion pricing, congestion increases with capacity. He assumes the utility function of user i to be $u_i(x_i, Y) := \sqrt{x_i} - \delta Y$, where $\delta > 0$ denotes the intensity of the disutility caused by congestion.

We now analyze equilibrium capacity and equilibrium congestion if the number of Internet users may vary. Equilibrium utility of a user without congestion pricing is given by

$$z_i(x_i^s) - D\left(\frac{X^s}{K^s}\right) - r(Y^s).$$

Whether the equilibrium utility without congestion pricing exceeds or is lower than the equilibrium utility with congestion pricing is not a priori clear since more packets are transferred in the absence of congestion prices, but at the same time congestion is higher.

Consider an alternative service which gives Internet user i the utility level v_i^*. Then, the participation constraint of user i is given by

$$z_i(x_i^s) - D\left(\frac{X^s}{K^s}\right) - r(Y^s) \geq v_i^*,$$

or,

$$z_i(x_i^s) - v_i^* \geq D\left(\frac{X^s}{K^s}\right) + r(Y^s). \tag{3.47}$$

Inequality (3.47) states that Internet user i does not subscribe to an ISP that charges a monthly flat fee if the net benefit from high usage is smaller than the sum of delay costs and the flat subscription fee. Thus, as the network becomes too congested, user i will cease to use the network and will exercise her outside option that provides the utility level v_i^*. Consequently, the number n of Internet users decreases. One can imagine user types generating high volumes of low-value traffic who only subscribe to an ISP if it charges a flat access fee only. In consequence, congestion would increase and other subscriber types might refrain from subscribing. Hence, if Internet users have the option to desist from subscribing, without congestion pricing, seemingly paradoxical at first sight, there will be less subscribers compared to the scenario where congestion prices are implemented. Figure 3.14 explains this result. Starting at the equilibrium with congestion prices, illustrated by the intersection of the curves $C'(K)K$ and $nD'(Y^*)Y^*$, a reduction in the number of Internet subscribers n shifts the curve $nD'(Y)Y$ to the left and results in the curve $nD'(Y^s)Y^s$. Note that a reduction in n may potentially lower X^s. A lower X^s would shift the curve $nD'(Y^s)Y^s$ even further to the left.

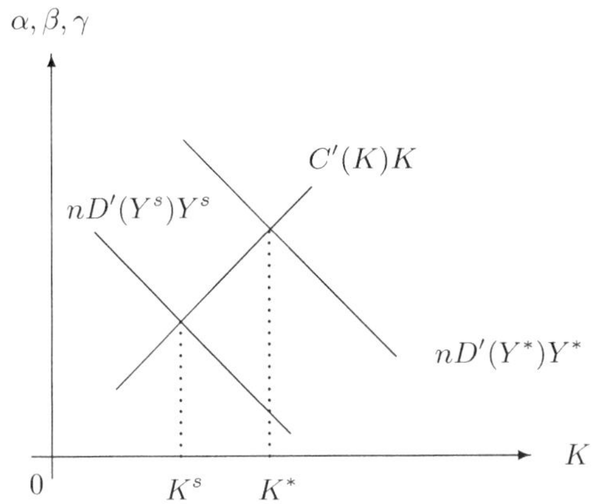

$\alpha := nD'(Y^*)Y^*, \quad \beta := nD'(Y^s)Y^s, \quad \gamma := C'(K)K$

Figure 3.14: Equilibrium capacity with a variable number of Internet users

Source: See MacKie-Mason and Varian ([148], p. 1146).

MacKie-Mason and Varian ([148], p. 1146) call this new equilibrium a 'Yogi Berra equilibrium' since Yogi Berra once stated that 'it's so crowded that no one goes there anymore.'[77] A Yogi Berra equilibrium is characterized by few very intensive and delay-tolerant users whose willingness to pay for capacity expansion is low. Delay-sensitive users with a high willingness to pay for Internet service with appropriate quality prefer to exit to alternative services. They may, for example, make phone calls over the traditional telephone network instead of using VoIP.

Let us summarize our findings from the comparison of the equilibria with and without congestion prices: If the number of Internet

77 MacKie-Mason and Varian ([148], p. 1146).

subscribers is fixed, both equilibrium capacity and equilibrium congestion are higher without congestion prices. If the number of Internet subscribers is allowed to vary the high congestion level may hinder delay-sensitive users from connecting to the Internet. The emerging Yogi Berra equilibrium is then characterized by a lower number of subscribers, but by higher congestion compared to the case with congestion prices.

Apostolopoulos et al. [5] apply congestion pricing to the Greek Academic Research Network. They assume the number of subscribers, which are institutions in their example, to be fixed.[78] As the scarce resource of the Greek Academic Research Network is the bandwidth of the incoming link that connects the Greek Academic Research Network to the rest of the Internet, congestion prices are applied only to traffic volumes conveyed on this link. The authors determine a different subscription fee for each subscriber, i.e., institution, that depends on different parameters such as the speed of Internet access to the Greek Academic Research Network and the size of the institution. They calculate the congestion price the institutions have to pay per unit of volume carried on the inbound circuit of the international connection as the ratio (costs of capacity expansion on the international link)/(traffic increase over the link during a given time period).

Hazlett [107] proposes an interim solution to Internet congestion, designed for institutions and organizations, that is intended to be implemented in the transition phase to congestion pricing. Her pricing proposal aims to generate an allocation which is approximately efficient and to approach an optimal capacity expansion. In particular, she proposes that organizations pay a subscription fee depending on the bandwidth of their Internet access link. Furthermore, each organization shall obtain a priority number which is defined as the ratio (dollar value of contributions to an organization's priority)/(bandwidth of the Internet access line). Note that the contributions of an institution with a fast Internet access link must be high relative to an institution with a slow Internet access link in order to obtain a high priority

78 This assumption is motivated by the fact that institutions in practice cannot operate without Internet connectivity. See Apostolopoulos et al. ([5], p. 595).

number. Any Internet user may contribute to an organization's priority, including the administration of the organization as well as users belonging to the organization, but also users outside the organization. One can imagine that an outside user wishes to make a contribution to a public archive in order to increase the priority of files she desires to download from that archive.

Priority contributions can be made at any time and are valid for a given time period.[79] During periods of congestion many contributions could be made by delay-sensitive users. The priority number falls with the expiration of contributions and rises with new contributions.

Note that the interim solution to Internet congestion exhibits an incentive compatibility problem that stems from two sources: First, the inverse dependency of the priority number on the capacity of the Internet access link may incite institutions to purchase slow Internet access links in order to obtain high priority numbers with low contributions relative to fast Internet access links. Moreover, within organizations with many Internet users a classic free rider problem may appear where nobody contributes to the priority number of the institution in the hope to be able to send packets with the priority numbers sponsored by other members. Hazlett ([107], p. 188) recognizes the latter problem and argues that the free rider problem is mitigated by the fact that contributions expire after a given time period.

We now evaluate congestion pricing. Refer to Table 3.8 for a synopsis of the following evaluation.

- *Allocative efficiency*
  From the welfare theoretic point of view, congestion pricing is the optimal pricing principle, i.e., it may serve as a benchmark for all other pricing proposals. Optimal congestion prices lead to an efficient allocation of resources since prices correctly reflect the scarcity thereof. Congestion externalities are internalized which

79 Hazlett ([107], p. 186) suggests setting a time period of three hours since a particular session on the Internet may generally be completed during this time interval.

Table 3.8: Evaluation of congestion pricing

ISP/Welfare	*Allocative efficiency*	▲
	Capacity expansion	▲
	Incentive compatibility	▲
ISP	*Cost-orientation*	▲
	Price discrimination	▲
	Feasibility	▼
	Accounting efficiency	▼
User	*Utility-orientation*	▲
	Price transparency	▼

▲ = very good, △ = good
◊ = satisfactory, ▽ = adequate, ▼ = inadequate

means that Internet users are charged the real costs of data transport. There are thus no cross-subsidies between user groups.

- *Capacity expansion*
  We showed that optimal congestion prices give correct monetary incentives for ISPs to expand capacity in bottlenecks.
- *Incentive compatibility*
  Congestion prices are incentive compatible since they induce Internet users to reveal their true willingness to pay for capacity. Confronted with the congestion price, users generate additional data traffic until their marginal utility of traffic generation equals the price for data transmission. Also, in a competitive market, congestion prices are profit maximizing and are thus incentive compatible for ISPs.

- *Cost-orientation*
  From the point of view of ISPs, congestion prices are also cost-oriented provided that marginal costs of capacity are not decreasing. Then, a two-part tariff, where the variable price component is the congestion price, allows ISPs to break even. We have seen that the ratio of marginal to average costs determines whether the subscription fee or the congestion revenue is the appropriate instrument to recover most of the costs. In case of decreasing marginal costs of capacity, marginal cost prices do not produce the necessary revenues to break even. As noted above, nonlinear tariffs or Ramsey prices may then be appropriate pricing instruments to prevent losses. Alternatively, if all users derive significant benefits from Internet connection, Shenker et al. ([219], pp. 185 f.) propose keeping the variable price component equal to marginal costs, but to raise the subscription fee.
- *Price discrimination*
  Congestion prices give ISPs the possibility to exploit different willingnesses to pay. Users who generate data traffic during peak periods have to pay more for data transport than users who use the Internet during off-peak periods. Furthermore, providers can adjust their price according to the QoS offered. A competitive market with free entry leads to efficient prices for each quality level. ISPs that ask low prices for traffic transport would offer low QoS with high congestion while others would charge high prices for high QoS and low congestion. Alternatively, a single ISP could offer multiple service qualities. This case will be further considered by the pricing proposals to be introduced below.[80]
- *Feasibility*
  We judge the feasibility of congestion pricing to be inadequate for the following reasons: System-wide information becomes necessary to charge packets appropriately for the congestion costs

80 In this context, Villasis ([248], pp. 98–103) proposes rate-of-transfer pricing, a pricing approach not analyzed in this work. Concretely, Villasis suggests making the variable price component of a two-part tariff dependent on the degree of the current network load, on the desired QoS, and on the size of the data transfer request.

caused along their path from the sender to the receiver.[81] Moreover, from the point of view of social welfare, congestion pricing should be implemented in as many networks as possible to have a broad impact on efficient use of Internet resources. This is difficult to achieve in the commercial and competitive Internet where independent ISPs determine their pricing strategies locally. Concerning the ease of implementation, one may point at the difficulty to assess congestion externalities correctly. To calculate congestion costs, both the utility functions of all Internet users and the current network load along the entire path from the sender to the receiver must be known. These informations are very difficult to obtain. However, as shown by expression (3.31), in equilibrium the optimal congestion price can be calculated without direct knowledge of the utility functions of individual subscribers. Alternatively, congestion costs, i.e., social costs of time, can be econometrically estimated. Gupta et al. [93, 95] estimate users' valuations of time through a non-parametric technique.

- *Accounting efficiency*
  Accounting efficiency is inadequate since, depending on the load of the network, potentially every packet is charged a different congestion price.
- *Utility-orientation*
  From the point of view of users, congestion pricing is utility-oriented since it maximizes individual utilities and social welfare at once. Recall that a competitive market with free entry leads to efficient prices for each quality level. Hence, quality differentiation is followed by price discrimination since ISPs which offer lower congestion and, therefore, higher quality, charge a higher congestion price. Internet users with a high willingness to pay select ISPs which can offer low delay on their network while Internet users with a low willingness to pay choose ISPs with high network utilization. Hence, there are no cross-subsidies between user groups.

81 Section 4.2.1 will analyze congestion pricing at the interconnection level.

- *Price transparency*
  In order to correctly reflect both direct and external costs of usage the congestion price p^* must vary with network utilization. As already mentioned in Section 2.2.2, network utilization may vary considerably over time. The consequential fluctuations of the congestion price make pricing intransparent. This drawback of missing price transparency is mitigated by the smart market approach which is a possible implementation of congestion pricing in the Internet. The smart market mechanism is presented in the following section.

3.3.2 Smart Market Approach: Vickrey Auctions

MacKie-Mason and Varian [149] propose the smart market mechanism in order to implement congestion pricing in the Internet. To motivate their pricing approach, the authors ([149], p. 126) first point at an ideal but impratical pricing mechanism to introduce congestion pricing in the Internet, namely at a Walrasian tâtonnement process. A Walrasian tâtonnement process is a successive price adaptation: At the beginning, an arbitrary price is set by an auctioneer. Then, users decide how much data traffic they would like to generate at this price. If the sum of traffic demands exceeds (is lower than) the available bandwidth, the price is adjusted upwards (downwards). This process is repeated until demand matches available bandwidth. In the Internet, one can imagine an intelligent agent who is performing real-time calculations to match supply of and demand for network resources. However, the application of the Walras tâtonnement process in the Internet faces a severe drawback: The current price of packet transmission has to be known to the users in order to make a decision about the amount of their traffic demand. To solve this problem, MacKie-Mason and Varian ([149], pp. 126–131) propose a smart market mechanism.

In a smart market, each user pays a flat fee depending on the bandwidth of the access link. The sum of flat fees collected should allow the ISPs to cover fixed costs. Moreover, an auction mechanism, which will be described in detail below, is implemented at congested resources. There are no usage-based charges when the network is free of congestion.

Concretely, in a smart market users are asked to indicate their maximum willingness to pay for the transmission of a data packet. The maximum willingness to pay is interpreted as the users' bid for the transmission of the respective packet. This bid is marked in the packet header of each packet. In the event that a router encounters congestion the current FIFO scheme is replaced with prioritisation. Routers inspect the bids in each packet header and rank the packets according to their bid. Packets with the highest bids obtain a prioritized transmission. All packets containing bids greater than some cutoff value are forwarded.

The determination of the cutoff value is illustrated in Figure 3.15. The course of the marginal cost of delay curve, or, the marginal cost of

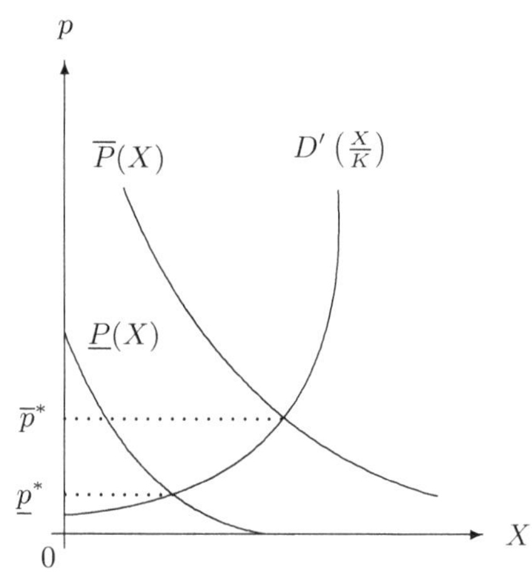

Figure 3.15: Cutoff value in the smart market
Source: See MacKie-Mason and Varian ([151], p. 290).

congestion curve, depicted by $D'(X/K)$, is assumed to be increasing and convex. As in Section 3.3.1, delay is assumed to depend on the utilization of the network, i.e., the ratio of the total use of the resource X to the capacity K.

Two demand scenarios are depicted in Figure 3.15: In a period with relatively low demand the inverse demand curve, or, the willingness to pay schedule, for bandwidth is illustrated by $\underline{P}(X)$ while $\overline{P}(X)$ reflects the inverse demand curve for bandwidth in a period with relatively high demand. The inverse demand curves reflect the number of packet transmissions demanded at each bid level, as indicated by p. The prices $\underline{p}^*$ and $\overline{p}^*$ are determined by the intersection of the inverse demand curves for bandwidth $\underline{P}(X)$ and $\overline{P}(X)$, respectively, and the marginal cost of congestion curve $D'(X/K)$, where the willingness to pay for an additional packet transmission equals the marginal increase in costs of delay caused by that packet. Therefore, the prices $\underline{p}^*$ and $\overline{p}^*$ are the bids of the marginal users in the respective demand scenario. The market-clearing congestion price $\underline{p}^*$ is relatively low when demand is low. Contrarily, $\overline{p}^*$ is relatively high when demand is high. The equilibrium prices $\underline{p}^*$ and $\overline{p}^*$ are charged to all users even if the bids indicated in the respective demand scenario exceed $\underline{p}^*$ and $\overline{p}^*$. Therefore, each inframarginal user, i.e., each user whose reservation price is higher than the equilibrium price, gets a consumer surplus.

We can conclude that the bid of the packet which is not forwarded by the router at the margin reflects current marginal costs of congestion. This bid determines the price charged for every packet at the respective router. Rejected packets, i.e., packets with a bid equal to or lower than the current congestion price, are dropped, buffered until network utilization decreases, or routed to a slower network.[82]

One can wonder why ISPs would have an incentive to implement the smart market mechanism. In other words, why should providers not skim off the total willingness to pay, i.e., charge each packet a price equal to the indicated bid, instead of setting a uniform price? The formal reason is that the smart market is set up like an auction:

82 Note that this last option connects the smart market approach with PMP.

Everybody agrees to the payment rules before the system starts. Providers charge the smart market price because that is what they agreed to do in their contract. But, then, why should everybody agree to implement the smart market mechanism in the first place? Above, we concluded that the bid of the packet, which is not forwarded by the router at the margin, determines the congestion price and reflects current marginal costs of congestion. Recall from the last section that, in a competitive market environment, prices reflecting current marginal costs of congestion at once maximize social welfare, individual utilities, as well as profits. Hence, all agents are given incentives to agree to the auction rules of the smart market.

The smart market mechanism has the following properties: First, the equilibrium price p^* reflects the bid of the marginal user. Every user is charged the equilibrium price. This leaves inframarginal users with a consumer surplus. Second, no iteration is necessary to determine the market-clearing price.

Third, bids may be interpreted as relative priority prices: Through their bids users implicitly communicate their desired priority for, i.e., quality of, data transmission since packets with higher bids are forwarded faster than low-bid packets whose senders potentially lose several auctions. However, no absolute service guarantees may be given.[83]

Fourth, the smart market is a version of the Vickrey auction, where the n highest bidders pay the $(n+1)$th highest bid to have their packet forwarded. The Vickrey auction goes back to Vickrey [247]. The Vickrey auction applies to an auction environment with sealed bids where individual valuations are private information. It assigns a good or service to the bidder who values it the most at a price equal to the second highest bid. It will be shown below that it is a dominant strategy for each bidder to bid her true valuation for packet transmission. In other words, it is an optimal strategy for each

83 Several contributions have extended the smart market to network environments which allow for QoS guarantees. However, the calculation of equilibrium prices turns out to be very costly. See Danielsen and Molka-Danielsen [58], Foukia et al. [78], MacKie-Mason [144], Reichl, Fankhauser, and Stiller [197], as well as Toutain and Huber [240].

bidder to bid her true valuation of packet transmission independently of the bidding strategies of all other users. The intuitive reason is that bidding more than one's true valuation only increases the chances of winning the auction in cases where the price exceeds one's true valuation while bidding less than one's true valuation only decreases the chances of winning the auction without any effect on the price.

To get an idea of the variation on the Vickrey auction, applied in the smart market mechanism, we will first consider the standard Vickrey auction where one good or service is auctioned off. Applied to a congested router in the Internet, this means that only one packet can be forwarded. This is not very realistic, but enhances further understanding. To simplify, consider two Internet users i, $i = 1, 2$, with a true valuation for packet transmission, measured in monetary terms, equal to v_i. Following the rules of the Vickrey auction each Internet user i has to indicate her bid b_i. Then, the packet with the highest bid in the packet header is forwarded at a price equal to the second highest bid. Suppose that both bidders derive zero utility if they lose the auction, i.e., if their packet is not forwarded. Then, Pareto efficiency requires that the data packet of the user with the higher valuation is transmitted. Given the above assumptions, the expected payoff of Internet user 1 equals the product of the probability of winning the auction and the utility obtained from winning the auction:

$$P(b_1 > b_2)(v_1 - b_2).$$

Suppose that $v_1 > b_2$. If bidder 1 bids $b_1 < b_2$ instead of $b_1 = v_1$, she loses the auction. Consequently, her utility level decreases by

$$(v_1 - b_2) > 0.$$

If, instead, bidder 1 bids $b_1 > b_2$, where $b_1 \neq v_1$, she wins the auction and her utility level remains unchanged compared to the case where she bids $b_1 = v_1$ since she pays a price equal to b_2. Hence, she can win the auction for sure if she bids $b_1 = v_1$.

Suppose that $v_1 < b_2$. Then, bidder 1 can only win the auction if $b_1 > b_2$. If she wins the auction, her utility level decreases by

$$(b_2 - v_1) > 0.$$

Hence, she does not want to win the auction. She would lose the auction for sure if she bid $b_1 = v_1$.

Finally, if $v_1 = b_2$ any bid is optimal. Bidder 1 now does not care about winning or losing the auction. Therefore, she has no reason not to bid $b_1 = v_1$. In all, we can conclude that the true revelation of one's willingness to pay is always an optimal bidding strategy independent of the bidding strategy of the other bidder. The same argument holds for bidder 2 as well as for the case with n bidders.[84]

Note that the second price to be paid in the traditional Vickrey auction equals the optimal congestion price: By winning the auction bidder i causes congestion and crowds out the consumption of bidder j, where $i, j = 1, 2$ and $i \neq j$. Social costs of that congestion equal the utility foregone by bidder j.[85]

We proceed with the variation on the Vickrey auction implemented by the smart market. This Vickrey auction is a sealed-bid multiple-units auction where multiple packets are forwarded by a congested router.[86] We therefore have to assume that the bids indicated in the packet headers that belong to the same packet stream are independent single-unit bids. In other words, we assume the bids not to depend on whether other packets belonging to the same packet stream win or lose the auction.[87] Without this assumption, the bid indication of one packet would be influenced by the price to be paid for another packet.[88]

The assumption of independent single-unit bids is not as restrictive as it seems. In the packet-switched Internet users do not know

84 See MacKie-Mason and Varian ([146], p. 1) and Tirole ([239], p. 453).

85 See MacKie-Mason and Varian ([146], p. 3).

86 The following analysis is based on Vickrey ([247], p. 26 f.) and on Wurman, Walsh, and Wellman ([259], p. 21).

87 The Generalized Vickrey Auction (GVA) is an extended Vickrey auction that allows the allocation of multiple units of a good where the bids are not independent single-unit bids. However, the GVA does not allow for a uniform price to be paid by all packets being forwarded if incentive compatibility has to be satisfied and if users desire multiple units. See Wurman, Walsh, and Wellman ([259], p. 22). For further information on the GVA consider MacKie-Mason and Varian [146], Takahshi and Tanaka [235], and Varian [244].

88 See Vickrey ([247], p. 27).

the path their packets follow on their way to the destination. Theoretically, it is possible that every packet of a packet stream follows a different path. In this case, the user bids for a single unit, i.e., for forwarding a single packet, at congested routers.

Assume that a congested router, which has ranked the packets according to their bids, can forward n packets at a price equal to the $(n+1)$th highest bid denoted by b_{n+1}. Let v_i be the true valuation for packet transmission of user i and let b_i be her corresponding bid. Again, all bidders i are assumed to obtain zero utility if their packets are not forwarded. The expected payoff of user i equals the product of the probability of having her packet forwarded and the utility obtained from winning the auction:

$$P(b_i > b_{n+1})(v_i - b_{n+1}).$$

Provided that $(v_i - b_{n+1}) > 0$, user i would want to maximize the probability of winning the auction. In this case, user i wins the auction with certainty when bidding $b_i = v_i$.

If, however, $(v_i - b_{n+1}) < 0$, user i would seek to minimize the probability of winning the auction. The probability of winning can be set to zero by bidding $b_i = v_i$. Consequently, bidding the true valuation v_i is always an optimal strategy. In other words, truth-telling is a dominant strategy since it is optimal independent of the bidding strategies of other users.

We now evaluate the smart market mechanism.[89] The subsequent evaluation is resumed in Table 3.9.

89 Our evaluation is partially based on Gerpott and Böhm ([84], p. 241).

Table 3.9: Evaluation of the smart market approach

ISP/Welfare	*Allocative efficiency*	▲
	Capacity expansion	▲
	Incentive compatibility	▲
ISP	*Cost-orientation*	▲
	Price discrimination	▲
	Feasibility	▼
	Accounting efficiency	▼
User	*Utility-orientation*	◊
	Price transparency	▽

▲ = very good, △ = good
◊ = satisfactory, ▽ = adequate, ▼ = inadequate

- *Allocative efficiency*
  As already noted, the smart market mechanism provides a way to implement congestion pricing in the Internet. As with congestion pricing, prices obtained by Vickrey auctions at routers correctly reflect the scarcity of capacity. These prices internalize congestion externalities since the bid of the first packet not transmitted determines the price and, at the same time, reflects marginal congestion costs. Forwarded packets are thus generated by users who are willing to pay the congestion price p^*, the marginal utility of packet transmission of the marginal user. Also, in the absence of congestion, there are no per packet charges. We can conclude that at each router the market is cleared at the equilibrium price that corresponds to the bid of the marginal user. Further, in con-

trast to an Walras tâtonnement process, no iteration is needed to determine the market-clearing price.

- *Capacity expansion*
  As with congestion pricing, we can now explain that the smart market mechanism gives correct monetary incentives to expand capacity in bottlenecks. The reason why the smart market price correctly signals the need for capacity expansion is the following:[90] The price in the smart market is the value of the first packet not forwarded. If the value of that packet exceeds marginal costs of capacity a marginal expansion of capacity is socially desirable. Similarly, imagine that several packets contain the same bid determining the price. Then, if the total value of these packets that are just not admitted to the network exceeds the costs of capacity expansion, necessary to forward these packets, it is desirable to invest in additional capacity. Hence, revenues derived from congestion prices should be invested in capacity expansion as long as they exceed the value of capacity assessed with marginal costs of capacity. Thereby, as pointed out in the last section, social welfare would increase.
- *Incentive compatibility*
  The smart market is incentive compatible for the following reasons: As explained above, all providers and users are given incentives to agree to the auction rules of the smart market. Then, once the smart market mechanism is implemented, it is a dominant strategy for each user to bid her true willingness to pay.

Interestingly, Gibbens and Kelly [86] show that the efficiency properties of the smart market in terms of allocation of scarce resources and maintenance of incentive compatibility may be replicated without the need for users to indicate a bid in each packet header. Instead, packets that encounter congestion on their path to the destination are marked at congested routers and are charged a fixed small amount for each mark received. That way, end-nodes, equipped with different transmission control algorithms according to user preferences (vari-

90 See MacKie-Mason and Varian ([147], p. 6).

ants of existing TCP algorithms) obtain both correct incentives and the necessary information to efficiently use the network.

- *Cost-orientation*
  From the point of view of providers, the smart market mechanism has the advantage of being cost-oriented: The fixed flat rate that depends on the bandwidth of the access link allows fixed costs to be covered. Moreover, the prices determined in the auctions are optimal prices in the sense that they cover marginal congestion costs and generate the necessary revenues to expand capacity if needed.
- *Price discrimination*
  The smart market allows different willingnesses to pay to be skimmed off: Apart from discriminating among subscribers with respect to volume the smart market allows ISPs to differentiate their prices according to the network load and, if bids are interpreted as relative priority prices, also with respect to the offered service quality. We can conclude that the smart market provides a very good possibility to price discriminate.
- *Feasibility*
  We judge the feasibility of the smart market to be inadequate for the following reasons: In order to determine the cutoff value the course of the marginal cost of congestion curve must be known, an information which may be rather difficult to obtain. Again, a technical drawback of the smart market concerns the fact that its implementation requires routers to be able to rank the packets according to their bid, to hold auctions, and to send accounting information to accounting machines in addition to their usual routing and transmission functions. Also, there is a 'deadweight loss of time:'[91] Routers have to sort the packets by their bids at frequent periodic time intervals. Consequently, a one period delay of packet queuing and bid sorting is induced on every packet before getting forwarded. The feasibility of the smart market is also inadequate for one more reason: The sender of a packet may win auctions at several routers, but later lose an auction and have her

91 Stahl ([227], p. 146).

packet dropped. However, users should not have to pay for unsuccessful packet transmission. Consequently, the implementation of the smart market requires a coordination between routers in periods of heavy network load. The necessity of coordination between routers during periods of congestion contradicts the requirement of decentralized implementation. Furthermore, the implementation of the smart market in the Internet obliges preferably all ISPs to adopt this pricing idea. It significantly cuts the flexibility providers have in setting prices for service. It is questionable whether numerous providers agree to adopt the smart market pricing model. We can conclude that the smart market approach lacks feasibility.

- *Accounting efficiency*
  An often mentioned drawback of the smart market approach is its accounting overhead. However, MacKie-Mason and Varian ([149], p. 129) argue that accounting does not slow down traffic much since, at each router, samples of packets can be transferred to a dedicated accounting machine. Concretely, the accounting information on every 1000th packet, for example, could be sent to an accounting machine that determines the price for each auction and records the usage for later billing.
- *Utility-orientation*
  From the point of view of customers, the smart market may be judged to be utility-oriented for the following reasons: Prices paid in Vickrey auctions are optimal congestion prices. Recall from the last section that they maximize individual utilities and social welfare at once. In times of network congestion, only users with a relatively high willingness to pay, i.e., users who are willing to pay the congestion price, are served. In consequence, there are no cross-subsidies between different user groups. Also, quality differentiation through prioritized forwarding is followed by price differentiation. However, there are also two negative effects influencing utility-orientation: The first critique concerns the assumption of independent single-unit bids. Shenker et al. ([219], p. 188) argue that 'it is impossible to independently set the valuation of a single packet in a file transfer, when the true valuation is for

the set of packets'. One can consider whether a smart agent, that determines the valuations of single packets on behalf of the users, could solve this problem. But even with a smart agent the problem is not fully taken care of for the following reason: The smart market ignores the fact that the value of packet transmission is contingent on other auctions held, i.e., is contingent on having other packets belonging to the same packet stream transmitted as well. Some packets may become worthless once other crucial packets belonging to the same packet stream have been dropped. Consequently, users may have to pay for worthless, but transmitted packets. Second, the auction mechanism only refers to links between two routers, i.e., is hop-by-hop oriented, to determine access at each hop. In contrast, users are interested in their packets reaching the final destination. They value packet transmission on an end-to-end basis. This means that their bids concern the entire path that can consist of many hops. But a packet could encounter congestion at several routers and its sender may be charged a congestion price at each of these routers. In this case, the final price to be paid for a packet could exceed the maximum willingness to pay for packet delivery.[92] This drawback might be eased if routers subtracted their price from the packet header of winning packets such that the maximum willingness to pay of bidders could not be exceeded by the cumulated congestion prices charged along the path. For these reasons, we can conclude that utility-orientation is only satisfactory.

- *Price transparency*
  Price transparency of the smart market mechanism is rather low since prices are not determined ex ante. The lack of price transparency is deteriorated by the bursty characteristic of Internet traffic. However, MacKie-Mason and Varian ([151], p. 297) conjecture that with congestion pricing, users have an incentive to smooth their data transport demand so that fluctuations of data traffic are eased. Moreover, prices charged to users at one router

92 If bottlenecks are only located at Internet access routers the smart market could only be implemented there which eliminates the 'end-to-end versus per-hop problem'. Shenker et al. ([219], p. 188).

only fluctuate down and can never exceed their maximum willingness to pay. Hence, price transparency is higher compared to congestion pricing, as introduced in the last section. In the case that retail customers refuse to bear the risk of price fluctuations, MacKie-Mason and Varian ([151], p. 296) propose insurance to be provided by the IAP, or by a third party, that assumes the risk of price fluctuations in exchange for an insurance premium. The insurer may again offer different subscription fees for different service qualities.

We close this section with a remark on the possibility of implementing the smart market model in network environments where QoS are guaranteed. Recall that in the smart market the sender of a packet may win auctions at several routers, but lose an auction later and have her packet discarded. This scenario must be excluded in networks that offer guaranteed QoS. In order to guarantee QoS, valid reservations must be set up along the entire path. Therefore, Toutain and Huber ([240], pp. 797 f.) propose simulating a smart market on each node along the path before resources are reserved and data is being transmitted. If the simulation is successful, i.e., if all auctions are won, the necessary resources are reserved along the path. Once a connection is set up, it has to be refreshed from time to time by repeating the auctions. Even if only one local auction is lost, the whole connection has to be torn down since resources must be guaranteed end-to-end.

The so-called Connection-Holder-is-Preferred-Scheme (CHiPS) deals with this problem while preserving the second-price character of the auctions. In the CHiPS model, holders of connections, that are already set up, are treated in a preferential way: If their bids have been too low in order to win the auction, they obtain a second chance to increase their bids. The running connections are not torn down until the bidders have made their decision on the second bid.[93]

93 See Foukia et al. ([78], pp. 3–8) and Reichl et al. ([197], pp. 72–75).

3.3.3 Dynamic Priority Pricing

Dynamic priority pricing that has been proposed by Gupta, Stahl, and Whinston [96, 98, 99] integrates both priority-based and congestion-based pricing. We first present the general idea of dynamic priority pricing before we introduce the formal model. Our aim is not to provide a detailed mathematical presentation of the dynamic priority pricing model, which can be found in Gupta, Stahl, and Whinston [99], but to present a simplified version thereof with the purpose of making the structure of the model understood.

The authors model the Internet as an economy where each node in the Internet is interpreted as a productive firm with input queues that charges for access. Congestion costs are the only costs introduced into the model. Then, as will be explained below, efficient resource allocation requires the prices at each node to reflect social marginal costs of congestion. Users are interpreted as customers of nodes who pay a congestion price and suffer a delay cost if they demand access to the nodes. The utility of users is assumed to depend on the service obtained and on the expected throughput time for that service. Each service can be provided by a series of nodes that are pooled in a so-called scheme.

Figure 3.16 provides a schematic representation of the network priority pricing model. Each node is associated with a priority queuing mechanism that allows for a predetermined number of priority classes. Each priority class is assigned an expected waiting time and a posted price. Whenever users require a service they are presented a menu of options specifying the monetary costs for each priority class and expected throughput times, i.e., the delay, associated with each priority class. The product of the number of schemes for a specific service and the number of priority classes yields the number of options each user can choose from when requesting that service.

User demand is modeled as a stochastic process. Service requests of users are associated with an instantaneous value and with a delay cost factor for this instantaneous value. There is an option, i.e., the minimum cost scheme, that minimizes monetary costs and total expected delay costs for some service request. If a user's instantaneous

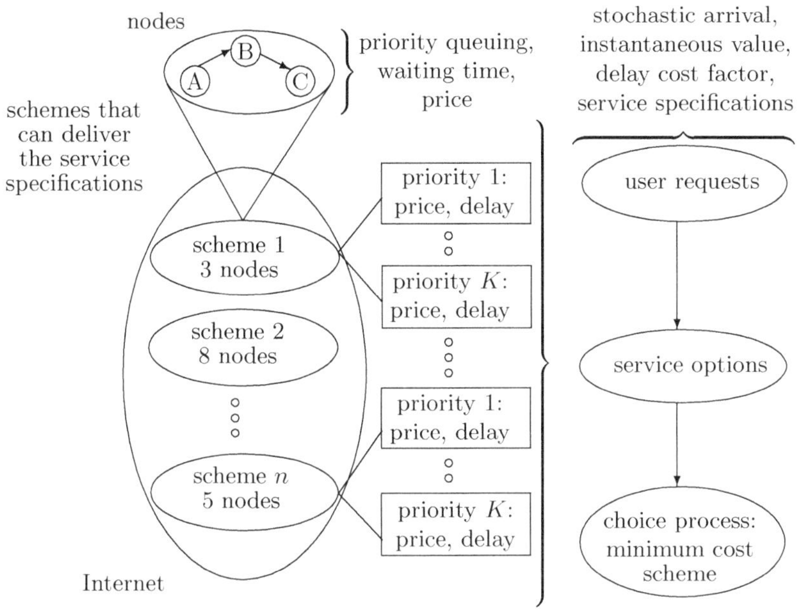

Figure 3.16: Schematic representation of the network priority pricing model

Source: See Gupta et al. ([93], p. 16).

valuation of the data transfer, i.e., of the service request, exceeds these minimal expected costs, she will demand the data transfer.[94] Contrarily, users who value the data transfer less will postpone their demand to a less congested time period. This behavior leads to a better distribution of traffic over time. The difficult task of choosing the minimum cost scheme may be automated with a personalized smart agent to which user preferences have been communicated.

Dynamic priority pricing is based on general equilibrium theory. A general equilibrium under uncertainty, e.g., in a volatile environment such as the Internet, is usually determined with the concept

94 We will explain below that if a user's instantaneous valuation of a service requests equals minimal expected costs she will submit the service request with a certain probability.

of an Arrow-Debreu equilibrium. An Arrow-Debreu equilibrium is a competitive equilibrium where so-called contingent commodities are traded. Contingent commodities are uncertain outcomes whose availability is conditional on a realized event, the so-called state of the world. In an Arrow-Debreu economy a commodity is defined for every contingency and every moment in time.[95] Applying the Arrow-Debreu framework to a volatile environment such as the Internet implies major informational and computational efforts. In order to prevent these efforts Gupta, Stahl, and Whinston [96] do not determine state-contingent equilibrium prices, but introduce the concept of a stochastic equilibrium. We will see below that in a stochastic equilibrium

> (i) user service requests are optimal for each user, given the [...] prices and anticipated waiting times, (ii) the anticipated delays are correct ex-ante expected waiting times, given the average flow rates [arrival rates of service requests], and (iii) the aggregate average flow rates are equal to the welfare-maximizing rates.[96]

The authors derive optimal prices that support the unique stochastic equilibrium. These derived prices are near-optimal prices since, due to major informational and computational efforts, a first-best solution of an Arrow-Debreu economy cannot be implemented in real-time.

As will be further explained below, in order to calculate the near-optimal prices of the stochastic equilibrium the authors develop a decentralized real-time mechanism in the form of a tâtonnement process, such as the Walras tâtonnement process described in the last section. By simulation Gupta, Stahl, and Whinston ([99], pp. 711–718) show that the tâtonnement process rapidly converges to the stochastic equilibrium prices.

Now that we have presented the general idea of dynamic priority pricing we proceed with the introduction of the formal model. Let $m \in \mathcal{M}$ denote a machine or a node, that can be a router or an information server, which belongs to the set $\mathcal{M}$ of all machines, where

---

95 Consider Mas-Colell, Whinston, and Green ([160], Section 19.C) for an explanation of the Arrow-Debreu equilibrium.

96 Gupta, Stahl, and Whinston ([99], p. 700).

$\mathcal{M} := \{1, \ldots, M\}$, $M \in \mathbb{N}$. Assume that each node m in the Internet offers the set $\mathcal{K} := \{1, \ldots, K\}$, $K \in \mathbb{N}$, of ordered priority classes k, where $k = 1$ depicts the highest priority. Let $q \in \mathbb{N}_0$ arbitrarily reflect a certain traffic volume and suppose that $q_j \in \mathbb{N}_0$ designates the traffic volume associated with a certain service $j \in \mathcal{J}$ such as video or audio on demand, teleteaching, or video conferences, where $\mathcal{J} := \{1, \ldots, J\}$, $J \in \mathbb{N}$. The capacity at node m shall be designated by $v_m \in \mathbb{R}_+$. Denote the expected (queue) waiting time at a node m for priority class k with $w_{mk} \geq 0$, measured in a given time unit, and let $\mathbf{W} := (w_{mk})$, where $m \in \mathcal{M}$ and $k \in \mathcal{K}$, designate the matrix of expected (queue) waiting times at the nodes. Expected throughput time for service j in priority class k shall be given by

$$\tau(q_j, k, \mathbf{W}) := \sum_{m \in \mathcal{S}} \left(w_{mk} + \frac{q_j}{v_m} \right), \tag{3.48}$$

where $\mathcal{S} \subseteq \mathcal{M}$ is the subset of nodes occupied by service request j, i.e., the subset of nodes that belong to a scheme which can deliver the service j, and where $\sum_{m \in \mathcal{S}}$ signifies that the sum is taken over all indices $m \in \mathcal{S}$. Expected throughput time for service j depends on the service time at each node along the path, determined by the ratio q_j / v_m, on the chosen priority class, and on the waiting time in the queues of the nodes along the path.

After having described how the Internet is modeled we proceed with characterizing users, preferences, and demands. For this purpose, we assume that the instantaneous value of service j to user i is given by a non-negative real numbered variable $V_{ij} \in \mathbb{R}_+$, where $i \in \mathcal{I}$, $\mathcal{I} := \{1, \ldots, I\}$, $I \in \mathbb{N}$. While V_{ij} is supposed to be a deterministic and known value to each user i it shall be a random variable to the system. Moreover, the delay cost factor, or the costs of waiting per unit of time, of customer i for service j shall be given by a non-negative real numbered variable $\delta_{ij} \in \mathbb{R}_+$. Again, we suppose δ_{ij} to be a deterministic and known value to each user i, but to be a random variable from the point of view of the system. The fact that V_{ij} and δ_{ij} are random variables to the system means that at different times user i may have distinct values and delay costs for the same service. Since, from the system's perspective, the random variables V_{ij} and δ_{ij} occur simultaneously $F_{ij}(V_{ij}, \delta_{ij})$ shall denote the joint cumulative distribution function of these random variables, where the associated joint density function is given by $f_{ij}(V_{ij}, \delta_{ij})$ which is supposed to exist and to have compact support.[97] Then, given that the expected throughput time for service j in priority class k is reflected by $\tau(q_j, k, \mathbf{W})$, the product $\delta_{ij}\tau(q_j, k, \mathbf{W})$ denotes total expected costs of delay of user i for service j in priority class k. Furthermore, the priority price matrix shall be given by $\mathbf{R} := (r_{mk}(q))$, where $m \in \mathcal{M}$ and $k \in \mathcal{K}$. Element $r_{mk}(q) \in \mathbb{R}_+$ depicts the priority price at node m in priority class k to process q units of data traffic. Then, total expected costs user i faces when she requests service j with priority k are given by the sum of total expected costs of delay and the monetary costs consisting of the prices summed across all nodes of the path:

$$c_{ijk}(\delta_{ij}, \mathbf{R}, \mathbf{W}) := \delta_{ij}\tau(q_j, k, \mathbf{W}) + \sum_{m \in \mathcal{S}} r_{mk}(q_j). \tag{3.49}$$

Customer i will prefer a scheme and a priority class minimizing total expected costs

$$c^*_{ij}(\delta_{ij}, \mathbf{R}, \mathbf{W}) := \min_{m,k} \quad c_{ijk}(\delta_{ij}, \mathbf{R}, \mathbf{W}), \tag{3.50}$$

where c^*_{ij} indicates the minimum cost scheme of user i for service j. Note that the minimum cost scheme of a user with a delay cost factor equal to zero will be determined by a service option with minimal monetary costs regardless of the associated expected throughput time while a user with a high delay cost factor is likely to select a service option offering faster throughput, albeit for higher monetary costs.

Let p_{ijkm} be the probability that the service request j of user i is submitted in priority class k at node m. Then, the expected net benefits of user i for receiving the service j in priority class k at node m, taking V_{ij}, δ_{ij}, $\mathbf{R}$, and $\mathbf{W}$ as given, can be expressed as

$$u_{ij}(p_{ijkm} | V_{ij}, \delta_{ij}, \mathbf{R}, \mathbf{W}) := (V_{ij} - c_{ijk}(\delta_{ij}, \mathbf{R}, \mathbf{W}))\, p_{ijkm}. \tag{3.51}$$

---

97 A function has compact support if its value equals zero outside of a compact set, i.e., outside of a bounded and closed set.

As already mentioned above, for each user i the instantaneous values V_{ij} and δ_{ij} are not random variables, but deterministic and known values. Each user seeks to maximize (3.51) with respect to p_{ijkm} while taking $\mathbf{R}$ and $\mathbf{W}$ as given.[98] The utility maximizing probability p_{ijkm} will then be characterized by

$$p_{ijkm}(V_{ij}, \delta_{ij}|\mathbf{R}, \mathbf{W}) \begin{cases} = 1 & \text{if} \quad V_{ij} > c^*_{ij}(\delta_{ij}, \mathbf{R}, \mathbf{W}) \\ \in [0,1] & \text{if} \quad V_{ij} = c^*_{ij}(\delta_{ij}, \mathbf{R}, \mathbf{W}) \\ = 0 & \text{if} \quad V_{ij} < c^*_{ij}(\delta_{ij}, \mathbf{R}, \mathbf{W}). \end{cases} \tag{3.52}$$

That is, user i will submit service request j in priority class k at node m with certainty if her instantaneous value of service j exceeds the associated minimized expected costs. In the opposite case, if $V_{ij} < c^*_{ij}(\delta_{ij}, \mathbf{R}, \mathbf{W})$, user i with certainty will not request the service. In the case that the instantaneous value of service j to user i equals the associated minimized expected costs the probabilistic choice function $p_{ijkm}(\cdot)$ can take any value from the interval $[0, 1]$.

User demand is modeled as a stochastic process. Concretely, service requests are supposed to follow a Poisson process[99] with a fixed arrival rate λ_{ij} of requests for service j from user i.[100] The resulting stochastic arrival rate, or, in other words, the average flow of requests for service j from user i in priority class k at node m is defined as the definite double integral

$$x_{ijkm} := \lambda_{ij} \int \int p_{ijkm}(V_{ij}, \delta_{ij}|\mathbf{R}, \mathbf{W}) f_{ij}(V_{ij}, \delta_{ij}) dV_{ij} d\delta_{ij}, \tag{3.53}$$

to be explained as follows: The limits of integration (not indicated explicitly) are the support of $F_{ij}(V_{ij}, \delta_{ij})$. Since we assumed V_{ij} and δ_{ij} to be non-negative the lower limits of integration must be non-negative while the upper limits can be both finite or infinite. The joint

98 This means that we assume users to be price and waiting time takers.

99 As already explained in Section 2.2.2, a Poisson process is a discrete stochastic process in continuous time which describes the total number of occurrences in an arbitrary time interval of a certain length t. Poisson processes are used to describe the occurrences of rare events such as service requests, for example.

100 The fixed arrival rate λ_{ij} is the expected value of a random variable that follows a Poisson distribution.

density function $f_{ij}(V_{ij}, \delta_{ij})$ is weighted by $p_{ijkm}(V_{ij}, \delta_{ij}|\mathbf{R}, \mathbf{W}) \in [0, 1]$. Without this weighting the average flow of requests would equal λ_{ij} since

$$\int\int f_{ij}(V_{ij}, \delta_{ij}) dV_{ij} d\delta_{ij} = 1.$$

Hence, with this weighting the values x_{ijkm} belong to the interval $[0, \lambda_{ij}]$.

We now focus on the optimal resource allocation and the stochastic equilibrium. Therefore, we must introduce some further definitions and notations. The arrival rate of service requests with the volume q at node m in priority class k shall be given by

$$\chi_{mkq}(\mathbf{X}) := \sum_{i=1}^{I} \sum_{j=1}^{J} x_{ijkm}(\mathbf{R}, \mathbf{W}), \tag{3.54}$$

where $\mathbf{X}(\mathbf{R}, \mathbf{W}) := (x_{ijkm}(\mathbf{R}, \mathbf{W}))$, with $i \in \mathcal{I}$, $j \in \mathcal{J}$, $k \in \mathcal{K}$, and $m \in \mathcal{M}$, is the matrix of the average flow of requests for service j from user i in priority class k at node m.

Define $\boldsymbol{\chi}_m(\mathbf{X}) := (\chi_{mkq}(\mathbf{X}))$, where $k \in \mathcal{K}$ and $q \in \mathbb{N}_0$, as the vector of all arrival rates of service requests with the volume q at node m in priority class k. We already mentioned that capacity at node m is designated by $v_m \in \mathbb{R}_+$. Now, we are ready to define the expected waiting time at node m for priority class k, for a given value of v_m, as

$$\Omega_k : \mathbb{R}^K \to \mathbb{R}; \quad w_{mk} := \Omega_k(\boldsymbol{\chi}_m(\mathbf{X})|v_m),$$

where the functions $\Omega_k(\boldsymbol{\chi}_m(\mathbf{X})|v_m)$ are supposed to be continuously differentiable, strictly increasing, and convex in the arrival rates $\chi_{mkq}(\mathbf{X})$. For users $\Omega_k(\boldsymbol{\chi}_m(\mathbf{X})|v_m)$ contains a trade-off between expected waiting time and throughput for priority class k: The higher the throughput $\chi_{mkq}(\mathbf{X})$ in priority class k the higher the expected waiting times users have to bear.

Suppose that incremental expected waiting times imposed on packets with priority l are not lower the lower the priority number, i.e., the higher the priority class, of newly arriving packets. Or, formally expressed,

$$\frac{\partial \Omega_l(\boldsymbol{\chi}_m(\mathbf{X})|v_m)}{\partial \chi_{mkq}} \geq \frac{\partial \Omega_l(\boldsymbol{\chi}_m(\mathbf{X})|v_m)}{\partial \chi_{mk'q}}, \quad \text{where} \quad k < k'. \tag{3.55}$$

To determine the optimal resource allocation and the stochastic equilibrium the social welfare function must be defined. We suppose that the social welfare function $W(\mathbf{P}, \mathbf{W})$ equals the sum of expected non-pecuniary user benefits, i.e., the difference between the total of instantaneous benefits and the sum of total expected costs of delay, where $\mathbf{P} := (p_{ijkm}(V_{ij}, \delta_{ij}))$, $i \in \mathcal{I}$, $j \in \mathcal{J}$, $k \in \mathcal{K}$, $m \in \mathcal{M}$:

$$W(\mathbf{P}, \mathbf{W}) :=$$

$$\iint \sum_{i=1}^{I} \sum_{j=1}^{J} \sum_{k=1}^{K} \sum_{m=1}^{M} \lambda_{ij} \left(V_{ij} - \delta_{ij}\tau(q_j, k, \mathbf{W})\right) p_{ijkm}(V_{ij}, \delta_{ij}) dF_{ij}(V_{ij}, \delta_{ij}), \tag{3.56}$$

where $dF_{ij}(V_{ij}, \delta_{ij}) = f_{ij}(V_{ij}, \delta_{ij}) dV_{ij} d\delta_{ij}$.

It is assumed that there are no operating costs in the Internet industry. The only costs are congestion costs. One may criticize the collective benefit function (3.56) on the grounds that ISPs usually maximize their profits rather than care about the collective benefits of the system. Gupta, Stahl, and Whinston ([98], p. 332) justify their approach with the argument that

> the market on the Internet can essentially be viewed as a service industry, and customer satisfaction is directly related to the market share in the service industry.

We proceed with the determination of the functions $p_{ijkm}(V_{ij}, \delta_{ij})$ and the values w_{mk} that maximize the welfare function (3.56) subject to

$$w_{mk} = \Omega_k(\boldsymbol{\chi}_m(\mathbf{X})|v_m). \tag{3.57}$$

The Lagrangian function is given by

$$L(\mathbf{P}, \mathbf{W}, \boldsymbol{\Gamma}) := W(\mathbf{P}, \mathbf{W}) + \sum_{m=1}^{M} \sum_{k=1}^{K} \gamma_{mk} \left(w_{mk} - \Omega_k(\boldsymbol{\chi}_m(\mathbf{X})|v_m)\right),$$

where γ_{mk} is the Lagrangian multiplier of the constraint (3.57), and where $\mathbf{\Gamma} := (\gamma_{mk})$, $m \in \mathcal{M}$, $k \in \mathcal{K}$. In order to set up the Kuhn-Tucker conditions[101] of this constrained benefit maximization problem we must consider the following: Optimal functions such as $p_{ijkm}(V_{ij}, \delta_{ij})$ are usually derived by means of the calculus of variations. However, since our objective function does not depend on the partial derivatives of $p_{ijkm}(V_{ij}, \delta_{ij})$ with respect to V_{ij} and δ_{ij} our optimization problem is a degenerate problem in the calculus of variations. In this case, the Euler equation,[102] which is a first-order condition for an optimum in the calculus of variations, is not a differential equation, but is reduced to a standard calculus first-order condition. Then, for our example, the optimal solution can be obtained by optimizing the integrand of the objective function with respect to $p_{ijkm}(V_{ij}, \delta_{ij})$ for all V_{ij} and δ_{ij}. Also, in order to derive condition (3.58a) down below one must keep in mind that, according to definitions (3.53) and (3.54), $p_{ijkm}(V_{ij}, \delta_{ij})$ indirectly affects the right-hand side of constraint (3.57) through x_{ijkm} and, with it, over χ_{mkq}. Moreover, note that w_{mk} indirectly enters the social welfare function via definition (3.48). In particular, we obtain

$$\frac{\partial \tau(\cdot)}{\partial w_{mk}} = \begin{cases} 1 & \text{if} \quad m \in \mathcal{S}, \\ 0 & \text{if} \quad m \notin \mathcal{S}. \end{cases}$$

To derive condition (3.59a) we will use the following definition of the average delay of user i for service j, weighted by the flow x_{ijkm}:

$$\bar{\delta}_{ij} := \frac{\lambda_{is} \int \int \delta_{ij} p_{ijkm}(V_{ij}, \delta_{ij}) dF_{ij}(V_{ij}, \delta_{ij})}{x_{ijkm}}.$$

Given the above considerations the Kuhn-Tucker conditions are:[103]

101 The Kuhn-Tucker conditions are presented in Chiang ([41], pp. 722–744).

102 See Kamien and Schwartz ([124], pp. 14-19) for an explanation of the Euler equation.

103 In order for the Kuhn-Tucker conditions to be sufficient to characterize a maximum the objective function must be quasiconcave and the constraints must be convex and qualified. Constraints are qualified if their gradients, i.e., the vectors of partial derivatives, are linearly independent. Here, $W(\cdot)$

$$
\begin{aligned}
\frac{\partial L(\cdot)}{\partial p_{ijkm}} &= \int\int \lambda_{ij}(V_{ij} - \delta_{ij}\tau(q_j, k, \mathbf{W}))dF_{ij}(V_{ij}, \delta_{ij}) \\
&\quad - \sum_{m=1}^{M}\sum_{l=1}^{K} \gamma_{ml}\left(\frac{\partial \Omega_l}{\partial \chi_{mkq}}\right)\lambda_{ij}\int\int dF_{ij}(V_{ij}, \delta_{ij}) \\
&= \lambda_{ij}\int\int \Bigg[(V_{ij} - \delta_{ij}\tau(q_j, k, \mathbf{W})) \\
&\quad - \sum_{m=1}^{M}\sum_{l=1}^{K} \gamma_{ml}\left(\frac{\partial \Omega_l}{\partial \chi_{mkq}}\right)\Bigg] dF_{ij}(V_{ij}, \delta_{ij}) \leq 0, \quad (3.58a) \\
\frac{\partial L(\cdot)}{\partial p_{ijkm}} p_{ijkm} &= 0, \quad (3.58b) \\
p_{ijkm} &\geq 0, \quad (3.58c)
\end{aligned}
$$

$$
\begin{aligned}
\frac{\partial L(\cdot)}{\partial w_{mk}} &= -\int\int \sum_{i=1}^{I}\sum_{j=1}^{J} \lambda_{ij}\delta_{ij}p_{ijkm}(V_{ij}, \delta_{ij})dF_{ij}(V_{ij}, \delta_{ij}) + \gamma_{mk} \\
&= -\sum_{i=1}^{I}\sum_{j=1}^{J} \lambda_{ij}\int\int \delta_{ij}p_{ijkm}(V_{ij}, \delta_{ij})dF_{ij}(V_{ij}, \delta_{ij}) + \gamma_{mk} \\
&= \begin{cases} -\sum_{i=1}^{I}\sum_{j=1}^{J} \overline{\delta}_{ij}x_{ijkm} + \gamma_{mk} \leq 0 & \text{if } m \in \mathcal{S}, \\ \gamma_{mk} \leq 0 & \text{if } m \notin \mathcal{S}. \end{cases} \quad (3.59a) \\
\frac{\partial L(\cdot)}{\partial w_{mk}} w_{mk} &= 0, \quad (3.59b) \\
w_{mk} &\geq 0, \quad (3.59c)
\end{aligned}
$$

---

is linear and, thus, (weakly) concave in $(\mathbf{P}, \mathbf{W})$. Moreover, the constraint is strictly convex in $p_{ijkm}(V_{ij}, \delta_{ij})$ since there is a linear relationship between $p_{ijkm}(V_{ij}, \delta_{ij})$ and x_{ijkm} as well as between x_{ijkm} and $\chi_{mkq}(\mathbf{X})$ while, by assumption, the constraint is strictly convex in $\chi_{mkq}(\mathbf{X})$. Also, the constraint is qualified since there is only one. Hence, the Kuhn-Tucker conditions are indeed sufficient to characterize a maximum.

$$\frac{\partial L(\cdot)}{\partial \gamma_{mk}} = w_{mk} - \Omega_k(\boldsymbol{\chi}_m(\mathbf{X})|v_m) \geq 0, \tag{3.60a}$$

$$\frac{\partial L(\cdot)}{\partial \gamma_{mk}}\gamma_{mk} = 0, \tag{3.60b}$$

$$\gamma_{mk} \geq 0. \tag{3.60c}$$

If (3.58a) is negative, by (3.58b), we have $p_{ijkm}(V_{ij}, \delta_{ij}) = 0$. Instead, if equality holds, then, $p_{ijkm}(V_{ij}, \delta_{ij}) \in [0, 1]$. Note that condition (3.58a) is satisfied if, for all V_{ij} and δ_{ij}, we have

$$V_{ij} - \delta_{ij}\tau(q_j, k, \mathbf{W}) - \sum_{m=1}^{M}\sum_{l=1}^{K}\gamma_{ml}\left(\frac{\partial \Omega_l}{\partial \chi_{mkq}}\right) \leq 0. \tag{3.61}$$

Furthermore, if $m \in \mathcal{S}$ and $w_{mk} > 0$, by conditions (3.59a) and (3.59b), the Lagrangian multiplier is given by

$$\gamma_{mk} = \sum_{i=1}^{I}\sum_{j=1}^{J}\bar{\delta}_{ij}x_{ijkm}. \tag{3.62}$$

In contrast, if $m \notin \mathcal{S}$, by conditions (3.59a) and (3.60c), we must have $\gamma_{mk} = 0$. Interpreted economically, expression (3.62) depicts the shadow price of expected waiting time for priority class k at router m. Moreover, by condition (3.61), in order for $p_{ijkm}(V_{ij}, \delta_{ij}) \in [0, 1]$, marginal expected net benefits of user i for service j in priority class k must equal total shadow costs of the induced marginal expected waiting times:

$$V_{ij} - \delta_{ij}\tau(q_j, k, \mathbf{W}) = \sum_{m=1}^{M}\sum_{l=1}^{K}\gamma_{ml}\left(\frac{\partial \Omega_l}{\partial \chi_{mkq}}\right).$$

Otherwise, we have $p_{ijkm}(V_{ij}, \delta_{ij}) = 0$.

The benefit maximizing allocation may be decentralized by a price mechanism if prices $r_{mk}(q)$ can be found that lead to probabilities, $p_{ijkm}(V_{ij}, \delta_{ij})$, which simultaneously maximize individual expected net benefits (3.51) for all $i \in \mathcal{I}$, $j \in \mathcal{J}$, as well as social welfare

(3.56). Recall from our analysis of individual utility maximization that, by (3.52), $p_{ijkm}(V_{ij}, \delta_{ij}|\mathbf{R}, \mathbf{W}) > 0$ requires

$$V_{ij} \geq \delta_{ij}\tau(q_j, k, \mathbf{W}) + \sum_{m \in \mathcal{S}} r_{mk}(q_j),$$

where, by definitions (3.49) and (3.50), the right-hand side of the inequality above is the minimum cost scheme of user i for service j. Given that $\gamma_{mk} = 0$ if $m \notin \mathcal{S}$, condition (3.61) satisfies this requirement provided that

$$\begin{aligned} r_{mk}(q) &= \sum_{l=1}^{K} \left(\frac{\partial \Omega_l(\cdot)}{\partial \chi_{mkq}} \right) \gamma_{ml} \\ &= \sum_{l=1}^{K} \left(\frac{\partial \Omega_l(\cdot)}{\partial \chi_{mkq}} \right) \sum_{i=1}^{I} \sum_{j=1}^{J} \overline{\delta}_{ij} x_{ijlm}. \end{aligned} \tag{3.63}$$

Hence, the benefit maximization allocation can be decentralized by the price mechanism (3.63). This price can be interpreted as follows: The term $\left(\frac{\partial \Omega_l(\cdot)}{\partial \chi_{mkq}} \right)$ is the derivative of the expected waiting time at node m for priority class l with respect to the arrival rate of service requests with the volume q at this node in priority class k. Further, the term $\left(\sum_{i=1}^{I} \sum_{j=1}^{J} \overline{\delta}_{ij} x_{ijlm} \right)$ reflects the summed delay costs of the system over all users i and services j or, alternatively, the shadow price γ_{ml} of expected waiting time at node m for priority class l. Thus, the optimal priority price $r_{mk}(q)$ at node m for priority class k to process q units of data traffic equals total shadow costs of caused incremental expected waiting times at node m. Therefore, the optimal prices derived are optimal congestion prices.

Recall that we assumed the expected waiting time to be strictly increasing in the arrival rates $\chi_{mkq}(\mathbf{X})$. Therefore, an increase in the arrival rate of service requests in priority class k increases the price for that priority class. Furthermore, our assumption given by (3.55) implies that higher priority classes are priced higher:

$$r_{mk} > r_{m(k+1)}.$$

One can imagine r_{mK} to be the base price for routing service at router m, and $(r_{mk} - r_{mK})$ to be the premium for higher service quality.

However, (3.63) does not explicitly solve for r_{mk} since r_{mk} enters the right-hand side of the formula via x_{ijlm}. Gupta, Stahl, and Whinston ([99], Appendix) solve this problem by showing that there exists a combination $(\mathbf{R}^*, \mathbf{W}^*)$ such that users submit their packets with the probability $p_{ijkm}(V_{ij}, \delta_{ij}|\mathbf{R}^*, \mathbf{W}^*)$ which maximizes their individual expected net benefits given in (3.51) for all $i \in \mathcal{I}$, $j \in \mathcal{J}$. The resulting stochastic arrival rates to the system, or, average flow rates, $x^*_{ijkm}(\mathbf{R}^*, \mathbf{W}^*)$ generate optimal expected waiting times w^*_{mk}. Furthermore, social welfare (3.56) is maximized by $\mathbf{P}^*$ and $\mathbf{W}^*$.

Interpreted alternatively, the authors prove that a combination $(\mathbf{R}^*, \mathbf{W}^*)$ exists such that demands for data traffic $\mathbf{X}(\mathbf{R}^*, \mathbf{W}^*)$ equal welfare maximizing stochastic arrival rates $\mathbf{X}^* := (x^*_{ijkm})$, where $i \in \mathcal{I}$, $j \in \mathcal{J}$, $k \in \mathcal{K}$, $m \in \mathcal{M}$, and that these demands generate optimal expected waiting times $\mathbf{W}^*$. Gupta, Stahl, and Whinston ([99], p. 710) call this alternative interpretation

> a 'stochastic equilibrium' in that expected waiting times are correct and 'excess demand' in terms of average flow rates $(\mathbf{X} - \mathbf{X}^*)$ is zero.

In other words, a stochastic equilibrium is reached if

1. stochastic arrival rates are optimal for each user given the prices and anticipated delays,
2. expected delays are correctly anticipated given the stochastic arrival rates, and if
3. stochastic arrival rates $\mathbf{X}$ equal optimal stochastic arrival rates $\mathbf{X}^*$.

In practice, to determine welfare maximizing prices, the flow rates x_{ijkm}, the expected waiting times w_{mk}, and the costs of delay parameters δ_{ij} must be known.[104] As explained in Section 3.3.2, in a static

104 Gupta et al. ([93], p. 15) emphasize that the priority price at each node only depends on measurable parameters at that node which implies that network-wide information is not necessary. Consequently, the complexity of price computation is independent of network size. This consideration will be discussed in our evaluation below.

environment a smart market can extract the necessary information to determine the delay parameters of users, or, the congestion costs, in an incentive-compatible way. However, Stahl [228] shows by an example that in a dynamic stochastic environment a second-price auction does not necessarily lead to truthful revelation of the value of time. Gupta et al. [93, 95] develop an estimation procedure to determine the congestion costs in a dynamic stochastic environment.[105]

Furthermore, Gupta, Stahl, and Whinston ([99], p. 710) propose estimating the average flow rates and the expected waiting time values by the current time-averaged flow rates measured at each node queue. Optimal prices are calculated during the interval $(t, t+1)$ through a real-time tâtonnement process. Prices at each node at time $(t+1)$ are estimated given the information on average flow rates and waiting times at time t. Denote the estimated new priority price using equation (3.63) at time $(t+1)$ by $\hat{r}_{mk}(t+1)$ and label the price implemented during the time $(t, t+1)$ by $r_{mk}(t)$. Then, the estimated price at time $(t+1)$ is set as

$$r_{mk}(t+1) = \alpha \hat{r}_{mk}(t+1) + (1-\alpha) r_{mk}(t),$$

with $\alpha \in [0, 1]$. Note that a lower value of the parameter α implies that price adjustments are smooth in time whereas a large value of α results in potentially large price jumps from period to period. The question then is how often the prices should be updated. Gupta, Stahl, and Whinston ([98], p. 339) argue that price updates should not be done too frequently for the following reasons: First, estimation results for waiting times and prices over a longer interval are more stable given less frequent price updates. Second, once estimated prices are close to the stochastic equilibrium, price fluctuations are small. Third, computational efforts may be mitigated.

105 For this purpose, the authors assume many Internet participants such that individual users cannot influence the market price. Consequently, they will not have an incentive to misrepresent their true costs of delay in order to manipulate network prices. The problem is then 'reduced to designing a statistical method of uncovering the critical information (users' values of time) from their observed market behavior'. Gupta et al. ([93], pp. 13 f.).

By constructing a computer simulation model Gupta, Stahl, and Whinston ([99], pp. 711–718) demonstrate that optimal dynamic priority prices can be implemented in a decentralized system. By simulation, they compare social benefits under a flat-rate pricing policy and under optimal priority pricing. They find that dynamic priority pricing significantly increases social benefits compared to the case where there is no usage-based pricing. In other papers, Gupta et al. ([92], pp. 41 f.) and Gupta, Stahl, and Whinston ([98], pp. 342–344) by simulation compare social benefits and consumer surplus, defined as social benefits less the aggregated prices paid, that result from different pricing schemes. The pricing schemes compared are a scheme without usage-based pricing, but with a potential flat fee, time-based pricing, and dynamic priority pricing. The authors find the following results: With an increasing level of congestion, social benefits are higher with dynamic priority pricing compared to time-based pricing. Additionally, social benefits with time-based pricing exceed social benefits with zero usage pricing. Furthermore, consumer surplus is highest with dynamic priority pricing. The reason is that dynamic priority pricing discourages low-value Internet customers from using the Internet during peak periods. Also, the authors find that during peak periods dynamic priority pricing yields higher revenues compared to time-based pricing and it yields comparable revenues during non peak periods. Moreover, dynamic priority pricing provides higher revenues compared to flat-rate pricing. The authors conclude that dynamic priority pricing is a resource allocation mechanism that is incentive compatible for both users and providers.

We proceed with an evaluation of dynamic priority pricing. Our evaluation is summarized in Table 3.10.

- *Allocative efficiency*
  Dynamic priority prices are welfare maximizing prices. It has been noted above that in a volatile environment such as the Internet it is not possible to achieve theoretically optimal pricing. At least, near-optimal prices can be determined in real-time. These near-optimal prices almost correctly reflect scarcity of resources since they are congestion prices that internalize congestion externali-

Table 3.10: Evaluation of dynamic priority pricing

ISP/Welfare	*Allocative efficiency*	▲
	Capacity expansion	▲
	Incentive compatibility	▲
ISP	*Cost-orientation*	△
	Price discrimination	▲
	Feasibility	▼
	Accounting efficiency	▼
User	*Utility-orientation*	▲
	Price transparency	▼

▲ = very good, △ = good
◊ = satisfactory, ▽ = adequate, ▼ = inadequate

ties. Given priority prices and expected throughput times, users adjust their demand for data traffic such that the value of the throughput increases while the volume decreases, which results in higher social welfare. Since prices discourage low-value Internet users from using the Internet during peak periods, traffic load is better distributed over time.

- *Capacity expansion*
  Dynamic priority prices give correct monetary incentives to expand capacity in bottlenecks since they reflect social marginal costs of congestion. Gupta et al. [94] by simulation compare the incentives to expand capacity in a scenario with dynamic congestion prices with a scenario where flat-rate pricing is applied, assuming one priority class. The results suggest that flat-rate pricing only

results in a higher level of optimal capacity compared to dynamic congestion pricing, given that the ratio of the average value which users have for a certain Internet service to the per unit costs of network capacity is high. These results are consistent with our findings in Section 3.3.1 where we analyzed equilibrium capacity with a variable number of Internet users. There, we found that optimal capacity without congestion pricing is lower than optimal capacity with congestion pricing if high-value users begin to substitute alternative services for Internet access. In consequence, ISPs are left with low-value users which means that the ratio of the average value which users have for a certain Internet service to the per unit costs of network capacity is low.

- *Incentive compatibility*
  Dynamic priority pricing is incentive compatible for users since, when confronted with dynamic priority prices, users generate optimal stochastic arrival rates to the system which, in turn, lead to optimal expected waiting times. Dynamic priority pricing is also incentive compatible for ISPs since, as already noted above, it yields higher revenues during peak periods compared to time-based pricing and it yields comparable revenues during off-peak periods. Moreover, dynamic priority pricing provides higher revenues compared to flat-rate pricing.
- *Cost-orientation*
  Dynamic priority prices meet the criterion of cost-orientation well since they appropriately reflect congestion costs. However, cost-orientation could be further enhanced if providers charged an additional flat fee in order to cover their fixed costs.
- *Price discrimination*
  We judge the possibility to price discriminate of dynamic priority pricing to be very good since providers can skim off different willingnesses to pay with respect to volume, quality, and network load.
- *Feasibility*
  For the following reasons we judge the feasibility of dynamic priority pricing to be inadequate: Even if priority prices set at one node only depend on measurable parameters observed at that specific

node, system-wide information becomes necessary to price data conveyance appropriately according to thc dynamic priority prices paid at each router along the path from the sender to the receiver, i.e., at each node belonging to a certain scheme. Moreover, from the point of view of social welfare, congestion pricing should be implemented in as many networks as possible in order to have a broad impact on allocative efficiency. This is difficult to achieve in a commercial and competitive Internet where independent ISPs determine their pricing strategies locally. Furthermore, dynamic priority pricing is difficult to implement: In order to dynamically calculate optimal prices at each router that belongs to a certain scheme, extensive information must be collected and processed, such as data about flow rates, the expected waiting times, and costs of delay parameters of the users. Moreover, this information must be updated in rather short time intervals in order to achieve near-optimal prices. The availability of these information requirements can hardly be guaranteed in the whole Internet.

- *Accounting efficiency*
  Accounting efficiency is inadequate given that prices vary dynamically. Recall that optimal prices set at nodes that belong to a certain scheme must be added in order to derive the final price for the data transport. To mitigate this drawback Gupta, Stahl, and Whinston ([97], p. 205) propose that users should not be billed by each node separately, but only by their IAPs. In turn, IAPs would be billed by their upstream providers and so on. That way, each network only has to communicate to adjacent networks the prices of data transports on its own network. Consequently, each ISP only has to keep accounts for adjacent providers. According to Gupta, Stahl, and Whinston ([99], p. 719), still another possibility for billing would be to leave revenue collection to content providers since the bulk of Internet traffic flows from content providers to users. Users would pay the content provider for both content and data transport. Then, the content provider would make payments to its IAP for data transmission. The latter would again pay its upstream provider and so on. We can conclude that dy-

namic priority pricing must be implemented both at the retail and at the interconnection pricing level.

Nevertheless, the amount of input data necessary to calculate near-optimal prices and the associated computational overhead may lead to the conclusion that dynamic priority pricing will not have much relevance for Internet pricing practices. Confronted with the critique on computational costs, Gupta, Stahl, and Whinston ([99], p. 719) argue that small services such as email that do not cause significant congestion should have zero dynamic priority prices. Consequently, there would be no need to account for such services. However, the authors ([99], p. 719) recognize that many tools for ISPs and users must be developed

> for measuring congestion and forecasting waiting times, estimating load requirements, making service and price offers, and for selecting the best deals.

- *Utility-orientation*
  From the point of view of Internet users, dynamic priority pricing is utility-oriented for the following reasons: Dynamic priority prices maximize individual expected net benefits as well as social welfare, defined as the sum of expected non-pecuniary user benefits. Also, quality differentiation is followed by price differentiation such that cross-subsidies between user groups are avoided.
- *Price transparency*
  The transparency of dynamic priority pricing is inadequate since prices may vary instantaneously which makes expenditures for Internet services hard to predict. Again, this problem may be mitigated by the introduction of smart agents.

Stahl ([227], pp. 144 f.) and Gupta, Stahl, and Whinston ([97], p. 206) introduce stepped pricing as a simplified approximation of dynamic priority pricing. Stepped pricing seeks to reduce accounting costs and to increase the feasibility and price transparency of dynamic priority pricing with the drawback of only approximating optimality. The authors note that congestion can either be measured in terms of expected delays or the percentage of bandwidth utilization. In the latter case, optimal prices increase smoothly with bandwidth utilization.

The authors propose approximating this smooth function by a step function where bandwidth is partitioned into exhaustive categories of utilization such as 0–50%, 50–75%, and 75–100%. Then, each category is assigned a price that rises with the degree of bandwidth utilization. The authors propose that prices of congested categories reflect an average of optimal dynamic prices for the range of congestion in that category and that congestion categories and prices be determined through theoretical investigation or via simulation modelling. They do not discuss the question of how often the utilization rate should be determined or how often the adjustment of the prices should occur. Another open question concerns how different utilization rates on the links between sender and receiver should be taken into account.[106] Nevertheless, stepped pricing remains a promising pricing idea.

3.3.4 Expected Capacity Pricing

Shenker et al. [219] criticize optimal congestion prices, endorsed in the last three sections, by pointing at the difficulty in assessing marginal congestion costs and at the potentially negative profits of ISPs when applying congestion prices rigourously if marginal costs of capacity are decreasing. Moreover, Shenker et al. ([219], p. 190) point out that maximization of social welfare requires a single pricing scheme, i.e., congestion pricing, to be implemented in the whole Internet. The authors argue that, instead, independent ISPs should be able to locally implement a wide variety of different pricing schemes, a requirement the optimality paradigm is inconsistent with.

Edge pricing proposed by Shenker et al. [219] addresses these difficulties. The authors argue that prices need not exactly reflect congestion costs, but only approximate them. Concretely, on the one hand, the authors suggest replacing the actual with the expected congestion status by making prices dependent on the time of day and the QoS provided. Prices are intended to increase in the QoS offered since the authors assume that packets that belong to a higher QoS class gener-

106 See Gerpott and Böhm ([84], p. 239).

ate more congestion externalities compared to packets of a lower QoS class. The approximation of congestion costs through expected congestion costs leads to time-of-day pricing which ignores instantaneous fluctuations in traffic levels: One can imagine a lightly loaded network in a period where expected congestion costs are high. On the other hand, the authors propose replacing transport costs along the actual path with those of the expected path. The price for data conveyance is then based on the source and on the destination of the data, but not on the particular route taken by the data. The idea of edge pricing is to combine these two approximations. Concretely, edge pricing requires prices to be 'based on the expected congestion along the expected path appropriate for the packet's source and destination.'[107] Consequently, prices can be calculated at the network access point, i.e., at the edge of the network, which gives the reason for the naming of the pricing proposal.

The possibility of determining prices locally is an attractive feature of edge pricing. Complexity can be reduced by making prices dependent on what happens at access nodes, but not on what happens at internal nodes as so far required by all pricing schemes presented in this section.

Shenker et al. [219] do not give an explicit formula for edge prices. Instead, they point out that edge pricing is flexible with respect to the form of pricing. In other words, edge prices can take many different forms, as long as congestion costs are appropriately approximated and as long as pricing is carried out at the edge.

Expected capacity pricing proposed by Clark [46] is a form of edge pricing. With his pricing model, Clark aims to capture the fact that marginal costs are non-zero only during periods of congestion without making the pricing mechanism sensitive to usage. The idea of expected capacity pricing is that users purchase a profile called expected capacity profile. Expected capacity can be contracted in many different forms. Clark ([46], p. 229) defines expected capacity as

107 Shenker et al. ([219], p. 192).

a maximum data object size that a user would like to transfer within some specified delay, together with an assumed duty cycle for these transfers.

As an example, consider a web browser whose expected capacity may be defined as a 1 MB object with minimal delay every ten seconds.

The proposed mechanism to implement an expected capacity service consists of traffic flagging and congestion management. Based on the contracted expected capacity profile, a traffic meter at the network access point examines the packets sent by a user and tags each packet as being either inside *(in)* or outside *(out)* of the expected capacity profile. Packets are always marked with a tag, regardless of whether the network is lightly or heavily loaded.

The implementation of traffic flagging is based on a token bucket concept: Imagine that the traffic meter at the network access point has a bucket filled with *in* tokens for each user. The tokens are created at the contracted average sending rate of the user. The unused *in* tokens are accumulated up to the bucket size. If the accumulated tokens exceed the bucket size they get discarded. Packets that arrive at the network access point are marked with an *in* token taken from the bucket as long as there are *in* tokens in the bucket. In case that there are no more tokens in the bucket arriving packets are marked with an *out* tag.

Turning back to our example with the web browser, the desired service for a web browser could be implemented by a token rate of 0.8 Mbps, since this rate accommodates a 1 MB object every ten seconds, and a bucket size of 1 MB.[108] If a user empties the bucket of tokens by sending an object of 1 MB, the bucket will be filled up within ten seconds, i.e., at the token rate. A user who rarely wants to send large files could negotiate a very small token rate, but a very large token bucket.

Apart from traffic flagging, congestion management is a crucial element of expected capacity pricing: In case of congestion, only packets with an *in* tag are forwarded while the senders of packets marked with an *out* tag obtain a congestion pushback notification. With today's routing technology, this would be done by discarding the packet.

108 One byte equals eight bits.

In consequence, there would be no Acknowledgments (ACKs) for dropped *out* packets. Due to the rate adaptation of TCP/IP dropped packets are sent again, but with a reduced sending rate. In the absence of congestion, there is no discrimination between *in* and *out* packets. Both packet groups are forwarded with the same service.

Users are only charged for the packets that lie within the specified expected capacity profile. If network congestion becomes severe such that even packets with an *in* tag have to be discarded the First-In, First-Out (FIFO) principle is applied to *in* packets. If many *in* packets must be rejected the expected capacity profile of users cannot be fulfilled. Capacity should then be expanded at these bottlenecks. Thus, the marking of packets gives ISPs valuable information on and a 'real-time feedback'[109] about the necessity of capacity expansion. In contrast, packets marked as being *out* are not an indicator for scarce capacity. Discarding *out* packets only points at the fact that users are overusing their expected capacity. Hence, by making users pay for expected capacity, users are charged for the privilege of sending data during periods of congestion when marginal costs of data transport are non-zero. Therefore, packets with an *in* tag represent the value users attach to sending their traffic during congestion.

Clark [46] does not determine how user profiles are assigned a certain price. Instead, he leaves it up to ISPs to define and to charge for expected capacity. Bucket size and token rate can be freely combined within a usage profile. Standard expected capacity pricing takes the form of cost-oriented flat subscription fees paid by users ex ante. These flat rates are not determined by the peak capacity of the access link as they usually are, but by the more complex expected usage profile for this link. The flat rate varies with the token rate and the size of the token bucket. These values are not fixed bounds, but thresholds to differentiate packets in case of congestion.

If expected capacity pricing takes the form of a flat rate, users do not pay for actual usage which implies that congestion costs can only be approximated. In this case, expected capacity pricing becomes similar to cumulus pricing introduced by Stiller et al. [231]. Within

109 Dolan ([63], p. 24).

the framework of cumulus pricing, contracts between IAPs and their subscribers specify the expected usage patterns in terms of bandwidth, delay, etc., i.e., the type of service, and the corresponding flat rate. There exists a feedback mechanism, based on so-called cumulus points, about actual usage patterns of customers which prevents the mismatch between actual and negotiated expected usage patterns exceeding a certain threshold. If usage discrepancies exceed the threshold specified in the contract the concerned customer receives feedback in the form of cumulus points. Cumulus points can either be red or green. A red cumulus point indicates that the user has exceeded her expected usage profile. In the opposite case, a green cumulus point is assigned. The number of cumulus points assigned increases with the difference between expected and actual usage. Cumulus points do not trigger an immediate reaction by the ISP, but only in the long run if accumulated red (positive) and green (negative) cumulus points exceed a certain reaction threshold.[110] In practice, this means that cumulus points remain valid for a certain number of consecutive billing periods before they finally trigger consequences. These consequences depend on the policies of ISPs. One can imagine that a certain number of accumulated cumulus points leads to a renegotiation of the original contract. Cumulus pricing is cumulative in the sense that not single bursts, but a permanent change of contracted behavior leads to price changes.[111]

After this excursion on cumulus pricing we want to focus on similarities between expected capacity pricing and a further pricing proposal. Note that expected capacity pricing does not try to internalize congestion externalities through pricing only, but through the combination of pricing with a technic traffic control mechanism. A similar approach is taken with the Simple Integrated Media Access (SIMA) system proposed by Kilkki, Kalervo, and Ruutu [132]. Within the SIMA system, users pay monthly flat rates that are associated with

110 The ISP has the option to define reaction thresholds multidimensionally such that peak rates or burst behavior can be taken into account.

111 Stiller et al. [231] present a feasible technical solution called Internet Charge Calculation and Accounting System (ICCAS) that supports the cumulus pricing scheme.

nominal bit rates. In case of congestion, routers first discard packets of those data streams with the highest mismatch between the momentary bit rate and the nominal bit rate, i.e., with the highest ratio of momentary to nominal bit rate. The ratio of momentary to nominal bit rate is measured at the network access point of each customer. Appropriate packet discarding requires packets to be marked with a priority number depending on this ratio. Moreover, each packet contains information to distinguish and support real-time applications. At each router, packets that belong to real-time applications are queued up in a separate buffer that is served before the non real-time buffer. In each buffer the FIFO principle applies. At any instant, there is an accepted priority level. The accepted priority level is calculated based on the buffer load levels of the real-time buffer and the non real-time buffer. Incoming packets are accepted if they have the same or a higher priority level than the accepted priority level. Otherwise, packets are discarded.

Clark ([46], p. 247) argues that the payment scheme for expected capacity may also be dynamic in the sense that users would pay for actual use under congestion.[112] The number of *in* packets could be counted at the network access point and be multiplied by a cost-oriented packet price. In this case, a usage profile would be installed before each data transfer.

Clark ([44], pp. 177 f.) also points at the possibility of creating a smart market for *in* packets in times of severe congestion in order to determine which *in* packets to drop. However, later on, Clark takes back his proposal for two reasons: First, he argues that the pricing scheme would get too complex. Second, he notes that it should only occur rarely that *in* packets must be discarded since ISPs obtain correct signals about where capacity expansion is desirable.

112 In this context, Singh et al. [222] extend the standard form of expected capacity pricing where a flat rate is paid ex ante and where congestion externalities are considered in a static way. They propose a so-called Dynamic Capacity Contracting (DCC) framework. DCC is based on short-term contracts between users and their IAPs and adds mechanisms that make the expected capacity pricing model congestion-sensitive.

Expected capacity pricing may also be implemented at the interconnection level between ISPs. Consider two interconnected providers A and B, where ISP A sends packets to ISP B. Imagine that ISP A has negotiated a specific expected capacity profile with ISP B. Then, ISP B would install a traffic meter device at the interconnection point with ISP A. The traffic meter checks incoming traffic and marks packets that exceed the specified capacity profile with an *out* tag. If packets are frequently marked with an *out* tag subscribers of ISP A would finally realize that they obtain congestion notifications even though they are sending within their expected capacity profile. If ISP A is reluctant to lose unsatisfied subscribers to its competitors it will adjust its expected capacity profile with ISP B. As an alternative to installing a traffic meter device at the interconnection point, ISP B may accept and meter all packets of provider A marked with an *in* tag. Provider B can then determine the amount of bandwidth consumed by traffic of value that should be forwarded during periods of congestion. This information gives a rational basis for determining interconnection payments. In particular, providers could agree to interconnect and settle based on the mutual provision of expected capacity for each other, rather than based on the actual transport of tagged packets.

Another advantage of expected capacity pricing is its compatibility with the receiver pays principle. If the receiver has to pay for data traffic conveyance she would contract a specific expected capacity profile with her IAP. This IAP would negotiate an expected capacity profile with other providers and so on. Then, the traffic flagging no longer occurs at the network access point of the sender. Instead, each packet is flagged when passing through a point of congestion on its way to the receiver. Before being delivered to the receiver, each packet passes a traffic meter at the network access point of the receiver. This traffic meter checks if the number of packets that encountered congestion exceeds the expected capacity profile of the receiver. If this is not the case, packets are delivered to the receiver. If the receiver did not purchase enough capacity, traffic adjustment is needed. This may be done by discarding packets that exceed the expected capacity profile. Thereby, the sending rate at the source is slowed down due to the rate adaptation of TCP. Alternatively, packets that exceed the expected capacity profile may be held back at the traffic meter until the traffic pattern matches the expected capacity profile.[113]

We now evaluate expected capacity pricing in its standard form with a flat subscription fee coupled with a technic traffic control mechanism.[114] Table 3.11 gives a synopsis of the subsequent evaluation.

Table 3.11: Evaluation of expected capacity pricing

ISP/Welfare	*Allocative efficiency*	◊
	Capacity expansion	△
	Incentive compatibility	▲
ISP	*Cost-orientation*	▲
	Price discrimination	◊
	Feasibility	△
	Accounting efficiency	▲
User	*Utility-orientation*	▲
	Price transparency	▲

▲ = very good, △ = good

◊ = satisfactory, ▽ = adequate, ▼ = inadequate

113 See Clark ([46], pp. 240–244). Further information on the receiver pays principle within the expected capacity framework can be found in Clark [45].

114 Our evaluation is partially based on Gerpott and Böhm ([84], pp. 241 f.).

- *Allocative efficiency*
  Although Clark [46] does not introduce a welfare function whose maximum serves as a benchmark, from the welfare theoretic perspective, expected capacity pricing is likely to lead to an approximation of allocative efficiency by including both an estimation of congestion costs and the network load into the pricing scheme: Expected capacity pricing considers that marginal costs of data conveyance are positive only during periods of congestion. In the absence of congestion, there is no discrimination between *in* and *out* packets. Primarily, only packets marked with an *out* tag are affected during peak periods. But, for two reasons, internalization of congestion externalities and allocative efficiency may only be approximated with expected capacity pricing. First, expected capacity pricing is not explicitly congestion-sensitive. This drawback is mitigated by the combination of flat-rate pricing with the technic congestion control mechanism. Second, on the one hand, in case of severe congestion, packets with an *in* tag may also be discarded. On the other hand, Internet users also pay for potential congestion when no congestion occurs. Moreover, users who exceed their expected capacity during periods of congestion do not have to pay more. The only consequence they face is an increase in delay of the transmission due to the dropping of *out* packets.
- *Capacity expansion*
  An advantage of the expected capacity pricing scheme is that ISPs are informed whether their network has sufficient overall capacity: If even *in* packets must be discarded during significant time periods, capacity expansion is needed. On the contrary, it is not an indication of insufficient capacity provision if *out* packets must be dropped since discarded *out* packets only indicate that customers are overusing their contracted expected capacity. Hence, congestion management of the expected capacity pricing approach provides a real-time feedback: Observing the tags of rejected packets appropriately signals the need for capacity expansion. If ISPs ignore these signals they risk losing unsatisfied subscribers to competitors. Furthermore, with appropriately designed expected ca-

pacity pricing, the necessary revenues to expand capacity in bottlenecks should approximately be generated.

- *Incentive compatibility*
  A further advantage of expected capacity pricing is its incentive compatibility since understatements of usage profiles lead to more frequent packet delays. In order to obtain a higher QoS a higher priced expected capacity profile has to be purchased.
- *Cost-orientation*
  From the point of view of providers, expected capacity pricing has the advantage of being cost-oriented. ISPs must have enough capacity to accommodate the expected capacity of their subscribers during busy periods. Therefore, the provisioning costs are directly related to the total amount of expected capacity sold.
- *Price discrimination*
  To a certain degree, expected capacity pricing allows different willingnesses to pay to be exploited by pricing distinct expected capacity profiles with different subscription fees.
- *Feasibility*
  An advantage of expected capacity pricing is its feasibility: Expected capacity is a form of edge pricing that can be implemented in a decentralized way. Many different pricing policies to allocate capacity among users may be implemented by IAPs. The design of the details of the expected capacity profiles can be determined by individual providers which enhances creativity and competition. What must be implemented globally is the preferential treatment of *in* packets compared to *out* packets at routers. Implementation is based on the token bucket principle that should not be very difficult to install. Rupp ([201], p. 40) claims that the expected capacity model can be integrated into the current Internet structure with minimal technical expense. Note that expected capacity pricing is compatible with the DiffServ concept. To see this, recall from Section 2.1.2 that in DiffServ environments, at the edge of the network, IP packets are classified by a mark in their header according the traffic profile of a customer. In Section 2.1.2, we stated that if a customer sends more packets than contracted, excess packets are marked as being out of profile. Such packets,

within the model of expected capacity pricing, would be market with an *out* tag. Just as within the concept of expected capacity pricing, out-of-profile packets in a DiffServ environment do not obtain the contracted service quality, but only best-effort service.

- *Accounting efficiency*
  We judge accounting efficiency of expected capacity pricing to be very good: Usage does not have to be measured. Hence, there is no need to implement accounting tools. Instead, subscription prices are determined by the expectation users have about their usage patterns.
- *Utility-orientation*
  From the subscriber's perspective, expected capacity pricing is utility-oriented in the sense that heterogeneous user preferences are taken into account. Different service qualities that result from distinct expected usage profiles are priced differently. Hence, there are no cross-subsidies between user groups and incentive compatibility is ensured. Occasionally, a user will not be able to exactly receive the expected capacity. This is the case if not every ISP has purchased enough expected capacity from the next one such that packets do not flow unimpeded along the path. This implies that there are no guaranteed QoS. The only guarantee given is that packets with an *in* tag have a higher probability not to be discarded along their path compared to packets marked with an *out* tag. Note that the critique on the missing service guarantee concerns all pricing schemes proposed in this section. It is not a deficiency of expected capacity pricing, but on the network technology installed.
- *Price transparency*
  Expected capacity pricing has the advantage of being transparent: First, tariff tables are known ex ante. Second, expected capacity prices are essentially Internet access subscription prices, except that they are not determined by the peak capacity consumption of the access link, but by a more complex expected usage profile for that link. Such flat rates make the pricing scheme predictable to users.

In sum, expected capacity pricing satisfies our criteria for Internet pricing fairly well. With the introduction of dynamic expected capacity pricing, allocative efficiency and the possibility to price discriminate, that are only satisfactory, can be improved. However, this can only be done at the expense of reduced price transparency as well as lower feasibility and accounting efficiency. Further positive aspects of expected capacity pricing are its compatibility with the receiver pays principle and its possible application at the interconnection level between providers.

Both the present and the previous section have focused on pricing proposals designed for a network environment that provides relative priorities. The next section will present pricing schemes for network environments where QoS can be guaranteed.

3.4 Pricing Proposals for Guaranteed Quality of Service

3.4.1 Adaptive Load-Sensitive Volume Pricing

Fankhauser, Stiller, and Plattner [70] introduce an Adaptive Load-Sensitive Volume Pricing (ALSVP) model, based on the contribution of Müller [169], for a network environment where QoS can be guaranteed. The authors propose making the price for a communication service, such as email or an IP call, dependent upon the amount of data generated, the QoS required, and upon the network load.

The authors distinguish between four different service classes, *SC*: First, there is a deterministically guaranteed service class, *DG*, that guarantees a certain throughput. Second, there is a statistically guaranteed service class, *SG*, such as controlled-load service which guarantees that a specific, very high fraction of transmitted packets, reaches the required throughput. Third, best-effort service with high priority, *HP*, is offered. Fourth, there is a best-effort service class with low priority, *LP*.

In order to implement these four service classes each router is assumed to have a separate queue for incoming packets of each service class. Packets are forwarded according to their priority, where the priority ordering is

$$DG \succ SG \succ HP \succ LP.$$

In each queue the FIFO principle applies. Suppose that algorithms for resource reservation and admission control exist to guarantee certain service levels for the first two classes.[115] The admission control algorithm determines which connection requests to grant and which to deny. Allocation of bandwidth occurs according to the principle of incremental growth, i.e., there is no fixed amount of bandwidth allocated to different service classes. The principle of incremental growth implies that a connection request for a deterministically or statistically guaranteed service class is only given if it does not affect any existing deterministic or statistic guaranteed connection. The class with deterministically granted QoS has a higher priority concerning admission than the class with statistically guaranteed service. Admission is always granted to best-effort service class packets. However, these packets are only forwarded if they do not affect any existing deterministically or statistically guaranteed connection.

The price for a communication service at time t depends on the price for the application A and on a time-variable traffic factor:

$$\text{price}(A, t) := \text{traffic factor}_{SC(A)}(t) \cdot \text{application price}(A).$$

We will look at each of these factors in turn.

The price for an application A is determined by the product of the base price for the required service class $SC(A)$ of the application, where

$$SC(A) \in \{DG, SG, HP, LP\},$$

115 This is a rather keen assumption for today's Internet. However, as will be mentioned below, Fankhauser, Stiller, and Plattner [70] succeeded in implementing their pricing proposal in a testbed.

and the data volume of the application, which is itself the product of throughput and the connection time:

$$\text{application price}(A) := \\ \text{base price}_{SC(A)} \cdot \text{throughput}(A) \cdot \text{connection time}(A).$$

Base prices for service classes are measured in monetary units per bit, where

$$\text{base price}_{DG} > \text{base price}_{SG} > \text{base price}_{HP} > \text{base price}_{LP},$$

in order to obtain a utility-oriented pricing structure which is incentive compatible. Base prices must be fixed quantitatively. The authors leave it up to ISPs to set the base prices for the different service classes. Given that the levels of base prices depend upon user behavior and on the configuration of the network, the authors argue that base prices have to be set quantitatively by simulation according to demand, business and market strategies, as well as by observing existing networks.

The time-variable traffic factor is given by the following formula, to be explained down below:

$$\text{traffic factor}_{SC(A)}(t) := \\ \begin{cases} f(\Delta\text{bandwidth}_{SC(A)}(t)), & \Delta\text{bandwidth}_{SC(A)}(t) > 0, \\ 1, & \Delta\text{bandwidth}_{SC(A)}(t) \leq 0. \end{cases}$$

The traffic factor is assumed to depend on

$$\Delta\text{bandwidth}_{SC(A)}(t) := \text{throughput}_{SC(A)}(t) - \text{bandwidth}_{SC(A)}(t),$$

i.e., on the difference between the actual throughput in service class $SC(A)$ required by application A at time t, or, in other words, the bandwidth allocated to the respective service class through the principle of incremental growth at time t, and the theoretically allocated bandwidth to that service class at time t which is denoted by $\text{bandwidth}_{SC(A)}(t)$. The theoretically allocated bandwidth to service class $SC(A)$ is defined as the ratio of requested bandwidth in this service class at time t to the overbooking ratio at time t. The overbooking ratio is the ratio between total demand of bandwidth at time t, measured at the admission control point, and available bandwidth at time t:

$$\text{bandwidth}_{SC(A)}(t) := \frac{\text{requested bandwidth}_{SC(A)}(t)}{\text{overbooking ratio}(t)},$$

$$\text{overbooking ratio}(t) := \frac{\text{total demand}(t)}{\text{available bandwidth}(t)}.$$

If the overbooking ratio exceeds 1 the network is congested. The theoretically allocated bandwidth to each service class ensures that bandwidth in each service class is available in proportion to its respective demand: In case of network congestion, demand for bandwidth of each service class is linearly reduced by the overbooking ratio. Instead of a linear reduction of the requested bandwidth of each service class one can imagine any other form of reduction such as a progressive or a degressive cut.

Actual throughput and the theoretically allocated bandwidth to a service class may diverge since allocation is done according to the principle of incremental growth. If actual throughput in a service class exceeds the allocated bandwidth to that service class, the demand for bandwidth is high. Then, the value of the traffic factor is determined by the penalty function $f(\cdot)$. As an example, consider the following penalty function:

$$f(\Delta\text{bandwidth}_{SC(A)}(t)) := (\Delta\text{bandwidth}_{SC(A)}(t) + 1)^2.$$

In practice, in order to influence user behavior significantly, any function rising faster than a linear one, where $f(0) = 1$, is applicable. The appropriate function must be found by simulation such that congestion externalities can be internalized and such that the necessary revenues are generated to expand capacity in bottlenecks.

We conclude that, if congestion occurs, the traffic factor takes a value greater than 1 which results in a higher price for the communication service. If the network is free of congestion the traffic factor equals 1 and does not influence the price for a communication service. Note that the traffic factor for the lowest service class LP always takes the value 1 since, according to the principle of incremental growth, the throughput of the lowest priority class cannot exceed the bandwidth theoretically allocated to that class.

The price of a communication service at time t is determined at the network access control point. Whenever a user requires service she is informed about the price and has the choice whether to demand the communication service at the respective moment, later, or not at all. She can select a price both through the required service class and through the time of data transmission.

One can imagine the price of a communication service changing until the user makes up her mind on whether to accept or to reject the price. There are three solutions to this problem. First, t may be a time interval rather than a point in time which gives the user enough time to react. The drawback of this solution is that it worsens allocative efficiency. Second, the ISP could bear the risk that the posted price differs from the actual one. Since price deviations can be both positive and negative the ISP may on average receive the same revenues as if users were always charged with the price at time t. Third, users may have a software agent that rapidly decides on their behalf whether to accept or to reject a posted price.

The authors do not address the question of how interconnection payments may be designed if ALSVP is implemented at the retail level. One could imagine that ISPs charge users an application price equal to the product of the data traffic volume and the sum of base prices charged by all ISPs along the path. Then, each ISP involved in data conveyance would receive an interconnection fee equal to the product of the traffic factor set by the IAP of the source and its own application price.

We proceed with an evaluation of ALSVP. A synopsis thereof can be found in Table 3.12.

Table 3.12: Evaluation of adaptive load-sensitive volume pricing

ISP/Welfare	*Allocative efficiency*	△
	Capacity expansion	△
	Incentive compatibility	▲
ISP	*Cost-orientation*	△
	Price discrimination	▲
	Feasibility	▽
	Accounting efficiency	▼
User	*Utility-orientation*	▲
	Price transparency	▽

▲ = very good, △ = good
◊ = satisfactory, ▽ = adequate, ▼ = inadequate

- *Allocative efficiency*
  The authors do not introduce a welfare function whose maximum serves as a benchmark to assess allocative efficiency of ALSVP. Nevertheless, we judge that, through the traffic factor, an efficient allocation of resources is likely to approximated if congestion costs can be estimated reliably. The traffic factor is larger than 1 only if the network is congested. Only in this case is the price of a communication service influenced by the traffic factor. An additional price instrument to approximate allocative efficiency would be obtained if base prices took the form of peak-load prices.
- *Capacity expansion*
  The traffic factor, if defined appropriately, generates about the necessary revenues for capacity expansion.

- *Incentive compatibility*
  A further advantage of ALSVP is its incentive compatibility. Since the price for a communication service depends on the amount of data generated, the service class required, and upon the network load users face the incentives necessary to reveal their true willingness to pay for bandwidth.
- *Cost-orientation*
  From the point of view of ISPs, ALSVP allows for cost recovery through appropriate choices of both base prices and the design of the penalty function. Note that base prices may be modified after some given period of time or that they can take the form of peak-load prices. At the same time, the traffic factor generates congestion revenues through short-term pricing. A flat rate to cover fixed costs would reduce financial risks of ISPs.
- *Price discrimination*
  Different willingnesses to pay can be creamed off since ISPs are able to price discriminate according to the data volume generated, the network load, and to the QoS required.
- *Feasibility*
  We judge the feasibility of ALSVP to be adequate: Implementation of ALSVP requires that all ISPs involved in data conveyance offer guaranteed QoS. Then, each ISP can specify its own base prices and its own penalty function or even adopt a different pricing scheme. However, implementation is not simple since the introduction of ALSVP requires many technical changes such as the filtering and classifying of packets, the implementation of the reservation protocol, and the admission control module at routers. But, Fankhauser, Stiller, and Plattner [70] have implemented their pricing proposal in a testbed and have demonstrated that the proposed pricing scheme does not imply intolerable processing and protocol overheads.[116]

116 For more on this consider Fankhauser et al. [67], Stiller, Fankhauser, and Plattner [232], as well as Stiller, Reichl, and Leinen [233].

- *Accounting efficiency*
  There is also a considerable accounting overhead since prices for communication services must be calculated at the admission control point. These prices vary dynamically according to the QoS required, the traffic volume, and the load of the network. To simplify implementation and to enhance accounting efficiency the authors propose focusing on pricing reserved resources, since these are the most expensive service classes, and point at the possibility of offering a mixed pricing scheme where the price for reservations is usage-based and the one for best-effort traffic is flat.
- *Utility-orientation*
  From the perspective of users, we judge ALSVP to be utility-oriented for the following reasons: Product differentiation, that even includes the offer of guaranteed QoS, is followed by price differentiation. Moreover, in times of network congestion, only users with a relatively high willingness to pay are served.
- *Price transparency*
  There is a lack of price transparency due to the traffic factor. But, as already mentioned, users have the possibility of denying or postponing the transmission of a communication service after knowing the price. Hence, users will not be charged for something they have not agreed to. Moreover, if base prices are peak-load prices, unpredictable short-term price fluctuations due to the traffic factor are likely to ease.

3.4.2 Dynamic Volume Pricing

Wang and Schulzrinne [251, 252] introduce volume pricing with a congestion-sensitive component which we call 'dynamic volume pricing'. The authors integrate their pricing proposal into a service negotiation environment called Resource Negotiation And Pricing (RNAP) protocol and architecture, but emphasize that the pricing proposal does not depend on any particular network architecture or protocol. ISPs can dynamically formulate service prices and communicate them to users. RNAP allows users to choose between available network services that offer different service qualities. Negotiation is done between a Host Resource Negotiator (HRN), acting on behalf of the user, and a local Network Resource Negotiator (NRN) that negotiates for the IAP. Hence, RNAP allows resource commitments to be automated for short negotiation periods where prices may be different in each period.[117]

We begin this section with the set up of the model. The authors assume a competitive market environment where routers distinguish between multiple service classes. Specifically, each router provides a distinct link bandwidth and a distinct buffer space for each service class.[118] Link bandwidth and buffer space supplied do not have to match the installed capacity. Rather, they represent targeted bandwidth and buffer space utilization.

Suppose that a representative user has a quasilinear utility function in the form of

$$U(x_1, \ldots, x_J, b) := \sum_{j=1}^{J} w_j \log x_j + b,$$

where x_j is the amount of bandwidth demanded, or, the demanded sending rate, of service class j, $j = 1, \ldots, J$, measured in data units per second, where w_j is a positive parameter that reflects the sensitivity of utility with respect to the amount of demanded bandwidth of service class j, and where b denotes the money a user has at

117 See Wang and Schulzrinne [250] for a detailed introduction to RNAP.

118 The provision of a distinct link bandwidth and a distinct buffer space for each service class makes dynamic volume pricing similar to PMP. However, it will be argued below that dynamic volume pricing allows unused resources to be utilized by lower service classes. That way, the loss of advantages of statistical multiplexing inherent in PMP is avoided.

her disposal to spend on all other goods apart from Internet traffic conveyance.[119] The budget constraint is given by

$$\sum_{j=1}^{J} p_j x_j + b = m,$$

where p_j is the price per unit of bandwidth of service class j, and where m depicts the budget of the user. Note that m and b are measured in monetary units per second. Solving the budget constraint for b and substituting the result for b in the utility function yields the unconstrained maximization problem of the consumer:

$$\max_{x_1,\dots,x_J} \quad \sum_{j=1}^{J} w_j \log x_j + m - \sum_{j=1}^{J} p_j x_j. \tag{3.64}$$

Note that the point where the function (3.64) reaches its maximum does not depend on the budget m. Hence, to find the utility maximizing value of x_j, rather than maximizing (3.64), we can as well maximize

$$\max_{x_1,\dots,x_J} \quad \sum_{j=1}^{J} w_j \log x_j - \sum_{j=1}^{J} p_j x_j. \tag{3.65}$$

We go on working with (3.65).

Differentiating (3.65) with respect to each x_j, setting the derivatives equal to zero, and rearranging terms yields the demand for bandwidth of each service class j:[120]

$$x_j = \frac{w_j}{p_j}. \tag{3.66}$$

---

119 Wang and Schulzrinne [251, 252] normalize the amount of bandwidth demanded of service class j as follows: They divide x_j by $\underline{x}_j$, where $\underline{x}_j$ represents the minimum bandwidth of service class j required by a user. If the minimum bandwidth $\underline{x}_j$ of service class j cannot be provided it is assumed that the user does not demand any data to be conveyed in this service class. In order to simplify the analysis, since this normalization does not alter the results derived below, we abstain from introducing it.

120 The unconstrained utility maximization problem (3.65) is concave in each x_j. Thereby, a second-order condition for a maximum is satisfied.

Note that wealth and cross-price effects of x_j are both zero. There is no wealth effect since the utility function is assumed to be quasilinear. The reason why there is no cross-price effect is that the nonlinear term of the utility function is the logarithm of a Cobb-Douglas utility function which generates demands characterized by zero cross-price effects. Furthermore, as

$$w_j = p_j x_j,$$

the parameter w_j can be interpreted as the willingness to pay for bandwidth of service class j.

We now introduce dynamic volume pricing. It consists of a fixed volume-based price component and of a congestion-sensitive price component. The fixed volume-based price component is again decomposed into a usage and into a holding price component. The usage price p_j^u is a uniform price per unit of data traffic that is distinct for each service class j and that allows ISPs to recover fixed and operating costs incurred to provide the respective service class.

Generally, a lightly loaded service class can offer higher QoS in terms of lower expected delays compared to a more heavily loaded service class. Therefore, Wang and Schulzrinne ([252], p. 946) propose estimating the usage price p_j^u of service class j as

$$p_j^u := \frac{p^{basic}}{\rho_j},$$

where p^{basic} denotes the basic price per unit of bandwidth if all bandwidth were utilized, and where ρ_j (> 0) depicts the expected load ratio of service class j. Here, in contrast to Wang and Schulzrinne [252], we assume p^{basic} to vary across service classes since the costs of a unit of bandwidth may increase with service quality given that for guaranteed service classes resource reservation and admission control become necessary.[121] Therefore, we define p_j^u as follows:

$$p_j^u := \frac{p_j^{basic}}{\rho_j},$$

121 Our approach results in optimal usage prices p_j^u different from those derived in Wang and Schulzrinne ([252], p. 947).

where p_j^{basic} denotes the basic price per unit of bandwidth of service class j if all its bandwidth were utilized. A low load ratio ρ_j is coupled with low expected delays and a high usage price p_j^u. Similarly, the authors define actual bandwidth consumption as

$$x_j^a := \frac{w_j}{p_j^u \rho_j}.$$

Wang and Schulzrinne ([252], pp. 946 f.) derive the equilibrium usage price for each service class that maximizes both the utility of a representative user and the profits of a representative ISP. Let $C(K)$ depict the cost function of a representative ISP, where K designates capacity. Given the utility maximizing demand for bandwidth of service class j depicted in (3.66), where $p_j := p_j^u$, the profit maximization problem of a representative provider can be written as

$$\max_{p_1^u,\ldots,p_J^u} \quad \sum_{j=1}^{J} \frac{w_j}{p_j^u} p_j^u - C(K), \quad \text{where} \quad p_j^u := \frac{p_j^{basic}}{\rho_j},$$

subject to the capacity constraint

$$\sum_{j=1}^{J} \frac{w_j}{p_j^u \rho_j} \leq K, \quad \text{where} \quad p_j^u := \frac{p_j^{basic}}{\rho_j}.$$

Note that provider profits do not depend on p_j^u since

$$\sum_{j=1}^{J} \frac{w_j}{p_j^u} p_j^u - C(K) = \sum_{j=1}^{J} w_j - C(K).$$

Hence, a representative provider only needs to satisfy the capacity constraint with equality in order to determine the optimal price p_j^u and, with it, p_j^{basic}:

$$p_j^u = \frac{w_j}{\rho_j \left(K - \sum\limits_{\substack{i=1 \\ i \neq j}}^{J} \frac{w_i}{p_i^{basic}} \right)}.$$

Therefore,

$$p_j^{basic} = \rho_j p_j^u = \frac{w_j}{K - \sum\limits_{\substack{i=1 \\ i \neq j}}^{J} \frac{w_i}{p_i^{basic}}}.$$

We can express the total usage charge $c_j^u(t)$ in service class j in period t, given that $q_j(t)$ data units have been transmitted in that period, as

$$c_j^u(t) := p_j^u q_j(t).$$

In addition to the usage price component, Wang and Schulzrinne ([252], p. 946) introduce a holding price component. Note that resources must be reserved to guarantee a certain QoS. This resource reservation imposes a potential cost on the network in the form of depriving other data traffic to be admitted to the network even if no data traffic is sent over the reserved resources. For this reason, Wang and Schulzrinne ([252], p. 946) introduce a holding price for services with explicit resource reservation and admission control, based on the following considerations: They assume that reserved resources, i.e., buffer space or bandwidth, of a service class that remain unused may be allocated to excess traffic of lower service classes. However, by selling the reserved resources at the lower usage price of a lower service class ISPs lose revenues. In order to reduce, or even to avoid, this loss of revenues, the authors propose setting the holding price in service class j, p_j^h, proportional to the difference between the usage price in service class j, p_j^u, and the next lower service class $(j-1)$, p_{j-1}^u:

$$p_j^h := \alpha_j (p_j^u - p_{j-1}^u).$$

The parameter α_j denotes the scaling factor of service class j. The holding charge $c_j^h(t)$ each user has to pay to reserve the bandwidth $x_j^r(t)$ in period t is given by

$$c_j^h(t) := p_j^h x_j^r(t) d_j,$$

where d_j depicts the duration of a period in class j. No holding charge is levied for services without explicit resource reservation or admission control such as best-effort service. Below, when evaluating dynamic volume pricing, we will argue that there is no obvious economic reason to introduce this holding charge.

So far, we explained how the fixed price component of dynamic volume pricing is determined. We proceed with the introduction of the congestion price component. If the average demand for bandwidth of a service class exceeds a certain threshold or if buffer occupancy reaches a certain level, users of the concerned service class are charged a congestion price. To make the latter point more explicit, consider the case of priority dropping of packets for an Assured Forwarding (AF) class in a DiffServ network environment. The dropping priority is only considered if the buffer occupancy reaches certain levels. Whenever such a level is reached packets with the corresponding dropping priority begin to be discarded with a certain probability and users with higher priority classes have to pay the additional congestion price. Lower priority users can then either accept the higher probability of dropped packets, adjust their sending rate, or, pay the congestion price that upgrades the priority level of their packets to avoid packet discarding.

For both potential sources of congestion, bandwidth and buffer space congestion, Wang and Schulzrinne ([252], p. 947) propose the following congestion price $p_j^c(t)$ of service class j in period t, to be explained below:

$$p_j^c(t) := \min\left\{\max\left\{p_j^c(t-1) + \sigma_j(D_j, S_j)\frac{(D_j - S_j)}{S_j}, 0\right\}, p_j^{max}\right\}, \tag{3.67}$$

where D_j and S_j denote the total demand for and supply of resources in service class j, respectively, where $\sigma_j(\cdot)$ is a convergence adjustment parameter, and where p_j^{max} is the upper bound of the congestion price. The convergence adjustment parameter $\sigma_j(\cdot)$ depends on D_j and S_j and increases with the level of congestion, i.e., with $(D_j - S_j)$. As already mentioned, the above formula shall be used to determine the congestion price for bandwidth as well as for buffer space. Hence, D_j and S_j will be distinct depending on the source of congestion.

Formula (3.67) is determined periodically. For the purpose of practicability Wang and Schulzrinne ([252], p. 947) propose determining a price adjustment threshold parameter θ_j for each service class j which limits the frequency of congestion price adjustments. In consequence, in period t the congestion price is updated if the calculated price deviation exceeds the threshold $\theta_j p_j^c(t-1)$. Note that formula (3.67) lets the congestion price only gradually fall to zero when congestion is removed. This protects the system from further congestion.

The maximum congestion price cannot exceed p_j^{max}. Whenever this congestion price level is reached, the service class admission control, if existing, rejects further service requests. Packets sent in service classes without admission control are dropped. If the level p_j^{max} is frequently reached more resources are required in service class j. Thus, the proposed pricing mechanism correctly signals where capacity expansion is needed.

The total congestion charge in period t for service class j can be written as

$$c_j^c(t) := p_j^c(t) q_j(t).$$

To sum up, at each router along the path, a representative user faces a total charge for an application, which may be a phone call or a complete movie, given by

$$c_j^s := \sum_{t=1}^{T} \left[p_j^h x_j^r(t) d_j + (p_j^u + p_j^c(t)) q_j(t) \right],$$

where T depicts the number of price update intervals at run time of the application. Total charges for an application incurred at each router along the path are transmitted to the Network Resource Negotiator (NRN) and are accumulated there to determine the final charge for the application. When data traffic traverses several different networks, resource negotiations are made between the NRNs of the concerned networks. To fulfill their task NRNs maintain routing and resource tables. Resource tables provide information on the availability and on the dynamic usage of the resources and allow the total charge c_j^s to be calculated at each router. Whenever a specific service request arrives the local NRN determines the path from its routing table and then calculates the accumulated price along this path with the per-router prices derived from the resource table.

Wang and Schulzrinne ([252], pp. 949–951) develop a simulation framework based on the Resource Negotiation And Pricing (RNAP) model and on an existing DiffServ implementation in order to compare the performance and the benefits of dynamic volume pricing with a static volume pricing scheme where a fixed price is charged per traffic unit. The comparisons focus on average user benefits, defined as the average of benefits obtained by all users, and on network performance in terms of packet delay and packet loss provided by each pricing schedule. The authors find that if data traffic burstiness and offered load, defined as the ratio between total user resource demand for a service type and the configured class capacity at the bottleneck, are increased, average user benefits are higher and network performance in terms of packet delay and packet loss is better under dynamic volume pricing compared to static volume pricing. Moreover, the authors find that the traffic load between the service classes is more balanced with dynamic volume pricing. The reason is that users may react to price fluctuations and network performance by migrating between service classes. However, the authors do not compare the profits of ISPs under the two pricing scenarios. One may expect that dynamic volume pricing yields higher profits compared to static volume pricing since it improves both network performance and user satisfaction. Moreover, with dynamic volume pricing and high network utilization, relatively high-value users ready to pay the congestion price use the network which may result in increased provider profits. In a different simulation study, Wang and Schulzrinne ([251], pp. 5 f.) indeed identify these effects. They consider a single service class and compare network revenues, defined as the total charge paid to a provider for all the admitted service demands during a simulation, under static and under dynamic volume pricing. They find that network revenues are higher under dynamic volume pricing.

We proceed with an evaluation of dynamic volume pricing which is summarized in Table 3.13.

Table 3.13: Evaluation of dynamic volume pricing

ISP/Welfare	*Allocative efficiency*	◊
	Capacity expansion	△
	Incentive compatibility	▲
ISP	*Cost-orientation*	▲
	Price discrimination	▲
	Feasibility	▼
	Accounting efficiency	▼
User	*Utility-orientation*	△
	Price transparency	▽

▲ = very good, △ = good

◊ = satisfactory, ▽ = adequate, ▼ = inadequate

- *Allocative efficiency*

  From the welfare theoretic point of view, we consider a holding price to be superfluous. In a network economy, where marginal costs of data transport tend to zero if the network is only lightly loaded, lower demand justifies lower usage prices and thus lower revenues. Even if there are periods where reserved resources remain unused ISPs should be able to break even since this risk is already taken into consideration by making the usage price component inversely proportional to the expected load ratio ρ_j such that fixed costs can be recovered by the usage price component.

  The congestion price component plays an important role in achieving economic efficiency. Note that congestion externalities are not introduced into the utility function. Instead, they are internalized separately by the congestion price p_j^c provided that the proposed congestion price correctly reflects social marginal costs of congestion. If p_j^c succeeds in approximately internalizing congestion externalities and given the usage prices p_j^u, which, by assumption, are equilibrium prices of a competitive market environment and which increase with the QoS offered, dynamic volume pricing approximates an efficient allocation of resources. However, this approximation is deteriorated by the introduction of the holding price.

- *Capacity expansion*
  As already noted above, dynamic volume pricing gives roughly correct signals where to expand capacity. These signals are given whenever the congestion price frequently reaches p_j^{max}. If ISPs ignored this signal resources would be overloaded. Consequently, the admission control would often have to deny service requests and packets would have to be dropped. Then, ISPs would lose potential revenues and unsatisfied customers to their competitors.
- *Incentive compatibility*
  Dynamic volume prices are incentive compatible. Prices induce Internet users to reveal their true willingness to pay for Internet resources as prices vary with the traffic volume, the QoS offered, and with the load of the network. Recall that simulation results suggest that dynamic volume pricing yields higher revenues compared to a static volume pricing scheme. Hence, ISPs have incentives to adopt dynamic volume pricing.
- *Cost-orientation*
  From the point of view of providers, dynamic volume pricing is cost-oriented since the usage-based price component is intended to recover fixed costs of network provisioning. Moreover, provided that the congestion price component correctly reflects social marginal costs of congestion, it can internalize congestion externalities at each node of the network and thereby generate the necessary revenues for capacity expansion.

- *Price discrimination*
  Dynamic volume pricing gives ISPs the possibility of creaming off different willingnesses to pay with respect to volume, network load, and the QoS provided.
- *Feasibility*
  For the following reasons one may argue that dynamic volume pricing can be implemented in a decentralized manner: Each network can determine its own usage, holding and congestion price components. Prices set at one node only depend on parameters observed at that specific node. Also, the concept is compatible with the DiffServ framework. However, system-wide information becomes necessary to calculate the final price of data conveyance that equals cumulated charges at each router along the path from the sender to the receiver. Feasibility is further deteriorated by the fact that QoS can only be guaranteed if all ISPs along the path from the source to the destination offer guaranteed service quality. Additionally, dynamic volume pricing is difficult to implement: Dynamic volume pricing, such as ALSVP, requires many technical changes. For all these reasons, we judge the feasibility of dynamic volume pricing to be inadequate.
- *Accounting efficiency*
  Furthermore, we judge accounting efficiency of dynamic volume pricing to be inadequate: Dynamic computation of the congestion price component necessitates the collection and processing of extensive information at the local NRNs. Prices set at routers along the path from the sender to the receiver must be added in order to determine the final price for an application. To reduce implementation as well as accounting difficulties Wang and Schulzrinne ([252], p. 947) limit too frequent price updates with the introduction of the price adjustment threshold parameter θ_j.
- *Utility-orientation*
  From the users' point of view, we judge utility-orientation of dynamic volume pricing to be good for the following reasons: Recall that simulation results suggest that average user benefits are higher under dynamic volume pricing compared to static volume pricing where a fixed price is charged per traffic unit. Moreover,

quality differentiation is followed by price differentiation such that there are no cross-subsidies between different groups of users. In particular, the causation principle is applied in a strict way: Prices vary with the traffic volume generated, the QoS required, and with the network load. However, the introduction of the holding price mitigates utility-orientation to a certain degree since users receive no value in terms of service quality in exchange for the holding price paid.

- *Price transparency*
  The transparency of dynamic volume pricing is rather low since prices may change dynamically with the state of the network. However, the local NRN periodically provides the Host Resource Negotiator (HRN) with updated prices. Hence, prices are known before a data transport service is claimed. The HRN then can choose the appropriate price-quality combination that best fits the preferences of the user.

3.4.3 Resource-Based Pricing

In a classical paper in the field Parris and Ferrari [191] present a pricing scheme for real-time connections, i.e., for connections with guaranteed performance.[122] Following Jordan and Jiang ([122], p. 1155) we call the proposed pricing scheme 'resource-based pricing'. The name of the pricing proposal points at the fact that the price for a connection is based on the resources reserved for that connection. The price for the reserved resources depends on the requested type of service or QoS, on the time of day, and on the duration of a connection.

We will argue below that the interesting feature about resource-based pricing consists in its combination of peak-load pricing with pricing for guaranteed QoS. Apart from this idea, we consider the contribution of Parris and Ferrari [191] to provide only few substantial insights into how to price reserved resources. We nevertheless

122 The description of the scheme for the establishment of such real-time connections, which the authors call 'channels', can be found in Ferrari and Verma [74].

present the approach since it is a classical paper in the field and, as already mentioned, since it combines peak-load pricing with pricing for guaranteed QoS.

To simplify, Parris and Ferrari [191] suppose that only real-time traffic must be transported and that all the nodes, constituting a network, are identical. A node, in our context, shall consist of a router and its associated link. Furthermore, the authors assume n different types of service. A connection which requires a type of service i, $i = 1, \ldots, n$, is called connection i. There is a fixed price per unit of time associated with every type of service i denoted by p_i^{tos}. Parris and Ferrari ([191], p. 4) propose pricing the reservation of resources that are necessary for the establishment of connection i as follows:

$$p_i^r := p_i^{tos} t_i tod_i,$$

where t_i denotes the duration of connection i and where tod_i depicts a factor that varies with the time of day. The price p_i^r compensates ISPs for reserving resources for connection i during t_i time units. The time-of-day factor, tod_i, encourages users to shift their traffic into off-peak periods. Note that resource-based pricing combines peak-load pricing with guaranteed QoS. Here, in contrast to Section 3.1.3, peak-load prices are not volume-based, but time-based. This is economically reasonable given that resources must be reserved in order to give guarantees on the quality provided.

The prices p_i^{tos} are determined just before a connection is set up. A price p_i^{tos} depends on the reserved network resources including bandwidth, buffer space, Central Processing Unit (CPU) time, and delay. Parris and Ferrari ([191], p. 6) propose to calculate p_i^{tos} as follows:

$$\begin{aligned} p_i^{tos} \quad := \quad & \alpha \cdot \text{bandwidth reserved}_i + \beta \cdot \text{buffers reserved}_i \\ & + \gamma \cdot \text{CPU time reserved}_i + \delta \cdot \text{delay resource reserved}_i. \end{aligned}$$

The constant coefficients α, β, γ, and δ are chosen by ISPs such that they reflect the relative scarcity of each resource. In other words, they are the prices for the four resources. If the bottleneck resource is, for example, the bandwidth, the coefficient α has to be larger than the other coefficients in order to induce users to efficiently use the network. The authors remain silent about how exactly to determine α, β, γ, and δ.

We proceed with introducing the functions used to calculate the reserved resources. Reserved bandwidth of a connection i is determined by the product of the maximal packet sending rate and the maximal packet size in bytes, S_i^{max}, summed across all N nodes of the path:

$$\text{bandwidth reserved}_i := N\left(\frac{1}{X_i^{min}}\right)S_i^{max},$$

where $1/X_i^{min}$ is the reciprocal of the minimum packet interarrival time, i.e., the minimal time elapsed between the arrival of packets, which equals the maximum packet sending rate. By multiplying the maximal sending rate of packets by the maximal packet size, the above definition ensures that the bandwidth reserved is adjusted to the worst case scenario, i.e., to the maximal bandwidth demand.

The buffer space reserved by a connection i equals the value of the buffer function, $\text{buffers}_i(\cdot)$, which calculates the number of buffers required by a connection at each node, summed across all N nodes of the path, multiplied by the maximal packet size in bytes:[123]

$$\text{buffer space reserved}_i := N\text{buffers}_i(\cdot)S_i^{max}.$$

The CPU time reserved for a connection i is the product of the maximum sending rate and the maximum service time at each node, T_i^{max}, needed to process the packets, summed across all N nodes on the path:

$$\text{CPU time reserved}_i := N\left(\frac{1}{X_i^{min}}\right)T_i^{max}.$$

While bandwidth, buffer space, and CPU time resources are directly related to QoS requirements, this is not the case for the delay

123 A detailed description of the function $\text{buffers}_i(\cdot)$ may be found in Parris and Ferrari ([191], p. 12).

resource reserved. Instead, the delay resource is a quantification of the opportunity costs of a network of creating a connection. With the integration of the delay resource reserved into the pricing scheme the authors consider that resource reservation imposes a potential cost on the network in the form of depriving other data traffic from being admitted to the network. The charge for the delay resource can be interpreted as a congestion fee. Formally, the authors calculate the delay resource reserved, summed across all N nodes on the path, as follows:

$$\text{delay resource reserved}_i := N\left(\frac{1}{D_i}\right) Z_i K(D_i, Z_i),$$

where D_i depicts the source-to-destination delay bound for the packets, where Z_i denotes the minimum probability that the delay of a packet is lower than a given bound D_i, and where $K(D_i, Z_i)$ is a delay function that depends on D_i and Z_i. The delay resource reserved is inversely proportional to the delay since lower delay requirements lower the probability of admission of further connection requests. For the same reason, the delay resource reserved is designed to increase with the probability of no lateness. The delay function $K(D_i, Z_i)$ is introduced to bias the values of D_i and Z_i of different connection types so that the amount of the delay resource consumed by each connection i correctly reflects its opportunity costs, i.e., the loss of potential to create other connections.

Parris and Ferrari [191] propose estimating the delay function by simulation. We do not outline this approach since we claim that the computational overhead to estimate the delay function can be avoided. In our opinion, congestion externalities can appropriately be internalized by one price instrument only, i.e., by setting the factor tod_i in accordance with the theory of peak-load prices studied in Section 3.1.3.

The authors do not address the question of how interconnection pricing might be done within the framework of resource-based pricing. Just as in the case of dynamic priority pricing one may imagine that users are either billed separately by each node or that users pay their

IAP for the entire connection. Then, the IAPs would compensate their upstream providers and so on.

We proceed with an evaluation of resource-based pricing. Refer to Table 3.14 to find a summary thereof.

Table 3.14: Evaluation of resource-based pricing

ISP/Welfare	*Allocative efficiency*	△
	Capacity expansion	△
	Incentive compatibility	▲
ISP	*Cost-orientation*	△
	Price discrimination	▲
	Feasibility	▼
	Accounting efficiency	◊
User	*Utility-orientation*	▲
	Price transparency	◊

▲ = very good, △ = good
◊ = satisfactory, ▽ = adequate, ▼ = inadequate

- *Allocative efficiency*
  The interesting feature about resource-based pricing consists in its combination of peak-load pricing with pricing for guaranteed QoS. Here, peak-load prices are not volume-based as in Section 3.1.3, but time-based. Since resources must be reserved to set up a connection it is economically reasonable to charge users for the duration of the connection. Although Parris and Ferrari [191] do not introduce a welfare function whose maximum serves as

a benchmark, resource-based pricing is likely to approximate an efficient resource allocation if the time-of-day factor tod_i is set in accordance with the theory of peak-load pricing discussed in Section 3.1.3. We argue that one instrument, i.e., the time-of-day factor tod_i, suffices to approximately internalize congestion externalities. The integration of the delay resource reserved into the price component p_i^{tos} is judged not to significantly better approximate allocative efficiency, but to considerably complicate implementation. Furthermore, the pricing scheme guarantees that connections requiring more reserved network resources are higher priced. Hence, resource-based prices are increasing both in network utilization and in the QoS provided such that Internet users are likely to be charged according to the real costs of data transport.

– *Capacity expansion*
  With an appropriate design of the time-of-day factor tod_i resource-based pricing gives monetary incentives for capacity expansion. Given that the time-of day factor, just like peak-load prices, is based on average rather than on actual network utilization, resource-based pricing only roughly provides the necessary revenues to expand capacity.
– *Incentive compatibility*
  Resource-based pricing is incentive compatible since it incites users to use the network efficiently: On the one hand, the price component p_i^{tos} motivates users with less stringent requirements for QoS to choose a type of service with a lower price. Users who reserve more resources than necessary, which would lead to inefficiencies, are penalized in the form of a higher price. On the other hand, the tod_i factor incites users to shift their demand to off-peak periods.
– *Cost-orientation*
  From the point of view of providers, an advantage of resource-based pricing is its cost-orientation. It allows ISPs to collect revenues commensurate with the QoS delivered to customers. The prices p_i^{tos} may be scaled in order to allow providers to break even. Moreover, the time-of-day factor, if designed in accordance with the theory of peak-load pricing, generates the revenues to fund

the costs of capacity expansion. An additional fixed subscription fee may be necessary to recover fixed costs and to reduce financial risks.

– *Price discrimination*
  We judge the possibility of resource-based pricing to cream off different willingnesses to pay to be very good: With the three price instruments given by p_i^{tos}, tod_i, and t_i providers can price discriminate between their clients with respect to the QoS offered, the network load, and the connect time.
– *Feasibility*
  Feasibility of resource-based pricing is inadequate: Recall that the total amount of reserved resources is equal to the sum of reserved resources in each node along the path from the sender to the receiver. This information has to be known by the IAP in order to determine the price p_i^r. Hence, system-wide information becomes necessary to calculate the final price for resource reservation. Moreover, the pricing scheme assumes a homogenous network, i.e., a network consisting of identical nodes, where the prices for the resources α, β, γ, and δ are constant in order to make p_i^{tos} solely dependent upon network utilization, a rather unrealistic assumption in today's Internet. Additionally, QoS can only be guaranteed if all ISPs along the path from the source to the destination offer guaranteed service quality. Furthermore, in the same way as ALSVP and dynamic volume pricing, resource-based pricing requires many technical changes to implement resource reservation in the Internet. Also, the calculation of the reservation charge requires the collection and processing of extensive information of reserved resources along the path from the sender to the receiver. This computational overhead could be mitigated if the delay resource reserved did not influence the price p_i^{tos}, but if, instead, only the time-of-day factor tod_i was used to internalize congestion externalities. Apart from this, as already noted in Section 3.1.3, it is not easy to correctly anticipate and estimate demand and therefore to set the time-of-day factor appropriately. Following this line of argumentation, Breker ([30], p. 3) points at the enormous amount of a priori information necessary to determine

the reservation charge for a connection. Moreover, she criticizes the fact that the necessary information is difficult to obtain.

- *Accounting efficiency*
  Once all the different pricing components are determined we judge accounting efficiency to be satisfactory: The price p_i^{tos} and the time-of-day factor tod_i are determined before the set up of each connection. During run-time, the IAP only has to keep track of the duration of the connection. One could argue that, compared to peak-load pricing, accounting efficiency is lower with resource-based pricing since it additionally depends on the QoS provided. However, the duration of a connection is easier to measure compared to the volume of data traffic.
- *Utility-orientation*
  From the point of view of users, through an appropriate design of the time-of-day factor tod_i, resource-based pricing is utility-oriented in the sense that in times of network congestion only users with a relatively high willingness to pay are served. Also, quality differentiation is followed by price differentiation. There are no cross-subsidies between user groups.
- *Price transparency*
  Price transparency of resource-based pricing is satisfactory since the prices p_i^{tos} and the tod_i values are available to users before the set up of a connection. The third price component, the duration of the connection t_i, is easily estimated and observed by the customer. Hence, users may predetermine the charges their connections will incur. Compared to peak-load pricing price transparency is lower due to the additional price component p_i^{tod} introduced even if connection time can be observed or estimated more easily than traffic volume. In comparison with ALSVP and dynamic volume pricing, price transparency is enhanced since resource-based pricing is time-based rather than volume-based.

3.4.4 Effective Bandwidth Pricing

Guaranteed QoS may also be given by Asynchronous Transfer Mode (ATM) networks. ATM is a packet-switching technology where packets have a fixed size, called cells. Moreover, ATM allows for statistical multiplexing. An ATM network offers a connection-oriented service in the sense that a virtual connection is set up before data is transmitted. This allows guaranteed QoS to be offered. ATM offers five different service classes, namely Constant Bit Rate (CBR), Variable Bit Rate – real-time (VBR-rt), Variable Bit Rate – non-real-time (VBR-nrt), Available Bit Rate (ABR), and Unspecified Bit Rate (UBR). While CBR and VBR-rt are deterministically guaranteed service classes, VBR-nrt offers statistically guaranteed service like controlled-load service within the framework of IntServ. ABR with its integrated congestion control and UBR offer best-effort services.[124]

In this section, a selected pricing proposal for charging in ATM networks[125] is presented for three reasons: First, both Internet and ATM services are packet transport services. Consequently, the same or similar pricing models may apply.[126] Second, running IP over ATM is a possible option to introduce guaranteed QoS in the Internet. Third, ATM technology is of major importance in the core of the Internet where it is used as the basic transport mechanism to carry IP traffic.[127]

Before we introduce a selected pricing proposal for ATM networks, namely effective bandwidth pricing, we want to point at two other often cited pricing proposals for ATM networks. Wang, Peha, and Sirbu [249] introduce a profit maximizing pricing policy called dynamic opportunity cost-oriented pricing. They show that under capacity constraints prices should equal the opportunity cost of providing a transport service that consist of the opportunity costs of reserving and the

124 See Peterson and Davie ([192], pp. 192–210 and pp. 513–517).

125 The common pricing practice for ATM networks is a monthly recurring charge depending on the access rate, the geographic distance, or on the number of virtual circuits used. See DaSilva, Petr, and Akar ([59], p. 357).

126 See Songhurst ([223], p. 6).

127 See Odlyzko ([185], p. 357).

opportunity costs of using network resources at different times. Gerpott and Böhm ([84], p. 240) criticize the fact that dynamic opportunity cost-oriented pricing assumes the availability of information which cannot be provided in the Internet. Therefore, they judge this theoretic concept as inapt to contribute to the solution of the Internet pricing problem in practice.

The pricing proposal of Murphy, Murphy, and Posner [170] aims to allocate bandwidth among users such that maximal ATM network efficiency, defined as the difference between total user benefits and costs, is achieved. The authors assume that utility functions of users depend on bandwidth and define a convex cost function in network utilization which may include congestion costs. They show that the optimal price that maximizes network efficiency as well as consumer surplus equals marginal costs. The optimal price varies dynamically depending on the network load. The pricing approach of Murphy, Murphy, and Posner [170] is similar to the contribution of MacKie-Mason and Varian [148] with the particularity that the former is explicitly applied to ATM network technology.

We now focus on effective bandwidth pricing, a tariff structure proposed by Kelly [127, 129]. We start our analysis with the introduction of the concept of effective bandwidth, first presented by Hui [111, 112]. Effective bandwidth of a connection is a proxy of its resource usage by bursty traffic, which explains the name of effective bandwidth.[128] The notion of effective bandwidth emerged from the field of traffic engineering and was obtained by means of large deviations theory that is a modern branch of probability theory and that seeks to estimate the probabilities of rare events.

Suppose that there are J Internet users who share a resource with a given capacity K. The traffic demand of each user j, $j = 1, \ldots, J$, is given by x_j. Suppose that user data demands x_j, $j = 1, \ldots, J$, are independent random variables with potentially distinct distributions. The question arises whether there is enough capacity to handle the aggregate data demand of all users, or, more specifically, whether a

128 By investigating real traffic Courcoubetis, Siris, and Stamoulis [53] show that the concept of effective bandwidth appropriately quantifies resource usage.

condition on the distributions of the individual data demands can be formulated which ensures that the probability P that the aggregate demand for data traffic exceeds the capacity K is smaller than $e^{-\gamma}$ for some given value γ:

$$P\left\{\sum_{j=1}^{J} x_j > K\right\} \leq e^{-\gamma}. \tag{3.68}$$

It was shown by Hui [111, 112] that condition (3.68) is satisfied for certain parameters C (depending on γ and K) and s (> 0), to be explained below, provided that

$$\sum_{j=1}^{J} B(x_j) \leq C,$$

where

$$B(x_j) := \frac{1}{s} \log Ee^{sx_j} \tag{3.69}$$

is called the effective bandwidth of user j.[129] The operator E denotes the statistical expected value operation.

We can conclude that, given that the sum of the effective bandwidths of the J sources using a resource does not exceed C, a performance guarantee can be given, where the performance guarantee is expressed in terms of an upper bound ($e^{-\gamma}$) on the probability that packets are dropped or that delay indeed occurs. Hence, the concept of effective bandwidth pricing allows the transportation of real-time traffic of delay-sensitive users who require such performance guarantees.

---

129 In the literature the relevant definition of effective bandwidth is often given by

$$B(x_j) := \frac{1}{st} \log E[e^{sx_j[0,t]}], \quad 0 < s, t < \infty,$$

where t is a time parameter which, for simplicity, is set equal to 1 in expression (3.69). The term $x_j[0,t]$ denotes the amount of traffic generated by user j during a random time interval of length t. See Songhurst ([130], p. 174).

In order to simplify notation we drop the index j for user j. Concerning the traffic characteristics of users, Kelly [127, 129] supposes that each source, alternately and for long periods in each case, is in an 'on' state, where it acts as a source with effective bandwidth, and in an 'off' state, where it generates no data traffic. When the user is 'on' she sends traffic at a peak rate h. Such an on/off source with peak rate h and mean rate M is characterized by

$$P\{x=0\} = 1 - \frac{M}{h}, \quad P\{x=h\} = \frac{M}{h},$$

where M/h depicts the probability that the source is 'on'. Consequently, the effective bandwidth given in (3.69) takes the form

$$\begin{aligned} B(M) &:= \frac{1}{s}\log\left(\left(1-\frac{M}{h}\right)e^0 + \frac{M}{h}e^{sh}\right), \\ &:= \frac{1}{s}\log\left(1+\frac{M}{h}(e^{sh}-1)\right). \end{aligned} \tag{3.70}$$

Note that effective bandwidth $B(M)$ is increasing and strictly concave in M:

$$\frac{\partial B(M)}{\partial M} > 0, \quad \frac{\partial^2 B(M)}{\partial M^2} < 0.$$

We will use this key property below when introducing effective bandwidth pricing.

A further important property of expression (3.70) is that effective bandwidth is bounded below by the mean rate M and is bounded above by the peak rate h. To see this, we will study how (3.70) is affected by a change of the parameter s. This parameter depends, among others, on the peak rate h relative to the link capacity K. Here, we do not want to formally introduce this dependency, but to point out how to interpret the parameter s: If the link capacity is much larger than the peak rate the parameter s tends to zero. Then, by the rule of Bernoulli-de l'Hospital, effective bandwidth (3.70) approaches M. In the opposite case, if the link capacity is not much larger than the peak rate, s approaches infinity. Then, by applying the rule of Bernoulli-de l'Hospital twice, it can be shown that effective bandwidth approaches the peak rate h. Moreover, effective bandwidth (3.70) is always increasing in s.[130] Hence, as s increases from zero to infinity effective bandwidth rises from the mean rate to the peak rate of traffic.[131]

Now that we have introduced the notion of effective bandwidth and have learned that it provides a way to assess resource usage, we will consider how it may be used to price Internet transport services, i.e., how effective bandwidth may be converted into a monetary charge.

Kelly [129] proposes a tariff structure, effective bandwidth pricing, which incites users to truly declare their expected mean traffic rate. We will see below that effective bandwidth pricing takes both static parameters known a priori and dynamic variables known a posteriori, such as the duration of a connection and the associated traffic volume, into consideration. While static parameters are determined in the traffic contract, dynamic variables are measured. The idea of effective bandwidth pricing is to bound the effective bandwidth by a linear function of the measured variables with coefficients depending on the static parameters.

Kelly ([129], p. 259) assumes that users know their peak rate h, but that the mean rate M is not known with certainty.[132] Furthermore, he supposes that each user has a prior distribution $G(M)$ for

---

130 To see this, note that by rearranging definition (3.70) we obtain

$$sB(\cdot) = \log\left(1 + \frac{M}{h}(e^{sh} - 1)\right).$$

By differentiating the right-hand side of this equation twice with respect to s one can show that the right-hand side increases disproportionate in s. Therefore, effective bandwidth $B(\cdot)$ must increase in s in order for equality to hold.

131 See Kelly ([129], p. 258). For a complete description of the concept of effective bandwidth consider Kelly [128].

132 Kelly ([129], pp. 265–267) extends his analysis to the case where users know neither their mean rate nor their peak rate with certainty. This extension will not be further developed here.

the mean rate M of the connection. The expected mean rate of the connection is given by

$$E_G M := \int_0^h z dG(z).$$

Provided that ISPs know the prior distribution $G(M)$ for the mean rate M they can define the effective bandwidth of the connection from equations (3.69) and (3.70) as

$$\begin{aligned} B(M) &:= \frac{1}{s} \log E_G \left(1 + \frac{M}{h}(e^{sh} - 1)\right), \\ B(E_G M) &:= \frac{1}{s} \log \left(1 + \frac{E_G M}{h}(e^{sh} - 1)\right). \end{aligned} \tag{3.71}$$

Note that expression (3.71) is equal to the effective bandwidth (3.70) provided that M is not a random variable, but equals its mean value under $G(M)$. Hence, given an on/off source with known peak rate h effective bandwidth only depends on the user's expected mean traffic rate. ISPs can derive the effective bandwidth if they know the user's expected mean rate $E_G M$. Further information about the distribution $G(M)$ does not change effective bandwidth and is therefore superfluous.

But how can ISPs obtain the necessary information about the expected mean rates to determine effective bandwidth? It will be shown below that effective bandwidth pricing incites users to truly reveal their expected mean rate. This implies that effective bandwidth pricing is incentive compatible.

Suppose that each user has to announce a mean rate m to its IAP before the admission of a connection. Given this declared mean rate the IAP charges a fee $f(m, M)$ per time unit, where M reflects the measured mean rate for the connection. Assume that users are risk neutral and that they minimize expected costs per time unit, $E_G f(m, M)$, with respect to m. We denote the minimizing value of m with $\underline{m}$.

From the point of view of ISPs, the optimal declared mean rate $\underline{m}$ should exhibit the following desirable properties: First, $\underline{m}$ should allow ISPs to derive the users expected mean rate $E_G M$ and with it the effective bandwidth (3.71) of a connection. Second, minimal expected costs per time unit should be proportional to the effective bandwidth of a connection. Equivalently, for a given choice of time units, minimal expected costs per time unit should equal the effective bandwidth of a connection such that users, for their consumption of Internet services, face charges that are proportional to their resource usage.

Kelly ([127], pp. 4 f.) shows that these two desirable properties determine a tariff $f(m, M)$ in the form of

$$f(m, M) := a(m) + b(m)M, \tag{3.72}$$

which, at $M = m$, is tangent, by appropriate selection of $a(\cdot)$ and $b(\cdot)$ to be explained below, to the curve (3.70) as depicted in Figure 3.17. The coefficient $a(m)$ depicts the price per time unit and the coefficient $b(m)$ the price per unit of volume.

To see that the tariff (3.72) fulfills the two desired properties mentioned above note that, when declaring a mean rate m, each user faces expected costs per time unit of a connection equal to

$$\begin{aligned} E_G f(m, M) &:= E_G \left(a(m) + b(m)M \right), \\ &:= a(m) + b(m) E_G M, \end{aligned} \tag{3.73}$$

i.e., equal to the value of the tangent (3.73) at $E_G M$. Recall from our analysis above that effective bandwidth $B(M)$ is increasing and strictly concave in M. Therefore,

$$E_G f(m, M) \geq f(E_G M, M) = B(E_G M),$$

i.e., at the point $E_G M$, where the costs of the expected mean rate equal effective bandwidth, expected costs per time unit are not smaller than the costs of the expected mean rate.

Equality holds if and only if $m = E_G M$ for all m. In other words, only in this case do expected costs per time unit equal effective bandwidth. This can also be seen graphically in Figure 3.17. Apart from the tangent through the point $(m, B(m))$ any tangent to the curve

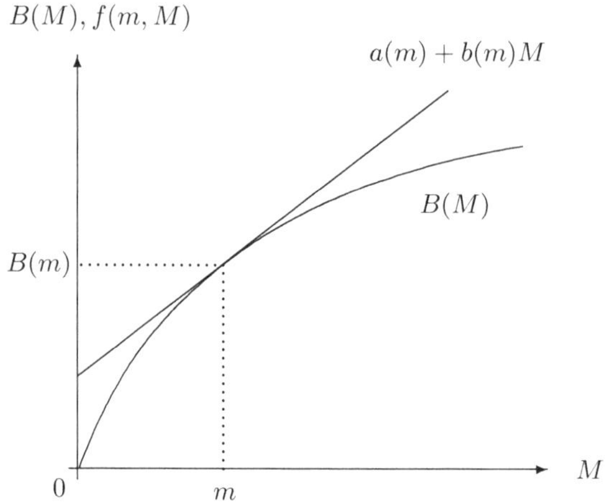

Figure 3.17: Effective bandwidth pricing
Source: See Kelly ([129], p. 261).

$B(M)$ generates costs higher than $B(m)$ per time unit when being measured at $M = m$.

We can conclude that expected costs per time unit are minimized at the declared mean rate $\underline{m} = E_G M$, where expected costs per time unit equal effective bandwidth $B(M)$. We have shown that, given the tariff (3.72), each user truthfully reveals her expected mean rate in order to minimize her expected costs per time unit. For a false declaration of the true expected mean rate users would have to pay a premium.

We can determine the coefficients in the tariff (3.72) by differentiating definition (3.70) with respect to M at $M = m$ to obtain

$$b(m) := \frac{e^{sh} - 1}{s(h + m(e^{sh} - 1))}.$$

Since, at $m = E_G M$, we have

$$f(m, M) = B(M),$$

we know that

$$a(m) := B(M) - mb(m).$$

The higher the declared mean rate m the lower $b(m)$ and the higher $a(m)$. Note that the higher the declared mean rate the lower the gain of statistical multiplexing. In this case, a tariff that relies more on the time-based pricing component relative to the volume-based price component is sensible. The opposite argument holds in the case of a low declared mean rate.

Recall that users truly reveal their expected mean rate m by the choice of a linear tariff (3.72). Kelly ([129], p. 260) proposes presenting users with a menu of different pairs $(a(m), b(m))$, with given prices per time unit and per unit of volume, users can choose from. Graphically, users would be free to choose any tangent from the menu to the effective bandwidth curve depicted in Figure 3.17. Then, each user faces a charge of $a(m)$ per time unit and a charge of $b(m)$ per unit of volume. Users have no incentive to disguise their true preferences by choosing a tangent to the effective bandwidth curve which is not consistent with their expected mean rate. If they did so, expected costs per time unit would not be minimized. The presentation of tariff choices $(a(m), b(m))$ eliminates the need to bother users with technical parameters such as s or the mean m. Technical parameters can be adjusted by the network operator. This makes the pricing approach easier to understand and more transparent to users.

Summing up, the effective bandwidth pricing concept charges users based on a combination of declared and measured traffic characteristics. The proposed tariff is linear in measurements of time and volume. It takes the form

$$a(m)T + b(m)V,$$

where $a(m)$ is the charge per time unit, where $b(m)$ is the charge per unit of volume, where T depicts the duration of the connection, and where V is the data transmission volume. While T and V are dynamic variables that are measured a posteriori, the coefficients $a(m)$ and $b(m)$ depend on the traffic contract parameter m. Due to the incentive compatibility of effective bandwidth pricing, tariffs of the form $a(m)T + b(m)V$ allow effective bandwidth to be approximated. Effective bandwidth pricing can be seen as a compromise between charging for reserved resources, i.e., charging for the policed peak rate of a connection, and charging for actually used resources.

Kelly ([129], p. 269 and p. 274) generalizes effective bandwidth pricing by the introduction of a charge $c(\cdot)$ levied per connection which compensates ISPs for the costs to set up a connection, i.e., for the costs incurred by the use of switching and signaling resources. Furthermore, additional contract parameters are introduced: The coefficients $a(\cdot)$, $b(\cdot)$, and $c(\cdot)$ may not only depend upon m, but also on other parameters such as the peak rate, the size of bursts, or the access line speed. Note that the introduction of further static contract parameters does not affect the incentive compatibility property of effective bandwidth pricing, given that with an on/off source with known peak rate effective bandwidth only depends on the users' expected mean rate $E_G M$, as illustrated by definition (3.71).

With the generalization of effective bandwidth pricing, the total charge a user faces for a connection can be expressed as

$$a(z)T + b(z)V + c(z), \qquad (3.74)$$

where z is the traffic contract of the connection. The charging mechanism characterized by (3.74) has been implemented within the CA$hMAN (Charging and Accounting Schemes in Multi-Service ATM Networks) project, undertaken by a consortium of network operators, equipment manufacturers, as well as participants from research institutes and universities.[133]

According to Kelly ([129], p. 276) the triple $(a(z), b(z), c(z))$ is determined whenever a connection for real-time data transport is set up. One can imagine smart agents acting on behalf of users which select the desired tariff option. Such a user/network interface has been implemented within the CA$hMAN project: A tariffing smart agent that acts on behalf of the network communicates traffic contract and tariff options to the purchasing agent. The purchasing agent, acting as a mediator between the user, the application, and the network, conveys the user's choice of the tariff and traffic contract back to the network.[134]

133 See Songhurst ([223], pp. 19–21).
134 See Songhurst and Kelly ([225], p. 35).

The results developed in this section focus on the characteristics of multiplexed traffic at some specific link in a network. Generally, Internet data traffic passes several links on the path from the sender to the receiver. If sender and receiver belong to different networks, interconnection pricing becomes a relevant issue. Songhurst ([224], pp. 155–157) extends effective bandwidth pricing to an interconnection pricing scheme. Songhurst distinguishes between per-connection charging and bulk charging. We first consider per-connection charging.

Suppose that two ISPs, ISP 1 and ISP 2, are involved in data conveyance from the sender to the receiver. Since effective bandwidth pricing is linear in time and in volume, tariff coefficients for a connection levied by different network providers can be added. To see this, suppose that ISP 1 pays network ISP 2 an amount equal to

$$a_2(z)T + b_2(z)V + c_2(z)$$

for terminating the connection. Then, ISP 1 can offer its retail customers tariffs in the form

$$(a_1(z) + a_2(z))\,T + (b_1(z) + b_2(z))\,V + (c_1(z) + c_2(z))\,,$$

where $(a_1(z), b_1(z), c_1(z))$ denotes the tariff levied by ISP 1. For this interconnection pricing scheme to work, interconnecting networks must agree on the traffic contract parameters before the set up of each connection. Moreover, accounting data must be exchanged between networks including duration, volume, and the selected tariff for each connection.

Higher accounting efficiency would be obtained by pricing for bulk use of capacity. Songhurst ([224], p. 156) proposes the following bulk interconnection charge in a time period T:

$$a(z)T + b(z)V_T + c(z)N_T,$$

where V_T depicts the interconnect traffic volume in time period T and where N_T reflects the number of connections in time period T. This bulk charge could either be levied after each time period or could only be applied to some defined peak periods. The tariff parameters $a(z)$, $b(z)$, and $c(z)$ have to be negotiated between the ISPs.

We proceed with an evaluation of effective bandwidth pricing.[135] The synopsis thereof can be found in Table 3.15.

Table 3.15: Evaluation of effective bandwidth pricing

ISP/Welfare	*Allocative efficiency*	△
	Capacity expansion	△
	Incentive compatibility	▲
ISP	*Cost-orientation*	△
	Price discrimination	△
	Feasibility	▽
	Accounting efficiency	▽
User	*Utility-orientation*	▲
	Price transparency	◊

▲ = very good, △ = good
◊ = satisfactory, ▽ = adequate, ▼ = inadequate

- *Allocative efficiency*
  Effective bandwidth pricing reflects effective resource usage. Note that we implicitly assumed the effective bandwidth function to be constant during the billing period. However, effective bandwidth can vary with the traffic mix, i.e., with the percentage of different data traffic types. Experimentation indicates that periods of

135 Our evaluation is partially based on Courcoubetis, Kelly, and Weber ([52], p. 536) and on Nagel ([171], pp. 21 f.).

the day can be identified during which the variation of the traffic mix is negligible.[136] Therefore, Courcoubetis et al. [51] propose complementing effective bandwidth pricing with peak-load pricing. This can be done by assigning different levels of effective bandwidth to different periods of the day. That way, differences in the use of resources are accurately reflected by different effective bandwidths and their corresponding tariff schemes. Although Kelly [127, 129] does not introduce a welfare function whose maximum serves as a benchmark, we judge that effective bandwidth pricing is likely to approximate an efficient allocation of resources since it appropriately reflects network usage.

- *Capacity expansion*
  We judge effective capacity pricing to give correct signals for network planning and network expansion since the contracted amount of effective bandwidth provides a measure for ISPs to estimate the required capacity for the future.
- *Incentive compatibility*
  The pricing scheme is incentive compatible in the sense that users reveal their true estimate of the mean rate of traffic by selecting a tariff $(a(\cdot), b(\cdot), c(\cdot))$.
- *Cost-orientation*
  For the following reasons, we judge that effective bandwidth pricing meets the criterion of cost-orientation well: Effective bandwidth pricing converts effective bandwidth into a monetary charge. This monetary charge is proportional to resource usage, i.e. to effective bandwidth. The coefficients $a(\cdot)$, $b(\cdot)$, and $c(\cdot)$ can be proportionally scaled, i.e., expressed in different monetary dimensions, in order to generate the necessary revenues to recover costs. Due to the concept of effective bandwidth ISPs know how much traffic a given link can handle without a loss of quality. Hence, they can multiplex traffic of different users up to a maximum amount of traffic while still providing performance guarantees. This maximizes network utilization and network revenues per link. However, fixed costs must be recovered by an additional subscription fee.

136 See Courcoubetis, Siris, and Stamoulis [53].

- *Price discrimination*
  ISPs are given the possibility to price discriminate in that they can offer users a menu of different pricing pairs, or, triples, that vary with the QoS demanded. In practice, users do not have to be offered a continuum of tariffs, but only a small number of the relevant tangents to the effective bandwidth function. If effective bandwidth pricing was complemented with peak-load pricing, ISPs could further discriminate among their subscribers with respect to the traffic mix and, hence, the network load.
- *Feasibility*
  The feasibility of effective bandwidth pricing is judged to be adequate: Guaranteed QoS may only be given by interconnected ISPs that have adopted the concept of effective bandwidth pricing. However, each ISP is free in the design of the menu of tariffs offered to its subscribers. The degree of difficulty in implementing effective bandwidth pricing depends on whether effective bandwidth is assumed to be constant or whether it varies periodically depending on the traffic mix. In any case, the effective bandwidth concept is complex. But, if effective bandwidth is fixed for a longer time period, effective bandwidth pricing should be less difficult to implement compared to other pricing schemes for guaranteed QoS.
- *Accounting efficiency*
  Accounting overhead of effective bandwidth pricing is considerable. If a connection spans over several networks from the sender to the receiver and if interconnection pricing is based on per-connection charging, ISPs have to exchange accounting data for each connection including duration, volume, and the selected tariff option. This results in rather inefficient accounting. As noted above, bulk interconnection charging helps to avoid some of the overheads associated with interconnection pricing on a per-connection basis. Given that the proposed tariff is based on relatively easily obtained measurements of connection time T and transmitted volume V, we judge accounting efficiency of effective bandwidth pricing to be higher compared to ALSVP and dynamic volume pricing.

- *Utility-orientation*
  From the point of view of Internet users, effective bandwidth pricing is utility-oriented in the sense that they can choose a tariff option in accordance with their preferences. There are no cross-subsidies between user groups: By making the costs $c(\cdot)$ to set up a connection dependent on static traffic contract parameters effective bandwidth pricing does not force users who demand a connection for a short time period to subsidize users who demand a connection for a long time period.
- *Price transparency*
  Transparency of pricing is satisfactory since the tariffs depend on static parameters which are known and chosen by users ex ante and on dynamic variables, i.e., on time and volume, which can relatively easily be observed by users.[137] Price transparency is lower compared to nonlinear tariffs since an additional variable, T, influences outlay. Moreover, tariffs may vary for each connection depending on the chosen contract parameters. If effective bandwidth is complemented with peak-load pricing, effective bandwidth pricing becomes intransparent. Once again, we can observe a trade-off between higher allocative efficiency, if actual network use is priced accurately, in exchange for lower price transparency, more accounting overhead, and less simple implementation.

3.5 Evaluation Synopsis of Pricing Models

Our evaluations of the pricing models proposed in this chapter are summarized in Tables 3.16 to 3.19. Our ratings of cost-orientation are downgraded if the pricing proposals do not ensure that fixed costs are covered and if prices are load-insensitive since, then, no revenues for capacity expansion are generated. Moreover, our ratings of the possi-

137 One can imagine a smart agent that provides the user with information about the volume transmitted.

bility to price discriminate and utility-orientation are downgraded if the concerned pricing proposal is not load-sensitive. But, these ratings are not demoted if pricing proposals for a single service Internet do not differentiate with respect to QoS since the lack of quality differentiation is a feature of the network technology, but not of the pricing scheme. Again, our assessments of feasibility are downgraded if a system-wide configuration of routers is necessary to provide relative priorities or guarantees on QoS. In the latter case our feasibility rating is even considerably demoted.

In order to understand our evaluation of peak-load prices reflected in Table 3.16 recall that in Section 3.1.3 we assumed demand patterns in the Internet to be predictable. If this was not the case, peak-load pricing would be unsatisfactory for all parties involved.

By inspecting Tables 3.16 to 3.19 we claim that from the welfare theoretic point of view optimal congestion pricing approaches, including congestion pricing, the smart market approach, and dynamic priority pricing, are favored. But pricing proposals for guaranteed QoS, peak-load pricing, and expected capacity pricing also come off well while flat-rate pricing, possibly combined with voluntary user declarations and a quota system to integrate priorities, perform the worst.

To evaluate the pricing proposals from the perspective of ISPs we also have to consider allocative efficiency, efficiency of capacity expansion, as well as incentive compatibility. Then, providers favor peak-load pricing and expected capacity. Static priority pricing and flat-rate pricing, possibly coupled with voluntary user declarations and a quota system, score rather badly.

One can wonder why flat rates are so popular given our unsatisfactory rating of flat-rate pricing. As already noted in Section 2.2.1, the popularity of flat-rated Internet access may have emerged with the need to achieve a critical mass. But, given the explosive growth of Internet subscribers in past years, the Internet no longer needs to be promoted by flat rates. Accordingly, results from an international study on the broadband market by the consulting company Arthur D. Little suggest that ISPs will have to switch from flat-rated pricing plans to usage-based pricing plans in order to recover costs.[138] Generally, however, subscribers do not appreciate metered Internet service. Instead, they prefer completely predictable and transparent prices. Recall from Section 2.2.2 that users are even ready to pay a premium for such prices. The fear that customers may switch to a competitor currently makes competitive providers reluctant to adopt usage-based pricing strategies. Further practical reasons for the popularity of flat-rate pricing, which also hold for nonlinear tariffs, are its feasibility and accounting efficiency. In the same way as flat rates, nonlinear tariffs are transparent and predictable to users. The two pricing schemes may have obtained their popularity for these reasons.[139]

When being evaluated with respect to practical criteria including feasibility and accounting efficiency, pricing proposals for guaranteed service quality and, in particular, optimal congestion pricing approaches lose attractiveness. However, for a comprehensive rating of the different pricing proposals one must know how individual ISPs assess the criteria for Internet pricing. This is especially true given the trade-off between the requirements concerning allocative efficiency, efficiency of capacity expansion, incentive compatibility, cost-orientation, and price discrimination and desired characteristics including feasibility and efficient accounting. This trade-off can best be observed when flat-rate pricing is opposed to congestion pricing. Expected capacity pricing, peak-load pricing, nonlinear tariffs, and PMP seem to be the best compromises.

Internet users favor expected capacity pricing. But peak-load pricing is also highly appreciated. But again, for a comprehensive rating of the different pricing proposals one must know how subscribers assess utility-orientation and price transparency. Often, a better utility-orientation can only be achieved at the cost of lower price transparency.

The bottom line is that several promising pricing schemes are available that can increase social welfare compared to current pricing solutions. However, so far, neither in practice nor in theory does a

138 See George et al. ([83], pp. 11 f.) and Baumann [18].

139 Further insights into why in practice Internet access is often priced at a flat rate will be provided in Section 4.1.1.

pricing proposal seem to exist which best meets all normative criteria set up in Section 2.2.3. Given the trade-off between our criteria, for a comprehensive rating of the different pricing proposals and in order to recommend a specific pricing system one must know how ISPs and subscribers assess the different normative criteria for Internet pricing. Nevertheless, we can conclude that expected capacity pricing and peak-load pricing do well from all points of view. We could combine the two approaches in order to cumulate the advantages of each pricing proposal. Unfortunately, at the same time, an advantage of one pricing proposal may be offset by a drawback of the other pricing proposal, or, even worse, drawbacks of the two pricing proposals may coincide. As an example of the latter possibility, consider the criterion of feasibility which both pricing proposals, considered individually, satisfy well. Through the combination of the two pricing approaches, however, a system-wide configuration of routers becomes necessary to provide relative priorities, that is not a prerequisite of peak-load pricing, and traffic demand patterns must be anticipated, which is not required by expected capacity pricing. In consequence, the feasibility of the combined pricing scheme is lower than the feasibility of each pricing proposal taken separately. Also, the combination of the two pricing approaches is characterized by lower accounting efficiency and price transparency compared to expected capacity pricing since prices, in the combined pricing scheme, are volume-based and vary with the time of day rather than being flat subscription fees for specific expected capacity profiles.

The combination of expected capacity pricing and peak-load pricing could take the following form: Users would still contract an expected capacity profile with their IAP. But instead of paying a flat rate for the contracting period the number of *in* packets would be counted at the network access point and be multiplied by appropriate peak-load prices as derived in Section 3.1.3. The expected capacity profile could be contracted before each data transfer or for a longer time period. In both cases, an additional monthly flat rate could be levied in order to recover fixed costs.

The combination of peak-load pricing with traffic flagging and technic congestion management results in very good allocative efficiency, incentive compatibility, cost-orientation, price discrimination, and utility-orientation. Also the criterion of efficient capacity expansion is met very well since peak-load prices, which themselves roughly provide the necessary revenues to expand capacity, are complemented with the real-time feedback, inherent in expected capacity pricing, that appropriately signals the need for capacity expansion. Price transparency is still good while feasibility and accounting efficiency are judged to be satisfactory. Feasibility is considered only to be satisfactory since a system-wide configuration of routers is necessary to provide relative priorities and since traffic demand patterns must be anticipated.

The combination of PMP with peak-load pricing is also promising, as already indicated in Section 3.2.3. That way, our rating of PMP concerning allocative efficiency, efficiency of capacity expansion, cost-orientation, the possibility to price discriminate, and utility-orientation would be upgraded. However, these upgradings are only possible in exchange for a lower price transparency as well as losses in accounting efficiency and in feasibility.

In this chapter, we also pointed at several promising variants of the proposed pricing proposals which shall be discussed here. In Section 3.1.1 we introduced percentile pricing that, in practice, is applied to burstable dedicated lines. Recall that, from the point of view of customers, the percentile pricing method has the advantage of disposing of uncapped bandwidth. However, it penalizes users who have bursty traffic since they pay high charges set by their peak traffic while their overall bandwidth usage may be substantially lower. The advantage to ISPs is that they can derive revenues based on the 95th percentile while their costs are calculated based on the 50th percentile. We already mentioned that, in the future, one might not only apply percentile pricing to dedicated Internet access lines, but also to broadband service.[140] We judge percentile pricing to be a good compromise between usage-based pricing and popular flat-rate pricing. Percentile pricing is likely to have a good chance of being adopted,

140 See Massey [162] and Semret ([211], p. 3).

possibly as an interim pricing solution in the transition phase to more elaborate pricing schemes.

In Section 3.1.1, apart from percentile pricing, we presented another pricing scheme that seeks to mitigate the drawbacks of flat-rate pricing, namely adaptive flat-rate pricing introduced by Flury et al. ([77], pp. 14–16). The idea is to make the flat rate volume-sensitive without the loss of price predictability. Recall that the authors propose periodically adapting the flat rate according to the volume of traffic generated during several past billing periods. The advantage of adaptive flat-rate pricing is its user acceptance, due to its predictability, and its simple implementation while providing users with small incentives not to overuse the network. Therefore, adaptive flat-rate pricing can be seen as a further interim pricing solution in the transition period from flat-rate pricing to more elaborate pricing approaches.

Further, in Section 3.1.2, we introduced an ex-post weighted-average Coase tariff as an alternative to optimal nonlinear tariffs. There, we argued that nonlinear prices in the form of ex-post weighted-average Coase tariffs, where the rental is a weighted average of total fixed costs, have the same desirable characteristics as optimal nonlinear tariffs, with the exception of price transparency. Price transparency would decrease as rentals would only be known ex post. But, at the same time, no information would be necessary concerning the distribution of different user types which simplifies implementation and thereby supports feasibility. Ex-post weighted-average Coase tariffs would lead to allocative efficiency if marginal costs were determined by congestion costs. Therefore, the variable price component must vary with the network load. One can imagine the variable price component to be an appropriate peak-load price.

Also, recall that in order to enhance user acceptance of PMP, this pricing model can partially accommodate flat-rate pricing by selling large blocks of transmission capacity. Concretely, an ISP would sell the right to generate a certain amount of data traffic within a given time period with a specified priority. In this case, PMP takes the form of a prepaid price plan. Alternatively, PMP could be implemented in the form of a flat rate where users commit themselves to using a fixed channel for a certain time period. This suggestion has the drawback that data traffic would no longer be separated according to tolerance of congestion. However, it may provide a further interim pricing solution on the way to usage-based priority pricing.

Moreover, recall from Section 3.3.3, that our rating of dynamic priority pricing with respect to feasibility, accounting efficiency, and price transparency could be upgraded through the introduction of stepped pricing, which is a simplified approximation to dynamic priority pricing. However, this is only possible at the cost of only approximating allocative efficiency as well as efficiency of capacity expansion.

A further interesting pricing approach, similar to expected capacity pricing, is cumulus pricing that we presented in Section 3.3.4. Recall that within the framework of cumulus pricing, contracts between IAPs and their subscribers specify the expected usage patterns and the corresponding flat rate. There exists a feedback mechanism based on cumulus points about actual usage patterns of customers which prevents the mismatch between actual and negotiated expected usage patterns exceeding a certain threshold. Stiller et al. [231] present a feasible technical solution called Internet Charge Calculation and Accounting System (ICCAS) which supports the cumulus pricing scheme. Also, the authors explain how to integrate cumulus pricing into a DiffServ environment. When being integrated into a DiffServ environment we judge cumulus pricing to have, with the one exception to be mentioned in a moment, the same advantages and drawbacks as expected capacity pricing. Solely accounting efficiency of cumulus pricing is lower compared to expected capacity pricing since cumulus points have to be counted at the edge of the network. If cumulus pricing is not integrated into a DiffServ environment, pricing is not complemented by technic congestion management. This lowers allocative efficiency as well as incentive compatibility since then, in periods of congestion, all packets are treated the same way, regardless of whether they created green or red cumulus points. Then, actual network loads that do not match contracted network loads neither influence current prices nor the service quality obtained. Only prices of the succeeding period may be affected.

Finally, one wonders which role will be assumed by service qualities in the future and which are likely to be the future pricing practices in the Internet. Recall that the introduction of QoS in the Internet requires system-wide coordination and agreements between providers concerning router technology and packet forwarding. Furthermore, when guaranteed QoS are offered, resource reservation and admission control become necessary. For these reasons, in the near future, data conveyance differentiated according to QoS may only be provided by intranets, extranets, or subnetworks of the Internet.[141] Over time the availability of different service qualities is likely to become more and more widespread.

In order to introduce quality differentiation in the Internet, users must begin to accept metered Internet service. In Section 2.2.2 we pointed at a simulated demand experiment suggesting that users accept volume-based and load-sensitive prices for Internet usage provided that congestion eases. We mentioned that the introduction of bandwidth-hungry real-time applications such as video on demand may enhance the acceptance of volume-based pricing. Necessary impulses to accustom users to volume-based prices rather than flat rates or time-based prices may be provided by packet-switched wireless communication technologies such as GPRS and, in the future, also UMTS, given that, today, data transport performed by GPRS is already predominantly brought to account on a volume basis.

As a compromise, one can imagine data traffic transported at the lowest priority level being priced at a monthly flat rate while higher-value users would have the option of receiving higher QoS, possibly on demand, at a usage-based price premium. To enhance user acceptability through enhanced predictability of expenses ISPs may sell prepaid cards which are debited whenever users require higher QoS on demand. That way, users can set up a monthly budget ceiling.

Also, we cannot expect a single pricing system to be implemented in the whole Internet. Instead, different pricing plans will coexist where individual providers opt for the pricing mechanism which best

141 Such a subnetwork will possibly be the result of Next Generation Internet (NGI) or Internet2 (I2), two projects that intend to establish a high-speed Internet which, in the framework of PMP, can be seen as a first-class network.

fits local conditions. Generally, we judge percentile pricing, adaptive flat-rate pricing, PMP in the form of a prepaid price plan, and cumulus pricing to be promising interim pricing solutions in the transition period from flat-rate pricing to more elaborate pricing schemes. Later, depending on the network technology, we expect peak-load pricing and expected capacity pricing to have a good chance of being adopted since they meet the normative criteria, established in Section 2.2.3, well from all points of view. Also, the combination of peak-load pricing with expected capacity pricing as well as peak-load pricing combined with PMP exhibit promising prospects of being implemented. In particular, we favor ex-post weighted-average Coase tariffs, where the variable price component is a peak-load price.

Table 3.16: Evaluation synopsis of pricing proposals for a single service Internet

		Flat rate pricing	*Nonlinear tariff*	*Peak-load pricing*
ISP/Welfare	*Allocative efficiency*	▼	▽	△
	Capacity expansion	▼	▼	△
	Incentive compatibility	▼	▲	▲
ISP	*Cost-orientation*	▽	△	△
	Price discrimination	▼	△	▲
	Feasibility	▲	△	△
	Accounting efficiency	▲	△	◊
User	*Utility-orientation*	▼	△	▲
	Price transparency	▲	△	△

▲ = very good, △ = good

◊ = satisfactory, ▽ = adequate, ▼ = inadequate

Table 3.17: Evaluation synopsis of load-insensitive priority pricing

		Voluntary user declarations	*Static priority pricing*	*PMP*
ISP/Welfare	*Allocative efficiency*	▼	◊	◊
	Capacity expansion	▼	▼	▼
	Incentive compatibility	▼	▲	▲
ISP	*Cost-orientation*	▽	◊	◊
	Price discrimination	▼	△	△
	Feasibility	△	▼	△
	Accounting efficiency	▲	◊	◊
User	*Utility-orientation*	▼	△	△
	Price transparency	▲	△	△

▲ = very good, △ = good

◊ = satisfactory, ▽ = adequate, ▼ = inadequate

Table 3.18: Evaluation synopsis of load-sensitive priority pricing

		Congestion pricing	*Smart market*	*Dynamic priority pricing*	*Expected capacity pricing*
ISP/Welfare	*Allocative efficiency*	▲	▲	▲	◊
	Capacity expansion	▲	▲	▲	△
	Incentive compatibility	▲	▲	▲	▲
ISP	*Cost-orientation*	▲	▲	△	▲
	Price discrimination	▲	▲	▲	◊
	Feasibility	▼	▼	▼	△
	Accounting efficiency	▼	▼	▼	▲
User	*Utility-orientation*	▲	◊	▲	▲
	Price transparency	▼	▽	▼	▲

▲ = very good, △ = good

◊ = satisfactory, ▽ = adequate, ▼ = inadequate

Table 3.19: Evaluation synopsis of pricing proposals for guaranteed QoS

		ALSVP	*Dynamic volume pricing*	*Resource-based pricing*	*Effective bandwidth pricing*
ISP/Welfare	*Allocative efficiency*	△	◊	△	△
	Capacity expansion	△	△	△	△
	Incentive compatibility	▲	▲	▲	▲
ISP	*Cost-orientation*	△	▲	△	△
	Price discrimination	▲	▲	▲	△
	Feasibility	▽	▼	▼	▽
	Accounting efficiency	▼	▼	◊	▽
User	*Utility-orientation*	▲	△	▲	▲
	Price transparency	▽	▽	◊	◊

▲ = very good, △ = good

◊ = satisfactory, ▽ = adequate, ▼ = inadequate

4. Internet Interconnection Pricing

> Any large multiprovider distributed service sector has to address the issue of cost distribution at some stage in its evolution.
>
> Huston ([114], p. 554)

4.1 Peering and Transit Pricing

4.1.1 Pricing Interconnection in the Dial-Up Internet Access Market

In the last chapter we focused on Internet retail prices. As already mentioned, Internet transport pricing is an issue on both the retail and the interconnection level. While some of the retail pricing approaches, namely dynamic priority pricing, expected capacity pricing, dynamic volume pricing, resource-based pricing, and effective bandwidth pricing, already provide a solution on how to design interconnection prices, all others remain silent on the issue. Therefore, we will now focus on interconnection pricing. First, a positive economic analysis of interconnection pricing will be given, suggesting that the interconnection market is inefficient due to the absence of accurate price signals and a lack of both price transparency and dynamics. Second, in Section 4.2, we will study optimal interconnection models and analyze their compatibility with the retail pricing models proposed in Chapter 3. These welfare maximizing interconnection models consider a single service Internet. The introduction of different service qualities at the interconnection level will be studied in Section 4.3.

In this first section a positive economic analysis will be given on peering and transit pricing, starting at the edge of the Internet. The Internet interconnection problem already occurs at the interconnection point of the Internet Access Provider (IAP) with the Public Switched Telephone Network (PSTN). Since, today, a majority of Internet users still accesses the Internet via dial-up, we will first analyze interconnection pricing in the dial-up Internet access market.[1] The analysis will provide insights into why, in practice, Internet access is often priced either flat or free. Moreover, the so-called reciprocal compensation problem occurring in the United States will be discussed. In this context, we will see that the standard U.S. interconnection model for Internet bound calls leads to substantial losses of the Incumbent Local Exchange Carriers (ILECs) and lacks incentives to adequately invest in capacity. Then, we will turn our attention to a higher level in the Internet hierarchy, to settlements between interconnecting ISPs. The question to be answered will be how the revenues from retail prices gained by IAPs are distributed to all other providers involved in the delivery of data. In a further step, peering arrangements of backbone providers will be analyzed with a bargaining model based on the Nash bargaining solution.

As already announced, we start this chapter with an analysis of interconnection pricing in the dial-up Internet access market. The players involved in the Internet dial-up model are the ILEC, Competitive Local Exchange Carriers (CLECs), also called Other Licensed Operators (OLOs), and IAPs. The ILEC is the local loop operator which provides the last mile from the central office to end-users and which originates all Internet bound calls. CLECs terminate calls to the modem banks of IAPs while IAPs provide the modem banks, access to the Internet, and customer service.

Internet bound calls have the special feature that they are essentially one-way, i.e., there are no return calls from the IAP to the end-user. Typically, they last longer than voice calls. Moreover, termination costs for Internet bound calls are lower than for voice calls. The reasons are that Internet bound calls require less switching and transmission resources, that IAP modem banks are more geographically concentrated compared to a typical customer base of the incum-

1 See pages 30 f. for statistics on the market penetration rates of broadband technologies.

bent, and that average per-minute costs are lower due to the longer call duration.[2] A general interconnection model in the dial-up Internet access market is depicted in Figure 4.1.[3]

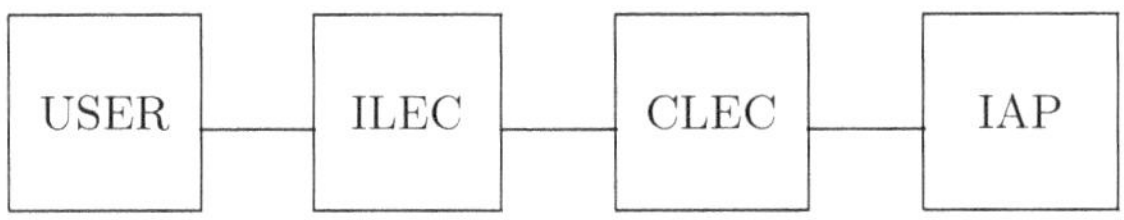

Figure 4.1: Interconnection in the dial-up Internet access market
Source: See Buisson, Sergent, and Frattaroli ([34], p. 11).

Chambouleyron [39] distinguishes between metered and unmetered interconnection models in the dial-up access market. In a metered interconnection model, telephone operators charge users for Internet bound calls while Internet bound calls are free of charge in unmetered models. Among the metered models, we will introduce the termination and the origination models that led to the free Internet model found in European countries. The standard U.S. interconnection model and the so-called Flat Rate Internet Access Call Origination (FRIACO) model, introduced in Great Britain, are unmetered models.

We first introduce the termination or direct model. In the termination model, the incumbent is responsible for the calls and bears the costs of the interconnection links. The competitive operator receives a termination fee from the incumbent for its termination service. End-users are billed on a per-minute basis by the incumbent for making local calls. IAPs charge users a monthly flat rate for Internet access,

2 See Wright ([258], pp. 5 f.).

3 In Switzerland, today, Internet bound calls are predominantly both originated and terminated on the PSTN of the Swiss incumbent, Swisscom. Possible reasons are that the telecommunications market in Switzerland was only liberalized in 1998 and that the Swiss surface and, with it, profit opportunities may be too small to incite entrants to rapidly build up their own networks. Hence, CLECs in Switzerland, such as Sunrise and Tele2, mainly act as resellers of network services they themselves buy from Swisscom.

for example. The IAP may obtain a negotiated part of the terminating revenues from the competitive operator.[4]

In the origination or indirect model, the competitive carrier is responsible for Internet bound calls. Therefore, it has to bear the costs of the interconnection links and bills the calls to end-users. The competitive operator then compensates the incumbent for originating the call. The competitive operator may share its call revenues with the IAP. The IAP charges end-users for Internet access. In the origination model, competitive carriers are in competition on call prices since they bill end-users. Often, the competitive carrier and the IAP are vertically integrated to a network provider which buys access to the origination service of the incumbent and offers joint service to end-users. Then, the integrated CLEC/IAP charges users a price per minute and typically a subscription fee for Internet access.

A problem arises if the incumbent wishes to offer Internet service itself at a flat rate while rival networks that purchase origination service face time-based prices. Rival networks are not able to offer the same service at a flat rate without incurring losses, given that flat rates provide no incentives for end-users to limit the time spent online. Such exploitation of the market power of the incumbent has led the British regulatory authorities to put pressure on British Telecom, the ILEC, to wholesale originating capacity to competitive carriers and IAPs at a flat rate.[5] This interconnection model is called Flat Rate Internet Access Call Origination (FRIACO).[6] Concretely, the competitive operator or the integrated CLEC/IAP charges end-users a monthly flat rate for Internet bound calls or for integrated call and Internet access service and compensates the incumbent for call

4 In Switzerland, Swisscom bills Internet users provided that they are not preselection customers of the CLEC. Then, currently, Swisscom assigns Sunrise, for example, an integrated CLEC/IAP, 92% of the proceeds from Internet bound calls. If Internet subscribers of Sunrise are also its preselection customers Sunrise is in charge of billing and pays Swisscom interconnection fees for the use of the PSTN. This is a form of the origination model introduced below.

5 See Wright ([258], pp. 26 f.). The same requirements were imposed by the German regulatory authorities on Deutsche Telekom, the incumbent in Germany, in June 2002.

6 See Oftel [187].

origination. This compensation has the form of a fixed charge based upon the contracted capacity. If the competitive operator and the IAP are not vertically integrated, IAPs charge end-users a monthly flat rate for Internet access. FRIACO enables competitive carriers to offer flat rate Internet access to their users which is not desirable from an economic point of view, but provides a further explanation for the popularity of flat-rated Internet access.[7]

Further, the termination and the origination models help to explain the economics of free Internet access where end-users only pay the price of a local call when accessing the Internet. In this case, there is no monthly Internet access fee levied by IAPs. Due to zero Internet access fees, there is no contract between IAPs and end-users. Users connect to the Internet by dialing the IAP's access number to reach the IAP's modems, but only pay the local calls to the competitive carrier in the origination model or to the incumbent in the termination model. The free Internet access model has become popular in an increasing number of European countries.[8] The way IAPs can still make money consists in obtaining a slice of the call revenues from the competitive carrier or the incumbent, according to the interconnection model applied. The amount of call revenues redistributed to the IAPs depends on the amount of call revenues generated by each IAP and is often undisclosed. Note that call redistribution would not be possible if the prices for originating and terminating calls reflected costs. Instead, there is a rent to be distributed. However, competition among IAPs forces them to give the rent back to their customers in the form of a zero Internet access fee.[9]

One may wonder why a profit maximizing firm such as the incumbent or a competitive operator should be ready to share the call revenues with IAPs. Haan [102] argues that telephone companies can solve a double marginalization problem by paying IAPs a certain lump-sum fee provided that the IAPs offer free Internet access. The intuition goes as follows: Without free Internet access, the

7 See Chambouleyron ([39], pp. 14 f.).

8 In Switzerland, Sunrise currently offers free Internet access with its product called sunrise freesurf.

9 See Cave and Mason ([38], p. 192).

dial-up retail price for Internet access is given by the sum of the price of a telephone call and the price set by the IAP. If the telephone operator and the IAP are both local monopolists they both charge monopoly prices. Hence, the retail price equals the sum of two marked-up monopoly prices. The resulting deadweight loss is larger than in the standard monopoly case: The loss in consumer surplus exceeds the one of single monopoly market. Moreover, monopolists do not maximize joint profits since they set their prices too high and therefore cannot sell the joint-profit maximizing quantity. This is the so-called double marginalization problem.[10] With the lump-sum transfer from the telephone company to the IAP the double marginalization problem can be eliminated such that the retail price equals the joint-profit maximizing price which is paid to the telephone company. The analysis of Haan [102] also holds if the IAP market is an oligopoly, provided that the Internet users' reservation price for Internet services is high enough, and, if the telephone company is regulated, provided that the regulated price is high enough.

Datta and Dixon [60] pick up the argument of Haan [102] and show that free Internet access is not efficient if there is a binding price cap regulation. However, the assumption that the incumbent can demand a monopolistic price is rather restrictive given the deregulation of the telecommunications market. Moreover, Haan ([102], p. 377) remarks that his results may change if alternative access technologies are integrated into the analysis.

In the United States the argument of Haan [102] does not hold since local telephone calls often are free of variable charges. Instead, due to regulatory constraints, many incumbents offer a monthly flat rate for local access.[11] Hence, there is no double marginalization problem. Consequently, telephone companies are not willing to pay a lump-sum transfer to IAPs if they offer Internet access for free.[12] Indeed, free Internet access offers are not common in the United States.[13]

10 See Tirole ([239], pp. 173–181).

11 See Didak and Spulber ([221], p. 351).

12 See Haan ([102], p. 377).

13 In the United States, free Internet access is also claimed to be offered by a number of providers such as AltaVista or Net Zero. However, free Internet

Instead, IAPs charge strictly positive access charges in the form of flat rates.

In the United States 'regulatory conundrums'[14] result in the so-called ISP reciprocal compensation problem. The origin of this problem is the U.S. Telecommunications Act of 1996 which does not make a distinction between Internet dial-up calls and regular local calls. Specifically, the act requires Local Exchange Carriers (LECs) to adopt the principle of reciprocity which states that termination charges between two interconnecting carriers must be identical. But as already noted above, Internet bound calls have the special features that they are essentially one-way and that they are less costly to terminate than voice calls.

The principle of reciprocity has allowed entrants, the CLECs, to specialize in terminating Internet traffic due to an arbitrage opportunity: Following the rule of reciprocal compensation, incumbents have to pay termination charges to entrants to terminate Internet bound calls even though incumbents do not collect any call revenue from Internet users.[15] These termination charges are likely to exceed termination costs for the following reason: Termination charges reflect the unit costs to terminate the average voice call of the incumbent. But, as mentioned above, termination costs of Internet bound calls are lower than for voice calls. Competitive carriers have entered the market solely to sign up IAPs and to exploit this arbitrage opportunity. Competitive pressure may force entrants to share their profits with the IAP industry. In the Internet industry, again, competitive forces may induce IAPs to give their share of profits back to end-users in the form of a lower Internet access fee.[16]

The ISP reciprocal compensation problem makes incumbents run losses since they only incur costs from the Internet dial-up business.

---

access has to be paid by users by tolerating permanent advertisements. Hence, Internet access is not actually free of charge. See Haan ([102], p. 360).

14 Banerjee and Ros [16].

15 Note that we implicitly suppose all Internet users to be connected to the PSTN and, hence, to pay a flat rate for local telephone service even if no Internet service were offered.

16 See Banerjee and Ros ([16], p. 211).

Consequently, they do not have monetary incentives to invest in Internet origination services which, together with the growth of demand for Internet services, results in congestion on the PSTN.[17] A further distortional effect of reciprocal compensation for Internet bound calls is the inefficient subsidization of Internet users by subscribers of the incumbent who do not use the Internet.

To restrict the arbitrage opportunity for competitive carriers, in 2001 the Federal Communications Commission (FCC) ad interim capped termination charges.[18] The FCC further proposed the Central Office Bill And Keep (COBAK) arrangement to avoid problems of regulatory arbitrage.[19] The COBAK proposal suggests abolishing the obligation to pay termination charges to competitive carriers. One may conjecture that the introduction of the COBAK proposal induces Internet access fees to increase.[20]

Banerjee and Ros [14, 15, 16] propose preventing the ISP reciprocal compensation problem by making the IAP responsible for Internet bound calls. The IAP would bill end-users for the joint service of Internet access and the local call to its modem bank. The IAP would then have to compensate the incumbent and the competitive operator for their originating and terminating service, respectively. Banerjee and Ros ([16], pp. 205–207) argue that the compensation should take the form of per-minute prices reflecting underlying costs. In consequence, one may conjecture that IAPs will no longer charge a flat rate to end-users since they would themselves face usage-sensitive costs.

We can conclude that regulatory artifacts of the PSTN are significant drivers of popular free and flat rates in the dial-up Internet access market. We conjecture that this is not likely to be a problem in the long run since, even if currently Internet dial-up access is still the most popular Internet access technology, alternative access technologies, i.e., broadband access technologies, are rapidly becoming more

17 See Sidak and Spulber ([221], pp. 351–360).
18 See FCC [73].
19 See DeGraba [61].
20 See Chambouleyron ([39], pp. 6–8).

popular.[21] With the market penetration of alternative unregulated access technologies different pricing models will be introduced which better reflect usage and underlying costs.

4.1.2 Settlements in Interconnection Arrangements

In this section, we want to stress the necessity that each provider is fairly compensated for its infrastructure investments and carriage services through appropriate inter-provider settlements.[22] Settlements are financial transfers between ISPs to receive interconnection and interoperability. The question to be answered is how the revenues from retail tariffs gained by IAPs are distributed to all other providers involved in the delivery of data.

Two basic types of interconnection relationships can be identified: Peering and transit.[23] In a peering arrangement two (bilateral peering) or several (multilateral peering) ISPs grant each other access to their networks. The peering relationship is non-transitive: A network does not accept traffic from a peer to convey it to another peer. There is no transit service offered to third parties. The only termination traffic accepted by a peer is destined to its own subscribers. Each ISP bears the costs of the use of its network by the customers of its peers and benefits from using the network of peers.

---

21 Statistics of market penetration rates of broadband technologies are provided on pages 30 f. in Section 2.1.3.

22 Settlements are also called interconnection, access, or termination charges.

23 Bailey ([9], pp. 160–165) provides a taxonomy of ISP interconnection agreements. He distinguishes between three variants of peering agreements, namely a peer-to-peer bilateral model and two multilateral peering models called cooperative and third-party administrator interconnection agreement models, as well as one transit interconnection agreement called hierarchical bilateral agreement. While in a cooperative agreement model ISPs share the responsibility for and the costs of the peering point, an independent profit-oriented operator runs the exchange point in the third-party administrator interconnection model. In Europe, most public exchange points are based on the cooperative agreement model while the Network Access Points (NAPs) in the United States predominantly rely on the third-party administrator model.

Traditionally, there have been no settlements between peers. This is the so-called Sender-Keep-All (SKA) model, also known as bill-and-keep model. In a first period of Internet growth, the SKA model promoted interconnection and the spreading of positive network externalities. However, peering based on the SKA model incites so-called hot-potato routing or 'shortest exit routing.'[24] Hot-potato routing refers to the strategy to pass traffic to other ISPs at the earliest point of exchange. This is possible since peering partners usually interconnect at several exchange points. By delivering traffic to the peer at the exchange nearest to the source the forwarding network can avoid transmission costs, i.e., congestion costs.[25]

Peering based on an SKA model may emerge if the interconnecting ISPs derive the same perceived benefit from interconnection, i.e., if two providers are of approximately the same size, measured, for example, in terms of the number of POPs in each network, have a similar network capacity and customer base, and have roughly identical experience and technology.[26] In other words, peering agreements under the SKA model are not observed if providers differ in size. The reason is that under the SKA regime small networks can benefit from large investments in backbone infrastructure and from a disproportionate number of routes at no cost. In the literature, this behavior is called 'backbone free-riding.'[27] Given the lack of appropriate pricing, ISPs, which invested heavily in their infrastructure, started to refuse to interconnect with smaller competitors. Major backbone providers set up administrative measures and rules-of-thumb to limit peering such as a minimum number of interconnection points or a minimum bandwidth capacity potential peer networks have to fulfill.[28]

In order to sustain interconnection and the associated positive network externalities, alternative settlement mechanisms to the SKA model are necessary. Where providers do not differ too much in size,

---

24 Crémer, Rey, and Tirole ([55], p. 439).

25 See Australian Competition and Consumer Commission (ACCC) ([1], p. 85).

26 See Australian Competition and Consumer Commission (ACCC) ([1], p. 48) and Kende ([131], p. 8).

27 Baake and Wichmann ([7], p. 90).

28 See Farnon and Huddle ([71], p. 383).

the trend in the ISP industry is to move toward paid peering in the form of bilaterally negotiated settlement structures.[29] One can imagine bilateral settlements where the peers agree on a price charged for traffic imbalances.[30] Alternatively, an entry threshold price to join the peering group or certain criteria potential peers must comply with may be adopted in order to induce a mutually perceived parity in the peering relationship.[31] In the case of multilateral peering, possible settlement models for traffic exchange range from SKA among all interconnected providers to a more complicated set of bilateral settlements.[32]

Networks of different sizes contract a transit agreement which is characterized by a hierarchical relationship between the supplier ISP and the customer ISP. According to Hwang and Weiss [116], today, transit agreements are the most pervasive interconnection model in the Internet. In a transit agreement the ISP with customer status obtains connectivity to all customers of the hierarchical superior, to all the other networks the supplier ISP peers with, as well as, if existing, to all its transit interconnections. In turn, supplier ISPs are compensated for the connectivity they provide. Generally, a customer ISP pays its supplier ISP a flat rate based on the capacity of the interconnection link, i.e., based on the potential peak throughput rate.[33] Usually, these flat rates are determined by negotiation and are intended to reflect recent and expected future traffic demands.[34] Halabi ([104], p. 42) observes that transit prices depend on the provider's relative strength and level of investment in a certain area, which means that transit prices are not cost-based.[35] This makes the transit model suffer from a lack of price transparency. Note that flat-rated settlements at the interconnection level match flat Internet access fees, possibly

29 See Laffont et al. ([134], p. 34) and Huston ([114], p. 566). In the next section, the economic rationales behind negotiated settlements in a peering arrangement will be analyzed.
30 See Telegeography ([237], p. 28).
31 See Huston ([114], p. 568).
32 See TeleGeography ([237], p. 28).
33 See Clark and Lehr ([47], p. 7) and Telegeography ([237], p. 31).
34 See Little and Wright ([143], p. 154).
35 See Weiss and Shin ([254], p. 12).

combined with voluntary user declarations and a quota system introduced in Section 3.2.1.

Apart from fixed transit prices, volume-based transit fees can also be observed. They are becoming increasingly popular.[36] In Australia, for example, transit fees are based on the amount of traffic, measured in megabytes, delivered by the upstream provider to the downstream provider. Also, some upstream providers offer a discount for increased amounts of traffic delivered to their client-providers. The discount settlement model relies on the assumption that the amounts of traffic received and sent by a downstream provider are positively correlated.[37]

Volume-based pricing at the interconnection level is compatible with nonlinear tariffs at the retail level: Where uniform volume prices are charged at the interconnection level, retail prices also have to be proportional to the volume of data generated in order to allow the IAP to recover interconnection costs. Similarly, if volume discounts are given at the interconnection level, the same pricing scheme must be applied at the retail level in order for revenues to match costs. ISPs which face volume-based transit prices can match the costs encountered in the interconnection market with the revenues derived from the retail market by offering appropriate nonlinear tariffs to their retail clients. One may imagine volume-based transit prices varying with the time of day to match them with peak-load pricing at the retail level.

Transit and peering agreements consist of negotiated agreements, so-called Service Level Agreements (SLAs), between interconnecting networks that describe the service provided, or, in other words, the commitment one ISP makes to the other to carry this other ISP's traffic.[38] Typically, observable performance metrics are specified in

36 See Antoniadis ([4], p. 9).

37 See Australian Competition and Consumer Commission (ACCC) ([1], pp. 46 f. and p. 49).

38 Lehr and McKnight ([141], p. 4) provide a taxonomy of SLAs. They distinguish between four SLA classes: Contracts between end-users and IAPs, transport agreements between upstream and downstream providers, peering agreements between Internet Backbone Providers (IBPs), and contracts between end-users and content or application service providers.

SLAs, but not guaranteed engineering metrics such as end-to-end delay limits which allow end-to-end service guarantees to be supported. If a supplier ISP cannot meet its SLA promises it has to pay a penalty or free its contract partner from a duty to pay. If customer ISPs overuse their contracted traffic profile they face increased charges or are denied service.[39]

SLAs can be both static or dynamic. While static SLAs extend over a relatively long time period, i.e., a month or a year, dynamic SLAs may change by the minute or by the hour and therefore require automated negotiation.[40]

Summing up, ISPs of similar size opt for a peering arrangement while transit arrangements dominate interconnection between networks of different size. In general, Internet Backbone Providers (IBPs) in the United States such as MCI's UUNET, Sprint, and Level3 collectively and exclusively peer under so-called non-disclosure agreements which means that peering conditions are kept secret.[41] Smaller ISPs peer with each other and buy transit from larger ISPs. Note that every downstream provider aims to become a peer in order to save transit fees and that every peer wants to be an upstream provider in order to collect transit fees.[42]

We are now ready to answer the question raised at the beginning of this section: Revenues from retail tariffs gained by IAPs are passed over to IBPs through transit fees to compensate upstream providers for infrastructure investments and carriage of data traffic. However, there have not been any systematic settlement policies. The question remains what an efficient settlement rule would look like. Sections 4.2 and 4.3 focus on the design of efficient settlements.

A reason why the Internet interconnection environment lacks the common use of a reasonable settlement system is that retail tariffs for

39 See Lehr and McKnight ([141], p. 3).

40 See Hwang ([115], pp. 74 f.). The interconnection settlement models proposed in Section 4.3 are based on dynamic SLAs.

41 See Little and Wright ([143], p. 152) and TeleGeography ([237], p. 27).

42 The economic rationales behind Internet interconnection decisions have been studied by Baake and Wichmann [7], Badasyan and Chakrabarti [8], Crémer, Rey, and Tirole [55], and by Dewan, Freimer, and Gundepudi [62], for example.

today's best-effort service do not fund the whole end-to-end carriage service. Instead, a partial path funding model is deployed. To see this, imagine a simplified topology of the Internet where local IAPs enter into transit agreements with some upstream providers. Then, the service domain offered to retail customers includes the union of the service domain of the respective local IAP, of the service domains of its upstream service providers, the service domains of their providers at a higher tier, and so on. Once the traffic sent by a retail customer leaves this vertical funding chain by passing a link where some upper tier ISPs peer or by being passed to another downstream provider, the original IAP ceases to fund transport costs. At this point, the IAP of the receiver begins to fund the traffic service. Hence, the ISP retail pricing structure is characterized by an implicit cost sharing of traffic carriage between the sender and the receiver. In contrast, financial settlement schemes typically assume an end-to-end funding to exist.[43]

Huston ([113], pp. 20–22) argues that, with the growing importance of QoS in the Internet, apart from the existing SKA mechanism and the partial path funding model a financial settlement mechanism corresponding to an end-to-end service model has to emerge. In this case, a client who requests a reservation of resources for traffic carriage would be charged for the whole end-to-end transaction. The originating IAP would distribute its retail revenues from the originating end-user to all other providers involved in the delivery of the respective traffic flow. According to Huston one can imagine that all providers along a path indicate their QoS offered as well as their applied unit settlement prices. Then, the initiator of a traffic flow, or, more likely, her smart agent may make an optimal decision by comparing the different combinations of prices and QoS offered. Recall that this is basically also the idea behind dynamic priority pricing.

To close the section, we summarize our considerations on the compatibility of settlement schemes in practice and the retail pricing proposals introduced in the last chapter. It has been noted that flat-rate pricing at the interconnection level is compatible with flat-rate pric-

43 See Huston ([114], pp. 573 f.).

ing, possibly combined with voluntary user declarations and a quota system, at the retail level. Volume-based prices levied at the interconnection level match nonlinear tariffs at the retail level. One can also imagine volume-based interconnection prices varying with the time of day which would make them compatible with peak-load pricing at the retail level.

4.1.3 A Bargaining Approach to Peering Arrangements

In this section Internet peering arrangements will be analyzed with a bargaining model proposed by Milgrom, Mitchell, and Srinagesh ([168], pp. 187–195). The model suggests that if sufficient Internet Backbone Providers (IBPs) of similar size compete for market share to maintain their bill-and-keep interconnection agreements, the prices of transit and Internet access will reflect costs. The analysis is based on the Nash bargaining solution.

Nash bargaining belongs to the class of bargaining games where a solution has to fulfill certain desirable axioms. The constructive idea of Nash [172] was to have a bargaining solution that is both fair and rational. Therefore, he set up five axioms, discussed below, that the bargaining solutions should satisfy: Individual rationality, Pareto efficiency, symmetry, independence of irrelevant alternatives, and independence of positive affine transformations. The idea of rationality and fairness fits peering contracts with a bill-and-keep agreement very well, given that they are only concluded if perceived benefits from peering are equal.

Apart from the Nash bargaining solution, there are many other solution concepts provided by the theory of cooperative games.[44] A justification for the choice of the Nash bargaining concept is that if side payments are possible and if the threat point, explained below, is given, it coincides with the Shapley value that also has an axiomatic

44 As already explained in Section 3.2.3, a game is called cooperative if players can enter binding commitments. This requires that players can communicate, negotiate an outcome, and that the agreement can be enforced by exogenous mechanisms.

foundation just as the Nash bargaining solution does. The Shapley value of a cooperative game always exists and is unique. Moreover, in the special case of two bargaining partners, as analyzed below, both the Nash solution and the Shapley value lie in the core. The core is a further important solution concept of the theory of cooperative games which, in the case of two bargaining partners, fulfills the axioms of individual rationality and Pareto efficiency.[45]

We assume that N identical customers subscribe to n IBPs. Each customer shall only subscribe to one IBP. Every IBP i, $i = 1, \ldots, n$, serves a fraction α_i of subscribers, where $\sum_{i=1}^{n} \alpha_i = 1$. The services provided by IBPs may be both access services to end-users and transit services to lower tier ISPs. An IBP i which is not connected to the Internet provides the utility $u(\alpha_i, N)$ to a representative customer while an IBP i which is connected to the Internet gives the utility $u(\alpha, N)$, where $\alpha \leq 1$ depicts the fraction of interconnected subscribers in the Internet economy. Hence, $u(\alpha, N)$ reflects the willingness to pay for connectivity of a representative customer. Positive network externalities make $u(\alpha, N)$ increase in α and in N. Suppose that N is constant. Then, we can define $f(\alpha) := u(\alpha, N)$. Furthermore, assume that the fractions α_1 and α_2 of customers subscribing to some IBP 1 and IBP 2, respectively, do not depend on whether there is an interconnection agreement between the two backbones or not. This assumption implies that a relatively small IBP does not lose customers to its relatively large switching costs between two IBPs are prohibitive.[46]

IBP 1 and IBP 2 are assumed to have negotiated peering agreements with all the other $(N - 2)$ backbone providers. If IBP 1 and IBP 2 obtain a peering agreement, full connectivity prevails. In this case, they can charge each subscriber a subscription fee $f(1)$. Then,

45 Owen ([189], pp. 262–265) proves the existence and the uniqueness of the Shapley value. The proof that the Nash bargaining solution coincides with the Shapley value if side payments are possible and if the threat point is known can be found in Harsanyi ([106], pp. 226–238). Jianhua ([121], pp. 112–117) explains the core solution concept.

46 We will see below that relaxing the assumption of prohibitive switching costs does not change our considerations.

abstracting from costs for simplicity,[47] profits equal revenues which amount to $N\alpha_i f(1)$, where $i = 1, 2$ and $i \neq j$. If IBP 1 and IBP 2 are disconnected, profits of IBP i are given by $N\alpha_i f(1 - \alpha_j)$, where $i, j = 1, 2$ and $i \neq j$. Thus, the gains from cooperation are given by

$$N\alpha_1(f(1) - f(1 - \alpha_2))$$

for IBP 1, and symmetrically,

$$N\alpha_2(f(1) - f(1 - \alpha_1))$$

for IBP 2.

Before deriving the solution of our bargaining game we present the axioms the cooperative Nash bargaining solution must satisfy.[48] The axiom of (strong) individual rationality requires that the equilibrium payoff of each player in case of cooperation, Π_i^*, exceeds the non-cooperative payoff:

$$\Pi_i^* > N\alpha_i f(1 - \alpha_j), \quad i, j = 1, 2.$$

The axiom of Pareto efficiency postulates that there exists no payoff vector $\hat{\Pi} := (\hat{\Pi}_1, \hat{\Pi}_2)$ which provides one bargainer a payoff higher than the equilibrium payoff without making another player worse off:

$$\nexists \quad \hat{\Pi} := (\hat{\Pi}_1, \hat{\Pi}_2) \quad \text{such that} \quad \hat{\Pi}_i \geq \Pi_i^*, \quad i = 1, 2.$$

The axiom of symmetry demands that if the two players IBP 1 and IBP 2 have the same non-cooperative payoff both bargainers receive the same equilibrium payoff:

$$N\alpha_1 f(1 - \alpha_2) = N\alpha_2 f(1 - \alpha_1) \Rightarrow \Pi_1^* = \Pi_2^*.$$

47 The introduction of costs does not change the analysis qualitatively if, for example, one assumes costs of IBP i to be $N\alpha_i C(1)$ if there exists a connection to IBP j and $N\alpha_i C(1 - \alpha_j)$ otherwise, where $i, j = 1, 2$ and $i \neq j$.

48 See Nash ([172], pp. 157–159) and Nash ([173], p. 136 f.).

The non-cooperative payoff vector $(N\alpha_1 f(1-\alpha_2), N\alpha_2 f(1-\alpha_1))$ is called threat point.

The axiom of independence of irrelevant alternatives states that the solution should not change if the original set of possible payoffs shrinks and if the original Nash solution is still an element of the shrunk set of possible payoffs. In other words, if a solution space containing the Nash solution is expanded by payoff options no bargainer is interested in, these additional payoff alternatives must be irrelevant.

The axiom of independence of positive affine transformations stipulates that the solution does not qualitatively change with the measurement of payoffs. In other words, if the payoffs Π_i are positive monotonically transformed such that

$$\hat{\Pi}_i := a_i + b_i \Pi_i, \quad b_i > 0,$$

then the equilibrium payoffs are given by

$$\hat{\Pi}_i^* = a_i + b_i \Pi_i^* \quad i, j = 1, 2.$$

The question arises if there are payoff vectors which satisfy all of the above axioms. The theorem of Nash[49] states that each solution (Π_1^*, Π_2^*) of a cooperative game that satisfies all five axioms, introduced above, maximizes the so-called Nash product

$$NP(\Pi_1, \Pi_2) := (\Pi_1 - N\alpha_1 f(1-\alpha_2))(\Pi_2 - N\alpha_2 f(1-\alpha_1)) \quad (4.1)$$

with respect to Π_1 and Π_2 subject to

$$\Pi_1 + \Pi_2 = N\alpha_1 f(1) + N\alpha_2 f(1), \quad (4.2)$$

where $\Pi_1, \Pi_2 \geq 0$. The payoffs of disconnection $N\alpha_1 f(1-\alpha_2)$ and $N\alpha_2 f(1-\alpha_1)$ are the payoffs in case of non-cooperation, the threat point. The constraint confines the payoff possibility set, i.e., the solution space. Pareto efficiency requires equilibrium allocations to be

49 See Nash [172].

located on the border of the payoff possibility set. Potential gains must be fully exploited.

Nash [172] showed that a unique Nash bargaining solution exits if its axioms are satisfied and if the solution space is convex and compact, i.e., bounded and closed. Our bargaining problem meets these requirements upon the solution space. To see this, note that the solution space, confined by the linear constraint (4.2) and by $\Pi_1, \Pi_2 \geq 0$ is convex. Moreover, the solution space is bounded since the payoffs Π_1 and Π_2, by the set up of the model, are non-negative and, given (4.2), cannot become infinite. Furthermore, the solution space is closed since its border belongs to the solution space as well.

The Lagrangian function of the bargaining problem is given by

$$\begin{aligned} L(\Pi_1, \Pi_2, \lambda) \;&:=\; (\Pi_1 - N\alpha_1 f(1-\alpha_2))(\Pi_2 - N\alpha_2 f(1-\alpha_1)) \\ &\quad + \lambda(N\alpha_1 f(1) + N\alpha_2 f(1) - \Pi_1 - \Pi_2). \end{aligned}$$

By differentiating the Lagrangian function with respect to Π_1, Π_2, and λ, setting the derivatives equal to zero, and solving for Π_1 and Π_2 we obtain the cooperative Nash bargaining solution which predicts that the two parties equally divide the gains from cooperation:[50]

$$\begin{aligned} \Pi_1^* &= \frac{1}{2}\left[N\alpha_1[f(1-\alpha_2) + f(1)] + N\alpha_2[f(1) - f(1-\alpha_1)]\right], \quad (4.3) \\ \Pi_2^* &= \frac{1}{2}\left[N\alpha_2[f(1-\alpha_1) + f(1)] + N\alpha_1[f(1) - f(1-\alpha_2)]\right]. \end{aligned}$$

Individual gains from cooperation for $i, j = 1, 2$ and $i \neq j$, are given by

$$\Pi_i^* - N\alpha_i f(1-\alpha_j) = \frac{1}{2}\left[N\alpha_i[f(1) - f(1-\alpha_j)] + N\alpha_j[f(1) - f(1-\alpha_i)]\right].$$

The sum of gains from cooperation amounts to

$$N\alpha_1[f(1) - f(1-\alpha_2)] + N\alpha_2[f(1) - f(1-\alpha_1)].$$

50 We can be sure to indeed find a maximum given that the level curves are convex and that the constraint is linear.

The first (second) term depicts the gain in revenues that IBP 1 (IBP 2) derives from an interconnection agreement with IBP 2 (IBP 1).

Above, we mentioned that given an interconnection agreement IBP 1 can charge the subscription fee $f(1)$ from each customer.[51] The corresponding profits

$$\Pi_1 = N\alpha_1 f(1)$$

differ from equilibrium profits depicted in expressions (4.3) by the bargained net payment from IBP 1 to IBP 2. The bargained net payment from IBP 1 to IBP 2 amounts to

$$\frac{1}{2}\left[N\alpha_1[f(1) - f(1-\alpha_2)] - N\alpha_2[f(1) - f(1-\alpha_1)]\right]. \tag{4.4}$$

Since we assumed away any costs a positive net payment can only be justified by an asymmetric bargaining power, i.e., by the existence of market power. Where there is a net payment from IBP 1 to IBP 2, the latter has more market power than the former. We will use the result (4.4) below when discussing conditions for a bill-and-keep agreement to realize and the bargaining power of IBPs.

The equilibrium outcome of the bargaining game is a bill-and-keep arrangement if both parties derive equal gains from interconnection. Then, equilibrium profits are given by

$$\Pi_i^* = N\alpha_i f(1), \quad i = 1, 2,$$

and no settlement payments are made by either IBP, i.e. the bargained net payment (4.4) equals zero. If the gains from interconnection are not identical the IBP with a greater advantage from interconnection has to pay its rival to obtain interconnection. Sufficient conditions for a bill-and-keep interconnection agreement are that either

- $\alpha_1 = \alpha_2$, or, that

---

51 Due to the symmetry of the problem the same argument holds for IBP 2 and its profits.

– f is (affin) linear:[52] $f(\alpha) = a + b\alpha$.

Formally, this can be shown by substituting α_1 (α_2) for α_2 (α_1) and $f(\alpha) = a + b\alpha$ for $f(\cdot)$ in expression (4.4), respectively. Then, in both cases, the bargained net payment (4.4) equals zero. Intuitively, when $f(\cdot)$ is linear, losses due to disconnection are equal since the smaller IBP loses more revenues per customer while the larger IBP incurs the loss over more subscribers.

Note that with fixed numbers of customers the larger network does not generally have more bargaining power since the shape of $f(\cdot)$ influences bargaining power as well. Consider equation (4.4) and note that if $\alpha_1 > \alpha_2$, without loss of generality, we have

$$f(1) - f(1 - \alpha_2) < f(1) - f(1 - \alpha_1). \tag{4.5}$$

Then, the shape of $f(\cdot)$ determines in which direction net payments flow. If $f''(\cdot) > 0$ the effect of inequality (4.5) on the bargained net payment is likely to dominate the effect of the market shares. If $f''(\cdot) < 0$ the effect of inequality (4.5) is likely to be dominated by the effect of the market shares.

In the early days of the Internet, $f(\cdot)$ may have been almost linear which justifies the common bill-and-keep arrangements in that time. With growing market penetration, one can imagine the value of connecting to additional subscribers to be decreasing, i.e., $f''(\cdot) < 0$. Then, customers of relatively large backbones have a low marginal value of being connected to additional subscribers. In consequence, relatively large IBPs may obtain a better bargaining position.

Remember that we have assumed switching costs between IBPs to be prohibitive. This was made operational by making the fraction α_i of subscribers to IBP i independent of the number of subscribers that can be reached through IBP i. If switching costs are low a small IBP loses at least some customers when getting disconnected from

52 One can show that this sufficient condition also holds if costs, as introduced in footnote 47 on page 257, are allowed for, provided that costs are also linear in $\alpha : C(\alpha) = a + b\alpha$. Intuitively, in the absence of any economies or diseconomies of scale, regardless of their size, IBPs are likely to derive the same perceived benefits from interconnection and, thus, opt for a bill-and-keep agreement.

the larger peering partner. The possibility for customers to switch IBPs potentially weakens the bargaining position of the smaller network. Hence, relaxing the assumption of prohibitive switching costs reinforces our presumption that relatively large IBPs may obtain a strong bargaining position.

The negotiation power of a relatively large IBP could be mitigated if smaller IBPs merged and increased their bargaining power that way. Alternatively, Besen et al. ([21], pp. 294 f.) demonstrate that the introduction of secondary peering, i.e., peering between downstream providers, into the model of Milgrom, Mitchell, and Srinagesh [168] reduces the bargaining power of large IBPs. The reason is that through secondary peering between customer ISPs of a small IBP and customer ISPs of a large IBP, connectivity between the customer ISPs prevails even if the two IBPs disconnect.

Nevertheless, dominant IBPs with a strong bargaining position may develop such that they can force smaller rivals to pay interconnection fees above the costs of interconnection. Then, smaller IBPs may try to recover these interconnection costs through higher access prices charged to end-users and higher transit prices charged to (downstream) ISPs.

Milgrom, Mitchell, and Srinagesh ([168], p. 192) argue that one remedy against this exercise of market power is vigorous competition among IBPs. Our bargaining model suggests that IBPs of similar size opt for a bill-and-keep agreement. Then, no IBP can successfully raise the costs of rivals by an increase in the interconnection fee. Simultaneously, each IBP wants to increase its market share in order to improve or to maintain its peering arrangements. With vigorous competition for (downstream) ISPs and end-users, prices for transit and Internet access should be kept at a low level.

To sum up, the bargaining model suggests that retail and transit prices reflect costs provided that there is a sufficient number of IBPs of comparable size competing for market share in order to preserve their bill-and-keep interconnection agreements. If one IBP obtains a dominant market position and if switching costs of consumers are low the above considerations indicate that a dominant IBP can charge transit fees to its IBP rivals. In consequence, retail and transit prices would no longer reflect costs.

To reduce the market power of backbone providers compared to downstream providers, Weiss and Shin [254] propose that interconnection prices be based on the maximum of inbound or outbound traffic volume. This criterion facilitates peering agreements by creating more symmetric traffic patterns. In consequence, market power of top-tiered backbone providers is mitigated since peering gives smaller providers more negotiation power against IBPs. Evidence of market power in the top-tier network is given by the fact that 80% of backbone data traffic is controlled by an oligopoly, the 'Big Five,'[53] consisting of MCI's UUNET, Level3, AT&T, Sprint, and Cable & Wireless.[54]

4.2 Optimal Interconnection Pricing

4.2.1 Congestion Pricing for Interconnected Networks

In Section 4.1 we conducted a positive economic analysis to explain Internet interconnection pricing in practice. We will now turn our attention to normative economics and ask how interconnection charges should be set to maximize social welfare. Moreover, the compatibility of retail pricing proposals presented in Chapter 3 with optimal interconnection pricing models will be investigated.

The paper of Lehr and Weiss [142] has its roots in the article of MacKie-Mason and Varian [151]. Lehr and Weiss analyze congestion pricing at the interconnection level. The authors concentrate on a situation where networks, providing a single type of service, do not have market power. Lehr and Weiss determine optimal congestion prices and examine the settlement problem between different networks. As explained in Section 3.3.1, an important characteristic of congestion

53 Weiss and Shin ([254], p. 16).
54 See Weinberg [253].

prices is that not only do they decrease usage when congestion occurs, but they also generate revenues for capacity expansion. We will extend the analysis of Lehr and Weiss [142] by showing that, just as in the case of a single network, congestion pricing and capacity expansion in a competitive market correspond to the social optimum.

We first introduce the set up of the model. Let $i \in \mathcal{M}$ denote a network which belongs to the set $\mathcal{M}$ of all networks, where $\mathcal{M} := \{1, \ldots, M\}$. Each network i is assumed to serve N_i subscribers. A subscriber of type (ij) originates a data transfer on network i and sends it to a subscriber to network j. The data sent is transported along the route (ij). The subset of networks involved in delivering the data on the route (ij) is denoted by $\mathcal{R}(ij) \subseteq \mathcal{M}$. To simplify, suppose that each subscriber sends a unique type of data traffic which follows a unique path through the Internet.[55] The set of all possible types of data traffic is given by $\mathcal{Z} := \{(ij) \mid i, j \in \mathcal{M}\}$. Moreover, $\mathcal{H}_i \subseteq \mathcal{M}$ shall denote the set of all routes $(lk) \in \mathcal{Z}$ which originate or terminate on some network i or cross this network. In other words, $\mathcal{H}_i \subseteq \mathcal{M}$ shall reflect all paths involving network i, or, equivalently, all subscriber types (lk) whose traffic is carried on network i.

Denote the number of subscribers of type (ij) to network i by N_{ij}. The total number of subscribers to network i is defined by

$$N_i := \sum_{j \in \mathcal{M}} N_{ij}.$$

55 These assumptions are not as restrictive as they may seem. A single subscriber who originates traffic along multiple paths may be modeled as several subscribers as long as there are no wealth effects and as long as cross-price effects between the traffic demands on different routes are zero. Wealth effects are eliminated by assumption given that, below, we will introduce quasilinear utility functions. The requirement of zero cross-price effects excludes the possibility that the traffic demands along different paths can be substituted. This requirement should generally be satisfied since the receiver of a message cannot easily be substituted. Unique routing fits the characteristic of the connectionless Internet traffic if $\mathcal{R}(ij)$ is allowed to change over time. See Lehr and Weiss ([142], p. 221).

The utility function of a subscriber type (ij) is assumed to be quasilinear:

$$U_{ij}(x_{ij}, Q_{ij}, b_{ij}) := u_{ij}(x_{ij}, Q_{ij}) + b_{ij}, \tag{4.6}$$

where x_{ij} denotes the number of data packets sent along a path (ij), where Q_{ij} indicates the experienced congestion along this path and where b_{ij} designates the money a subscriber of type (ij) disposes of to spend on all other goods apart from data transport along a path (ij). The matrix of demanded data transfers along a path (ij) shall be defined by $\mathbf{X} := (x_{ij})$ where $i, j \in \mathcal{M}$. We further assume that the utility is weakly increasing in the amount of data transferred and weakly decreasing in the level of congestion, i.e.,

$$\frac{\partial u_{ij}(\cdot)}{\partial x_{ij}} \geq 0 \quad \text{and} \quad \frac{\partial u_{ij}(\cdot)}{\partial Q_{ij}} \leq 0.$$

The level of congestion, Q_{ij}, is an inverse indicator for the QoS along a path (ij). We expect Q_{ij} to increase with the volume of data traffic and to decrease with the capacity of each network. The level of congestion is measured in terms of average delay which we define to be the sum of the (expected) average delay at each network interconnection point along a path (ij):

$$Q_{ij} := \sum_{k \in \mathcal{R}(ij)} D(Y_k),$$

where $D(Y_k)$ depicts the average delay of network $k \in \mathcal{R}(ij)$ and where $Y_k := X_k / K_k$ denotes network utilization which is itself defined as the aggregate traffic X_k on network k, to be defined down below, divided by the capacity K_k, where $X_k \leq K_k$. Packets may have to be dropped in order for the condition $X_k \leq K_k$ to hold. We further assume $D(\cdot)$ to be identical across networks and to be a continuous, monotonically increasing function of network utilization. We suppose that each network can be characterized by one level of delay.

Aggregate traffic on network i, X_i, consists of on-net and Internet data traffic. Whereas sender and receiver of on-net data traffic

$$X_i^{on} := N_{ii} x_{ii} \tag{4.7}$$

belong to the same network, they are distinct for Internet data traffic. Internet data traffic is composed of off-net and in-net data traffic, X^{off} and X^{in}, respectively. Off-net data traffic originates on network i and terminates on another network k:

$$X_i^{off} := \sum_{\substack{k \in \mathcal{M} \\ i \neq k}} N_{ik} x_{ik}. \tag{4.8}$$

In-net data traffic originates on some network k and transits or terminates on network i:

$$X_i^{in} := \sum_{\substack{(kj) \in \mathcal{H}_i \\ k \neq i}} N_{kj} x_{kj}. \tag{4.9}$$

Total traffic originating on network i is the sum of on-net and off-net traffic while the aggregate traffic carried on network i is given by

$$X_i := X_i^{on} + X_i^{off} + X_i^{in}. \tag{4.10}$$

Suppose that there are two-part tariffs with a fixed access charge to network i denoted by r_i and a variable congestion price p_{ij} per unit of data traffic transported along a path (ij). Then, the budget constraint of a subscriber type (ij) is given by

$$p_{ij} x_{ij} + r_i + b_{ij} = m_{ij},$$

where m_{ij} denotes the exogenous income of a subscriber type (ij). Solving the budget constraint for the numeraire b_{ij} and substituting the result for b_{ij} in the utility function (4.6) yields the unconstrained maximization problem of a subscriber type (ij):

$$\max_{x_{ij}} \quad u_{ij}(x_{ij}, Q_{ij}) + m_{ij} - p_{ij} x_{ij} - r_i. \tag{4.11}$$

The point where the function (4.11) reaches its maximum does not depend on m_{ij}.[56] Hence, to find the utility maximizing value x_{ij}^*, i.e.,

56 We assume all $u_{ij}(x_{ij}, Q_{ij})$ to be increasing and (strictly) concave in x_{ij} as well as to be decreasing and sufficiently (strictly) concave in Q_{ij} such that

the optimal number of data packets sent along a path (ij), rather than maximizing (4.11), we can as well maximize

$$\max_{x_{ij}} \quad u_{ij}(x_{ij}, Q_{ij}) - p_{ij}x_{ij} - r_i. \tag{4.12}$$

We go on working with (4.12).

We further assume voluntary participation. This means that the outside utility level, i.e., the utility level a consumer would obtain if she did not demand traffic type (ij), equals zero. Moreover, we suppose the sender to pay for the data traffic sent. Consequently, the equilibrium surplus realized by a consumer demanding traffic type (ij) satisfies

$$u_{ij}(x_{ij}^*, Q_{ij}) - p_{ij}x_{ij}^* - r_i \geq 0.$$

The costs of capacity provision of network i are depicted by the differentiable function $C_i(K_i)$ which we assume to be increasing and convex in K_i. For the moment, we neglect the possibility of settlement charges and define the profit functions of ISPs as the sum of the flat subscription fees and usage revenues net of network costs:

$$\Pi_i(x_{i1}, \ldots, x_{iM}, K_i) := N_i r_i + \sum_{j \in \mathcal{M}} N_{ij} p_{ij} x_{ij} - C_i(K_i).$$

We now analyze optimal congestion pricing and capacity expansion in a network environment with multiple competing ISPs where data packets potentially pass several networks on their path from the

---

(4.11) has a unique maximum. In other words, for small quantities of x_{ij} we suppose the direct effect of x_{ij} on utility to dominate while for large quantities of x_{ij} the indirect effect of x_{ij} over all Y_k, where $k \in \mathcal{R}(ij)$, and, with them, over Q_{ij} on utility shall dominate. That is, we suppose marginal utility of data transport to be decreasing in x_{ij} and marginal disutility of network utilization to be increasing in Q_{ij}.

origin to the destination computer. Social welfare for given levels of capacity K_i is defined as the sum of consumer and producer surplus:

$$W(\mathbf{X}) := \sum_{i\in\mathcal{M}}\sum_{j\in\mathcal{M}} N_{ij}(u_{ij}(x_{ij}, Q_{ij}) - p_{ij}x_{ij} - r_i) + \sum_{i\in\mathcal{M}} \Pi_i(\cdot), \quad (4.13)$$

$$\text{where} \quad Q_{ij} := \sum_{k\in\mathcal{R}(ij)} D(Y_k) \quad \text{and} \quad Y_k := \frac{X_k}{K_k}.$$

In order to determine the social optimum, the welfare function (4.13) must be maximized with respect to each x_{ij}. For this purpose, note that the increase in congestion Q_{ij} along a path (ij) generated by a marginal increase in data traffic demand along this path is given by

$$\begin{aligned}\frac{\partial Q_{ij}}{\partial x_{ij}} &= \frac{\partial\left(\sum_{k\in\mathcal{R}(ij)} D(Y_k)\right)}{\partial x_{ij}} \\ &= \sum_{k\in\mathcal{R}(ij)}\left(\frac{dD(Y_k)}{dY_k}\frac{\partial Y_k}{\partial x_{ij}}\right) \\ &= \sum_{k\in\mathcal{R}(ij)}\left(\frac{dD(Y_k)}{dY_k}\frac{1}{K_k}\right). \end{aligned} \quad (4.14)$$

A first-order condition for the social optimum for each type of traffic (ij) is given by[57]

$$\begin{aligned}\frac{\partial W(\mathbf{X})}{\partial x_{ij}} &= N_{ij}\frac{\partial u_{ij}}{\partial x_{ij}} + \sum_{\substack{(lk)\in\mathcal{Z}\\(lk)\neq(ij)}}\left(N_{lk}\frac{\partial u_{lk}}{\partial Q_{lk}}\frac{\partial Q_{lk}}{\partial x_{ij}}\right) + N_{ij}\frac{\partial u_{ij}}{\partial Q_{ij}}\frac{\partial Q_{ij}}{\partial x_{ij}} \\ &\quad - N_{ij}p_{ij} + N_{ij}p_{ij} \\ &= N_{ij}\frac{\partial u_{ij}}{\partial x_{ij}} + \sum_{\substack{(lk)\in\mathcal{Z}\\(lk)\neq(ij)}}\left(N_{lk}\frac{\partial u_{lk}}{\partial Q_{lk}}\frac{\partial Q_{lk}}{\partial x_{ij}}\right) + N_{ij}\frac{\partial u_{ij}}{\partial Q_{ij}}\frac{\partial Q_{ij}}{\partial x_{ij}} = 0. \end{aligned} \quad (4.15)$$

57 By our assumptions in footnote 56 about the shape of $u_{ij}(x_{ij}, Q_{ij})$ all addends of the social welfare function (4.13) are concave in x_{ij}. Hence, social surplus – the sum of concave functions – is concave. We can conclude that condition (4.15) indeed identifies a maximum.

The second term on the right-hand side of condition (4.15) reflects the negative externalities in form of additional congestion imposed by subscribers of type (ij) on subscriber types other than (ij) whose traffic is carried on a network belonging to path (ij). The third term on the right-hand side of expression (4.15) represents the marginal costs type (ij) subscribers impose on each other. Condition (4.15) states that type (ij) consumers should use the system until marginal utility from sending data traffic equals marginal costs created through their traffic.

In order to force a type (ij) subscriber to internalize all the negative externalities caused by her, congestion prices should amount to

$$p_{ij}^* := -\sum_{\substack{(lk)\in\mathcal{Z}\\(lk)\neq(ij)}} \left(N_{lk} \frac{\partial u_{lk}}{\partial Q_{lk}} \frac{\partial Q_{lk}}{\partial x_{ij}} \right) - (N_{ij}-1) \frac{\partial u_{ij}}{\partial Q_{ij}} \frac{\partial Q_{ij}}{\partial x_{ij}},$$

where the added term $\frac{\partial u_{ij}}{\partial Q_{ij}} \frac{\partial Q_{ij}}{\partial x_{ij}}$ reflects the own, or direct, costs of a user type (ij). Note that for large N_{ij} these direct costs of a user type (ij) are negligible relative the marginal costs imposed on all other type (ij) subscribers. To simplify notation, we assume N_{ij} to be sufficiently large such that we can ignore these direct costs of usage of a type (ij) subscriber. Therefore, we go on working with the congestion price

$$p_{ij}^* := -\sum_{\substack{(lk)\in\mathcal{Z}\\(lk)\neq(ij)}} \left(N_{lk} \frac{\partial u_{lk}}{\partial Q_{lk}} \frac{\partial Q_{lk}}{\partial x_{ij}} \right) - N_{ij} \frac{\partial u_{ij}}{\partial Q_{ij}} \frac{\partial Q_{ij}}{\partial x_{ij}}. \tag{4.16}$$

Recall expression (4.14), denote the marginal increase in delay by $D_{Y_n} := \frac{dD(Y_n)}{dY_n}$, denominate the marginal disutility of congestion with $u_{lk}^Q := \frac{\partial u_{lk}}{\partial Q_{lk}}$, and rearrange expression (4.16) to obtain

$$p_{ij}^* := -\sum_{n\in\mathcal{R}(ij)} \frac{D_{Y_n}}{K_n} \left(\sum_{(lk)\in\mathcal{H}_n} N_{lk} u_{lk}^Q \right). \tag{4.17}$$

Imagine the simple case with only two networks, i.e., $M = 2$. We can then distinguish between four types of data traffic: On-net traffic (11) and (22) as well as Internet traffic (12) and (21). According to expression (4.17), the optimal congestion prices are

$$\begin{aligned}
p_{11}^{*} &= -\frac{D_{Y_1}}{K_1}(N_{11}u_{11}^{Q} + N_{12}u_{12}^{Q} + N_{21}u_{21}^{Q}), \\
p_{22}^{*} &= -\frac{D_{Y_2}}{K_2}(N_{22}u_{22}^{Q} + N_{12}u_{12}^{Q} + N_{21}u_{21}^{Q}), \\
p_{12}^{*} &= -\frac{D_{Y_1}}{K_1}(N_{11}u_{11}^{Q} + N_{12}u_{12}^{Q} + N_{21}u_{21}^{Q}) \\
&\quad - \frac{D_{Y_2}}{K_2}(N_{22}u_{22}^{Q} + N_{12}u_{12}^{Q} + N_{21}u_{21}^{Q}) = p_{21}^{*} = p_{11}^{*} + p_{22}^{*}.
\end{aligned}$$

We can conclude that optimal congestion prices for Internet data traffic equal the sum of the congestion prices for on-net traffic of each network along the path. The same result can be obtained if there are M networks: Then, the optimal congestion price along a path (ij) is the sum of the congestion prices for on-net traffic levied by each network which belongs to the subset $\mathcal{R}(ij)$.

The result comes from our assumption that each network can be characterized by one level of delay. Each packet traversing the respective network, independently of its direction, causes a certain level of congestion externalities, reflected in the optimal congestion price for on-net traffic. Hence, each packet is charged the sum of on-net congestion prices encountered on the path from the sender to the receiver.

Our conclusion satisfies intuition: While Internet data traffic congests all networks along the path, on-net data traffic only loads the originating network. Consequently, it seems sensible that Internet data traffic is charged a price equal to the sum of the congestion prices for on-net traffic, levied by each network belonging to the subset $\mathcal{R}(ij)$, while on-net data traffic is only charged the congestion price of the originating network. The optimal solution thus requires Internet traffic to be priced at least as high compared to on-net traffic since the former potentially causes more congestion.

We now examine when capacity expansion in each network is desirable from the welfare theoretic point of view. To determine the welfare maximizing levels of capacity for each of the M networks we differentiate maximal welfare

$$\overline{W}(K_1, \ldots, K_M) := \max_{x_{ij}} W(\mathbf{X})$$

with respect to the capacity of the corresponding network. When determining conditions of first order we can ignore indirect effects of K_i on the maximal welfare over x_{ij} due to the envelope theorem. In other words, terms involving $\frac{\partial x_{ij}}{\partial K_i}$ drop out due to condition (4.15) which must hold for each x_{ij}. Hence, a necessary condition for welfare maximization for each network K_i is given by:[58]

$$\frac{\partial \overline{W}(\cdot)}{\partial K_i} = \sum_{(lk) \in \mathcal{H}_i} \left(N_{lk} u_{lk}^Q \frac{\partial Q_{lk}}{\partial K_i} \right) - \frac{dC_i(K_i)}{dK_i} = 0. \tag{4.18}$$

Note that we have

$$\begin{aligned}
\frac{\partial Q_{lk}}{\partial K_i} &= \frac{\partial \left(\sum_{n \in \mathcal{R}(ij)} D(Y_n) \right)}{\partial K_i} \\
&= \sum_{n \in \mathcal{R}(ij)} \left(\frac{dD(Y_n)}{dY_n} \frac{\partial Y_n}{\partial K_i} \right) \\
&= \frac{dD(Y_i)}{dY_i} \left(-\frac{X_i}{K_i^2} \right) \\
&= -D_{Y_i} \frac{X_i}{K_i^2}.
\end{aligned}$$

58 We suppose a maximum to exist which is the case if the mapping $\overline{W}(\cdot)$ is continuous and if the domains of all K_i are compact, i.e., bounded and closed, where the lower bounds are at $K_i = X_i$ for all K_i. Also, we assume the Hessian matrix of the welfare function $\overline{W}(\cdot)$ to be negative semidefinite. This second order condition is satisfied if all $u_{ij}(x_{ij}, Q_{ij})$, where $Q_{ij} := \sum_{k \in \mathcal{R}(ij)} D(Y_k)$ and $Y_k := X_k / K_k$, are increasing and concave in K_i. Moreover, by assumption, all cost functions are convex in K_i such that all terms $-C_i(K_i)$ are concave. Then, maximal welfare – the sum of concave functions – is concave.

Therefore, we can rewrite condition (4.18) as follows:

$$\frac{\partial \overline{W}(\cdot)}{\partial K_i} = -\frac{X_i D_{Y_i}}{K_i^2}\left(\sum_{(lk)\in\mathcal{H}_i} N_{lk} u_{lk}^Q\right) - \frac{dC_i(K_i)}{dK_i} = 0. \tag{4.19}$$

Condition (4.19) can be expressed as

$$-\frac{D_{Y_i}}{K_i}\left(\sum_{(lk)\in\mathcal{H}_i} N_{lk} u_{lk}^Q\right) = \frac{dC_i(K_i)}{dK_i}\frac{K_i}{X_i}.$$

Compare the left-hand side of the above result to expression (4.17) to conclude that

$$p_{ii}^* = -\frac{D_{Y_i}}{K_i}\left(\sum_{(lk)\in\mathcal{H}_i} N_{lk} u_{lk}^Q\right) = \frac{dC_i(K_i)}{dK_i}\frac{K_i}{X_i}. \tag{4.20}$$

This is the same result as presented by expression (3.31) in Section 3.3.1: Equation (4.20) states that at equilibrium optimal on-net congestion charges can be calculated based on local information only, without knowledge of the utility function of subscribers.

Substituting the price p_{ii}^* for the corresponding term in condition (4.19) yields

$$\frac{\partial \overline{W}(\cdot)}{\partial K_i} = p_{ii}^* \frac{X_i}{K_i} - \frac{dC_i(K_i)}{dK_i} = 0. \tag{4.21}$$

We can conclude that as long as network i charges the congestion price (4.20) for each packet carried its total congestion revenues properly signal possible needs for capacity expansion. Capacity expansion is socially desirable if and only if congestion revenues exceed the value of the capacity of a certain network expressed in terms of marginal costs of capacity:

$$\frac{\partial \overline{W}(\cdot)}{\partial K_i} = p_{ii}^* X_i - \frac{dC_i(K_i)}{dK_i} K_i > 0.$$

This is the same result we obtained in expression (3.32) in Section 3.3.1. The comments on the shape of the cost curve concerning cost recovery made in Section 3.3.1 apply in this context as well. Again, as already mentioned above, we assume marginal costs of capacity to be non-decreasing.

So far, in the above analysis, we have not introduced settlement fees. We will see that the optimal pricing solution requires a settlement process between providers for two reasons: First, networks have to share information on efficient local congestion prices such that the originating networks can know what price to set for an end-to-end service in order to bill the senders for the transport services. A settlement process that requires networks to bill each other for terminating data traffic offers one mechanism to convey this information. Second, it will be shown below that with appropriate settlements the private optimum in a competitive market corresponds to the social optimum.

Lehr and Weiss ([142], pp. 224 f.) propose two possibilities for billing subscribers: The first billing solution is a 'pay-as-you-go'[59] scheme where ISPs directly charge and bill senders with congestion prices. Alternatively, the originating network could bill each subscriber. To set the appropriate price the originating ISP i needs information about the sum of congestion prices along the rest of the path, i.e., about $(p^*_{ij} - p^*_{ii})$.

If at most two networks, for example, network 1 and network 2, are involved in data conveyance the networks could bill each other for traffic termination: Imagine that traffic demand is originated on network 1. Then, network 1 would charge its subscribers of type (12) a price equal to $(p^*_{11} + p^*_{22})$ per data packet and pay network 2 the price p^*_{22} per unit of terminated data traffic.

If there are more than two networks involved in the delivery of data traffic the originating network could calculate p^*_{ij} directly provided that networks continuously update each other with information about their congestion prices. One mechanism to convey the necessary information is a settlement process which requires networks to bill each other for traffic termination. In this case, the originating network does not have to know the congestion status of all other networks involved in data delivery, but only the total congestion price charged

59 Lehr and Weiss ([142], p. 224).

at the next point of interconnection, which is the sum of congestion charges of all networks involved in terminating the data traffic. If, for example, a data packet passes the networks 1, 2, and 3, network 2 charges provider 1 the price $(p_{22}^* + p_{33}^*)$. This allows provider 1 to charge the final price to its subscribers of type (13) without knowing how the sum of p_{22}^* and p_{33}^* is split between terminating ISPs.

We will now extend the analysis of Lehr and Weiss [142] by examining, by analogy with Section 3.3.1, whether congestion pricing and capacity expansion in a competitive market correspond to the social optimum. Therefore, we introduce the following assumptions: Suppose the ISP market to be competitive. Each provider i owns a network with capacity K_i and carries X_i packets, where $i = 1, \ldots, M$. The price per packet on network i is given by p_{ii}. Each provider i charges a user type (ij) the two-part tariff

$$T_{ij} := r_i + p_{ij}x_{ij}, \quad \text{where} \quad p_{ij} := \sum_{k \in \mathcal{R}(ij)} p_{kk}, \tag{4.22}$$

i.e., where the variable price component equals the sum of prices for on-net traffic of each network along the path (ij). Retail revenues from on-net traffic of provider i, by definition (4.7), are given by

$$p_{ii}N_{ii}x_{ii} = p_{ii}X_i^{on}.$$

Retail revenues from off-net traffic amount to

$$\sum_{\substack{k \in \mathcal{M} \\ i \neq k}} p_{ik}N_{ik}x_{ik}.$$

We suppose that ISP i pays settlements to other providers for transit or terminating services of data traffic originated on network i. By definition (4.8), these settlements equal

$$\sum_{\substack{k \in \mathcal{M} \\ i \neq k}} (p_{ik} - p_{ii})N_{ik}x_{ik} = \sum_{\substack{k \in \mathcal{M} \\ i \neq k}} p_{ik}N_{ik}x_{ik} - p_{ii}X_i^{off}.$$

Provider i receives settlements from other providers for terminating or transiting data traffic originated on another network which, by definition (4.9), are given by

$$p_{ii} \sum_{\substack{(kj) \in \mathcal{H}_i \\ k \neq i}} N_{kj} x_{kj} = p_{ii} X_i^{in}.$$

We can conclude that the total retail revenues derived from data conveyance of each ISP i, by definition (4.10), amount to

$$p_{ii} X_i^{on} + \sum_{\substack{k \in \mathcal{M} \\ i \neq k}} p_{ik} N_{ik} x_{ik} - \sum_{\substack{k \in \mathcal{M} \\ i \neq k}} p_{ik} N_{ik} x_{ik} + p_{ii} X_i^{off} + p_{ii} X_i^{in} = p_{ii} X_i.$$

Then, the profits of a representative provider i can be written as

$$\Pi_i(X_i, K_i) := N_i r_i + p_{ii} X_i - C_i(K_i).$$

There are many providers with possibly different utilization levels Y_i and, therefore, with different offers of QoS. A two-part tariff of a representative provider with utilization Y_i shall be given by

$$[p_{ij}(D(Y_i)), r_i(D(Y_i))], \tag{4.23}$$

where $p_{ij}(D(Y_i)) := \sum_{k \in \mathcal{R}(ij)} p_{kk}(D(Y_k))$. We express the variable price $p_{ij}(\cdot)$, levied by a provider i, solely as a function of the delay on network i since this provider cannot influence the utilization levels Y_k, where $k \neq i$, of all other networks involved in data delivery. As above, we assume the average delay function $D(\cdot)$ to be identical across networks. Moreover, we assume that

$$\frac{dp_{ii}}{dD} \frac{dD}{dY_i}, \quad \frac{dr_i}{dD} \frac{dD}{dY_i} < 0.$$

That is, we suppose that the higher the average delay of network i, the lower the QoS provided and, given a fixed delay on all other networks $k \in \mathcal{R}(ij)$, $k \neq i$, the lower the two-part tariff. The two-part tariff (4.23) is determined by the competitive market and is therefore outside of the control of the individual ISPs. For simplicity, suppose that each provider offers only one class of service, i.e., one level of Y_i. Moreover, subscribers are assumed to be both price and quality takers. This means that the amount of traffic sent by one user has no influence on the price.

We first consider the maximization problem of consumers. Consumers must decide which network to choose and how much to use it. The utility maximization problem for a consumer type (ij) is given by

$$\max_{x_{ij},Y_i} \quad u_{ij}\left(x_{ij}, Q_{ij}\right) - x_{ij} \sum_{k \in \mathcal{R}(ij)} p_{kk}(D(Y_k)) - r_i(D(Y_i)),$$

where $Q_{ij} := \sum_{k \in \mathcal{R}(ij)} D(Y_k)$. Given our assumption about subscribers being quality takers we can ignore the effect of x_{ij} on Y_i when solving the utility maximization problem. First-order conditions with respect to x_{ij} and Y_i are[60]

$$\frac{\partial u_{ij}}{\partial x_{ij}} - \sum_{i \in \mathcal{R}(ij)} p_{ii} = 0, \qquad (4.24)$$

$$\left(\frac{\partial u_{ij}}{\partial Q_{ij}} \frac{dD}{dY_i}\right) - \left(\frac{dp_{ii}}{dD} \frac{dD}{dY_i}\right) x_{ij} - \left(\frac{dr_i}{dD} \frac{dD}{dY_i}\right) = 0. \qquad (4.25)$$

Equation (4.24) says that each consumer uses the Internet until the marginal utility of packet transfer equals its total price. Equation (4.25) shows that a subscriber's choice of network utilization satisfies the condition that the marginal disutility of increased network utilization must be compensated by reduced expenditures

$$\left(\frac{dp_{ii}}{dD} \frac{dD}{dY_i}\right) x_{ij} + \left(\frac{dr_i}{dD} \frac{dD}{dY_i}\right).$$

60 We assume the Hessian matrix of the utility function of a consumer type (ij) to be negative semidefinite. In particular, this sufficient condition for a maximum requires marginal utility of network usage to be non-increasing and marginal disutility of network utilization to be non-decreasing. The former requirement essentially corresponds to Gossen's First Law introduced in Section 3.3.1.

Adding up condition (4.25) over the all users whose traffic is carried on network i yields

$$\sum_{(lk)\in\mathcal{H}_i} N_{lk}\left(\frac{\partial u_{lk}}{\partial Q_{lk}}\frac{dD}{dY_i}\right)-\left(\frac{dp_{ii}}{dD}\frac{dD}{dY_i}\right)X_i-N_i\left(\frac{dr_i}{dD}\frac{dD}{dY_i}\right)=0,$$

or, equivalently,

$$\sum_{(lk)\in\mathcal{H}_i} N_{lk}\left(\frac{\partial u_{lk}}{\partial Q_{lk}}\frac{dD}{dY_i}\right)=\left(\frac{dp_{ii}}{dD}\frac{dD}{dY_i}\right)X_i+N_i\left(\frac{dr_i}{dD}\frac{dD}{dY_i}\right). \quad (4.26)$$

Consider now the maximization problem of ISPs in this competitive market. Providers maximize their profits with respect to X_i, i.e., the amount of aggregate traffic carried, and with respect to the capacity K_i:

$$\max_{X_i,K_i} \quad N_i r_i(D(Y_i))+p_{ii}(D(Y_i))X_i-C_i(K_i), \quad \text{where} \quad Y_i:=\frac{X_i}{K_i}.$$

First-order conditions with respect to X_i and K_i are[61]

$$\begin{aligned}\frac{N_i}{K_i}\left(\frac{dr_i}{dD}\frac{dD}{dY_i}\right)+p_{ii}+\left(\frac{dp_{ii}}{dD}\frac{dD}{dY_i}\right)\frac{X_i}{K_i} &= 0,\\ -N_i\left(\frac{dr_i}{dD}\frac{dD}{dY_i}\right)\frac{X_i}{K_i^2}-\left(\frac{dp_{ii}}{dD}\frac{dD}{dY_i}\right)\left(\frac{X_i}{K_i}\right)^2-\frac{dC_i(K_i)}{dK_i} &= 0.\end{aligned}$$

By factoring out the ratios $1/K_i$ and $-X_i/K_i^2$, respectively, and rearranging terms we obtain

$$p_{ii}+\frac{1}{K_i}\left(\left(\frac{dp_{ii}}{dD}\frac{dD}{dY_i}\right)X_i+N_i\left(\frac{dr_i}{dD}\frac{dD}{dY_i}\right)\right) = 0, \quad (4.27)$$

$$-\frac{X_i}{K_i^2}\left(\left(\frac{dp_{ii}}{dD}\frac{dD}{dY_i}\right)X_i+N_i\left(\frac{dr_i}{dD}\frac{dD}{dY_i}\right)\right) = \frac{dC_i(K_i)}{dK_i}. \quad (4.28)$$

61 We assume the Hessian matrix of the profit function to be negative semidefinite. In particular, this requires marginal profits to be non-increasing in both X_i and K_i.

Substituting the left-hand side of formula (4.26) for the corresponding term in expression (4.27) and rearranging terms yields

$$p_{ii} = \frac{1}{K_i} \sum_{(lk) \in \mathcal{H}_i} N_{lk} \left(\frac{\partial u_{lk}}{\partial Q_{lk}} \frac{dD}{dY_i} \right), \tag{4.29}$$

or, equivalently,

$$p_{ii} = -\frac{D_{Y_i}}{K_i} \sum_{(lk) \in \mathcal{H}_i} N_{lk} u_{lk}^{Q}. \tag{4.30}$$

By comparing expression (4.30) to formula (4.20) we find that the competitive price of network i results in the optimal degree of congestion, i.e., that the competitive price equals the optimal price. Moreover, solving condition (4.27) for p_{ii}, substituting p_{ii} for the corresponding term in condition (4.28), and rearranging terms yields

$$p_{ii} = \frac{dC_i(K_i)}{dK_i} \frac{K_i}{X_i}. \tag{4.31}$$

Accordingly, just as the optimal price, the competitive price can be calculated based on local information only, without knowledge of the utility function of subscribers. Moreover, view condition (4.21) to note that the competitive price engenders the optimal level of capacity.

We can conclude that in a competitive market where a two-part tariff is charged for Internet access and usage, both the equilibrium price and the equilibrium capacity maximize social surplus. Since the competitive price engenders the optimal level of capacity this price must give correct monetary incentives for capacity expansion. To make this statement more explicit, by analogy with Section 3.3.1, we will now consider two different scenarios where a competitive ISP has to decide whether to add capacity.

In the first scenario, assume that ISP i, which has to decide whether to invest in additional capacity, has already maximized its profits with respect to X_i and, therefore, takes X_i as given. Then, the only choice variable of the ISP is K_i. If ISP i increases capacity, network utilization decreases and, in consequence, this ISP can charge a higher price. By the two-part tariff (4.22), the extra amount ISP i can charge a subscriber type (ij) by a marginal increase in K_i is

$$\frac{dT_{ij}(\cdot)}{dK_i} = \left(\frac{dr_i}{dD} \frac{dD}{dY_i} + \frac{dp_{ii}}{dD} \frac{dD}{dY_i} x_{ij} \right) \frac{dY_i}{dK_i}.$$

Using equation (4.25) and observing that

$$\frac{dY_i}{dK_i} = -\frac{X_i}{K_i^2}$$

we obtain

$$\frac{dT_{ij}(\cdot)}{dK_i} = -\frac{1}{K_i} \left(\frac{\partial u_{ij}}{\partial Q_{ij}} \frac{dD}{dY_i} \right) \frac{X_i}{K_i}.$$

Summing the right-hand side of this equation over all subscribers whose traffic is carried on network i yields

$$-\frac{1}{K_i} \sum_{(lk) \in \mathcal{H}_i} N_{lk} \left(\frac{\partial u_{lk}}{\partial Q_{lk}} \frac{dD}{dY_i} \right) \frac{X_i}{K_i}.$$

Substituting the price (4.29) for the corresponding term in the above expression yields total additional revenues from capacity expansion which amount to

$$p_{ii} \frac{X_i}{K_i}.$$

These revenues cover costs of expanding capacity if

$$p_{ii} \frac{X_i}{K_i} - \frac{dC_i(K_i)}{dK_i} = p_{ii} \frac{X_i}{K_i} - \frac{dC_i(K_i)}{dK_i} \geq 0.$$

Comparing this expression to equation (4.21) and bearing in mind that, according to expressions (4.30) and (4.20), we have $p_{ii} = p_{ii}^*$, we find that a competitive provider expands its capacity if and only if it is socially optimal to do so. Profits increase if and only if net social benefits increase.

In the second scenario, ISP i keeps its price offering

$$[p_{ij}(D(Y_i)), r_i(D(Y_i)]$$

at a fixed level and expands its capacity by ΔK (> 0). In a competitive market environment the price offering can only be kept constant if, given a fixed delay on all other networks $k \in \mathcal{R}(ij)$, Y_i remains constant. With X_i^* and K_i^* as optimal values of an initial equilibrium, by definition of Y_i, we have

$$Y_i^* := \frac{X_i^*}{K_i^*}.$$

In order to keep Y_i^* fixed at $Y = Y_i^*$ and, therefore, to keep the two-part tariff constant the additional number of packets must satisfy

$$\Delta X_i = Y_i^* \Delta K_i.$$

Increase in profits amounts to

$$p_{ii} Y_i \Delta K_i - \frac{dC_i(K_i)}{dK_i} \Delta K_i = \left(p_{ii} \frac{X_i}{K_i} - \frac{dC_i(K_i)}{dK_i} \right) \Delta K_i.$$

Once again, we find that capacity expansion is optimal if and only if it increases profits. We can draw the same conclusion as in Section 3.3.1, namely, that a competitive provider expands its capacity if and only if it is socially optimal to do so. Hence, efficient congestion prices and settlements in the competitive market give correct monetary incentives for capacity expansion.

To summarize, the rationale behind settlement processes is twofold: First, settlements are an instrument to reveal the necessary congestion pricing information of different networks such that the originating networks can calculate the final optimal congestion price charged to the sender. Second, appropriate settlements make the decentralized private optimum correspond to the social optimum.

In this section we have analyzed how optimal congestion pricing introduced in Section 3.3.1 can be extended to optimal settlement payments. It has been shown that optimal congestion prices for Internet data traffic equal the sum of the congestion prices for on-net traffic of each network along the path from the sender to the receiver.

Interconnection congestion pricing is compatible with retail congestion pricing if each individual provider can be characterized by one specific level of delay, or, congestion. Also, interconnection congestion pricing matches the smart market approach. To see this recall that prices obtained by Vickrey auctions reflect marginal congestion costs.

To conclude this section we elaborate some points of criticism of congestion pricing already mentioned in Section 3.3.1: It has been noted above that, at the optimum, local congestion prices can be calculated based solely on local demand and cost information.[62] However, in practice it may be difficult to calculate the marginal costs of capacity necessary to determine the optimal congestion prices.[63] A further point of criticism of the proposed concept concerns the lack of price transparency. Recall that users wish to know the congestion price before sending a data packet. This requires all price information to be available to all users at all times. Therefore, the paths packets take have to be known in advance. This is problematic in a connectionless environment such as the Internet where packets of a certain data stream can follow different paths to the destination. A smart market where each router on the path subtracts its price from the bid in the header of winning packets may mitigate this problem. That way, the maximum willingness to pay cannot be exceeded by the cumulated congestion prices charged along the path. A final criticism of congestion pricing for interconnected networks concerns the fact that networks with market power may emerge, as already mentioned in Section 4.1.3. In this case, pricing and decisions to interconnect or to expand network capacity can be biased as a consequence of extracting rents.[64]

4.2.2 Extra-Capacity Pricing

Little and Wright [143] introduce welfare maximizing settlement payments in a model of horizontal product differentiation with two competing providers. Competition between providers takes place through two-part tariffs. We will start our analysis with setting up the model

62 See expression (4.20).
63 See Lehr and Weiss ([142], p. 228).
64 See Lehr and Weiss ([142], p. 228).

of network competition. Then, welfare maximizing prices and capacity will be determined. It will be shown that optimal usage-sensitive prices exceed marginal costs of data transport of each provider. These prices take into consideration that additional usage requires appropriate capacity expansion in order to prevent congestion. The optimal level of infrastructure provision frees the network from congestion. It will be shown that an efficient outcome can be realized if a settlement regime is implemented where net providers of capacity charge net demanders of capacity for the use of their network at a rate equal to the incremental costs of the provided infrastructure. Therefore, in this work, we will call the interconnection pricing proposal 'extra-capacity pricing'. Below, we will also find that if traffic flows are approximately balanced there are no settlement flows ex post.

Imagine two competing ISPs, ISP 1 and ISP 2. They both charge two-part tariffs composed of a price p_i per unit of data traffic and of a fixed fee, or rental, r_i, $i = 1, 2$. Both ISPs provide an amount K_1 and K_2, respectively, of infrastructure or capacity. Hence, a total capacity of $(K_1 + K_2)$ is available to a subscriber. To provide the capacity K_i, ISP i incurs the costs $C_i(K_i)$, where $C_i'(K_i) > 0$ and $C_i''(K_i) > 0$. The costs $C_i(K_i)$ include the costs of laying cable or buying satellite bandwidth to handle the average bandwidth requirements of customers as well as the costs of routers. Each ISP incurs fixed costs f per customer. The fixed costs f include the costs of connecting a new customer to the modem pool at a POP, adding server capacity for email and caching, as well as the costs of billing and customer service. Moreover, we assume each customer to generate marginal costs c which are the costs an additional unit of traffic imposes on the network. Given that, in equilibrium, the network is free of congestion, marginal costs c are likely to be negligible. Following Little and Wright [143] we include these costs nevertheless in order to emphasize, at the end of this section, the compatibility of extra-capacity pricing at the interconnection level with peak-load pricing at the retail level.

Suppose a fixed number of subscribers normalized to 1. Each subscriber to ISP i demands x_i units, megabytes, for example, of data transfer. The utility of subscribers is represented by the following quasilinear utility function:

$$U(x_i, \theta_i) := u(x_i) + \theta_i, \tag{4.32}$$

where the utility associated with usage, $u(x_i)$, is identical across subscribers and where the taste parameter θ_i reflects the benefits of belonging to a particular network that relate to factors other than the provision of Internet access.[65]

To specify θ_i, the model of the so-called linear city, introduced by Hotelling [109], is adopted.[66] The linear city is depicted in Figure 4.2. The ISPs shall be located at opposite ends of the unit interval [0, 1].

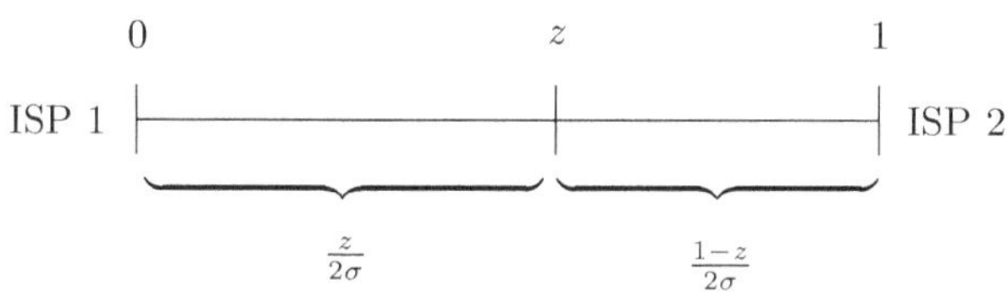

Figure 4.2: Linear city
Source: Own illustration.

Moreover, subscriber types, reflected by different values of z, are assumed to be distributed uniformly along this interval. The value z on the unit interval determines the most preferred network type for each type of subscriber. As will be made clear below, σ reflects the substitutability between the networks. A higher σ means a stronger substitutability between the networks. Subscribers incur a utility loss $\frac{1}{2\sigma}$ per unit of distance between their most preferred network type and

65 As $u(x_i)$ is the same across users the marginal utility $u'(x_i)$ is the same for all subscribers. In this case, the optimal choice of ISPs is a two-part tariff structure, where the variable price component reflects marginal costs and where the rental is set such that all consumer surplus is extracted. See Laffont et al. ([136], p. 20).

66 See Tirole ([239], pp. 279–282) for an illustration of the linear city model of Hotelling.

the location of the ISPs. Hence, a subscriber of type z incurs costs equal to $\frac{z}{2\sigma}$ and $\frac{1-z}{2\sigma}$ when she chooses ISP 1 and ISP 2, respectively.

The utility loss $\frac{1}{2\sigma}$ per unit of distance measures the relative importance of non-price competition, i.e., the horizontal product differentiation. One source of horizontal differentiation is the mode of Internet access.[67] If $\frac{1}{2\sigma} = 0$, i.e., if σ, reflecting the substitutability between networks, tends to infinity, only price differentials matter and Bertrand competition[68] prevails. The higher $\frac{1}{2\sigma}$, i.e., the lower the substitutability between the networks, the better the possibility of an ISP to successfully increase its price above that of its competitor without dropping out of the market. Hence, increasing substitutability implies a growing influence of price differences on the size of the market shares.

Suppose that subscribers to ISP 1 of type $z \in [0, 1]$ obtain a taste benefit

$$\theta_1(z) := \frac{\beta}{2\sigma} + \frac{(1-z)}{2\sigma}. \tag{4.33}$$

Subscribers to ISP 2 of type $z \in [0, 1]$ receive a taste benefit proportional to z:

$$\theta_2(z) := \frac{z}{2\sigma}. \tag{4.34}$$

The expressions $\frac{1-z}{2\sigma}$ and $\frac{z}{2\sigma}$ reflect the avoided utility losses if a subscriber of type z chooses ISP 1 instead of ISP 2 and ISP 2 instead of ISP 1, respectively. In other words, $\frac{1-z}{2\sigma}$ and $\frac{z}{2\sigma}$ represent the avoided utility losses from getting a service which does not exactly fit the subscriber's ideal type of service.

To introduce some asymmetry into the model of horizontal product differentiation, the parameter $\beta \in [-1, 1]$ is added to the benefits of belonging to ISP 1. The parameter β reflects the vertical Internet access differentiation. It can be interpreted as a measure of brand loyalty for network 1 or may reflect value added services or the QoS

67 Consider Section 2.1.3.

68 Bertrand competition refers to a game with simultaneous moves where players seek to maximize their profits using the prices as their strategic variables. If the offered goods are perfect substitutes, equilibrium prices equal marginal costs and there is no profit opportunity. See Tirole ([239], pp. 209–211).

provided by ISP 1. With equal prices and $\beta > 0$, more customers prefer ISP 1. With equal prices and $\beta < 0$ more subscribers choose ISP 2. If $\beta = 0$ networks are symmetric from the subscribers' perspective. If $\beta = 1$, we have

$$\theta_1(z) = \frac{2 - z}{2\sigma}.$$

Then, since $z \in [0, 1]$, all subscribers, regardless of their type, prefer ISP 1 or are just indifferent between the two providers such as consumers of type $z = 1$. If $\beta = -1$, we obtain

$$\theta_1(z) = -\frac{z}{2\sigma}.$$

In this case, all subscribers, regardless of their type, prefer ISP 2 or are just indifferent between the two providers such as consumers of type $z = 0$.

Subscribers maximize their utility function (4.32) with respect to x_i subject to their budget constraint $r_i + p_i x_i + \theta_i = m$, where m denotes the exogenous income and where θ_i is considered as the consumption of the numeraire good whose price equals 1. Solving the budget constraint for the numeraire θ_i and substituting the result for θ_i in the utility function (4.32) yields the unconstrained maximization problem of subscribers to ISP i:

$$\max_{x_i} \quad u(x_i) + m - r_i - p_i x_i. \tag{4.35}$$

The point where the function (4.35) reaches its maximum whether depends on the budget m nor on the rental r_i. Hence, we can define the indirect utility function $v(p_i)$ associated with network usage as

$$v(p_i) := \max_{x_i} \; u(x_i) - p_i x_i.$$

We denote the Marshallian demand functions, i.e., the utility maximizing demand functions, of each subscriber to ISP i by $x_i^* - x(p_i)$. The demand for data transfer is assumed to be decreasing in p_i: $x'(p_i) < 0$. Further, net surplus w_i of subscribers to ISP i shall be given by

$$w_i := v(p_i) - r_i. \tag{4.36}$$

We will now determine the market shares s and $(1-s)$ of ISP 1 and ISP 2, respectively. For this purpose, note that, since z is uniformly distributed on the interval $[0, 1]$, the market share s of ISP 1 equals z: $s = z$. A potential customer is indifferent in her choice between the two ISPs if

$$v(p_1) - r_1 + \theta_1(z) = v(p_2) - r_2 + \theta_2(z), \tag{4.37}$$

where $\theta_1(z)$ and $\theta_2(z)$ are defined by (4.33) and (4.34). Then, by solving for z, we obtain the market share s:

$$s(w_1, w_2) = \frac{1}{2} + \frac{\beta}{2} + \sigma(w_1 - w_2). \tag{4.38}$$

If there is no brand loyalty, i.e., if $\beta = 0$, and if two-part tariffs offered are identical, i.e., if $p_1 = p_2$ and $r_1 = r_2$, the two ISPs share the market equally. If $p_1 = p_2$, $r_1 = r_2$, and $\beta > 0$, ISP 1 has a larger market share than its competitor. The market share of ISP 1 is also larger compared to ISP 2 if $p_1 < p_2$, $r_1 = r_2$, and $\beta = 0$.

The profit functions of the providers are defined as

$$\begin{aligned} \Pi_1(p_1, r_1, K_1) &:= s(p_1 - c)x(p_1) + s(r_1 - f) - C_1(K_1), \\ \Pi_2(p_2, r_2, K_2) &:= (1 - s)(p_2 - c)x(p_2) + (1 - s)(r_2 - f) - C_2(K_2). \end{aligned}$$

As the sum $(K_1 + K_2)$ is the total capacity provided, the capacity constraint is given by

$$sx(p_1) + (1 - s)x(p_2) \leq K_1 + K_2. \tag{4.39}$$

If the capacity constraint is violated congestion occurs and data transport is delayed which lowers the utility of subscribers. To simplify, we assume that no utility is obtained if usage exceeds capacity.

We now introduce the benchmark model that determines efficient pricing and efficient supply of capacity. In order to determine total welfare, defined as the sum of consumer and provider surplus, we first introduce consumer surplus, given by

$$\begin{aligned} CS(p_1, p_2, r_1, r_2) &:= sw_1 + (1 - s)w_2 + \int_0^s \theta_1(z)dz + \int_s^1 \theta_2(z)dz \\ &:= sw_1 + (1 - s)w_2 + \frac{s(1 - s)}{2\sigma} + \frac{\beta s}{2\sigma} + \frac{1}{4\sigma}, \end{aligned}$$

and provider surplus, defined as joint profits $(\Pi_1(\cdot) + \Pi_2(\cdot))$. Hence, total welfare is

$$W(p_1, p_2, r_1, r_2, K_1, K_2) :=$$
$$sw_1 + (1-s)w_2 + \frac{s(1-s)}{2\sigma} + \frac{\beta s}{2\sigma} + \frac{1}{4\sigma} + \Pi_1(\cdot) + \Pi_2(\cdot).$$

To obtain the social optimum the welfare function has to be maximized with respect to the choice variables p_1, p_2, r_1, r_2, K_1, and K_2 subject to the capacity constraint (4.39). We simplify the problem by changing variables: According to definition (4.36) the choice variables r_1 and r_2 are replaced by $(v(p_1) - w_1)$ and $(v(p_2) - w_2)$, respectively. Since there is a one-to-one relationship between r_i and w_i one can find the optimal values w_i, and then derive the optimal rentals r_i which lead to the net surpluses w_i. Therefore, we will maximize welfare with respect to w_i rather than with respect to r_i, $i = 1, 2$.

The Lagrangian is given by

$$\begin{aligned}
&L(p_1, p_2, w_1, w_2, K_1, K_2, \lambda) := \\
&sw_1 + (1-s)w_2 + \frac{s(1-s)}{2\sigma} + \frac{\beta s}{2\sigma} + \frac{1}{4\sigma} + s(p_1 - c)x(p_1) \\
&+ s(v(p_1) - w_1 - f) - C_1(K_1) + (1-s)(p_2 - c)x(p_2) \\
&+ (1-s)(v(p_2) - w_2 - f) - C_2(K_2) \\
&+ \lambda(K_1 + K_2 - sx(p_1) - (1-s)x(p_2)).
\end{aligned}$$

By our assumption about increasing marginal costs of capacity it can be shown by differentiation that an interior solution exists where both firms provide some capacity. Below, to derive conditions (4.40) and (4.41) we will use the envelope theorem. By the envelope theorem we can conclude that that $v'(p_i) = -x(p_i)$. Having these considerations in mind we can derive conditions of first order of our welfare maximization problem:[69]

$$
\begin{aligned}
\frac{\partial L(\cdot)}{\partial p_1} &= s(p_1 - c)x'(p_1) - \lambda s x'(p_1) = 0, && (4.40)\\
\frac{\partial L(\cdot)}{\partial p_2} &= (1-s)(p_2 - c)x'(p_2) - \lambda(1-s)x'(p_2) = 0, && (4.41)\\
\frac{\partial L(\cdot)}{\partial w_1} &= \sigma\Big[w_1 - w_2 + \frac{(1-2s)}{2\sigma} + \frac{\beta}{2\sigma} + (p_1 - c)x(p_1) \\
&\quad + (v(p_1) - w_1 - f) - (p_2 - c)x(p_2) - (v(p_2) - w_2 - f) \\
&\quad - \lambda(x(p_1) - x(p_2))\Big] = 0, && (4.42)\\
\frac{\partial L(\cdot)}{\partial w_2} &= -\sigma\Big[w_1 - w_2 + \frac{(1-2s)}{2\sigma} + \frac{\beta}{2\sigma} + (p_1 - c)x(p_1) \\
&\quad + (v(p_1) - w_1 - f) - (p_2 - c)x(p_2) - (v(p_2) - w_2 - f) \\
&\quad - \lambda(x(p_1) - x(p_2))\Big] = 0, && (4.43)\\
\frac{\partial L(\cdot)}{\partial K_1} &= \lambda - C_1'(K_1) = 0, && (4.44)\\
\frac{\partial L(\cdot)}{\partial K_2} &= \lambda - C_2'(K_2) = 0, && (4.45)\\
\frac{\partial L(\cdot)}{\partial \lambda} &= K_1 + K_2 - sx(p_1) - (1-s)x(p_2) = 0.
\end{aligned}
$$

Solving conditions (4.40) and (4.41) for p_1 and p_2, respectively, yields

$$
\begin{aligned}
p_1 &= c + \lambda, && (4.46)\\
p_2 &= c + \lambda. && (4.47)
\end{aligned}
$$

We can conclude that $p_1 = p_2$. Given equal variable price components and given that the utility $u(x_i)$ associated with usage x_i is

69 A second-order condition for a constrained maximum is satisfied if all successive bordered principal minors, starting with the second principal minor, of the bordered Hessian matrix of the optimization problem alternate in algebraic sign, starting with a positive sign. The determinantal test for a constrained maximum is presented in Chiang ([41], pp. 381–387). In our case, this sufficient condition to hold requires in particular that marginal costs of capacity are increasing, which holds by assumption.

identical across consumers, we have $v(p_1) = v(p_2)$ and $x(p_1) = x(p_2)$. Furthermore, conditions (4.44) and (4.45) imply that the capacity constraint is binding, since $\lambda = C_i'(K_i) > 0$, and that

$$C_1'(K_1) = C_2'(K_2).$$

Hence, at the optimum, incremental costs of infrastructure of the two ISPs are equal. If, for example, ISP 1 records greater diseconomies of scale up to a certain level of capacity, then it is efficient for ISP 1 to supply less than half of the infrastructure.

Substituting (4.46) and (4.47) for the prices in conditions (4.42) and (4.43) and cancelling common terms yields

$$\begin{aligned} \frac{\partial L(\cdot)}{\partial w_1} &= \sigma \left[\frac{(1-2s)}{2\sigma} + \frac{\beta}{2\sigma} \right] = 0, \\ \frac{\partial L(\cdot)}{\partial w_2} &= -\sigma \left[\frac{(1-2s)}{2\sigma} + \frac{\beta}{2\sigma} \right] = 0. \end{aligned}$$

For these conditions to hold, for $\sigma > 0$, we must have

$$\frac{(1-2s)}{2\sigma} + \frac{\beta}{2\sigma} = 0.$$

Solving for s yields

$$s = \frac{1}{2} + \frac{\beta}{2}. \tag{4.48}$$

Given the market share (4.48), by equation (4.38), for $\sigma > 0$, we can conclude that $w_1 = w_2$. Moreover, by definition (4.36) and by the fact that $p_1 = p_2$ we obtain

$$r_1 = r_2.$$

From the welfare theoretic perspective, the level of the lump-sum fees r_1 and r_2 is indeterminate since they are only transfers between consumers and providers. However, if ISPs have to cover fixed costs, the rentals r_i may not be lower than f in order to allow the ISPs to break even. That is, the rentals r_i are bounded from below by $r_i \geq f$. Note that both providers offer their services for the same two-part tariff and let consumers pick their preferred brand.

Our considerations can be summarized as follows:[70]

$$\begin{aligned} p_1 &= p_2, && (4.49)\\ p_1 &= c + C_1'(K_1), && (4.50)\\ p_2 &= c + C_2'(K_2), && (4.51)\\ C_1'(K_1) &= C_2'(K_2), && (4.52)\\ K_1 + K_2 &= x(c + C_i'(K_i)), \quad i = 1, 2, && (4.53)\\ r_1 &= r_2. \end{aligned}$$

This solution gives an important insight: The unit prices charged to subscribers are identical across providers and take the incremental costs of the demanded capacity provision into consideration. Optimal unit prices signal true costs of additional capacity. Moreover, the solution determines the total amount of capacity ($K_1 + K_2$) to be provided. The division of infrastructure supply between the two ISPs depends on the cost functions. With decreasing returns to scale, as assumed in our analysis, both ISPs should supply some infrastructure. As already noted above, if one ISP has lower marginal costs of capacity up to a certain level of capacity it is efficient for that ISP to provide more than half of the infrastructure. In the presence of economies of scale a corner solution would be efficient with one ISP providing all capacity.[71] With constant returns to scale and identical cost functions, the division of infrastructure provision between the two providers would be undetermined.

Little and Wright ([143], pp. 158–162) show that the optimal solution cannot be achieved without settlements. Without settlements there is an under-investment in capacity due to a free-rider problem in the following sense: In order to maximize individual profits, providers are reluctant to build up their own infrastructure, but are eager to

70 Equation (4.53) is obtained from the binding constraint (4.39) and by using expressions (4.49) to (4.52).

71 A corner solution does not solve the first-order conditions (4.44) and (4.45) with respect to K_1 and K_2 since these conditions hold for interior solutions.

use the capacity of the competitor for free. Moreover, usage is priced too low. Both consequences of the settlement-free environment result in excessive congestion.

The same result is derived by Manenti [156] who shows that in the presence of congestion externalities a peering agreement based on the SKA model leads to a suboptimal level of investment in capacity. To alleviate the problem of under-investment in capacity Manenti ([156], p. 24) proposes that each peering partner pays its peer an interconnection fee which is inversely proportional to its own installed capacity.

Following Little and Wright ([143], pp. 162–165) we proceed to show that the efficient outcome can be decentralized, i.e., that it can be realized in a competitive environment if the appropriate settlement scheme is adopted. Therefore, we suppose a three stage game where in the first stage the settlement rule is put in place by negotiation between the ISPs before they maximize profits with respect to capacity in the second stage and with respect to prices in the third stage of the game. The game will be solved by backward induction. It will be shown that the efficient outcome may be achieved under the following settlement rule: If one ISP uses more capacity than it provides it has to pay its competitor a rate a on its net capacity demand. Under this settlement rule there are two scenarios to distinguish, namely an asymmetric and a symmetric scenario. While in the asymmetric case one ISP is a net user of capacity, in the symmetric case both providers supply exactly the amount of capacity to cover their own usage. We will consider each scenario in turn.

Assume that ISP 1 is a net supplier and ISP 2 a net user of capacity. With the settlement rule specified above the profit functions take the following forms:

$$\Pi_1(p_1, r_1, K_1) :=$$
$$s(p_1 - c)x(p_1) + s(r_1 - f) + a[(1 - s)x(p_2) - K_2] - C_1(K_1),$$

$$\Pi_2(p_2, r_2, K_2) :=$$
$$(1-s)(p_2-c)x(p_2)+(1-s)(r_2-f)-a[(1-s)x(p_2)-K_2]-C_2(K_2).$$

Substituting $(v(p_i) - w_i)$ for r_i yields

$$\begin{aligned} \Pi_1(p_1, w_1, K_1) &:= s(p_1 - c)x(p_1) + s(v(p_1) - w_1 - f) \\ &\quad + a[(1-s)x(p_2) - K_2] - C_1(K_1), \quad (4.54) \\ \Pi_2(p_2, w_2, K_2) &:= (1-s)(p_2 - c)x(p_2) + (1-s)(v(p_2) - w_2 - f) \\ &\quad - a[(1-s)x(p_2) - K_2] - C_2(K_2). \quad (4.55) \end{aligned}$$

In the third stage of the game, ISP 1 maximizes its profits with respect to the variables p_1 and w_1 subject to the constraint that it can meet the bandwidth demand of its competitor with its excess capacity $(K_1 - sx(p_1)) > 0$:

$$(1-s)x(p_2) - K_2 \leq K_1 - sx(p_1). \quad (4.56)$$

ISP 2, in the third stage of the game, faces an unconstrained maximization problem in the choice variables p_2 and w_2. In the second stage of the game, ISP 1 maximizes its profits with respect to K_1 whereas ISP 2 maximizes its profits with respect to K_2. The Lagrangian for the optimization problem of ISP 1 in the third stage of the game is given by

$$\begin{aligned} &L(p_1, w_1, \lambda) := \\ &s(p_1 - c)x(p_1) + s(v(p_1) - w_1 - f) + a[(1-s)x(p_2) - K_2] - C_1(K_1) \\ &+ \lambda[K_1 - sx(p_1) + K_2 - (1-s)x(p_2)], \end{aligned}$$

where s is defined by (4.38).

We solve the game by backward induction. For this purpose, we will first determine conditions of first order in the third stage of the game. Below, to derive conditions (4.57) and (4.59), the envelope theorem is used to conclude that $v'(p_i) = -x(p_i)$. Also, to determine conditions (4.58) and (4.60) one has to keep in mind that w_i influences the endogenous variables in a direct way and in a indirect manner over s since s depends on w_i. Moreover, we will see below that the capacity constraint is indeed binding. For an interior solution conditions of first order for both providers are given by[72]

$$\begin{aligned}
\frac{\partial L(\cdot)}{\partial p_1} &= s(p_1 - c)x'(p_1) - s\lambda x'(p_1) = 0, && (4.57)\\
\frac{\partial L(\cdot)}{\partial w_1} &= -s + \sigma[(p_1 - c)x(p_1) + (v(p_1) - w_1 - f) - ax(p_2)\\
&\quad - \lambda x(p_1) + \lambda x(p_2)] = 0, && (4.58)\\
\frac{\partial L(\cdot)}{\partial \lambda} &= K_1 - sx(p_1) + K_2 - (1-s)x(p_2) = 0,
\end{aligned}$$

$$\begin{aligned}
\frac{\partial \Pi_2(\cdot)}{\partial p_2} &= (1-s)(p_2 - c)x'(p_2) - (1-s)ax'(p_2) = 0, && (4.59)\\
\frac{\partial \Pi_2(\cdot)}{\partial w_2} &= -(1-s) - \sigma[-(p_2 - c)x(p_2) - (v(p_2) - w_2 - f)\\
&\quad + ax(p_2)] = 0. && (4.60)
\end{aligned}$$

Solving conditions of first order yields[73]

$$\begin{aligned}
p_1 &= c + \lambda, && (4.61)\\
p_2 &= c + a, && (4.62)\\
r_1 &= f + \frac{s}{\sigma} + (a - \lambda)x(p_2), && (4.63)\\
r_2 &= f + \frac{(1-s)}{\sigma}, && (4.64)\\
K_1 + K_2 &= sx(p_1) + (1-s)x(p_2). && (4.65)
\end{aligned}$$

72 A sufficient condition for a constrained maximum of ISP 1 is fulfilled if $\sigma > 0$: In this case, the first bordered principal minor of the bordered Hessian matrix is positive. We suppose the Hessian matrix of the profit function of ISP 2 to be negative semidefinite such that a second-order condition is satisfied. In particular, this assumption requires $(p_2 - c)x''(p_2) + x'(p_2) < 0$.

73 To obtain equations (4.63) and (4.64) we use formulas (4.61) and (4.62), respectively.

By substituting expressions (4.61) to (4.65) for the corresponding terms in the profit functions (4.54) and (4.55), by definition (4.36), we obtain the maximum profits

$$\overline{\Pi}_1(K_1, a, \lambda) := \frac{s^2}{\sigma} + s(a - \lambda)(x(c + a) - x(c + \lambda)) + aK_1 - C_1(K_1), \tag{4.66}$$

$$\overline{\Pi}_2(K_2, a) := \frac{(1 - s)^2}{\sigma} + aK_2 - C_2(K_2). \tag{4.67}$$

Suppose that in the first stage of the game the interconnection price a is chosen to equal λ. Then, maximum profit functions are given by

$$\overline{\Pi}_1(K_1, \lambda, \lambda) := \frac{s^2}{\sigma} + \lambda K_1 - C_1(K_1), \tag{4.68}$$

$$\overline{\Pi}_2(K_2, \lambda) := \frac{(1 - s)^2}{\sigma} + \lambda K_2 - C_2(K_2). \tag{4.69}$$

In the second stage of the game ISPs maximize the functions (4.68) and (4.69) with respect to K_1 and K_2. Conditions of first order,[74]

$$\frac{\partial \overline{\Pi}_1(K_1, \lambda, \lambda)}{\partial K_1} = \lambda - C_1'(K_1) = 0,$$

$$\frac{\partial \overline{\Pi}_2(K_2, \lambda)}{\partial K_2} = \lambda - C_2'(K_2) = 0,$$

yield[75]

$$\lambda = C_1'(K_1),$$

$$\lambda = C_2'(K_2),$$

74 Conditions of second order are satisfied by assumption: $C_i''(K_i) > 0$.

75 The following equations imply that the capacity constraint (4.56) must be binding since $C_i'(K_i) > 0$.

and therefore

$$C_1'(K_1) = C_2'(K_2).$$

Hence, if $a := \lambda$, we can summarize our results as follows:

$$\begin{aligned} p_1 &= p_2, && (4.70)\\ p_1 &= c + C_1'(K_1), && (4.71)\\ p_2 &= c + C_2'(K_2), && (4.72)\\ C_1'(K_1) &= C_2'(K_2), && (4.73)\\ K_1 + K_2 &= x(c + C_i'(K_i)), \quad i = 1, 2, &&\\ r_1 &= f + \frac{s}{\sigma}, && (4.74)\\ r_2 &= f + \frac{(1-s)}{\sigma}. && (4.75) \end{aligned}$$

Note that the solution we have just obtained satisfies the optimal results (4.49) to (4.53) derived above. However, the lump-sum payments or rentals are generally distinct. Imagine that σ approaches infinity. This is the case when horizontal product differentiation becomes impossible. Then, the rentals are just high enough to cover the fixed costs f of connecting a subscriber to the Internet. Moreover, in this case, rentals are identical across providers. Rentals are also identical across subscribers if $s = \frac{1}{2}$. By substituting the results (4.70), (4.74), and (4.75) for the corresponding terms in definition (4.36) and bearing in mind that $\lambda = a$ one can show that $s = \frac{1}{2}$ if $\beta = 0$, which means that there is no asymmetry in networks from the subscribers' point of view.

The basic result is that the efficient outcome can be achieved if the capacity provider, ISP 1, charges the capacity user, ISP 2, for the capacity supplied a price equal to the incremental costs of providing capacity:

$$a := C_1'(K_1).$$

An important question is whether in the first stage of the game the ISPs voluntarily agree on the efficient level of $a = \lambda$. Little and

Wright ([143], pp. 171 f.) show that the two ISPs have an incentive to set the interconnection price a at a level above incremental costs of capacity. This results in higher retail prices and therefore in a higher provider surplus at the expense of consumer surplus.[76]

To show this problem of incentive compatibility, we differentiate maximal profits (4.66) and (4.67) with respect to a at $a = \lambda$. Then, we obtain the following results:

$$\left.\frac{d\overline{\Pi}_1(K_1^*, a, \lambda)}{da}\right|_{a=\lambda} = K_1^*,$$
$$\left.\frac{d\overline{\Pi}_2(K_2^*, a)}{da}\right|_{a=\lambda} = K_2^*,$$

where K_1^* and K_2^* denote the optimal levels of capacity determined in the second stage of the game. We can conclude that both ISPs have an incentive to raise the settlement price a in proportion to the level of bandwidth they provide. The intuition of that result is the following: The rise in profits of ISP 2 due to its higher usage price $(c + a)$ is offset by the increase in the settlement fee a. The only way to increase its profit is to provide its own capacity for which it does not have to pay settlement fees. ISP 1 can increase its profits by serving its own demand and by serving the excess capacity demand of ISP 2 with its excess capacity. The profits of ISP 1 are therefore proportional to its total amount of capacity.

Little and Wright ([143], p. 164) argue that the rise in profits at the expense of consumer surplus is not likely to be a problem in the long run. ISPs mostly have large fixed costs to cover and face intensive retail competition. Then, settlement fees above marginal costs are necessary to break even. In this case, the optimal first-best solution is not feasible any more and one has to search for a second-best solution such as the Ramsey optimum. In the Ramsey optimum settlement charges would just be high enough to cover fixed costs. Little and Wright ([143], p. 164) argue that by competitive forces the Ramsey optimum is likely to be attained in the ISP industry:

76 See Little and Wright ([143], pp. 153 f.).

In reality, there are not just two, but multiple ISPs in competition which limits the possibility of setting the interconnection price above marginal costs of capacity. Moreover, with free entry into the industry, the ISP market is likely to be contestable and any profit opportunity will be eliminated through more entry and infrastructure investments.

In the symmetric scenario, both ISPs use exactly the capacity they provide and no settlement payment takes place ex post. However, in order to achieve the efficient solution it is indispensable that in the first stage of the game the appropriate settlement rule, specified above, is implemented. That is, if an ISP should become a net user of capacity, it has to compensate its competitor for the usage of its network. The existence of this settlement rule is critical to prevent incentives to free-ride.

In the symmetric game, ISPs maximize their profits with respect to the variables p_i and r_i in the third stage of the game subject to their capacity constraints:[77]

$$\Pi_1(p_1, r_1, K_1) := s(p_1 - c)x(p_1) + s(r_1 - f) - C_1(K_1)$$

subject to

$$sx(p_1) \leq K_1 \tag{4.76}$$

and

$$\Pi_2(p_2, r_2, K_2) := (1 - s)(p_2 - c)x(p_2) + (1 - s)(r_2 - f) - C_2(K_2)$$

subject to

$$(1 - s)x(p_2) \leq K_2. \tag{4.77}$$

In the second stage of the game, maximal profit functions are maximized with respect to K_i. Backward induction yields the same results (4.70) to (4.75) as obtained in the asymmetric scenario. Recall that these results correspond to the optimal results (4.49) to (4.52).

77 Second-order conditions for constrained maxima are fulfilled if $\sigma > 0$: Then, the first bordered principal minors of the bordered Hessian matrices of the two optimization problems are both positive.

Equilibrium capacities supplied equal the demand for capacity in each network:

$$\begin{aligned} sx(p_1) &= K_1, \\ (1-s)x(p_2) &= K_2. \end{aligned}$$

By the results (4.70) to (4.73), adding these two equations yields the same result given in (4.53). We can conclude that our results in the symmetric scenario are equal to the optimal solution, except that rentals need not be equal in the decentralized solution.

We close this section by examining which retail pricing schemes proposed in Chapter 3 match the extra-capacity pricing model. We will explicate that extra-capacity pricing is compatible with congestion pricing and with peak-load pricing, provided that the firm peak case prevails. To see this, recall, first, that retail prices in the extra-capacity pricing model equal

$$p_i = c + C_i'(K_i), \quad i = 1, 2,$$

where $C_i'(K_i) = \lambda$. To recognize that extra-capacity pricing fits peak-load pricing, provided that the firm peak case prevails, note that in an off-peak period the capacity constraints (4.39), (4.56), (4.76), and (4.77) are not binding. Hence, $\lambda = 0$ and optimal extra-capacity prices equal off-peak prices:[78]

$$p_i = c.$$

In the peak period, the capacity constraints are binding and optimal extra-capacity prices equal peak prices:[79]

$$p_i = c + \beta,$$

where $\beta = C_i'(K_i)$.

Extra-capacity pricing is compatible with congestion pricing if the capacity constraints (4.39), (4.56), (4.76), and (4.77) are binding. Then, demand for capacity equals supply of capacity. Refer to equation (3.31) to see that the optimal congestion price p^* equals marginal

---

78 See equation (3.15).

79 See equation (3.14).

costs of capacity if $X = K$, i.e., if the demand for capacity equals the supply of capacity. As already noted above, in the extra-capacity pricing model, marginal costs of data transport, c, are negligible in equilibrium given that in the optimum the network is free of congestion. Hence, if $X = K$, the optimal congestion price equals retail prices of the extra-capacity pricing model. Note that the choice of the retail pricing model brings about the mentioned advantages and drawbacks discussed in Sections 3.1.3 and 3.3.1.

4.2.3 Off-Net-Cost Pricing Principle

So far, we assumed that either the sender or the receiver pays for data conveyance. In this section, we suppose that the sender and the receiver share the costs of data transport. Moreover, websites are explicitly introduced as one type of retail customer. It is characteristic of websites or content hosting providers that their traffic flow is mostly unidirectional: The few incoming data packets from user requests trigger a flood of outbound audio, video, image, and text traffic. Typically, content hosting providers do not maintain a large network infrastructure. Therefore, they must buy connectivity to the Internet from an upstream ISP.[80]

The following analysis is based on two papers of Laffont et al. [134, 135] and on an article by Armstrong [6]. We will first present a benchmark model with perfect Bertrand competition between ISPs for two types of subscribers, namely consumers and website providers with inelastic demand for and inelastic supply of webpages, respectively. We will see that Bertrand competition drives down retail prices until they equal marginal costs. In equilibrium, the ISP industry is characterized by zero profits. Our analysis leads to the so-called off net cost pricing principle[81] introduced by Laffont et al. [134]. Then, the assumption of inelastic demand for or inelastic supply of webpages will

80 See Telegeography ([237], p. 267).

81 The name is derived from the fact that retail prices will turn out not to alter depending on whether data transports are originated and terminated on the same or on distinct networks.

be relaxed and the socially optimal interconnection charge will be derived.

To begin with, imagine two types of subscribers, i.e., consumers who wish to view and download information and website providers that post information and content of various kinds. There is relatively little traffic between consumers, such as email exchanges, and from consumers to websites, such as information requests, compared to the data downloaded and conveyed from websites to consumers. To capture this traffic pattern and to simplify, data is assumed to only flow from websites to consumers. We suppose a balanced traffic pattern, i.e., that each consumer demands one unit of data traffic from each website.

Consumers shall derive the utility u per website visited. Websites are assumed to gain the utility $\hat{u}$ from each consumer visit. The utility $\hat{u}$ may take the form of a commercial or a reputational benefit such as the utility derived from money obtained for posting advertisements, from saving money for postage when content is downloaded, or from knowing the number of consumer visitors who viewed the posted information. Suppose that there is no payment from the visitor to the website for accessing content. The number of consumers and websites shall be exogenously determined with the number in each group normalized to 1.

We assume that identical ISPs compete for subscribers in a perfectly competitive market. Total marginal costs of traffic conveyance from a website to a consumer shall amount to

$$c := c_o + c_t, \tag{4.78}$$

where c_o depicts the marginal costs of originating data traffic and where c_t reflects the marginal costs of terminating data traffic. If data traffic is originated and terminated on distinct networks the marginal costs incurred by the network of the website are depicted by c_o while c_t reflects the marginal costs the terminating network has to bear. For simplicity, we abstain from introducing any fixed costs.

If a consumer accesses a website which subscribes to a different ISP the ISPs charge each other an interconnection fee a per unit of data exchanged. Interconnection pricing is assumed to be reciprocal, i.e., the two operators charge each other the same interconnection fee.[82] It is not obvious whether the originating or the terminating network should bear the interconnection price since website visits benefit both parties. We assume that traffic originating ISPs bear the interconnection charge a. Consequently, all the costs involved in completing a data transport are allocated onto the website segment of the market. Note that if the interconnection fee a is negative, i.e., if $a < 0$, the ISP of the website is compensated for the costs incurred for originating the data transport. We can conclude that the originating network faces unit costs equal to $(c_o + a)$ while the unit costs of the terminating network amount to $(c_t - a)$.

Assume that ISP i, $i = 1, \ldots, n$, charge the retail price p_i per unit of data delivered to its consumer subscribers and the retail price $\hat{p}_i$ to websites for each consumer visit. The market shares for consumers and websites of ISP i are denoted by s_i and $\hat{s}_i$, respectively. Moreover, the market shares for consumers and websites of all providers except provider i are denoted by $(1 - s_i)$ and $(1 - \hat{s}_i)$, respectively.

Putting it all together, the profits of ISP i consist of the profits from websites, the profits from terminating data traffic and the profits from consumer retail prices, to be further explained below:

$$\Pi_i(p_i, \hat{p}_i) := \hat{s}_i(\hat{p}_i - c_o - s_i c_t - (1 - s_i)a) + s_i(1 - \hat{s}_i)(a - c_t) + s_i p_i. \quad (4.79)$$

Profits derived from websites are reflected by the first term on the right-hand side in definition (4.79), where $s_i c_t$ stands for the transport costs incurred for terminating data traffic on one's own network and where $(1 - s_i)a$ displays the interconnection fees ISP i has to pay to its rivals for terminating traffic. The second term on the right-hand side in (4.79) indicates the profits from data termination while the third term reflects profits from consumer retail prices. Note that in (4.79) costs are arbitrarily allocated onto the website segment of the market. By simplifying, the profit function becomes

$$\Pi_i(p_i, \hat{p}_i) := s_i(p_i + a - c_t) + \hat{s}_i(\hat{p}_i - a - c_o).$$

82 This assumption will be discussed below.

In this definition, the first term on the right-hand side depicts the profits derived from the consumer business and the second term the profits obtained from the website market segment.

Imagine a three stage game where in the first stage the interconnection charge is determined by a bilateral agreement, for example, where retail prices are set in the second stage and where end-users choose their network in the third stage of the game. Given a perfectly competitive provider market, in each business segment Bertrand competition drives down retail prices until they equal marginal costs:

$$\begin{aligned} p_i &= c_t - a \quad \forall \quad i, \\ \hat{p}_i &= c_o + a \quad \forall \quad i. \end{aligned}$$

In equilibrium, the ISP industry is characterized by zero profits:

$$\Pi_i = 0 \quad \forall \quad i.$$

For these results to be valid, the reservation values of subscribers must not be lower than the retail prices:

$$c_t - a \leq u \quad \text{and} \quad c_o + a \leq \hat{u}.$$

To see this, note that if $(c_o + a) > \hat{u}$ the maximal price $\bar{\hat{p}}_i$ each ISP i can charge its website subscribers is given by $\bar{\hat{p}}_i = \hat{u} < (c_o + a)$. In this case, no ISP can offer its services to websites without incurring a loss. Therefore, ISPs will cease to sell their services to website customers. The same argument holds for the consumer business. Consequently, there would be no data traffic at all.

Our analysis leads to the so-called off-net-cost pricing principle introduced by Laffont et al. ([134], p. 7):

Off-net-cost pricing principle: If $u \geq c_t - a$ and $\hat{u} \geq c_o + a$, there exists a unique price equilibrium which is symmetric and satisfies:

$$\forall \quad i \qquad p_i = p^* = c_t - a, \tag{4.80}$$

$$\forall \quad i \qquad \hat{p}_i = \hat{p}^* = c_o + a, \tag{4.81}$$

$$\forall \quad i \qquad \Pi_i = \Pi^* = 0.$$

Laffont et al. ([134], p. 8) prove the off-net-cost pricing principle by the standard Bertrand argument, introduced above, which applies to each market segment. Note that ISPs set their equilibrium retail prices as if all originating traffic were terminated on a rival network and as if all terminating traffic came from a competitor network. But websites are also visited by consumers belonging to the same network. Nevertheless, the origination and termination prices for data traffic are $(c_o + a)$ and $(c_t - a)$, respectively, which reflect the marginal costs of sending the traffic to a rival network and the marginal costs of terminating traffic coming from a competitor network. This explains the name 'off-net-cost pricing principle'.

The off-net-cost pricing principle implies that retail prices reflect the opportunity costs of having a customer subscribe to one's own network rather than to a rival network. To see this, we will consider the net costs of stealing website or consumer traffic from a competitor. Assume two ISPs i, $i = 1, 2$. The market shares of the two networks in the consumer business are given by s_1 and s_2, where $s_1 + s_2 = 1$. By analogy, the market shares of the two ISPs in the website business are given by $\hat{s}_1$ and $\hat{s}_2$, where $\hat{s}_1 + \hat{s}_2 = 1$.

Consider first the case where a website customer of network j switches to network i, where $i, j = 1, 2$. By definition (4.78), net costs incurred by ISP i are given by

$$s_i[c - (c_t - a)] + s_j[(c_o + a) - 0] = c_o + a.$$

Let us explain this equation: A fraction s_i of consumer subscribers to ISP i demands content from the new website customer. To accommodate this demand ISP i incurs the costs c for originating and terminating the traffic on its own network. At the time when the website still subscribed to ISP j, ISP i only terminated data traffic from that website to its consumer subscribers at marginal costs equal to $(c_t - a)$. Moreover, a fraction s_j of consumers subscribing to the rival network now requests content from the stolen website. To serve these consumers, ISP i incurs marginal costs equal to $(c_o + a)$ for originating traffic. Before, no such costs arose. We can conclude that the opportunity costs of attracting a website of the rival equal off-net costs $(c_o + a)$.

Similarly, by definition (4.78), net costs of network i amount to $(c_t - a)$ whenever a consumer is stolen from the rival:

$$\hat{s}_i[c - (c_o + a)] + \hat{s}_j[(c_t - a) - 0] = c_t - a.$$

The fraction $\hat{s}_i$ of website subscribers to ISP i are visited by the new consumer. With the new consumer, ISP i incurs the costs c for the transportation of on-net traffic. Before the consumer switched her provider, ISP i only originated data traffic to that consumer at marginal costs equal to $(c_o + a)$, i.e., the sum of marginal costs for traffic origination c_o and the interconnection price a payed to ISP j for traffic termination. Moreover, the stolen consumer now requests content from a fraction $\hat{s}_j$ of websites subscribing to the rival network. Consequently, ISP i incurs the costs c_t for traffic termination, but receives the interconnection fee a for each unit of traffic terminated. Before, no costs arose since data traffic was internal to ISP j. We can conclude that the opportunity costs of attracting a consumer of the rival equal off-net costs $(c_t - a)$.

A further implication of the off-net-cost pricing principle is that retail prices cover marginal costs of data conveyance whatever the level of a:

$$\hat{p}^* + p^* = (c_o + a) + (c_t - a) = c_o + c_t.$$

The interconnection charge a only determines how the cost burden of traffic is shared between senders and receivers, i.e., between websites and consumers.

Note that the off-net-cost pricing principle includes the Sender-Keep-All (SKA) regime if $a = 0$. Then, consumers bear the costs of terminating traffic while website providers are charged the traffic originating costs. If $a = c_t$ consumers can access websites free of charge while the latter bear the whole costs of traffic conveyance. The reverse argumentation holds if $a = -c_o$.

In particular, the level of a does not influence the level of social welfare $W(\cdot)$ defined as the sum of subscriber surplus and provider profits which, in equilibrium, equal zero:

$$W(p^*, \hat{p}^*) := (u - p^*) + (\hat{u} - \hat{p}^*) + \sum_{i=1}^{n} \Pi_i(\cdot) = u + \hat{u} - c_o - c_t. \quad (4.82)$$

Recall that we have assumed data traffic to be unidirectional. Laffont et al. ([134], p. 10) claim that the off-net-cost pricing principle is also compatible with mixed traffic patterns where traffic may also flow from consumers to websites. In this case, a perfectly competitive network provider i charges both types of customers the tariff

$$T_i(x, q) := (c_t - a)x + (c_o + a)q,$$

where x and q depict the incoming and outgoing traffic of a customer, respectively.

However, the off-net cost pricing principle no longer holds if the assumption of reciprocal interconnection prices is relaxed. To see this, suppose for simplicity that there are only two competing ISPs, ISP 1 and ISP 2, and that a_1 and a_2 denote the interconnection fees levied by ISP 1 and ISP 2, respectively, for terminating off-net traffic. Furthermore, it is assumed that, without loss of generality, $a_1 > a_2$. Profits of ISP i can be written as

$$\begin{aligned} \Pi_i(p_i, \hat{p}_i) &:= s_i[p_i - (c_t - (1 - \hat{s}_i)a_i)] + \hat{s}_i[\hat{p}_i - (c_o + (1 - s_i)a_j)] \quad (4.83) \\ &:= s_i[p_i - (c_t - a_i)] + \hat{s}_i[\hat{p}_i - (c_o + a_j)] + s_i\hat{s}_i(a_j - a_i). \quad (4.84) \end{aligned}$$

The first term on the right-hand side of the profit function (4.83) depicts the profits derived from the consumer business. Given asymmetric interconnection fees, marginal costs of traffic termination equal $(c_t - (1 - \hat{s}_i)a_i)$, where the term $(1 - \hat{s}_i)a_i$ indicates the interconnection fees obtained for terminating traffic that is originated on the rival's network. The second term on the right-hand side of the profit function (4.83) reflects the profits obtained from the website market segment. Due to the asymmetry in interconnection fees marginal costs of originating traffic equal $(c_o + (1 - s_i)a_j)$, where $(1 - s_i)a_j$ are the interconnection fees paid to the rival to terminate off-net traffic.

Given that the difference $(a_j - a_i)$ is positive for ISP 2, but negative for ISP 1, the latter has an incentive to concentrate its business on one market segment only, such that either $s_i = 0$ or $\hat{s}_i = 0$ and, therefore, $s_i\hat{s}_i(a_j - a_i) = 0$ in definition (4.84). In contrast, for network 2 it is profitable to be present on both market segments.

By totally differentiating profits with respect to market shares one can show that ISP 2 gains more by a simultaneous increase in s_2

and $\hat{s}_2$ compared to specializing on one market segment. In contrast, ISP 1 gains more by a simultaneous increase in market share in one market segment and a reduction of its market share in the other market business. These conflicting interests imply that there is no equilibrium in pure strategies.[83]

Consequently, Laffont et al. ([134], pp. 15 f.) claim that interconnection fees should be reciprocal, i.e., symmetric. They define reciprocity in a broad sense which allows termination costs of networks to differ: Imagine that ISP 1 has a more expensive hot-potato routing strategy[84] than ISP 2. Then, the termination costs for off-net data traffic of ISP 1, c_t^1, are relatively higher than those of ISP 2, c_t^2:

$$c_t^1 := c_t^2 + \Delta, \quad \Delta > 0.$$

Since

$$c := c_o^1 + c_t^2 = c_o^2 + c_t^1,$$

where c_o^1 and c_o^2 depict the origination costs of ISP 1 and ISP 2, respectively, we can conclude that

$$c_o^2 = c_o^1 - \Delta.$$

An equilibrium in pure strategies with the competitive retail prices

$$\begin{aligned} p^* &= c_t^1 - a_1 = c_t^2 - a_2, \\ \hat{p}^* &= c_o^1 + a_2 = c_o^2 + a_1 \end{aligned}$$

that fulfills the off-net-cost pricing principle only exists if the ISPs consider this cost asymmetry when setting their interconnection prices, i.e., if

$$a_1 := a_2 + \Delta.$$

That is, the ISP with the less aggressive hot-potato routing policy should be compensated for carrying off-net traffic longer on its network compared to the competitor by having to pay a lower interconnection fee which, in our example, means that $a_2 < a_1$.

83 Pure strategies are deterministic strategies: Players do not randomize when faced with a choice of strategies, but choose exactly one choice option.

84 Recall from Section 4.1.2 that hot-potato routing refers to the strategy of passing traffic on to other networks at the earliest point of exchange.

Our benchmark model is characterized by inelastic demand. With inelastic demand no normative analysis of the level of the interconnection charge a is possible since a does not influence social welfare.[85] Now, we suppose consumer demand to be elastic while still assuming an inelastic website demand for posting information. In this case, the interconnection price a plays an important role in achieving economic efficiency.

Assume the utility function of a representative consumer to be quasilinear:

$$U(x, b) := u(x) + b,$$

where $u(x)$ is the utility a representative consumer obtains from the data traffic x received, and where b denotes the money a representative consumer disposes of to spend on all other goods apart from website visits. Suppose that $u'(x) > 0$ and $u''(x) < 0$. Solving the budget constraint $px + b = m$, where m indicates the income of a consumer, for b and substituting the result for b in the utility function above yields the unconstrained maximization problem of a representative consumer:

$$\max_x \quad u(x) + m - px. \tag{4.85}$$

The point where the function (4.85) reaches its maximum does not depend on the budget m. Hence, to find the utility maximizing value $x^* = x(p)$, rather than maximizing (4.85), we can as well maximize

$$\max_x \quad u(x) - px. \tag{4.86}$$

We go on working with (4.86). Then, the indirect utility or the consumer surplus function is

$$v(p) := \max_x \; u(x) - px,$$

where, according to the envelope theorem, $v'(p) = -x(p)$.

85 To see this, recall equation (4.82).

We suppose that $x'(p) < 0$. Furthermore, we denote the average retail price of consumers who subscribe to networks other than ISP i by p_{-i}. Then, the profits of ISP i can be written as

$$\Pi_i(p_i, \hat{p}_i) := s_i x(p_i)(p_i + a - c_t) + \hat{s}_i \left[s_i x(p_i) + (1 - s_i)x(p_{-i})\right](\hat{p}_i - a - c_o). \tag{4.87}$$

The term $[s_i x(p_i) + (1 - s_i)x(p_{-i})]$ is the sum of visits to websites demanded by consumer subscribers to ISP i and consumer subscribers to all other networks at prices p_i and p_{-i}, respectively. Hence, the term

$$\hat{s}_i \left[s_i x(p_i) + (1 - s_i)x(p_{-i})\right]$$

depicts the volume of traffic generated by the website market segment of ISP i.

Again, Bertrand competition leads to retail prices that equal marginal costs of data conveyance and to zero equilibrium profits. Hence, the off-net-cost pricing principle still holds. To see this, imagine that all ISPs sell their services at a price above marginal costs. Then, in a perfectly competitive market, one ISP can profitably undercut that price and corner the market.

We now derive the optimal level of the interconnection price a. In our welfare analysis we can ignore aggregate profits $\sum_{i=1}^{n} \Pi_i(\cdot)$ since in equilibrium there are no profit opportunities. We will simplify the welfare maximization problem by changing variables. That is, we will not maximize welfare with respect to a, but with respect to p, the consumer retail price. Since there is a one-to-one relationship between a and p, one can find the ideal consumer price p^*, and then derive the interconnection charge a^* which leads to this price.

Given the consumer retail price p, social welfare is

$$W(p) := v(p) + [\hat{u} - \hat{p}]x(p). \tag{4.88}$$

The first term on the right-hand side of equation (4.88) denotes the surplus consumers obtain from visiting websites. Recall that websites gain the utility $\hat{u}$ from each consumer visit and have to pay the retail price $\hat{p}$ for each consumer visit. Hence, the second term on the right-hand side of equation (4.88) describes the surplus of websites.

Recall from our analysis above that the off-net-cost pricing postulates

$$\hat{p} = c_o + a \quad \text{and} \quad a = c_t - p.$$

Therefore, we can rewrite equation (4.88) as

$$v(p) + [\hat{u} - c_o - a]x(p) = v(p) + [p + \hat{u} - c_o - c_t]x(p) =: W(p). \quad (4.89)$$

Maximizing the welfare function (4.89) with respect to p and substituting $-v'(p)$ for $x(p)$ yields a following condition of first order:

$$\frac{dW(p)}{dp} = x'(p)(p + \hat{u} - c_o - c_t) = 0. \quad (4.90)$$

By our assumption $x'(p) < 0$ and by condition (4.90) we can conclude that

$$(p + \hat{u} - c_o - c_t) = 0.$$

Note that a second-order condition is satisfied since

$$\frac{d^2W(p)}{dp^2} = x'(p) + x''(p)(p + \hat{u} - c_o - c_t) = x'(p) < 0.$$

Solving for the equilibrium price yields

$$p^* = c_o + c_t - \hat{u}. \quad (4.91)$$

To determine the interconnection charge which leads to this price, substitute the right-hand side of expression (4.80) for p^* in equation (4.91) and rearrange terms to conclude that the welfare maximizing level of the interconnection price must satisfy

$$a^* = \hat{u} - c_o. \quad (4.92)$$

Then, according to equation (4.81), the price for data traffic origination amounts to

$$\hat{p}^* = \hat{u}.$$

We can conclude that in the welfare maximizing equilibrium the websites are deprived of any gains from trade. According to the principles of Ramsey pricing, introduced in Section 3.1.2, this result is to be expected since they suggest burdening price-cost markups on the inelastic side of the market. Note that the optimal interconnection charge given in (4.92) may also be negative if $\hat{u}$ is small. Then, the originating ISP is compensated for conveying valuable information to consumers.

Imagine the mirror case where consumer demand is inelastic while the websites' demand for posting information is elastic. Then, in accordance with the principles of Ramsey pricing, as much of the cost burden as possible should be allocated to consumers. This requires the consumer retail price to equal the willingness to pay of consumers

$$u = p^* = c_t - a,$$

and the socially optimal access charge to amount to

$$a^* = c_t - u.$$

Laffont et al. ([134], pp. 11 f.) remark that the off-net-cost pricing principle also holds when different service qualities are introduced. Therefore, the authors denote originating and terminating marginal costs of priority service with c_o^+ and c_t^+, respectively. We have $c_o^+ > c_o$ and $c_t^+ > c_t$ since priority service requires both more bandwidth due to overprovisioning and bandwidth of a higher quality. By analogy, denote the interconnection fee and the retail prices for consumers and websites for priority service with a^+, p^+, and $\hat{p}^+$, respectively. Applying the off-net-cost pricing principle to priority service yields

$$p^+ = c_t^+ - a^+ \quad \text{and} \quad \hat{p}^+ = c_o^+ + a^+.$$

Moreover, if demand of consumers for viewing websites is elastic while demand of websites for posting information is inelastic,

$$a^{*+} = \hat{u}^+ - c_o^+,$$

where a^{*+} depicts the interconnection price per unit of priority data exchanged and where $\hat{u}^+$ denotes the utility level of websites from each consumer visit requiring enhanced quality of data transport. In the mirror case,

$$a^{*+} = c_t^+ - u^+,$$

where u^+ reflects the utility level of consumers demanding priority service when accessing a website.

The fact that the off-net-cost pricing principle also holds in a network environment with different service qualities makes it compatible with static priority pricing, Paris Metro Pricing (PMP), and with congestion pricing. Within the framework of PMP, the levels of $p, \hat{p}$, and a would be distinct, depending on the quality provided by the chosen channel. If c_o and c_t reflect marginal congestion costs the off-net-cost pricing principle is compatible with congestion pricing.

Also peak-load pricing matches the off-net-cost pricing principle: Peak retail prices and interconnection charges would amount to $p^+, \hat{p}^+$, and a^{*+} while in the off-peak period these measures would be given by $p, \hat{p}$, and a^*. Again, note that the choice of the retail pricing model brings about the mentioned advantages and drawbacks discussed in the corresponding sections in the last chapter.

4.3 Automated Bandwidth Trading

4.3.1 Automated Bandwidth Trading Based on Double Auctions

So far, except in the last section when we studied how the off-net-cost pricing principle may be extended to include multiple service classes, different Quality of Service (QoS) requirements have not been considered in either of our previous Sections 4.1 and 4.2. In this section, QoS requirements will be accounted for. The direction of the analysis is given by Bailey and McKnight ([10], p. 320) who stated that when introducing different service qualities 'only a usage-sensitive pricing scheme may prevent a tragedy of the commons'. Hence, flat-rated interconnection fees will no longer be sustainable.

First, we will discuss how current Service Level Agreement (SLA) negotiation can be extended to support end-to-end service guarantees. Then, we will present a proposal on how to organize an automated bandwidth exchange based on a double auction mechanism.

Today, interconnection agreements are mainly based on standard best-effort service.[86] Recall from Section 4.1.2 that transit and peering agreements consist of negotiated SLAs. These SLAs are the basis for the introduction of end-to-end guaranteed service qualities which are necessary to support real-time services across the Internet. An end-to-end guarantee can be given if there exists a hierarchy of appropriate bilateral SLAs.[87] It is claimed that automated SLA negotiation should be introduced and replace SLAs negotiated by humans. That way, SLAs can be contracted dynamically and cover a wide range of service levels from best-effort to virtual leased line.[88]

Following this idea, Fankhauser [66] introduces automated SLA trading. For this purpose, he assumes that both a basic interconnection contract and a physical connection exist between two ISPs. With variations of demand and the traffic load on the networks, software entities called SLA traders, also named bandwidth brokers, dynamically set up new bilateral agreements and thereby exchange information about bandwidth allocation between adjacent networks. In the framework of the Differentiated Services Architecture (DiffServ), SLAs specify the profile for aggregated flows needed to appropriately mark packets.[89]

SLA traders can purchase and sell SLAs. Fankhauser ([66], pp. 113 f.) proposes that SLA traders submit asks for their offered SLAs based on residual bandwidth pricing. The residual bandwidth price

86 See Laffont et al. ([135], p. 288).

87 See Lehr and McKnight ([141], p. 1).

88 See Fankhauser and Plattner ([68], p. 2).

89 Nichols et al. [176] also propose bandwidth brokers for the DiffServ framework. They state that bandwidth brokers can set up both static agreements as in the case of classical transit and peering agreements and dynamic contracts even for a single flow.

function assures that bandwidth prices increase with the amount of SLA capacity sold and is chosen such that the price-volume product of all resources of a network operator is maximized. When acting as buyers, SLA traders select the most profitable SLA offered by their neighbor providers. Concerning the compatibility of SLA trading with different retail pricing models, Fankhauser, Schweikert, and Plattner ([69], p. 14) state that within the framework of SLA trading, Internet Access Providers (IAPs) can choose any retail pricing structure for their end-users, including the popular flat rate.

Instead of focusing on the idea of a hierarchy of bilateral contracts in order to support end-to-end guarantees, we will analyze institutionalized electronic market places where submitted bids and asks are matched in auctions. Auctions can be considered as a particular type of multilateral negotiation.

The idea of electronic bandwidth trading is not new. Companies such as Arbinet in New York (USA), Enron in Houston (USA), RateXchange in Los Angeles and New York (USA), InterXion in Amsterdam (Netherlands) and Frankfurt (Germany), or Asia Capacity Exchange (ACE) in Hong Kong (China) have become global capacity traders. Electronic bandwidth exchanges allow sellers to sell their installed excess capacity and enable buyers to purchase bandwidth on demand.

However, the granularity of traded units is still rather coarse. Besides IP minutes, the most current unit of sale is physical bandwidth on a monthly basis, or longer, or in terms of Mbps or faster. One could also imagine packets being the unit of sale instead of leasing a circuit for ten minutes, for example. Until today, networks neither meter nor bill at the packet level. However, there are companies such as Orologic in Morrisville, North Carolina, that are developing packet billing services.[90]

Promising electronic market places can be created by Merkato, a software platform which is used commercially to automate buying, selling, and allocating bandwidth dynamically in real-time. Recently, Telefonica, one of the world's largest telecommunication carriers, has

90 See Grigonis [91].

deployed the platform. Merkato conducts auctions to allocate bandwidth using the progressive second price auction mechanism presented in the next section.

With the emergence of bandwidth exchanges, derivative securities may be developed that will allow for distributing and allocating risk given the uncertain future demand for bandwidth.[91] RateXchange and Hanse-X, located in Frankfurt (Germany), for example, claim to offer standardized futures and options for bandwidth or plan to introduce these instruments.[92] One can imagine a buyer who, in a network where capacity allocation is determined through a spot market every minute, leading to variable prices, wishes to establish a connection at a maximum cost of $10 per hour of use. For this kind of resource reservation Semret ([209], Chapter 4) introduces a new derivative, a hold option. Semret derives the price of the hold option by extending the Black-Scholes option pricing approach.[93]

We proceed with the automated bandwidth trading approach introduced by Rupp ([202], pp. 39–58). Based on competitive bidding, the Automated Bandwidth Exchange (ABAX) allocates capacity using a continuous double auction mechanism, described below, with the goals of achieving efficiency, fast allocation, transparency, fairness, and decentralization while supporting quality-differentiated services. We will discuss these five goals down below.

ABAX allocates bandwidth on the wholesale level. Unmanageable complexity forbids the application of the mechanism for individual traffic flows between end-users. It is limited to allocate link capacity from one interconnection point to another. Hence, participation in the ABAX market is restricted to large regional, national, and international carriers maintaining their own permanent links between exchange points.

At exchange points two or several participants of the ABAX connect to exchange traffic. Every exchange point is a local marketplace for the capacity of links connecting the respective interconnection point with adjacent exchange points. In the proposed model, ABAX

91 See Lehr and McKnight ([141], p. 5).

92 See Gerpott and Massengeil ([85], p. 600).

93 See Black and Scholes [23].

is an organization built up by participating parties combining several federated local markets. ABAX runs, coordinates, and controls local auctions at each exchange point.

Sellers are ISPs owning links with various capacities and delay characteristics between exchange points. Buyers bid for links between different interconnection points. Their bids can embrace several links with specified quality requirements such as minimum bandwidth or delay. Sellers and buyers trade standardized bandwidth commodity contracts which enable fast, automated transactions. ABAX conducts hourly local auctions of link capacity.

Buyers and sellers can participate in the auction through smart agents, i.e., software programs that run on the computers of the bidders and that have been configured in accordance to the buying and selling strategies of individual buyers and sellers, respectively.[94] Smart agents accept offers of and requests for link capacity subject to QoS requirements. Then, the ABAX organization matches bids and asks based on a continuous double auction mechanism.

Double auctions are two-sided auctions that allow multiple buyers and sellers to bid simultaneously for a commodity, bandwidth in our case, to be exchanged. In a continuous double auction, compatible bids are matched immediately.[95] The best ask price, i.e., the minimum ask, is referred to as the market ask while the best bid price, i.e., the maximum bid, constitutes the market bid. Current market bid and ask prices are public information.[96] Whenever a new buy bid arrives the auctioneer examines whether it matches the lowest existing sell bid, i.e., the market ask price, and vice versa. If bids are matching the commodity is traded immediately at the price of the existing bid and a new price quote is generated. Hence, transactions are completed if

---

94 Rupp ([202], p. 42) calls these smart agents 'brokers'. Since we have used and will use this term in a different context we abstain from naming smart agents brokers.

95 In contrast, in the periodic double action, also named call market or clearing house, bids are collected over a specified interval of time and the market is cleared at the expiration of the bidding interval at a price that maximizes revenues. See Bichler ([22], p. 97).

96 See Friedman ([79], pp. 61 f.).

an open bid or ask is accepted by another seller or buyer.[97] Double auctions have not been intensively studied theoretically even though many important stock markets such as the New York Stock Exchange and commodity markets such as the Chicago Mercantile Exchange are conducted as double auctions.[98] Experimental studies on double auctions have shown that in many market environments prices quickly converge to a competitive equilibrium price.[99]

We now describe the auction design introduced by Rupp ([202], pp. 43–51) including the set up of the model, the properties of the proposed mechanism, and the auction rules. Suppose that N buyers i and M sellers j demand and offer bandwidth in the Internet, respectively. Denote interconnection points with A, ..., Z. The capacity, i.e., the total bandwidth of the physical connection, between any two interconnection points is given by $K \in [0, \bar{K}]$. A link l, $l = 1, \ldots, L$, where L is the number of links, with $K > 0$ connects two interconnection points. Let q depict the bandwidth quality in terms of delay, jitter,[100] and loss ratio. The costs to sellers of providing one unit of capacity K at quality q is depicted by $s_j(l, K, q)$. These costs can either be interpreted as variable costs or as opportunity costs of the sale of the capacity. Buyers only have a valuation for a certain link if it belongs to a complete path $w_h^{\mathrm{O,D}}$, $h = 1, \ldots, H$, where H is the number of paths, from the origin or sender O to the destination D. Buyers consider links that belong to a path as complements.

An interconnection $r^{\mathrm{O,D}}$ connects the points O and D through an arbitrary path $w_h^{\mathrm{O,D}}$. There may be several paths $w_h^{\mathrm{O,D}}$ constituting

---

97 See Bichler ([22], p. 97).

98 Friedman [79] shows that double auctions are efficient if the traded commodity is divisible and provided that there would be no trade if the auction was prolonged. The latter requirement states that bidders must be able to reach a Nash equilibrium in their final actions. Gjerstad and Dickhaut [89] provide a model of information processing and strategy choice of bidders in order to demonstrate the convergence to competitive equilibrium prices and allocations in double auctions. Consider Friedman [80] for more information on the theory and evidence of double auctions.

99 See Gjerstad and Dickhaut ([89], pp. 1 f.).

100 Recall from Section 2.1.2 that jitter refers to the variation in the delay of packets belonging to the same application.

an interconnection $r^{O,D}$. The valuation of buyer i of the connection $r^{O,D}$ with capacity K and quality q is given by $v_i(r^{O,D}, K, q)$. Since buyers do not bother which path is taken by their traffic, paths that connect the same points O and D are perfect substitutes.

According to Rupp ([202], pp. 44–48) the auction design should be efficient and should allow for a fast allocation of capacity. Moreover, it should be transparent, fair, as well as decentralized. Note that the desirable property of incentive compatibility is neglected since, according to Rupp ([202], p. 45), incentive compatible mechanisms do not in general meet the mentioned properties. This lack of incentive compatibility inherent in the automated bandwidth trading approach potentiates strategic manipulation by the bidders. However, in the literature it is claimed that the problem of strategic behavior diminishes with a rising complexity of the allocation mechanism.

For the mechanism to be efficient, on the one hand, buyers must obtain sufficient capacity along the path from the sender to the receiver. To see this, remember that buyers only have a valuation for a certain link if it belongs to a complete path from the sender to the receiver and, therefore, that all links making up a specific path are complements. Thus, a path with a missing link becomes worthless from the point of view of buyers. If such a path is indeed allocated to a buyer, allocative efficiency decreases. On the other hand, efficiency requires capacity to be allocated to buyers who have the highest valuation of bandwidth. The first requirement of the efficiency property may be fulfilled if one allows for combinatorial bids.[101] In combinatorial auctions bidders may bid on combinations of goods. Hence, combinatorial bids allow for all-or-nothing allocations of bandwidth. Allowing bidders to express complementarities in their bids potentially makes allocations more efficient compared to those of traditional auctions. However, winner determination becomes a complex

101 Expressed differently, links are considered to be combinatorial goods. Goods are called combinatorial goods if the value of a bundle of goods differs from the sum of the values of the same goods unbundled, i.e., if the valuations of bidders are not additive. See Bichler ([22], p. 120).

problem for the auctioneer.[102] So far, combinatorial auctions have not been very well understood theoretically. Rassenti, Smith, and Bulfin ([195], p. 406) state that, generally, combinatorial auctions are not incentive compatible and refer to Vickrey ([247], p. 26) who finds that bidders who acquire multiple units in an auction do not truthfully reveal their preferences. The intuitive reason is that a buyer who bids for multiple units cannot be modeled as an aggregate agent of multiple single-unit buyers. The combination of multiple buyers into one gives rise to collusion and a community of interest. In consequence, the bid submitted for a second or third unit, for example, will be influenced by the potential effect of these bids on the price to be paid for the first unit, for example.

To ensure a fast allocation of bandwidth, in the proposed model, the duration of the spot market for bandwidth exchange is set to be less than one hour. Every hour t, $t = 1, \ldots, T$, a new market opens. The time interval between the closing of an auction and the opening of a new one is used to update routing tables. Rupp ([202], p. 50) introduces an activity rule, to be explained down below, that forces bidders to increase or decrease their bids or asks, respectively, fast enough such that the auction indeed ends within the specified time interval.

To ensure transparency, buyers and sellers can observe submitted bids and asks, i.e., current prices, any time. Matching bids and asks are processed immediately. At any moment during the auction, bidders are able to match an observed bid or ask. Moreover, the amount of already traded bandwidth can be observed by all bidders at all times during the auction.

Apart from the criteria concerning a fast allocation of bandwidth and transparency the proposed auction mechanism fulfills the requirement of fairness since discrimination between bidders is solely based on their willingness to pay. Moreover, the auction mechanism is considered to be decentralized since it combines multiple local auctions: Buyers do not have to observe all bids and asks for links but, instead,

102 See Sandholm ([204], p. 175). Rothkopf, Pekeč, and Harstad [199] consider the computational problem of evaluating combinatorial bids.

specify the submarkets, i.e., the local marketplaces, they are interested in to observe all relevant information during the auction. These submarkets must at least consist of the connections that buyers bid for.

We now consider the auction rules. Before an auction starts the auctioneer determines reservation prices, i.e., the minimum bid $\underline{b}$ and the maximum ask $\overline{a}$. There is an activity rule which prescribes that buyers and sellers must increase and decrease their bids and asks by at least a minimum increment every minute in order to prevent dropping out of the market. This minimum increment and the interval $[\underline{b}, \overline{a}]$ are set such that the auction ends within an hour. Once the auction has started, sellers and bidders simultaneously submit their asks $a_j(l, K, q)$, specifying the unit price of seller j for the offered capacity K and quality q on link l, and bids $b_i(r^{\mathrm{O,D}}, K, q)$, indicating the willingness to pay of buyer i for one unit of capacity for an interconnection $r^{\mathrm{O,D}}$ with capacity K and quality q.

While sellers bid for links buyers bid for entire paths. Then, how can sellers know the market bid, i.e., the maximum bid, for a certain link? The market bid β_l for a certain link l is determined by the difference between the market bid for an interconnection provided by a path $w_h^{\mathrm{O,D}}$ which contains the link l and the sum of market asks, i.e., minimum asks, for the other links $\hat{l}$, $\hat{l} = 1, \ldots, L$, $\hat{l} \neq l$, belonging to the path $w_h^{\mathrm{O,D}}$. The market bid for link l can be expressed as

$$\beta_l := \max_h \left[\max_{\substack{i \\ l \in w_h^{\mathrm{O,D}}}} b_i(w_h^{\mathrm{O,D}}, K, q) - \sum_{\substack{\hat{l} \in w_h^{\mathrm{O,D}} \\ \hat{l} \neq l}} \min_j a_j(\hat{l}, K, q) \right].$$

A bid and one or several asks match if the bid for an interconnection $r^{\mathrm{O,D}}$ equals or exceeds the sum of asks for the links constituting this interconnection for a certain capacity K and a certain quality q:

$$b_i(r^{\mathrm{O,D}}, K, q) \geq \sum_{l \in r^{\mathrm{O,D}}} a_j(l, K, q).$$

Matching bids and asks are processed instantly. For almost one hour buyers and sellers have the opportunity to increase and decrease their bids and asks, respectively.

Note that the auction design and the auction rules are very complex, too complex for human bidders. This is the reason why configured smart agents bid on behalf of buyers and sellers of bandwidth. Smart bidders are permanently connected to the network and can obtain and offer capacity to accommodate short-term demand. Due to the complexity of the automated bandwidth exchange, Rupp [202] does not give a formal proof of its efficiency characteristic, but contents himself with running computer simulations to validate his model. Theoretical optimal allocations which maximize realized willingnesses to pay are compared with bandwidth allocations conducted by the automated bandwidth exchange. Rupp ([202], pp. 51–57) shows that the automated bandwidth exchange works well.[103]

We can conclude that the proposed automated bandwidth exchange ensures a fast allocation of bandwidth, transparency, fairness, as well as decentralization while the goal of efficiency is likely to be achieved. However, the proposed mechanism is not incentive compatible. But, as already mentioned above, the problem of strategic behavior of bidders diminishes with a rising complexity of the allocation mechanism; and the automated bandwidth exchange is indeed complex.

Theoretically, automated bandwidth trading is compatible with any of the retail pricing mechanisms proposed in Chapter 3. It is left up to individual providers how to design their retail pricing plans. However, it is to be expected that pricing proposals that are load-sensitive and take QoS into consideration are likely to be preferred by IAPs given that they are able to offer guaranteed QoS and that they themselves face load and quality sensitive interconnection prices.[104]

103 Similarly to ABAX, Parameswaran, Stallaert, and Whinston [190] propose an allocation mechanism for the DiffServ framework where bandwidth brokers conduct combinatorial sealed-bid periodic double auctions (call markets) in each network.

104 The prices determined by ABAX are load-sensitive since they vary according to current demand for data traffic conveyance.

The possibilities of IAPs of purchasing bandwidth on demand from the source to the destination and of offering guaranteed QoS makes ABAX compatible with adaptive load-sensitive volume pricing, for example. IAPs would then charge end-users in accordance with their specified base prices and penalty function while they themselves face the costs determined by ABAX.

4.3.2 Automated Bandwidth Trading Based on Progressive Second Price Auctions

Lazar and Semret [139] propose a new auction mechanism called Progressive Second Price (PSP) auction for network bandwidth sharing. In contrast to the Vickrey auction in the smart market model introduced in Section 3.3.2, where the bidders bid for one indivisible unit of a resource, the two-dimensional bids in the PSP auction, consisting of a bid quantity and a bid price, can ask for arbitrary shares of the total available resource quantity. The PSP mechanism generalizes the idea of the Vickrey auction in that the total charge for the purchased capacity each bidder i faces equals the willingness to pay of all other bidders who are excluded by the bid of bidder i. Hence, for a marginal share of the network resource the winning bidder pays a price equal to the next highest bid. The PSP mechanism has the desirable features of achieving economic efficiency and being incentive compatible as well as being implementable with reasonable overhead.

Semret [209] and Semret et al. [214] extend the work of Lazar and Semret [139] and study the feasibility of auctioning capacity in a Diff-Serv Internet model. Through a game theoretic analysis the authors determine optimal strategies for buyers and sellers of capacity and show that the PSP auction leads to an efficient equilibrium in Diff Serv bandwidth markets. As already noted in Section 4.3.1 the PSP auction is adopted by Merkato, a software platform which creates electronic market places to automate purchase, sale, and allocation of bandwidth dynamically in real-time. Bandwidth on demand is auctioned off every five minutes. Configured intelligent software agents act on behalf of buyers and sellers. Merkato enables buyers not to have to set up long-term fixed contracts as in the case of classic peering and transit agreements. Sellers can sell their excess capacity and shift traffic from peak to off-peak periods via price signals.[105]

Semret et al. [214] model the Internet economy as a set of interconnected networks. They assume that each network can be represented by a single bottleneck capacity. Each network consists of a two-tier wholeseller and retailer market. Multiple differentiated service classes are offered in each network. The players in the modeled Internet economy are one Raw Bandwidth Seller (RBS) per network, one Service Bandwidth Broker (SBB) per service class per network, and users. The players represent a wholeseller of bandwidth, Internet Access Providers (IAPs), and end-users, respectively. Semret ([209], p. 76) argues that end-users are likely to be large subscribers such as websites, intranets, or virtual private networks rather than individual retail customers. Semret ([209], p. 9) states that in practice bidders are most likely to be automated agents.

It is assumed that players interact in a non-cooperative manner. The non-cooperative game formulation is motivated by the competition among SBBs. SBBs that offer different service classes do not buy capacity from each other. But SBBs offering distinct service classes within the same network compete with each other for purchasing bandwidth from the RBS. The RBS does not buy capacity from any other player. The two-tier auction pricing framework is depicted in Figure 4.3 for the case where two service classes are offered in each network.[106]

We proceed with the introduction of the game theoretic model. The set of players is depicted by $\mathcal{I} := \{1, \ldots, I\}$. A superscript indicates that a player with identity $i \in \mathcal{I}$ is a seller. In contrary, a subscript states that player i is a buyer. Brokers are buyers and sellers at once. If player i desires to purchase from seller j she places a bid $\mathbf{b}_i^j := (x_i^j, p_i^j)$, where x_i^j depicts the desired amount of bandwidth to be purchased and where p_i^j denotes the price buyer i is willing to pay for each unit. Without loss of generality, suppose that all players

105 See InvisibleHand Networks [118].

106 The coefficients r_i^j, r_j^i, r_k^l, and r_l^k will be introduced below.

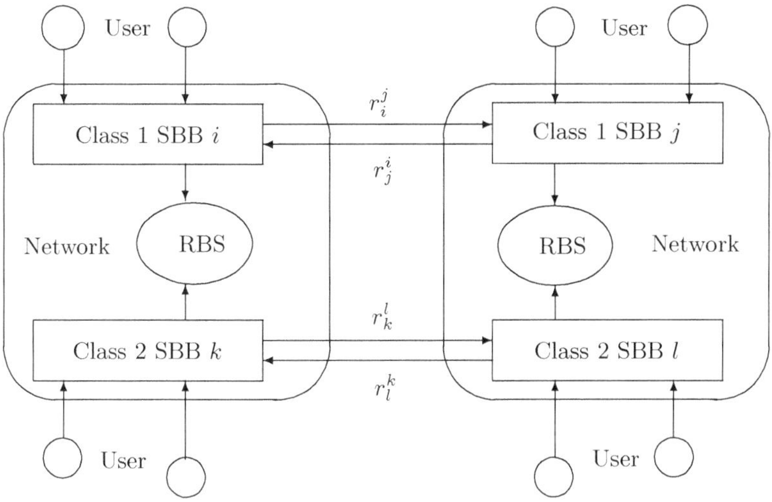

Figure 4.3: Two-tier auction pricing framework
Source: See Semret et al. ([214], p. 2501).

bid in all auctions. If a player i does not wish to purchase from seller j the bid is set to $\mathbf{b}_i^j := (0, 0)$. A seller j sets an ask $\mathbf{b}_j^j := (x_j^j, p_j^j)$ meaning that she is ready to sell the quantity x_j^j at the minimal unit price p_j^j. Hence, p_j^j depicts the reserve price of the bandwidth offered by seller j. Note that if the superscript and the subscript are identical a bid is to be understood as an ask.

In the following analysis omitted superscripts and/or subscripts indicate that the respective superscript or subscript ranges over all possible values. An omitted superscript results in the $(1 \times I)$ vector of quantities $\mathbf{x}_i$ demanded by player i, for example. Similarly, $\mathbf{X}$ denotes the $(I \times I)$ matrix of quantities. The $(I \times 1)$ profile of bids placed by a buyer j is depicted by $\mathbf{B}_j := (\mathbf{b}_j^1, \ldots, \mathbf{b}_j^I)^T$, where the superscript T indicates that the vector is transposed.[107] Similarly, the $(1 \times I)$ profile of bids seller j faces is denoted by $\mathbf{B}^j := (\mathbf{b}^j_1, \ldots, \mathbf{b}^j_I)$.[108] Also, the $(1 \times I)$ vector of profiles of bids placed by all buyers j, $j \in \mathcal{I}$, is given by $\mathbf{B} := (\mathbf{B}_1, \ldots, \mathbf{B}_I)$.[109] Moreover, the $(1 \times (I-1))$ bid vector when player i is elided is indicated by $\mathbf{B}_{-i} := (\mathbf{B}_1, \ldots, \mathbf{B}_{i-1}, \mathbf{B}_{i+1}, \ldots, \mathbf{B}_I)$.[110] Furthermore, a^j_i indicates the quantity allocated by player j to player i while c^j_i denote the total costs associated with this allocation. The $(I \times I)$ matrix of allocated quantities shall be designated by $\mathbf{A} := (a^j_i)$, where $i, j \in \mathcal{I}$.

Confronted with the profile of bids $\mathbf{B}^j := (\mathbf{b}^j_1, \ldots, \mathbf{b}^j_I)$ seller j determines an allocation $(\boldsymbol{a}^j, \mathbf{c}^j) := A^j(\mathbf{B}^j)$ according to her allocation rule $A^j(\cdot)$. An allocation rule is feasible provided that $a^j_i \leq x^j_i$ and $c^j_i \leq p^j_i x^j_i$. The progressive second price auction, introduced below, is an example of a feasible allocation rule.

We proceed with the analysis of bandwidth sellers and focus on their provisioning and peering constraints. Suppose that player $k \in \mathcal{I}$ represents an RBS. The strategy of such a player k to always ask $\mathbf{b}^k_k := (x^k_k, p^k_k)$, where x^k_k equals the physical bottleneck capacity[111] of her network, and where p^k_k reflects the unit price of bandwidth, i.e., the reserve price. We suppose that reserve prices are always strictly positive. Players representing an RBS only act as sellers. Therefore, $\mathbf{b}^j_k := (0, 0)$ for all $j \neq k$.

Assume player j, $j \in \mathcal{I}$, to be an SBB. Each SBB offers the quantity x^j_j to her customers. To be able to allocate the quantity

107 Note that the elements of the vector $\mathbf{B}_j$ are again (1×2) vectors. We can also express the profile of bids $\mathbf{B}_j$ as a matrix of dimension $(I \times 2)$ with respect to the scalar elements x^i_j and p^i_j, where $i \in \mathcal{I}$.

108 To be precise, the profile of bids $\mathbf{B}^j$ also includes the ask $\mathbf{b}^j_j$ set by player j. The bid profile $\mathbf{B}^j$ is a matrix of dimension $(I \times 2)$ with respect to the scalar elements x^j_i and p^j_i, where $i \in \mathcal{I}$.

109 This vector becomes a matrix of dimension $(I \times 2I)$ if it is expressed with respect to the scalar elements x^i_j and p^i_j, where $i, j \in \mathcal{I}$, rather than with respect to $\mathbf{B}_j$, where $j \in \mathcal{I}$.

110 When expressed with respect to scalar elements this vector becomes a matrix of dimension $((I-1) \times (2I-2))$.

111 Remember that by assumption each network can be represented by a single bottleneck capacity.

$\sum_{i \in \mathcal{I}} a_i^j$ to her buyers on her sell-side each SBB j must have obtained enough bandwidth from the RBS k in her network. The provisioning constraint of SBB j is given by

$$\sum_{i \in \mathcal{I}} a_i^j \leq a_j^k. \tag{4.93}$$

SBB j also sells interconnection service. Therefore, she must buy enough capacity on the buy-side from interconnecting SBBs, called peers,[112] which offer the same QoS. Player l, $l \in \mathcal{I}$, shall be a peer. Assume that the fraction of incoming traffic at SBB j, generated by her customers, which is routed to the interconnected network l is given by the provisioning coefficient r_j^l.[113] Then, the peering constraint of SBB j is given by

$$r_j^l \sum_{\substack{i \in \mathcal{I} \\ i \neq l}} a_i^j \leq a_j^l, \tag{4.94}$$

for all peers l. The peering constraint (4.94) for a peer l states that the capacity allocated to SBB j by this peer l must equal or exceed the sum of capacity sold by SBB j to all players except to peer l multiplied by the fraction of incoming traffic at SBB j that is routed to peer l. That is, in order for SBB j to honor her contracts the capacity she actually obtains from a peer l constrains the quantity player j can offer to her peers i, $i \neq l$. In other words, player j must obtain enough capacity from each peer l offering the same service quality in order to provide this service quality also to her own customers.

To simplify notation, set $r_j^k = 1$ if k is the RBS of SBB j. Then, since $a_k^j = 0$, constraint (4.93) is a special case of constraint (4.94) for $l = k$. In the case that player l is neither a peer of player j nor her RBS $r_j^l = 0$.

112 In this section the term 'peer' is used for all interconnected networks, regardless of whether the respective networks are in a peering or in a transit relationship.

113 A more specific interpretation of the provisioning coefficients will be given below.

We now determine the bandwidth SBB j can sell to her customers. Therefore, define

$$e_j^l(a_j^l, a_l^j) := \frac{a_j^l}{r_j^l} + a_l^j \tag{4.95}$$

to be the capacity of the link between SBB j and SBB l that SBB j offers to her customers. Let

$$e_j(\mathbf{A}) := \min_{l \neq j} \; e_j^l(a_j^l, a_l^j) \tag{4.96}$$

be the bottleneck capacity at player j.

We can now specify the broker's sell-side constraints: An SBB $j \in \mathcal{I}$ shall have the buy-side allocation $(\boldsymbol{a}_j, \mathbf{c}_j)$. Then, the quantity sold on the sell-side can be shown to be constrained by

$$x_j^j \leq \min_{l \neq j} e_j^l(a_j^l, a_l^j).$$

To see this, suppose that $x_j^j > e_j^l(a_j^l, a_l^j)$ for a player $l \neq k$. Hence, if all the offered capacity is sold

$$\sum_{i \in \mathcal{I}} a_i^j = x_j^j > e_j^l(a_j^l, a_l^j) := \frac{a_j^l}{r_j^l} + a_l^j.$$

Therefore,

$$\sum_{\substack{i \in \mathcal{I} \\ i \neq l}} a_i^j > \frac{a_j^l}{r_j^l},$$

is obtained which violates the constraint (4.94).

A further constraint for a broker j on the sell-side is that he does not sell at a loss. Broker j faces total costs $\sum_{l \in \mathcal{I}} c_j^l$ of the capacity purchased. Therefore, the price per unit of capacity which yields non-negative profits must satisfy

$$p_j^j \geq \frac{1}{x_j^j} \sum_{l \in \mathcal{I}} c_j^l, \quad \text{for} \quad x_j^j > 0. \tag{4.97}$$

We will explain below that in equilibrium the peering constraint (4.94) is satisfied as an equality. For the moment, suppose that this equality holds. Then, solving the constraint (4.94) for a_j^l/r_j^l and substituting the result for this quotient in definition (4.96) determines the following equilibrium conditions for all brokers j, $j \in \mathcal{I}$:

$$e_j(\mathbf{A}) = \sum_{\substack{l \in \mathcal{I} \\ l \neq j}} a_l^j, \tag{4.98}$$

$$a_j^l = (e_j(\mathbf{A}) - a_l^j) r_j^l. \tag{4.99}$$

These conditions require that at equilibrium, broker j does not sell more capacity than her bottleneck capacity and that she does not buy more capacity from her peers than necessary. Concretely, the left-hand side of equation (4.98) reflects the offered quantity $e_j(\mathbf{A})$ of broker j that she purchased on the buy-side. The right-hand side of equation (4.98) depicts the capacity sold by broker j to her users on the sell-side. Hence, the right-hand side cannot exceed the left-hand side of equation (4.98). If the left-hand side exceeds the right-hand side, broker j has purchased more capacity than can be sold. She can increase profits by reducing her bids on the buy-side. Therefore, equality holds in equilibrium. For the same reason, constraint (4.94) holds with equality in equilibrium: Broker j will not buy more capacity from a peer l on the buy-side than necessary to allocate the quantities $\sum_{\substack{i \in \mathcal{I} \\ i \neq l}} a_i^j$ to her peers on the sell-side, given the provisioning coefficient r_j^l.

The left-hand side of equation (4.99) depicts the capacity broker j is buying from broker l while the right-hand side is the capacity broker j must buy from player l in order to offer a bottleneck capacity of at least $e_j(\mathbf{A})$. From definition (4.96) it follows that the right-hand side cannot exceed the left-hand side of equation (4.99). If the left-hand side is greater, broker j cannot rise her bottleneck capacity $e_j(\mathbf{A})$ offered on the sell-side by buying extra capacity from broker l. Hence, broker j will decrease her purchases from broker l until equality holds.[114]

114 See Semret et al. ([213], p. 416).

We proceed with the interpretation of the vector of provisioning coefficients $\mathbf{r}_j := (r_j^1, \ldots, r_j^I)$. Within the framework of our model, broker j can only differentiate herself through the vector of provisioning coefficients $\mathbf{r}_j$. A broker is characterized by the type of her Service Level Agreement (SLA) offered. Distinct SLAs are determined by different vectors $\mathbf{r}_j$. Semret et al. ([214], p. 2502) distinguish between three different types of SLAs, namely expected capacity SLAs, worst-case capacity SLAs, and local SLAs:

- With an expected capacity SLA, users on average obtain the capacity they contracted for even if their traffic traverses several networks. The Assured Forwarding (AF) service, for example, could be contracted with an expected capacity SLA. With this SLA, the coefficient r_j^l depicts the fraction of traffic which enters SBB j and is forwarded to SBB l while the coefficient r_j^j reflects the on-net traffic fraction of SBB j, i.e., the fraction of traffic which is originated and terminated on the network of player j. Moreover, $\sum_{\substack{l \in \mathcal{I} \\ l \neq k}} r_j^l = 1$, where k denotes the RBS of SBB j's network. Note that so far we implicitly supposed that SBBs offered expected capacity SLAs.
- With a worst-case capacity SLA, users are always allocated the bandwidth they pay for. Then, for all peers l of broker j the provisioning coefficient fulfills $r_j^l = 1$. The Expedited Forwarding (EF) service, for example, could be contracted with a worst-case capacity SLA.
- In a local SLA, SLAs are only applied in the local network. In this case, $r_j^j = 1$ and $r_j^l = 0$ for all $l \neq j$.

Note that the potential engineering need of SBBs to overprovision their network may be included into the model by factoring overprovisioning into each provisioning coefficient. If, for example, SBB j wishes to overprovision a virtual leased line by 5%, which needs a worst-case capacity SLA, then $\mathbf{r}_j = (1.05, 1.05, \ldots)$. We can conclude that by (4.95) the bottleneck capacity depends, among other things, on the service offered by SBB j.

We now focus on the decision-making problem of buyers. Buyers are modeled as bottleneck buyers where each buyer $i \in \mathcal{I}$ maximizes her unconstrained quasilinear (monetary) utility

$$U_i(\mathbf{B}) := \theta_i(e_i(\mathbf{A}(\mathbf{B}))) - \sum_{j \in \mathcal{I}} c_i^j(\mathbf{B}), \tag{4.100}$$

where $e_i(\cdot)$ is defined as in expression (4.96) and where $\theta_i(\cdot)$ depicts the bandwidth valuation function of buyer i, i.e., her willingness to pay for a scalar bottleneck $e_i(\cdot)$. The bandwidth valuation function $\theta_i(\cdot)$ is the private knowledge of each buyer i. The allocation matrix $\mathbf{A}$ and the costs c_i^j depend on the bid matrix $\mathbf{B}$ since each seller j determines an allocation $(\boldsymbol{a}^j, \mathbf{c}^j)$ depending on the profile of bids $\mathbf{B}^j$. These dependencies will be made more explicit below when we introduce the allocation rule, i.e., the PSP auction.

If the buyer is an end-user i subscribing to SBB j, then we have $r_i^j = 1$, $r_i^l = 0$ for all $l \neq j$, and $a_j^i = 0$ for all j. Hence, according to expressions (4.95) and (4.96), $e_i(\mathbf{A}) = a_i^j$ and the utility function (4.100) simplifies to

$$U_i(\mathbf{B}) := \theta_i(a_i^j(\mathbf{B})) - c_i^j(\mathbf{B}).$$

If the buyer is a broker j, the utility function (4.100) is to be interpreted as the potential profit function of broker j, where $\theta_j(\cdot)$ depicts the broker's buy-side valuation of bandwidth and is taken as the potential revenue function from selling on the sell-side the capacities purchased on the buy-side. Hence, capacity allocations are only valuable to brokers if they increase their bottleneck capacity $e_j(\mathbf{A})$.

The demand on the sell-side yields potential revenues. Define the demand on the sell-side of broker j at each given unit price y by

$$d^j(y) := \sum_{p_k^j \geq y} x_k^j \quad \forall \quad y \geq 0.$$

The inverse demand function is defined by

$$f^j(z) := \sup\{y \geq 0 : d^j(y) \geq z\}, \qquad (4.101)$$

reflecting the highest unit price at which broker j could sell the zth unit of capacity, i.e., the marginal value of capacity at z. The price to be paid for the zth unit of capacity is a supremum since the inverse demand curve that broker j faces is a step function as depicted in Figure 4.4. An arbitrary step of the inverse demand function indicates the quantity broker j sells to an SBB i at a corresponding unit price p_i^j. The realized prices depend on the allocation mechanism $A^j(\cdot)$ used.

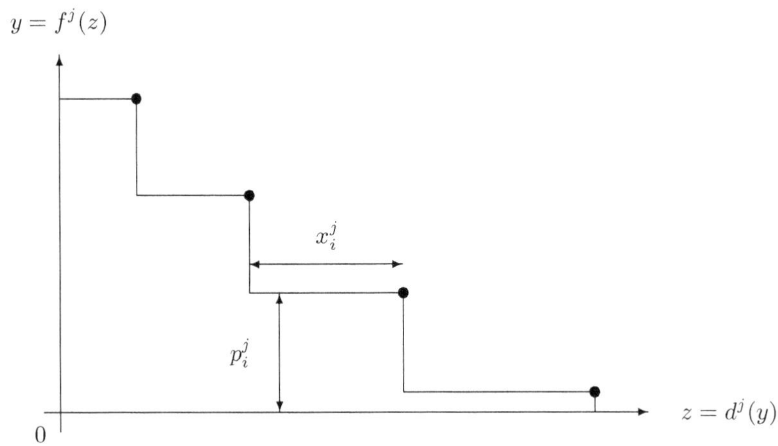

Figure 4.4: Inverse demand curve for broker j
Source: Semret et al. ([214], p. 2503).

If broker j is a profit maximizer she sells as much as possible for a given allocation $\mathbf{A}$. Hence, $x_j^j = e_j(\mathbf{A})$. Consequently, potential revenues of broker j are given by

$$\theta_j(e_j(\mathbf{A})) := \int_0^{e_j(\mathbf{A})} f^j(z)dz. \qquad (4.102)$$

We now determine the utility-maximizing bidding strategies for end-users and brokers as well as the resulting equilibrium. Therefore, we must introduce the PSP allocation mechanism and the equilibrium concept applied which is the ϵ-Nash equilibrium.

We first introduce the notion of an ϵ-Nash equilibrium. The bidding profile $(\mathbf{B}_i; \mathbf{B}_{-i})$ is an ϵ-Nash equilibrium if, for all bidders i and bidding strategies $\mathbf{B}'_i$,

$$U_i(\mathbf{B}_i; \mathbf{B}_{-i}) \geq U_i(\mathbf{B}'_i; \mathbf{B}_{-i}) - \epsilon,$$

where $\mathbf{B}_i$ is the ϵ-best bidding strategy of player i. In an ϵ-Nash equilibrium no player can gain more than ϵ by deviating from the ϵ-best bidding strategy.[115] Note that if $\epsilon = 0$ the ϵ-Nash equilibrium and the Nash equilibrium concept are identical. Within an auction framework where the auction is played dynamically, $\epsilon > 0$ may be interpreted as a bid fee each bidder has to pay when submitting a bid. Users submit new bids as long as they can increase their utility by more than ϵ. Hence, the game ends in an ϵ-Nash equilibrium. We will explain below that the level of ϵ plays an important role in achieving economic efficiency.

We will now introduce the design of the PSP allocation mechanism. The PSP auction is designed with a two-dimensional bid space consisting of price and quantity indications. The PSP auction allocates player i the bandwidth

$$a_i^j(\mathbf{B}^j) := \min \left\{ x_i^j, \left[x_j^j - \sum_{\substack{p_k^j \geq p_i^j \\ k \neq i}} x_k^j \right]^+ \right\} \tag{4.103}$$

and charges player i

$$c_i^j(\mathbf{B}^j) := \sum_{k \neq i} p_k^j \left[a_k^j(0; \mathbf{B}_{-i}^j) - a_k^j(\mathbf{b}_i^j; \mathbf{B}_{-i}^j) \right]$$

115 See Fudenberg and Tirole ([81], pp. 134 f.).

for all $i, j \in \mathcal{I}$. Expression

$$\left[x_j^j - \sum_{\substack{p_k^j \geq p_i^j \\ k \neq i}} x_k^j \right]^+$$

depicts the available capacity after all bidders with a higher bid than p_i^j are served. In other words, it depicts the maximum available capacity at a bid price of p_i^j. The capacity allocated to bidder i may not exceed the residual bandwidth after all bidders outbidding player i have been served. To understand how the PSP mechanism determines the costs c_i^j associated with the allocation a_i^j imagine that bidder i withdraws her bid. Then, one or several bidders who submitted lower bid prices may be allocated additional bandwidth units for which they are willing to pay their indicated bid prices. These potential revenues foregone by broker j by allocating an amount of capacity a_i^j to bidder i determine the costs c_i^j charged to bidder i. Hence, the PSP auction allocates the capacity to the highest bidders at costs equal to the declared willingness to pay of bidders who are excluded by the bid of a player i.

Consider the following example to better understand the PSP auction: Assume that $x_j^j = 100$ and that there are four bidders with the bidding strategies $\mathbf{b}_1^j = (30, 6)$, $\mathbf{b}_2^j = (30, 4)$, $\mathbf{b}_3^j = (50, 3)$, and $\mathbf{b}_4^j = (20, 1)$. The PSP mechanism determines

$$\begin{aligned}
a_1^j &= \min\{30, 100\} = 30, \\
a_2^j &= \min\{30, 100 - 30\} = 30, \\
a_3^j &= \min\{50, 100 - 30 - 30\} = 40, \\
a_4^j &= \min\{20, 100 - 30 - 30 - 40\} = 0, \\
c_1^j &= 4[30 - 30] + 3[50 - 40] + 1[20 - 0] = 50, \\
c_2^j &= 6[30 - 30] + 3[50 - 40] + 1[20 - 0] = 50, \\
c_3^j &= 6[30 - 30] + 4[30 - 30] + 1[20 - 0] = 20, \\
c_4^j &= 6[30 - 30] + 4[30 - 30] + 3[40 - 40] = 0.
\end{aligned}$$

We can conclude that $(a_1^j, c_1^j) = (30, 50)$, $(a_2^j, c_2^j) = (30, 50)$, $(a_3^j, c_3^j) = (40, 20)$, and $(a_4^j, c_4^j) = (0, 0)$.[116]

The idea behind the PSP auction is an exclusion-compensation principle: The amount paid for capacity by player i equals the willingness to pay of all other bidders who are excluded by the bid of player i. The willingness to pay of excluded bidders can be interpreted as social opportunity costs. At the same time, the PSP mechanism compensates the seller for the maximal lost potential revenues from the excluded bidders.

The exclusion-compensation principle is illustrated in Figure 4.5. This figure depicts the price-quantity bids of six bidders, where the bids are ranked according to bid prices. The market price function $P_i^j(\cdot)$ from the point of view of user i will be defined below. The costs c_i^j bidder i faces are illustrated by the shaded area. Her costs c_i^j equal the social opportunity costs due to the exclusion of bidder 3 and bidder 2. Bidder i does not get all the capacity requested at the bid price p_i^j, but, in accordance with equation (4.103), receives only

$$a_i^j = x_j^j - x_6^j - x_5^j$$

since bidder 5 is ready to pay a higher price for the quantity $(x_i^j - a_i^j)$ compared to bidder i.[117]

The PSP mechanism is a generalization of the second-price Vickrey auction: For a marginal unit of capacity each bidder is charged

116 Lazar and Semret ([139], p. 9) remark that if players bid the same price and if the sum of the required capacity exceeds the available capacity the PSP allocation rule does not allocate all the capacity available. This case would be relevant if, for example, $x_j^j = 100$, $\mathbf{b}_1^j = (60, 4)$, and $\mathbf{b}_2^j = (70, 4)$. The PSP mechanism determines $a_1^j = \min\{60, 100 - 70\} = 30$ and $a_2^j = \min\{70, 100 - 60\} = 40$. Tuffin [241] solves this problem by slightly changing the allocation rule such that, in the case of equal bid prices, the remaining bandwidth is divided among users in proportion to their requested quantities. The contribution of Tuffin [241] does not change the results derived by Lazar and Semret [139], Semret [209], and Semret et al. [214]. The reason is that the latter introduce a technicality such that at equilibrium the problem of unallocated capacity will never arise.

117 In Figure 4.5 the bid price of bidder 1 is so low that she does not obtain any capacity while the bid price set by bidder 2 is not high enough to ensure that she is allocated all the capacity demanded.

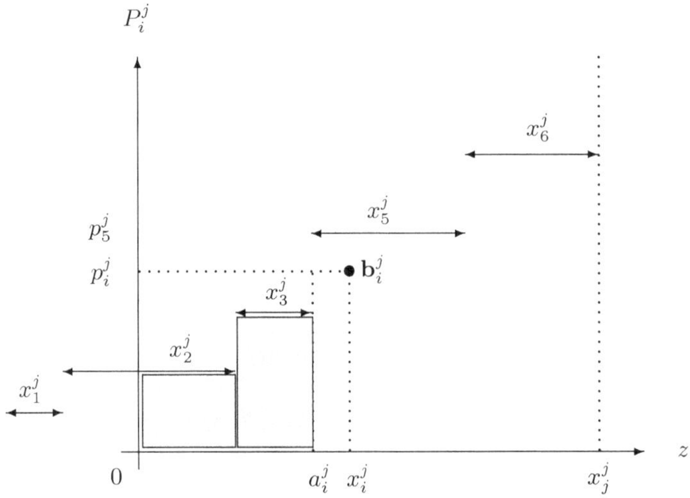

Figure 4.5: Exclusion-compensation principle
Source: See Semret ([209], p. 18).

the price the next highest bidder is ready to pay for it. If all bidders i bid $x_i^j = x_j^j$ the winning bidder would be charged the second highest price just as in the Vickrey auction. In contrast to the standard Vickrey auction the second highest price is potentially charged for several units of capacity instead of for just one unit of capacity.[118]

Note that with the PSP auction each seller determines the quantity allocated to each buyer solely from the bids for her resources, i.e., solely from local information. Allocations determined in one network of the Internet depend on the resources available in that network and on the bids for capacity of the respective network only.

118 See Semret ([209], pp. 18 f.).

The market price function of broker j from the point of view of user i depicted in Figure 4.5 is defined as

$$P_i^j(z) := \inf \left\{ y \geq 0 : x_j^j - \sum_{\substack{p_k^j > y \\ k \neq j}} x_k^j \geq z \right\},$$

where

$$c_i^j = \int_0^{a_i^j} P_i^j(z) dz.$$

The market price is defined as the infimum of the term in braces since the market price function is a step function as illustrated in Figure 4.5. In this figure, at $z = x_i^j$, for example, the market price equals

$$P_i^j(x_i^j) = \inf \left\{ y \geq 0 : x_j^j - x_6^j \right\} = p_5^j.$$

It has already been noted above that the PSP auction has the desirable properties of incentive compatibility and efficiency. We first consider incentive compatibility. We will argue that truth-telling, i.e., submitting a bid price equal to the marginal valuation of bandwidth, is a dominant strategy for both users and brokers. In turn we will look at the dominant bidding strategies of users and brokers.

Lazar and Semret ([139], pp. 12 f.) formally show that, under reasonable assumptions, the dominant bidding strategy for each user i is to bid the largest possible quantity v_i^j where the marginal valuation of bandwidth still exceeds the market price, and to bid a price w_i^j equal to the marginal valuation of bandwidth. Hence, revealing the true willingness to pay is optimal. We will content ourselves with a geometrical illustration to explain why truth-telling is a dominant strategy for each user.

Given a marginal valuation curve $\theta_i'(\cdot)$ depicted in Figure 4.6, user i maximizes her utility by setting the truthful bid $\mathbf{t}_i^j = (v_i^j, w_i^j)$, where v_i^j is the highest quantity where the marginal valuation for bandwidth, $\theta_i'(\cdot)$, still exceeds the market price, and where $w_i^j = \theta_i'(v_i^j)$. According to the PSP auction mechanism, the costs associated with this bid are depicted by the shaded area: These costs equal the declared willingness to pay of all other bidders who are excluded by the bid of player i. The utility of bidder i associated with the truthful bid $\mathbf{t}_i^j = (v_i^j, w_i^j)$ equals the area between the costs associated with her bid and the marginal valuation curve $\theta_i'(\cdot)$ up to the quantity v_i^j.

We will now explain that bidder i cannot increase her utility by deviating from the truthful bid $\mathbf{t}_i^j = (v_i^j, w_i^j)$: If, for the bid quantity v_i^j, user i set a bid price higher than her marginal valuation of bandwidth $\theta_i'(v_i^j)$ she would risk outbidding the next bidder above her which, due to the PSP auction mechanism, would result in higher costs being paid for the allocated units of bandwidth. Similarly, if user i lowered the bid quantity and adjusted the bid price according to her marginal valuation of bandwidth, i.e., set a bid $\mathbf{b}_i'^j$, user i could outbid the next bidder above her. In consequence, user i would be allocated a lower quantity of bandwidth at higher costs which decreases her utility.

In contrast, if, for the bid quantity v_i^j, user i set a bid price lower than her marginal valuation of bandwidth $\theta_i'(v_i^j)$ the chances of being outbid by the next bidder below her increase. If this happens to be the case the utility of user i would decrease relative to the scenario where user i sets the bid price equal to the marginal valuation of bandwidth. The same argument holds if user i rose the bid quantity and adjusted the bid price according to her marginal valuation of bandwidth, i.e., set a bid $\mathbf{b}_i^j$. Hence, in equilibrium for all $\mathbf{b}_i^j$ we have

$$U_i(\mathbf{t}_i^j; \mathbf{B}_{-i}^j) \geq U_i(\mathbf{b}_i^j; \mathbf{B}_{-i}^j) - \epsilon.$$

A similar line of reasoning applies to the dominant bidding strategy of brokers: Brokers are simultaneously involved in several auctions. Remember from expression (4.102) that a broker i can only increase her revenues if she manages to raise her bottleneck capacity $e_i(\mathbf{A})$. Hence, brokers have to coordinate their buy-side bids in order to maximize their profits. In consequence, they cannot directly determine the optimal bid quantity, but must first determine their optimal bottleneck e^*. The optimal bottleneck e^* is the largest bot-

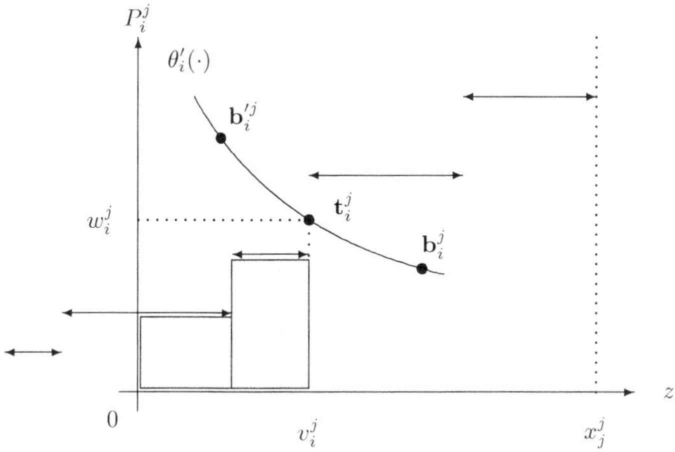

Figure 4.6: Truthful ϵ-best reply
Source: See Lazar and Semret ([139], p. 12).

tleneck such that the marginal value of capacity of broker i, which, according to expression (4.102), is given by

$$\theta_i'(e^*) = f^i(e^*),$$

just exceeds the market price from the point of view of broker i. This market price is defined by the average of the market prices realized at the different auctions, weighted by the provisioning factors:

$$P_i := \sum_{j \neq i} P_i^j(v_i^j) r_i^j.$$

A broker i who has a given sell-side ask $\mathbf{b}_i^i$ and who is confronted the bidding strategies of all other players $\mathbf{B}_{-i}$, which together determine $\boldsymbol{a}^i$, obtains her optimal bids at each buy-side market by transforming the desired optimal bottleneck e^* into the corresponding bidding quantities

$$v_i^j = (e^* - a_j^i) r_i^j,$$

to submit at each buy-side market. According to the equilibrium condition (4.99),

$$v_i^j = a_i^j = (e^* - a_j^i) r_i^j.$$

The same as for end-users, Semret et al. ([214], p. 2505) show that truth-telling is optimal for each broker. The marginal value of capacity of broker i at each buy-side market j is given by her marginal value of capacity at e^*, $f^i(e^*)$, divided by the fraction of incoming traffic at broker i that is routed to peer j. Hence, at each buy-side market broker i sets the bid price

$$w_i^j = \frac{1}{r_i^j} f^i(e^*)$$

which reveals her true willingness to pay per unit of capacity from broker j.

Then, the ϵ-best strategy for broker i is given by the profile of truthful bids $\mathbf{T}_i := (\mathbf{v}_i, \mathbf{w}_i)$. Hence, in equilibrium we have for all $\mathbf{B}_i$

$$U_i(\mathbf{T}_i; \mathbf{B}_{-i}) \geq U_i(\mathbf{B}_i; \mathbf{B}_{-i}) - \epsilon.$$

Semret ([209], p. 66) proves that a game with arbitrarily networked PSP auctions, where, among other things, all buyers have utilities given by (4.100), where sellers are static, i.e., set fixed asks $\mathbf{b}_i^i$ with positive reserve prices p_i^i, there exists a truthful network-wide ϵ-Nash equilibrium for any $\epsilon > 0$. However, such an equilibrium does not have to be unique.

An ϵ-Nash equilibrium is efficient in the sense that resources are allocated to players who value them the most. The intuition goes as follows: In a PSP auction, the marginal valuation for capacity of each excluded player cannot exceed the bid price of any opponent who obtains a positive allocation. Stated differently, if the marginal valuation of capacity of player j is smaller than the marginal valuation of capacity of player i and if player j is allocated a positive amount of capacity player i can take away some of the resources allocated to player j by paying a price lower than her own marginal valuation of capacity. Thereby, both the utility of player i and total social welfare increase since the marginal value of capacity of player i exceeds the one of player j. In equilibrium, no player can increase her utility by more than ϵ by unilaterally deviating from her bidding strategy. Total social surplus $\sum_{i \in \mathcal{I}} U_i(\cdot)$ is (almost) maximized. As will be further explained in a moment, the smaller the parameter ϵ, the closer we can get to maximal social surplus.[119]

Through the parameter ϵ the PSP auction is characterized by a trade-off between engineering and economic efficiency, measured by convergence time and by total user value, respectively. To see this, note that the smaller ϵ, the closer we get to a Nash equilibrium, i.e., to allocations maximizing social surplus. However, if the costs of a bid are small, i.e., if ϵ is small, more iterations are needed until equilibrium is reached. Given that there are more iterations with a small ϵ, convergence time to equilibrium is longer.[120] By simulation, Semret et al. ([214], pp. 2507–2511) study the DiffServ PSP auction framework and validate the analytical results presented above.

We conclude this section with an evaluation of the PSP auction with respect to the criteria established in Section 2.2.3 since the PSP auction constitutes a novel way for pricing large retail customers. Our evaluation is summarized in Table 4.1. As will be explained below, from the welfare theoretic point of view the PSP auction mechanism fulfills all criteria very well.

- *Allocative efficiency*
  As explained above, the PSP auction leads an allocation which is arbitrarily close to maximum efficiency.
- *Capacity expansion*
  Prices give correct monetary incentives to expand capacity in bottlenecks: If necessary, brokers will buy more capacity to accommodate the demand of their customers and to, thereby, increase their profits.

119 Lazar and Semret ([139], pp. 17–19) provide a formal proof of the efficiency of the PSP auction.

120 Lazar and Semret ([139], pp. 19–21) investigate the trade-off between engineering and economic efficiency by simulation.

Table 4.1: Evaluation of the progressive second price auction

ISP/Welfare	*Allocative efficiency*	▲
	Capacity expansion	▲
	Incentive compatibility	▲
ISP	*Cost-orientation*	▲
	Price discrimination	▲
	Feasibility	◊
	Accounting efficiency	◊
User	*Utility-orientation*	▲
	Price transparency	▽

▲ = very good, △ = good
◊ = satisfactory, ▽ = adequate, ▼ = inadequate

- *Incentive compatibility*
  The PSP mechanism is incentive compatible in that each player sets a truthful bid price equal to the marginal valuation of bandwidth. In equilibrium, no player can increase her utility by more than ϵ by unilaterally deviating from her bidding strategy.
- *Cost-orientation*
  From the point of view of ISPs, the PSP auction mechanism is cost-oriented if RBSs sell the capacity at cost-oriented prices. Then, brokers trade the amount of capacity which maximizes their profits. Occasionally, brokers may be unprofitable if the capacities bought and sold are not synchronized. In this case, the equilibrium conditions (4.98) and (4.99) are not met for all brokers j,

$j \in \mathcal{I}$. However, in the long run the sell-side constraint (4.97) ensures that brokers break even.

Generally, the PSP auction is not revenue-maximizing since the price paid is always lower than the bid.[121] However, Lazar and Semret ([138], pp. 11 f.) demonstrate that the PSP auction rule tends to maximize revenues as the ratio of demand to supply becomes large.

- *Price discrimination*
  A further advantage of the PSP auction mechanism is that providers, i.e., RBS and SBBs, are given the possibility to price discriminate. Depending on the bid price and, consequently, on the marginal valuation of bandwidth, each bidder may potentially pay a different unit price.
- *Feasibility*
  We judge the feasibility of the PSP mechanism to be satisfactory: On the one hand, Semret ([209], p. 12) claims that the PSP auction is feasible regarding the load of signalling, billing, and a priori information. His claim is based on the facts that the auction rule is computationally inexpensive[122] and that the preferences of buyers do not have to be known. With two-dimensional bids, the market price can be derived directly from the bids only. Evidence is given by the fact that the PSP auction has been implemented in the framework of Merkato. Also, as already mentioned above, the PSP mechanism allows auctions to be held in a decentralized manner since each seller determines the allocations solely from the bids for her resources, i.e., solely from local information. However, on the other hand, in order to give end-to-end service guarantees all over the Internet, the PSP auction mechanism must be adopted by each provider in the Internet, a rather unlikely scenario. But

121 Note that even first price auctions where the winner of the auction pays a price equal to her bid yield exactly the same revenues as the Vickrey auction where the winner pays the second highest bid. This is the so-called revenue equivalence theorem. See Jehle and Reny ([120], pp. 383–403).

122 The complexity of computing an allocation $(\boldsymbol{a}^j, \mathbf{c}^j)$ is $\mathcal{O}(I^2)$. This means that the complexity of computing an allocation $(\boldsymbol{a}^j, \mathbf{c}^j)$ is a quadratic polynomial in the number of players. See Semret ([209], p. 20).

the PSP auction model at the same instant provides a solution to both the retail and the interconnection pricing problem. Both (large) end-users and interconnected networks buy network access through a PSP auction.

- *Accounting efficiency*
  We judge accounting efficiency to be satisfactory since, as already mentioned above, the determination of the costs $\mathbf{c}^j$ can be done with reasonable computational overhead. Also, accounting units, i.e., units of bandwidth, are rather coarse compared to packets, for example. However, compared to other pricing schemes, such as flat-rate pricing or expected capacity pricing, the overhead costs involved in calculating the prices are still considerable.
- *Utility-orientation*
  From the point of view of users, the PSP auction mechanism is utility-oriented for the following reasons: Prices determined by a PSP auction maximize individual utilities and social welfare at once, whereas users with the highest willingness to pay are allocated the bandwidth at a price lower than their marginal willingness to pay. Also, there are no cross-subsidies between user groups. In particular, differentiated services are offered fitting heterogeneous user preferences. Semret et al. ([212], p. 6) note that their model also accommodates best-effort traffic in that best-effort traffic could use any unallocated or allocated, but unused capacity. The authors propose not applying the PSP mechanism to this traffic class, but instead charging a flat rate.
- *Price transparency*
  Price transparency of the PSP auction is rather low. Depending on the market conditions, prices may vary considerably. But, prices are always lower than the respective bid. Hence, users know the maximum costs of an allocation in advance.

In sum, the PSP auction mechanism is a very promising pricing approach. It meets many of our criteria for Internet pricing to complete satisfaction. The question remains open how small retail customers should be priced within the context of the PSP auction framework. The same compatibility considerations conducted in the previous section apply to the PSP auction: Theoretically, it is compatible with any of the retail pricing mechanisms proposed in Chapter 3. The choice of the retail pricing model brings about the mentioned advantages and drawbacks summarized in Section 3.5. It is left up to individual providers how to design their retail pricing plans. However, it is to be expected that pricing proposals that are load-sensitive and take QoS into consideration are likely to be preferred by IAPs since they are able to offer guaranteed QoS and they themselves face load and quality-sensitive interconnection prices.[123] It is conceivable that IAPs are only ready to offer a flat rate or load and quality-insensitive usage prices at a risk premium.

4.4 Synopsis of Internet Interconnection Pricing

The Internet is all about connectivity. To ensure interconnection of various networks, each ISP must be compensated for its investments in infrastructure and for conveyed data. There may be many ISPs involved in the delivery of data to an end-user who purchases the service from one ISP only, namely from her Internet Access Provider (IAP). Therefore, inter-provider financial settlements become necessary. Such interconnection settlements were the focus of this chapter. We explained that wholesale interconnection pricing agreements are closely related to retail pricing models: An ISP that pays volume-based interconnection fees incurs a financial risk when offering flat rates to its end-users. Both interconnection fees and retail pricing schemes have to be compatible in order to transmit appropriate incentives. This implies in particular that a multi service network requires interconnection charges to be differentiated with respect to the QoS offered.

For some retail pricing proposals, namely for dynamic priority pricing, expected capacity pricing, dynamic volume pricing, resource-

123 The prices determined by the PSP auction are load-sensitive since they vary according to current demand, i.e., current bids, for data traffic conveyance.

based pricing and effective bandwidth pricing, the issue of interconnection pricing was addressed in Chapter 3 in the form of a bottom-up approach. That is, given a certain retail pricing proposal a matching interconnection pricing solution was presented. In this chapter we conducted a top-down approach and thereby focused on interconnection settlements and analyzed which retail pricing structures match the proposed interconnection pricing models. This section summarizes our analysis and findings in Chapter 4.

In Section 4.1, we conducted a positive economic analysis of interconnection pricing, suggesting that the interconnection market is inefficient due to the absence of accurate price signals and a lack of both price transparency and dynamics. We pointed at the necessity that each provider is fairly compensated for its infrastructure investments and carriage services through appropriate inter-provider settlements.

The starting point of our analysis was the dial-up Internet access market. Our considerations provided important insights into why, in practice, Internet is often priced either flat (due to the FRIACO model) or free (due to the double marginalization problem). Also, we discussed the so-called reciprocal compensation problem occurring in the United States. In this context, we saw that the standard U.S. interconnection model for Internet bound calls leads to substantial losses of the Incumbent Local Exchange Carriers (ILECs) and lacks incentives to adequately invest in capacity. We then presented two solutions to the reciprocal compensation problem, proposed by the FCC and by Banerjee and Ros [14, 15, 16]. We concluded that regulatory artifacts of the Public Switched Telephone Network (PSTN) are significant drivers of popular free and flat rates in the dial-up Internet access market. We conjectured that this is not likely to be a problem in the long run since alternative access technologies, i.e., broadband access technologies, are rapidly becoming more popular. With the market penetration of alternative unregulated access technologies different pricing models will be introduced which better reflect usage and underlying costs.

In Section 4.1.2 we turned our attention to a higher level in the Internet hierarchy, to settlements between interconnecting ISPs. The question to be answered was how the revenues from retail tariffs gained by Internet Access Providers (IAPs) are distributed to all other providers involved in the delivery of data. We identified two basic types of interconnection relationships: Peering and transit. We found that ISPs of similar size opt for a peering arrangement while transit arrangements dominate interconnection between networks of different size. Also, peering agreements are often based on a Sender-Keep-All (SKA) model while, in a transit agreement, a customer ISP compensates its supplier ISP for the provided interconnection service. Our considerations led to the following result: Revenues from retail tariffs gained by IAPs are passed over to Internet Backbone Providers (IBPs) through transit fees to compensate upstream providers for infrastructure investments and carriage of data traffic. However, there have not been any systematic settlement policies. Therefore, the question remained what an efficient settlement rule looks like.

In Section 4.1.2 we also studied the compatibility of settlement schemes in practice with the retail pricing proposals introduced in Chapter 3. Our considerations can be summarized as follows: Flat-rate pricing at the interconnection level is compatible with flat-rate pricing, possibly combined with voluntary user declarations and a quota system, at the retail level. Volume-based prices levied at the interconnection level match nonlinear tariffs at the retail level. One can also imagine volume-based interconnection prices varying with the time of day making them compatible with peak-load pricing at the retail level.

In Section 4.1.3 we analyzed peering arrangements based on a bargaining model proposed by Milgrom, Mitchell, and Srinagesh ([168], pp. 187–195). The model suggests that if there is a sufficient number of IBPs of similar size competing for market share in order to preserve their interconnection agreements, retail and transit prices reflect costs. If one IBP obtains a dominant market position and if switching costs of consumers are low a dominant IBP can charge transit fees to its IBP rivals. In consequence, retail and transit prices no longer reflect costs. Remember that the authors abstracted from costs for simplicity. We outlined how one could introduce costs without changing the results of the analysis qualitatively.

In Section 4.2 we turned our attention to normative economics and asked how interconnection charges should be set to maximize social welfare. Based on an article by Lehr and Weiss [142] we first studied congestion pricing at the interconnection level. An important characteristic of these congestion prices is that not only do they decrease usage when congestion occurs, but they also generate the revenues necessary for capacity expansion. We found that optimal congestion prices for Internet data traffic equal the sum of the congestion prices for on-net traffic of each network along the path. Hence, an originating network should pay the provider in charge of forwarding the data traffic an interconnection fee equal to the sum of on-net congestion prices of all networks involved in terminating the data traffic. A further result was that, at equilibrium, optimal on-net congestion prices can be calculated based on local information only, without knowledge of the utility function of subscribers. This is the same finding as derived in Section 3.3.1. We then extended the analysis of Lehr and Weiss [142] by showing that with appropriate settlements the private optimum in a competitive market corresponds to the social optimum just as in the case of a single network examined in Section 3.3.1. Moreover, we could preserve a result obtained for the optimal price, namely that the competitive price can also be calculated based on local information only, without knowledge of the utility function of subscribers. Furthermore, we could draw the same conclusion as in Section 3.3.1, i.e., that a competitive provider expands its capacity if and only if it is socially optimal to do so. Hence, efficient congestion prices and settlements in the competitive market give correct monetary incentives for capacity expansion. Again, we considered that interconnection congestion pricing is compatible with retail congestion pricing and the smart market approach.

In Section 4.2.2 we presented extra-capacity pricing introduced by Little and Wright [143]. These authors determine welfare maximizing settlement payments in a model of horizontal product differentiation with two competing providers. The solution of the benchmark problem that determines efficient pricing and efficient supply of capacity gave important insights: Optimal prices exceed marginal costs of data transport of each provider. These prices take into consideration that additional usage requires appropriate capacity expansion in order to prevent congestion. Hence, optimal unit prices signal true costs of additional capacity. Furthermore, optimal level of infrastructure provision frees the network from congestion. The authors show that the optimal solution cannot be achieved without settlements. The reasons are that without settlements there is an under-investment in capacity due to a free-rider problem and the fact that usage is priced too low. Both consequences of the settlement-free environment result in excessive congestion. We then demonstrated that the efficient outcome can be decentralized, i.e., it can be realized in a competitive environment, if a settlement regime is implemented where net providers of capacity charge net demanders of capacity for the use of their network at a rate equal to the incremental costs of the provided infrastructure. An important question was whether competing ISPs voluntarily agree on the efficient settlement rule. We showed that this is not the case. Instead, the two ISPs have an incentive to set the interconnection price at a level above incremental costs of capacity, i.e., to raise the settlement price in proportion to the level of bandwidth they provide. This results in higher retail prices and, therefore, in a higher provider surplus at the expense of consumer surplus. We then elucidated why this is not likely to be a problem in the long run. We closed the section with an explanation that extra-capacity pricing is compatible with congestion pricing and with peak-load pricing, provided that the firm peak case prevails.

In Section 4.2.3 we abandoned our assumption that either the sender or the receiver pays for data conveyance. Instead, following Laffont et al. [134, 135] and Armstrong [6], we supposed that the sender and the receiver share the costs of data transport. We first presented a benchmark model with perfect Bertrand competition between ISPs for two types of subscribers, namely consumers and website providers with inelastic demand for and inelastic supply of webpages, respectively. We argued that Bertrand competition drives down retail prices until they equal marginal costs. In equilibrium, the ISP industry is characterized by zero profits. Our analysis led to the so-called off-net-cost pricing principle introduced by Laffont et al. [134]. This name is derived from the fact that retail prices turned out not to alter depending on whether data transport was originated and terminated on the same or on distinct networks.

We saw that the off-net cost pricing principle no longer holds if the assumption of reciprocal, i.e., symmetric, interconnection prices is relaxed. However, reciprocity can be defined in a broad sense where termination costs of networks are allowed to differ. We explained that, then, the ISP with the less aggressive hot-potato routing policy should be compensated for carrying off-net traffic longer on its network compared to the competitor by having to pay a lower interconnection fee.

An implication of the off-net-cost pricing principle is that retail prices cover marginal costs of data conveyance whatever the level of the interconnection price. In particular, we demonstrated that the level of the interconnection price does not influence the level of social welfare if demand is inelastic. This no longer holds true when relaxing our assumption about inelastic demand. If consumer demand is supposed to be elastic while website demand is inelastic, in the welfare maximizing equilibrium, the websites are deprived of any gains from trade. According to the principles of Ramsey pricing this result is to be expected since they suggest burdening price-cost markups on the inelastic side of the market. We explained that in the mirror case, where consumer demand is inelastic while the websites' demand for posting information is elastic, as much of the cost burden as possible should be allocated to consumers.

We closed the section in pointing out that the off-net-cost pricing principle also holds when different service qualities are introduced. This property makes the off-net-cost pricing principle compatible with peak-load pricing, static priority pricing, paris metro pricing, and congestion pricing.

Both Sections 4.1 and 4.2 on positive and normative economic analysis of interconnection pricing, respectively, focus on network environments with one service class. In Section 4.3, which is also based on normative economics, we introduced different service qualities into the analysis of interconnection pricing. In this context, we presented two auction mechanisms for electronic market places: The double auction and the progressive second price auction.

We started Section 4.3.1 with a discussion about how current Service Level Agreement (SLA) negotiation can be extended to support end-to-end service guarantees. We then presented an automated bandwidth trading approach, named Automated Bandwidth Exchange (ABAX) that was introduced by Rupp [202]. In the proposed model, ABAX matches (combinatorial) bids and asks based on a continuous double auction mechanism with the goals of achieving efficiency, fast allocation, transparency, fairness, and decentralization while supporting quality-differentiated services. We concluded that the proposed automated bandwidth exchange ensures a fast allocation of bandwidth, transparency, fairness, as well as decentralization while the goal of efficiency is likely to be achieved. However, the proposed mechanism is not incentive compatible which potentiates strategic manipulation by the bidders. But, we explained that the problem of strategic behavior of bidders diminishes with a rising complexity of the allocation mechanism; and the automated bandwidth exchange is indeed complex.

Concerning the compatibility of ABAX with retail pricing schemes we found that, theoretically, automated bandwidth trading matches any of the retail pricing mechanisms proposed in Chapter 3. It is left up to individual providers how to design their retail pricing plans. However, it is to be expected that pricing proposals that are load-sensitive and take QoS into consideration are likely to be preferred by IAPs given that they are able to offer guaranteed QoS and that they themselves face load and quality sensitive interconnection prices. The possibilities of IAPs of purchasing bandwidth on demand from the source to the destination and of offering guaranteed QoS makes ABAX compatible with adaptive load-sensitive volume pricing, for example. IAPs would then charge end-users in accordance with their specified base prices and penalty function while they themselves face the costs determined by ABAX.

In Section 4.3.2 we presented a new auction mechanism, called Progressive Second Price (PSP) auction, introduced by Lazar and Semret [139]. In contrast to the Vickrey auction in the smart market model introduced in Section 3.3.2, where the bidders bid for one indivisible unit of a resource, the two-dimensional bids in the PSP auction, consisting of a bid quantity and a bid price, can ask for arbitrary shares of the total available resource quantity. The PSP mechanism generalizes the idea of the Vickrey auction in that the total charge for the purchased capacity each bidder i faces equals the willingness to pay of all other bidders who are excluded by the bid of bidder i. Hence, for a marginal share of the network resource the winning bidder pays a price equal to the next highest bid. We explained that the willingness to pay of excluded bidders can be interpreted as social opportunity costs. At the same time, the PSP mechanism compensates the seller for the maximal lost potential revenues from the excluded bidders.

Based on the extended work of Lazar and Semret [139] by Semret [209] and Semret et al. [214] we determined optimal strategies for buyers and sellers of capacity and showed that the PSP auction leads to an efficient equilibrium in DiffServ bandwidth markets, where the equilibrium concept applied is an ϵ-Nash equilibrium. Particularly, we demonstrated that truth-telling, i.e., submitting a bid price equal to the marginal valuation of bandwidth, is a dominant strategy for all bidders. As already noted in Section 4.3.1, the PSP auction is adopted by Merkato, a software platform which creates electronic market places to automate purchase, sale, and allocation of bandwidth dynamically in real-time. Merkato enables buyers not to have to set up long-term fixed contracts as in the case of classic peering and transit agreements. Instead, sellers can sell their excess capacity and shift traffic from peak to off-peak periods via price signals.

We closed the section with an evaluation of the PSP auction with respect to the criteria established in Section 2.2.3 since the PSP auction constitutes a novel way for pricing large retail customers. We judged the PSP auction mechanism to be a very promising pricing approach. It meets many of our criteria for Internet pricing to complete satisfaction.

Then, we answered how small retail customers should be priced within the context of the PSP auction framework. We obtained the same results as with ABAX, namely that the PSP auction mechanism is theoretically compatible with any of the retail pricing mechanisms proposed in Chapter 3. The choice of the retail pricing model brings about the mentioned advantages and drawbacks summarized in Section 3.5. Just as with ABAX, it is to be expected that pricing proposals that are load-sensitive and take QoS into consideration are likely to be preferred by IAPs. It is conceivable that IAPs are only ready to offer a flat rate or load and quality-insensitive usage prices at a risk premium. Table 4.2 summarizes our compatibility analysis of interconnection and retail pricing schemes conducted in this chapter.

Table 4.2: Compatibility analysis of interconnection and retail pricing schemes

Interconnection pricing	*Retail pricing*
Flat-rate pricing	Flat-rate pricing
Volume-based pricing	Nonlinear tariffs
Congestion pricing	Congestion pricing Smart market approach
Extra-capacity pricing	Peak-load pricing (firm peak) Congestion pricing
Off-net-cost pricing principle	Peak-load pricing Static priority pricing Paris metro pricing Congestion pricing
ABAX PSP auction	Theoretically all retail pricing schemes

5. Critical Appreciation and a Primer on Bundling

> As long as [... your willingness to pay] for your flat fees [... is] very high, then they can persist. But if you want e-mail to be cheap and Internet access to be cheap, then it's going to have to be pay as you go.
>
> Bob Metcalfe ([117], p. 16)

With the progressive commercialization of the Internet that must satisfy heterogeneous user demand, prices for Internet usage play an important role. This work analyzed the pricing of Internet transport services and interconnection. We explained that appropriate pricing requires popular flat rates to be abandoned. They should be replaced by usage-based prices which are load-sensitive and take different service qualities into consideration. That way, first, negative congestion externalities can be internalized according to the costs-by-cause principle. This is a prerequisite for an efficient allocation of scarce resources. Second, prices differentiated with respect to quality allow the introduction of different service qualities in the Internet and take account of heterogeneous user demand. Third, usage-based prices are essential to allow ISPs to recover costs.

A welcome side-effect of the replacement of flat-rate pricing by usage-based pricing is that, thereby, the problem of spam in the Internet can be combated. According to the U.S. company Brightmail more than half of all emails sent worldwide were spam messages in 2003. Experts alert that this quota is likely to reach 65% to 75% in the next few years. The spam menace, apart from congesting electronic mail boxes, also consumes scarce bandwidth through needless data transports. The Swiss provider Green.ch estimates that already 20% of its bandwidth is loaded with spam. The technology research company Forrester Research judges prices to be the only successful instrument against spam. That way, spammers themselves, rather than Internet users, have to bear the costs of their activities. Forrester Research finds that the business idea of spammers, who are paid by companies to spread their sales messages, would already be vitiated if an email costed a fourth of a cent.[1]

The aim and the contribution of this work were to give a systematic overview of Internet pricing proposals, to evaluate these pricing schemes and to analyze relations between them. Given the wide and heterogeneous literature on Internet pricing this overview was not exhaustive. However, in Chapter 3, we analyzed classical and essential pricing schemes while pointing at and outlining related pricing approaches. Most of the presented pricing proposals are designed for the Internet environment. The two exceptions are nonlinear outlay schedules and peak-load pricing which stem from the theory of public utility pricing. In Sections 3.1.2 and 3.1.3 we applied these two pricing schemes to the Internet environment. In particular, as an alternative to optimal nonlinear tariffs, we proposed an ex-post weighted-average Coase tariff where fixed costs are allocated according to usage and an additional variable price component is charged which reflects marginal costs of data transport. Moreover, in Section 3.3.3, our contribution consisted of presenting a simplified version of dynamic priority pricing with the purpose of making the structure of the model understood. Also, when introducing dynamic volume pricing in Section 3.4.2, we abandoned the assumption of identical basic prices across service classes with the consequence of having obtained optimal usage prices different from those derived by the authors.

We consecutively evaluated each pricing scheme presented in Chapter 3 according to normative criteria for Internet pricing, set up in Section 2.2.3, from the points of view of social welfare, ISPs, and Internet users. Our evaluations were based on a rating scheme ranging over five categories from 'very good' to 'inadequate'. Section 3.5 gave a synopsis of these evaluations. The basic result is that several auspicious pricing proposals allow social welfare to be enhanced compared to current pricing solutions. However, we did not identify a pricing plan which at the same time satisfies all normative criteria for Internet pricing at best. Instead, there is a trade-off between achieving the desired characteristics including allocative efficiency,

1 See Settele [216].

efficient capacity expansion, incentive compatibility, cost-orientation, price discrimination and utility-orientation and the requirements concerning feasibility, accounting efficiency, as well as price transparency. Comparing the ratings of flat-rate pricing and congestion pricing accentuates this trade-off. Also, due to this trade-off, pricing proposals for guaranteed service quality and, in particular, optimal congestion pricing approaches become less recommendable when being evaluated with respect to practical criteria including feasibility and accounting efficiency. Given this trade-off, a concluding rating of the different pricing schemes and a possible recommendation of a specific pricing system require information about how ISPs and subscribers appraise the different normative criteria for Internet pricing. Nevertheless, we concluded that expected capacity pricing and peak-load pricing do well from all perspectives. We pointed at the possibility of combining these two approaches. We also indicated that the combination of Paris Metro Pricing (PMP) with peak-load pricing shows promise. In our evaluation, popular flat rates turned out to be inadequate in particular from the welfare theoretic point of view. We gave reasons why flat rates are so popular despite our bad rating.

We also discussed several promising variants of pricing schemes, presented in Chapter 3, that can be interim pricing solutions in the transition phase from flat-rate pricing to more sophisticated pricing approaches. These pricing variants include percentile pricing, adaptive flat-rate pricing, a version of PMP in the form of a prepaid price plan, as well as cumulus pricing.

We then addressed the question to what extent different service qualities will actually be offered and which Internet pricing practices are likely to be found in the future. We explained that in order to implement different service qualities in the Internet, router technology and packet forwarding must be coordinated system-wide and that service requirements must be contracted in interconnection agreements. Additionally, when introducing guaranteed QoS, resource reservation and admission control are requisite. For these reasons, in the near future, we expect different service qualities to only be provided in intranets, extranets, or subnetworks of the Internet. Over time, more and more carriers are likely to offer different service qualities.

A further requisite for the introduction of quality differentiation in the Internet is user acceptance of metered Internet service. Results of a simulated demand experiment, presented in Section 2.2.2, suggest that users accept volume-based and load-sensitive prices for Internet usage if congestion decreases and the quality of data transmission thereby improves. Thus, the question remained how to incite Internet users to prefer volume-based tariffs to flat rates. We mentioned that necessary impulses to increase user acceptance of volume-based prices may be released by packet-switched wireless communication technologies such as GPRS and, in the future, also UMTS, given that, today, data transport processed by GPRS is already predominantly brought to account on a volume basis.

As a compromise, a monthly flat rate could be charged for data traffic transports at the lowest priority level while higher-value users would be offered higher QoS, possibly on demand, at a usage-based price premium. Additionally, to assist user acceptance through a higher predictability of their spending, ISPs may sell prepaid cards which are debited whenever users require higher QoS on demand. That way, users can cap their budget for Internet usage.

Given that we did not identify a pricing proposal which best meets our normative criteria on Internet pricing, we cannot expect a single pricing scheme to be implemented in the whole Internet. Instead, different pricing plans will coexist which take particular local circumstances into consideration. Generally, we appraise percentile pricing, adaptive flat-rate pricing, and PMP in the form of a prepaid price plan to be opportune interim pricing solutions in the transition period from flat-rate pricing to more sophisticated pricing schemes. Later, depending on the network technology, we estimate peak-load pricing and expected capacity pricing to bear good prospects of being implemented since they meet our normative criteria on Internet pricing well from all points of view. Also, interlinking peak-load pricing with expected capacity pricing as well as the combination of peak-load pricing with PMP feature good chances of being adopted. In particular, we recommend ex-post weighted-average Coase tariffs, where the variable price component is a peak-load price.

In Chapter 4 we focused on interconnection pricing. Interconnection is essential for successful data carriage. For various networks to interconnect, each ISP must be compensated for its investments in infrastructure and for data carriage. Many ISPs may be involved to convey data to an end-user who buys the service from her Internet Access Provider (IAP). For this reason, financial settlements between providers are fundamental. We first conducted a positive economic analysis of interconnection pricing, where we explained why each provider must be fairly compensated for its infrastructure investments and transport services through appropriate inter-provider settlements. Our study suggested that the absence of appropriate price signals and missing price transparency and dynamics lead to inefficiencies in the interconnection market. In Section 4.2 we turned our attention to normative economics and analyzed efficient settlement rules. In particular, in Section 4.2.1 we extended the model by Lehr and Weiss [142] by showing that with appropriate settlements the private optimum in a competitive market and the social optimum coincide. Section 4.3 was also based on normative economics, but additionally accounted for different service qualities. Specifically, we analyzed two auction mechanisms for automated bandwidth pricing, i.e., the double auction and the Progressive Second Price (PSP) auction. We evaluated the latter with respect to the criteria established in Section 2.2.3 since the PSP auction is a new mechanism for pricing large retail customers. We concluded that the PSP auction mechanism has promise since it completely satisfies many of our criteria for Internet pricing.

We expounded that one cannot focus on wholesale interconnection pricing agreements only without bearing in mind retail pricing models: Pricing schemes on both levels have to be compatible in order to transmit appropriate incentives. In Chapter 3 we discussed interconnection pricing solutions for some retail pricing proposals including dynamic priority pricing, expected capacity pricing, dynamic volume pricing, resource-based pricing and effective bandwidth pricing. This analysis took the form of a bottom-up approach: Starting with a certain retail pricing proposal we presented a compatible interconnection pricing scheme. In Chapter 4 we followed a top-down approach, where the focus was on interconnection settlements. Given the proposed interconnection pricing models, we identified matching retail pricing structures. Our compatibility analysis in Chapter 4 can be summarized as follows:[2] Flat-rate pricing at the interconnection level matches flat-rate pricing at the retail level, possibly combined with voluntary user declarations and a quota system. Moreover, volume-based prices charged at the interconnection level comply with nonlinear tariffs at the retail level. If these volume-based interconnection prices varied with the time of day they would be compatible with peak-load pricing at the retail level. Besides, interconnection congestion pricing matches congestion pricing and the smart market approach. Extra-capacity pricing fits congestion pricing and peak-load pricing in the event of the firm peak case. Again, the off-net cost pricing principle is compatible with peak-load pricing, static priority pricing, PMP, and congestion pricing. Both automated bandwidth trading mechanisms theoretically match all of the retail pricing schemes presented in Chapter 3. Providers can individually determine their favored retail pricing plans. However, pricing proposals that are load-sensitive and that consider different service qualities are likely to be preferred by IAPs since they themselves face load and quality-sensitive interconnection prices.

We close this work with a primer on bundling. In Section 3.1.2 price discrimination has been introduced as an instrument to induce consumers to truly reveal their preferences. Recall that nonlinear pricing, i.e., quantity discounts, can increase usage and revenues at once. This is a form of bundling which will be the focus of our final considerations.[3]

Bundling refers to the strategy of selling two or several distinct goods in a package at a single price. Many software packages such as Microsoft Office consist of bundled individual components. Other examples of bundling are academic journals or newspapers where articles are sold as a package.[4] Very low marginal costs of information

2 Refer to Table 4.2.
3 See Shapiro and Varian ([218], p. 81).
4 See Bichler ([22], p. 60).

products make bundling especially attractive.[5] At the limit, if marginal costs are zero and if consumers do not negatively value any of the bundled goods, each purchase creates some benefits at no incremental costs. Hence, efficiency is increased.[6] We will illustrate below that apart from low marginal costs, negatively correlated consumer valuations of the bundled goods enhance the desirability of the bundling strategy. Further drivers of the bundling strategy are positive network externalities: Goods producing positive network externalities that would not be purchased by a broad set of consumers may be sold in a bundle. Remember that in the presence of network externalities the value of a good can be increased this way.

Bundling has become a popular marketing strategy in the Internet environment. Optus and Telstra, two large telephone operators in Australia, for example, bundle fixed network telephony, mobile telephony, Internet access, and pay TV. They offer the bundle, consisting of substitute goods, at a discount.[7] Another example is Comcast, the largest cable operator of the United States, which decided to offer both its Internet access and regular television services at a discount. One may expect to observe video, voice, and high-speed Internet access services increasingly bundled together by cable, satellite, telephone, and wireless operators. Competition in the digital multichannel marketplace fosters discounts on offered bundles which benefits consumers in terms of lower prices and single bills.[8]

Not only substitutes may be bundled, but also complements: Swisscom, the Swiss incumbent, is planning to introduce UMTS bundled with GPRS and WLAN for its business customers at a flat rate. Users equipped with either a laptop or a handheld PC obtain access to all technologies: At so-called hotspots such as hotels, stations, or congress centers the WLAN technology will be applied. In areas

---

5 Kahin and Varian [123] edited a collection of articles that analyze bundling digital products. This collection consists of contributions by Bakos and Brynjolfsson [12], Chuang and Sirbu [43], Fisburn, Odlyzko, and Siders [76], and MacKie-Mason and Riveros [145]. Consider also Bakos and Brynjolfsson [11, 13] and Varian [245].

6 See Bakos and Brynjolfsson ([12], p. 117).

7 See Thomas [238].

8 See May [165].

outside hotspots, depending on the availability, UMTS or GPRS will perform data conveyance. All three technologies in the bundle are complements in the sense that every technology covers a distinct area such that area-wide access to the Internet can be offered. Swisscom assumes that such a bundled solution provides considerable added value to its business customers.[9] Similarly, online service providers like AOL sell Internet access bundled with proprietary content and specialized commerce at a flat rate.[10]

Alternatively, Internet access and transmission service can be sold together with information services. As an example, a user would pay the information service provider a certain amount for downloading a video. The content service provider in turn would pay the network provider for the transmission service.[11] A historic example of selling network transport service together with the application as a single unit is cable TV.

Why has bundling become increasingly popular in the Internet environment? At first sight, from the economic point of view, bundling does not seem to be a sensible strategy since flat-rate pricing has been heavily criticized in this work. To answer this question, we will look at the economic rationales behind the bundling strategy and investigate the optimality thereof. We will first introduce some definitions.

We can distinguish between price and product bundling.[12] Price bundling refers to the strategy of selling two or several separate goods in a package. In contrast to product bundling introduced below, the bundle does not provide any added value to the consumers. Hence, if the goods in the bundle are also available separately on markets, the bundle must be sold at a discount to induce some consumers to purchase the bundle. The reservation price for a price bundle equals the sum of the conditional reservation prices of the goods in the bundle. The conditional reservation price of a product is its reservation price conditional on the consumer purchasing another product.

---

9 See NZZ ([180], p. 25).

10 See Telegeography ([237], p. 31).

11 See Kausar, Briscoe, and Crowcroft ([126], p. 34).

12 See Stremersch and Tellis [234]. In the literature previous to the article of Stremersch and Tellis these two terms have been used as synonyms.

Product bundling refers to the strategy of integrating two or several products or services and selling the product bundle at any price. Product integration provides value added, such as interconnectivity in the Internet environment. Further examples of product bundles are PC systems or the Internet access technology bundle offered by Swisscom. The value added makes the reservation price for the product bundle exceed the sum of the conditional reservation prices of the individual products.[13]

We can further distinguish between pure bundling, mixed bundling, and unbundling. Pure bundling, sometimes called tying, refers to the strategy where the goods are only sold in the bundle while in the case of mixed bundling the goods are available both individually and bundled together in a package. The sale of separate goods only is called unbundling.

The economic literature of bundling focuses on a profit maximizing monopolist.[14] Following Stremersch and Tellis [234], however, we will consider bundling strategies in a competitive environment and account for the cost structure of the firm. Stremersch and Tellis [234] conduct a separate analysis for price and product bundling. Given that the selected results presented here do not differ much in substance depending on whether price or product bundling is considered, we will only examine price bundling and content ourselves with pointing out possible differences between price and product bundling.

Stremersch and Tellis ([234], p. 62) show that a price bundling strategy yields higher revenues compared to unbundling provided that conditional reservation prices are asymmetric. Their result holds for both pure and mixed price bundling strategies. Conditional reservation prices of two products X and Y are asymmetric if there is

---

13 Whether the bundle can be sold at a premium price depends on the degree of competition. In practice, product bundles are typically sold at a discount. The Microsoft Office bundle, for example, costs significantly less than the individual software components would cost if purchased separately. See Odlyzko ([186], p. 504).

14 See Adams and Yellen [2], McAfee, McMillan, and Whinston [166], and Schmalensee [206], for example.

a consumer group[15] which has a lower conditional reservation price for product X than another consumer group and the latter consumer group has a lower conditional reservation price for product Y than the former consumer group. Stated differently, if conditional reservation prices are asymmetric there is a negative correlation between conditional reservation prices for two products across consumer groups.

We now demonstrate the pricing advantage of pure price bundling when conditional reservation prices are asymmetric. Table 5.1 depicts the conditional reservation prices of two consumers, consumer A and consumer B, that represent different consumer groups, for monthly Internet access and for pay TV. Suppose that consumer A is ready

Table 5.1: Conditional reservation prices for Internet access and pay TV

Consumer	*Internet access*	*Pay TV*
A	20	15
B	15	20

Source: See Stremersch and Tellis ([234], p. 63).

to pay \$20 per month for Internet access, but is only willing to spend \$15 on pay TV while consumer B values monthly Internet access at \$15 and pay TV at \$20.

What is the revenue maximizing strategy? A carrier offering both services could sell both Internet access and pay TV for \$20 per month. Then, total revenues amount to \$40 since consumer A only subscribes to the Internet service while consumer B exclusively subscribes to the pay TV service. Alternatively, the carrier could sell both Internet access and pay TV for \$15. In this case, total revenues amount to \$60 since both customers subscribe to both services. But, if Internet access and pay TV are sold in a bundle for \$35, total revenues amount to \$70.

15 A consumer group is defined as an identifiable group of consumers within a market who have relatively homogeneous conditional reservation prices. See Stremersch and Tellis ([234], p. 62).

In order to see that, in our example, also a mixed bundling strategy dominates an unbundling strategy consider the following: In addition to the bundle priced at $35 the carrier could sell the two services individually at $20 each, thereby adopting a mixed bundling strategy. Then, both subscribers would still purchase the bundle which results in total revenues equal to $70.

In our example, price bundling increases revenues since the willingness to pay for the bundle is less dispersed than the willingness to pay for the components of the bundle. Hence, price bundling allows significantly better exploitation of the willingness to pay of consumers if it lessens the dispersion in their willingness to pay.[16] This may be the reason why British Telecom (BT), in June 2003, decided to bundle broadband access with IP Virtual Private Networks (VPNs) for their corporate customers given that it was not always financially sensible for large companies to link smaller branch offices and homeworkers directly to an IP VPN.[17]

So far, we saw that pure and mixed price bundling yield higher revenues compared to unbundling provided that conditional reservation prices are asymmetric.[18] The question arises whether companies prefer mixed or pure bundling. Stremersch and Tellis ([234], p. 67) claim that if markets are competitive a mixed price bundling strategy dominates a pure price bundling strategy. Their statement is supported by Matutes and Regibeau [164] who investigate optimal bundling strategies in a duopoly. The reason for the dominance of mixed price bundling is that, in competitive markets, firms cannot use bundling strategies to differentiate themselves from their competitors. Competitive markets preclude differentiated products since differentiated products are imitated immediately with the consequence of pricing pressures. Moreover, competitive markets ensure that any

16 See Shapiro and Varian ([218], p. 75).

17 See British Telecommunications [31].

18 Based on simulation results, Stremersch and Tellis ([234], p. 64) show that in the case of product bundling, independently of whether conditional reservation prices are symmetric or asymmetric, both pure and mixed product bundling yield higher revenues than unbundling. However, the difference in revenues from product bundling compared to unbundling is higher with asymmetric conditional reservation prices.

profitable consumer taste is served. A mixed bundling strategy is thus likely to be adopted since it increases product variety.

Even if pure bundling was more profitable, competitors of the firm choosing a pure bundling strategy would adopt a mixed bundling strategy since, due to the enhanced product variety, it is more attractive to consumers. Thereby, the market share of a company offering pure bundling would be reduced. Hence, it is optimal for that company to likewise adopt a mixed bundling strategy.

Empirical evidence of the result that mixed bundling dominates pure bundling can be found in the telecommunications industry: There is a pronounced asymmetry in the conditional reservation prices of consumers. The products offered are predominantly substitutes, such as cellular versus fixed telephony versus VoIP. Thus, there is a considerable revenue potential when choosing price bundling strategies. Due to intense competition, rather than pure bundling one observes mixed bundling.

In the presence of economies of scale, Stremersch and Tellis ([234], p. 68) argue that both pure and mixed price bundling are more profitable compared to unbundling.[19] The reason is that if economies of scale prevail price bundling increases sales while marginal costs decrease with additional sales. Large economies of scale can be found in markets with high development costs and large sunk costs, such as in the market for digital goods and in transmission networks as long as they are not congested.

In the so-called New Economy, an often stated objective of firms, apart from profit maximization, is maximization of market penetration. The reason is that the Internet market often displays positive feedback. 'Positive feedback makes the strong get stronger and the weak get weaker.'[20] Positive feedback in network economies comes

19 In the case of product bundling, the same argument holds if the costs of product bundling are subadditive. Costs of product bundling are subadditive if it costs less to produce the product bundle than to produce the goods integrated in the bundle separately. One can show that industries that are characterized by economies of scale, such as the market for digital goods and data transmission networks, as long as they are not congested, exhibit decreasing average costs which in turn imply subadditivity.

20 Shapiro and Varian ([218], p. 175).

from positive network externalities.[21] In a network economy with positive feedback, market penetration is critical to survive. Then, it can be successful to bundle a new product with an existing one.

We can conclude that, today, bundling becomes increasingly popular in the Internet since it may allow providers to increase both revenues and market penetration. However, if the bundled goods or services suffer from congestion if usage is too high, such as in the case of transmission services, benefits from bundling are tempered. In other words, high marginal costs, i.e., high marginal congestion costs, make bundling strategies unattractive. Once again, this is the reason why flat-rate pricing for Internet access, which is a bundle of a specific or unlimited amount of data transfers, is not a sensible pricing strategy in networks where bandwidth is not installed in excess.

A further topic to be investigated in the context of Internet transport pricing that is not explicitly covered in this work is how to price multicasting. In multicasting one source sends data traffic to multiple receivers. The source sends its data stream only once. Packets are replicated by the network where delivery paths diverge.

Unbundling the last mile, is another intensively discussed topic that influences the way Internet access is priced. Three forms of unbundling can be distinguished: Bitstream access, shared line access, and full unbundling, also called full access. With bitstream access, the incumbent keeps control over the copper lines and the appendant technical installations, i.e., the modems and the DSLAMs. The incumbent then leases the last mile to entrants, where the lease prices on the last mile are regulated. With shared line access, also called nonexclusive bitstream access, data and voice transmission frequencies are divided. The incumbent does not rent the entire bandwidth to a single entrant, but only pieces of this bandwidth, i.e., the high frequency bandwidth for DSL data transmission, to different entrants at some access price per unit of bandwidth. Telephone service is still controlled by the incumbent. With full unbundling, entrants collocate with the incumbent, place their own modems at the central office of the incumbent, and rent the copper line from the home to the cen-

21 See Shapiro and Varian ([218], p. 183).

tral office of the incumbent operator for exclusive use at a regulated price.[22]

To conclude, pricing of Internet data highways is a research area that needs more study. A pricing system that simultaneously meets all normative criteria set up in Section 2.2.3 at best does not (yet) exist. Thereby, we do not claim that our criteria for Internet pricing cannot be met by any pricing plan. However, such a pricing plan has yet to be invented. In the meantime, a wide variety of pricing schemes will be implemented, depending on temporal and spatial demand for and supply of capacity. The general trend will be that 'users will get what they pay for – even if they have to pay a lot.'[23]

22 See Fischer, Nicolet, and Sciarini ([75], p. B9), Laffont and Tirole ([137], pp. 267 f.), and Schmid ([207], p. B3).

23 Sagawa ([203], p. 128).

APPENDIX

A. Determinantal Test for a Relative Maximum

Above, we analyzed several optimization problems which require conditions of second order to be checked. Generally, we refrained from explicitly specifying sufficient conditions for relative extrema and contented ourselves with considering in which cases these conditions are satisfied. In this appendix, we exemplarily consider the maximization problem of consumers in a competitive market, analyzed in Section 3.3.1, in order to illustrate how to test whether conditions of second order are met. For this purpose, we adopt the same notation as in Section 3.3.1:

x_i := Number of packets generated by user i, $i = 1, \ldots, n$,
Y := Utilization of the network,
$u_i(\cdot)$:= Utility of user i expressed in monetary terms,
$p(Y)$:= Usage price of a representative provider with utilization Y,
$r(Y)$:= Subscription fee of a representative provider with utilization Y.

Recall from Section 3.3.1 that in our model consumers must decide how much traffic to generate and which provider to subscribe to, whereas different providers are characterized by different levels of Y. Hence, each user i has the choice variables x_i and Y. The unconstrained (monetary) utility function of a representative consumer i is given by

$$U_i(x_i, Y) := u_i(x_i, Y) - p(Y)x_i - r(Y).$$

Differentiating this utility function with respect to x_i and Y and setting the derivatives equal to zero yields

$$\frac{\partial U_i(x_i, Y)}{\partial x_i} = \frac{\partial u_i(x_i, Y)}{\partial x_i} - p(Y) = 0, \qquad (A.1)$$

$$\frac{\partial U_i(x_i, Y)}{\partial Y} = \frac{\partial u_i(x_i, Y)}{\partial Y} - p'(Y)x_i - r'(Y) = 0. \qquad (A.2)$$

In order to be sure to indeed find a local maximum the Hessian matrix $\mathbf{H}$ of the utility function of user i, given by

$$\mathbf{H} = \begin{pmatrix} \frac{\partial^2 U_i(x_i, Y)}{\partial x_i^2} & \frac{\partial^2 U_i(x_i, Y)}{\partial x_i \partial Y} \\ \frac{\partial^2 U_i(x_i, Y)}{\partial Y^2} & \frac{\partial^2 U_i(x_i, Y)}{\partial Y \partial x_i} \end{pmatrix},$$

must be negative semidefinite. This means that all successive principal minors of the Hessian determinant

$$|\mathbf{H}| = \begin{vmatrix} \frac{\partial^2 U_i(x_i, Y)}{\partial x_i^2} & \frac{\partial^2 U_i(x_i, Y)}{\partial x_i \partial Y} \\ \frac{\partial^2 U_i(x_i, Y)}{\partial Y^2} & \frac{\partial^2 U_i(x_i, Y)}{\partial Y \partial x_i} \end{vmatrix}$$

must alternate in algebraic sign, starting with a non-positive sign.[1] Thus, for our example, among other things, we must have

$$\frac{\partial^2 U_i(x_i, Y)}{\partial x_i^2} = \frac{\partial^2 u_i(x_i, Y)}{\partial x_i^2} \leq 0. \tag{A.3}$$

Condition (A.3) requires marginal benefits of network usage to be non-increasing. This condition essentially corresponds to Gossen's First Law introduced in Section 3.3.1.

For the Hessian matrix $\mathbf{H}$ to be negative semidefinite all of its diagonal elements must be non-positive such that the first principal minor of $\mathbf{H}$ is negative independently of the numbering of the choice variables. Hence,

$$\frac{\partial^2 U_i(x_i, Y)}{\partial Y^2} = \frac{\partial^2 u_i(x_i, Y)}{\partial Y^2} - p''(Y)x_i - r''(Y) \leq 0,$$

or, equivalently,

$$\frac{\partial^2 u_i(x_i, Y)}{\partial Y^2} \leq p''(Y)x_i + r''(Y).$$

1 See Chiang ([41], pp. 332–337).

must also hold true. In Section 3.3.1 we assumed $u_i(x_i, Y)$ to be decreasing and concave in Y. Therefore, we must have

$$p''(Y)x_i + r''(Y) \geq \frac{\partial^2 u_i(x_i, Y)}{\partial Y^2} \leq 0. \tag{A.4}$$

Condition (A.4) requires that, at the maximum, the increase in marginal disutility due to a marginal increase in Y does not exceed the variation in the marginal reduction of expenditures due to a marginal increase in Y.

Furthermore, the second principle minor, or, the Hessian determinant $|\mathbf{H}|$, must be non-negative:

$$\frac{\partial^2 U_i(x_i, Y)}{\partial x_i^2}\frac{\partial^2 U_i(x_i, Y)}{\partial Y^2} - \frac{\partial^2 U_i(x_i, Y)}{\partial x_i \partial Y}\frac{\partial^2 U_i(x_i, Y)}{\partial Y \partial x_i} \geq 0.$$

As long as the two cross-partial derivatives are both continuous, by Young's theorem[2] we have

$$\frac{\partial^2 U_i(x_i, Y)}{\partial x_i \partial Y} = \frac{\partial^2 U_i(x_i, Y)}{\partial Y \partial x_i} = \frac{\partial^2 u_i(x_i, Y)}{\partial x_i \partial Y} - p'(Y).$$

Hence, in order for the Hessian determinant $|\mathbf{H}|$ to be non-negative

$$\frac{\partial^2 u_i(x_i, Y)}{\partial x_i^2}\left(\frac{\partial^2 u_i(x_i, Y)}{\partial Y^2} - p''(Y)x_i - r''(Y)\right) \geq \left(\frac{\partial^2 u_i(x_i, Y)}{\partial x_i \partial Y} - p'(Y)\right)^2$$

must be satisfied.

If both successive principal minors of $|\mathbf{H}|$ duly alternate in sign we can conclude that the Hessian matrix $\mathbf{H}$ of the utility function is negative semidefinite and, therefore, to indeed find a relative maximum.

2 Consider Chiang ([41], p. 313).

B. Acronyms

ABAX	Automated Bandwidth Exchange
ABR	Available Bit Rate
ACK	Acknowledgment
ADSL	Asymmetric Digital Subscriber Line
AF	Assured Forwarding
ALSVP	Adaptive Load-Sensitive Volume Pricing
AOL	America Online
ATM	Asynchronous Transfer Mode
CBR	Constant Bit Rate
CIX	Commercial Internet Exchange
CLEC	Competitive Local Exchange Carrier
COBAK	Central Office Bill And Keep
CPU	Central Processing Unit
DiffServ	Differentiated Services Architecture
DSL	Digital Subscriber Line
DSLAM	Digital Subscriber Line Access Multiplexer
DVD	Digital Video Disc
DWDM	Dense Wavelength Division Multiplexing
EF	Expedited Forwarding
FCC	Federal Communications Commission
FIFO	First-In, First-Out
FRIACO	Flat Rate Internet Access Call Origination
FTP	File Transfer Protocol
Gb	Gigabits
GB	Gigabytes
Gbps	Gigabits per second
GPRS	Generalized Packet Radio Service
GSM	Global System for Mobile Communications
HRN	Host Resource Negotiator
HSCD	High-Speed Circuit-Switched Data
I2	Internet 2

IAB	Internet Architecture Board
IAP	Internet Access Provider
IBP	Internet Backbone Provider
IEEE	Institute of Electrical and Electronics Engineers
IETF	Internet Engineering Task Force
ILEC	Incumbent Local Exchange Carrier
INDEX	Internet Demand Experiment
IntServ	Integrated Services Architecture
IP	Internet Protocol
IPnG	Internet Protocol next Generation
IPv4	Internet Protocol version 4
IPv6	Internet Protocol version 6
ISDN	Integrated Services Digital Network
ISP	Internet Service Provider
LAN	Local Area Network
Kb	Kilobits
KB	Kilobytes
Kbps	Kilobits per second
MAE	Metropolitan Area Exchange
Mb	Megabits
MB	Megabytes
Mbps	Megabits per second
NAP	Network Access Point
NGI	Next Generation Internet
NRN	Network Resource Negotiator
NSF	National Science Foundation
OLO	Other Licensed Operator
PC	Personal Computer
PHB	Per-Hop Behavior
PMP	Paris Metro Pricing
POP	Point Of Presence
PSP	Progressive Second Price
PSTN	Public Switched Telephone Network
PWLAN	Public Wireless Local Area Network
QoS	Quality of Service
RADSL	Rate-Adaptive Digital Subscriber Line

RBS	Raw Bandwidth Seller
RNAP	Resource Negotiation And Pricing
RSVP	Resource Reservation Protocol
SBB	Service Bandwidth Broker
SDSL	Symmetric Digital Subscriber Line
SKA	Sender-Keep-All
SLA	Service Level Agreement
TCP	Transmission Control Protocol
TOS	Type Of Service
TV	Television
UBR	Unspecified Bit Rate
UMTS	Universal Mobile Telecommunications System
VBR-nrt	Variable Bit Rate – non-real-time
VBR-rt	Variable Bit Rate – real-time
VPN	Virtual Private Network
WLAN	Wireless Local Area Network
WLL	Wireless Local Loop
WWW	World Wide Web

C. Glossary

The terms explained in this glossary are literal citations drawn from MacKie-Mason and Varian ([149], pp. 132–134), Newton [175], and Peterson and Davie ([192], pp. 715–742) if not indicated otherwise.

ACK	In data communications, the transmission of acknowledgement (ACK) characters from the receiving device to the sending device indicates the data sent has been received correctly.
ADSL	Asymmetric Digital Subscriber Line. ADSL is designed to deliver more bandwidth downstream (from the central office to the customer site) than upstream.
AF	Assured Forwarding. One of the per-hop behaviors proposed for Differentiated Services.
ATM	Asynchronous Transfer Mode. Very high speed transmission technology. ATM is a high bandwidth, low-delay, connection-oriented, packet-like switching and multiplexing technique.
Best-Effort	A term for a Quality of Service (QoS) class with no specified parameters and with no assurances that the traffic will be delivered across the network to the target device.
Bit Rate	The number of bits of data transmitted over a [...network] line per second.

Buffer	A temporary storage location for information being sent or received, and serves the purpose of flow control. Usually located between two different devices that have different abilities or speeds for handling the data.
Bursty Traffic	Communication traffic characterized by short periods of high intensity separated by fairly long intervals of little or no utilization.
Caching	A process by which information is stored [...] on the server in anticipation of the next request for information.
Central Office	A telephone company building where subscribers' lines are joined to switching equipment for connecting other subscribers to each other, locally and long distance.
Circuit	A connection or line between two points.
Circuit Switching	A communication paradigm in which a dedicated communication path is established between two hosts, and on which all packets travel.
CLEC	Competitive Local Exchange Carrier. The term and concept was coined by the Telecommunications Act 1996. Essentially the idea of the CLEC was that it would be a new local phone company that would [...] compete with the incumbent, i.e. existing, monopoly local phone company.
Congestion	A state resulting from too many packets contending for limited resources (e.g., link bandwidth and buffer space on routers [...]), which may force the router [...] to discard packets.
Connectionless	The data communication method in which communication occurs between hosts with no previous setup. Packets between two hosts may take different routes, as each is independent of the other.

Connection Oriented Transmission	Data transmission technique involving setting up a connection before transmission and disconnecting it afterward. A type of service in which information always traverses the same pre-established path or link between two points.
Data Flow	[A sequence of packets that follow the same path through the network, i.e., it is a] 'sequence of packets of end-to-end associations.'[1]
Data Stream	Collection of characters and data bits transmitted through a channel.
Default Route	A routing table entry that is used to direct any data addressed to any network numbers not explicitly listed in the routing table.
EF	Expedited Forwarding. One of the per-hop behaviors proposed for Differentiated Services.
Ethernet	A popular local area network technology.
Extranet	A[n] Internet-like network which a company runs to conduct business with its employees, its customers and/or its suppliers. [...] It is called an extranet because it typically uses the technology of the public Internet (TCP/IP and browsers) and customers and suppliers often access the extranet through the Internet via their local ISP.
FIFO	First-In, First-Out. A buffering scheme in which the first [... packet] that enters the buffer is also the first [... packet] retrieved.
Filtering Traffic	The process of determining which traffic is transmitted first, then next, and so on. The traffic is compared to a filter, or a set of specifications, to determine if it can pass through or not.

1 Stiller, Reichl, and Leinen ([233], p. 152).

FTP	File Transfer Protocol. The standard protocol of the Internet architecture for transferring files between hosts.
Header	The portion of a packet, preceding the actual data, containing source and destination addresses, and error checking and other fields.
Hop	Each short, individual trip that packets make many times over, from router to router, on their way to their destinations.
Hop-by-Hop Route	A route that is created by having each [...router] along the path use its own routing knowledge to determine the next hop of the route, with the expectation that all [...routers] will choose consistent hops such that the [...packet] will reach the desired destination.
Host	A computer attached to one or more networks that supports users and runs application programs.
Hotspot	A small geographic area of several hundred square feet in which you can get access to a 802.11b [or 802.11a or 802.11g] wireless local area network.
IAB	Internet Architecture Board. The main body that oversees the development and standardization of protocols of the Internet architecture.
IEEE	Institute for Electrical and Electronics Engineers. A professional society for engineers that also defines network standards.
IETF	Internet Engineering Task Force. A task force of the IAB, responsible for providing short-term engineering solutions for the Internet.
Internet Backbone	[The] network spanning the world from one major metropolitan area to another [which] is provided by a handful of national Internet Service Providers (ISPs).

Intranet	A private network that uses Internet software and Internet standards.
Jitter	Variation in network latency. Large jitter has a negative impact on the quality of video and audio applications.
LAN	Local Area Network. A network based on any physical network technology that is designed to span distances of up to a few thousand meters.
Last Mile	An imprecise term that typically means the link [...] between an end-user and the telephone company central office [...]. It doesn't mean a 'mile', since [...this] 'mile' could be less than a mile or several miles.
Latency	A measure of how long it takes a single bit to propagate from one end of a link or channel to the other. Latency is measured strictly in terms of time.
Logical Channel	A software based connection through which data is sent.
Modem	Modems comprise equipment which converts digital signals to analog signals and vice versa. Modems are used to send digital data signals over the analog PSTN (Public Switched Telephone Network).
Modem Pool	A collection of modems which a user can dial up from his terminal, access one and use [... it] to make a data call over the switched telephone network. Modem pools are [...] designed to allow many users to share few modems, thus saving on modems.
OLO	A European term that stands for 'Other Licensed Operators' referring to all Public Telecommunications Operators – except for the one that was originally the PTT [Post Telephone & Telegraph administration].

Oversubscription	'Scheduling a network line to carry a greater volume of data than the line is designed to carry at any one time. Oversubscribing a line assumes that it is unlikely that any one subscriber (or group of subscribers) will use all of the line's capacity at any one time, and relies on methods such as quality of service to prioritize subscriber traffic during periods of congestion.'[2]
P2P	'Peer-to-peer refers to any relationship in which multiple, autonomous devices interact as equals. A peer-to-peer network is a type of network in which workstations may act as clients (requesting data), servers (offering data) and/or servents (both a client and a server). P2P technology enables the sharing of computer resources and services, including information, files, processing cycles and storage by direct exchange between systems (without the use of central servers).'[3]
Packet	A data unit sent over a packet-switched network.
Packet Switching	A communication paradigm in which packets (messages) are individually routed between hosts, with no previously established communication path.
PHB	Per-Hop Behavior. Behavior of individual routers in the Differentiated Services architecture. AF and EF are two proposed PHBs.
Point-To-Point	A connection with only two endpoints.
POP	Point Of Presence. A physical place where a carrier has a presence for network access, a POP generally is in the form of a [...] router.

2 CIENA Corporation Glossary, http://www.ciena.com/resources/resources_glossary.htm (28.10.03).

3 Sandvine ([205], p. 3).

Portal Site	In the Internet/World Wide Web, a portal is a site, which the owner positions (through marketing and heavy promotion) as an entrance to other sites on the Internet. The concept is that he convinces visitors to the Internet to visit his site first, and savor the advertising on his site (his major way of making money). A portal typically has, at minimum, search engines, free email, instant messaging and chat, personalized home pages and Web hosting.
Protocol	Protocols define the rules by which devices talk with each other, or more formally, a protocol is a set of rules governing the format of messages that are exchanged between computers and people.
PSTN	Public Switched Telephone Network. The entire interconnected collection of local, long distance and international phone companies.
QoS	Quality of Service. Packet delivery guarantees provided by a network architecture. Usually related to performance guarantees, such as bandwidth and delay.
Route	The path a message takes.
Router	A network node connected to two or more networks that forwards packets from one network to another.
Routing	The process of selecting the circuit path for a message.
Routing Table	The table maintained in a router that lets it make decisions on how to forward packets.

RSVP	Resource Reservation Protocol. An IETF standard designed to support resource (for example, bandwidth) reservations through networks of varying topologies and media. Through RSVP, a user's quality of service requests are propagated to all routers along the data path, allowing the network to reconfigure itself [...] to meet the desired level of service. The RSVP protocol engages network resources by establishing flows throughout the network.
Server Colocation	An ISP/web hoster service in which a client places their server on the Internet at an ISP's office for a monthly fee. In return, the server is, theoretically, always connected via multiple redundant high speed connections to the Internet.
Session	An active communication, measured from beginning to end, between devices or applications over a network.
SLA	Service Level Agreement. An agreement between a user and a service provider, defining the nature of the service provided and establishing a set of metrics [...] to be used to measure the level of service provided, measured against the agreed level of service.
Statistical Multiplexing	A multiplexing technique that differs from simple multiplexing in that the share of the available transmission bandwidth allocated to a given user varies dynamically. In other words, in statistical multiplexing, a channel is assigned only to devices (e.g., telephone, data terminal or fax machine) which are active and seeking to communicate.
Switch	A network node that forwards packets [...] based on header information in each packet. Differs from a router mainly in that it typically does not interconnect networks of different types.

T-1	Also spelled T1, which stands for Trunk Level 1. A digital transmission link with the signaling speed of 1.544 Mbps [...] in both directions (i.e. send and receive).
TCP/IP	Transmission Control Protocol/Internet Protocol. A networking protocol that provides communication across interconnected networks, between computers with diverse hardware architectures and various operating systems.
Telnet	Remote terminal protocol of the Internet architecture. Telnet allows [...users] to interact with a remote system as if [...their] terminal is directly connected to that machine.
Throughput	The observed rate at which data is sent through a channel. The term is often used interchangeably with bandwidth.
TOS	Type Of Service. The header of an IPv4 (Internet Protocol version 4), the version currently deployed most widely, contains an eight-bit TOS field. That field can be used to identify to the various [...] routers in an IP-based network those packets which would like preferential treatment on a Class of Service (COS) basis.
Virtual Circuit	A communication link – voice or data – that appears to the user to be a dedicated point-to-point circuit. Virtual circuits are generally set up on a per-call basis and disconnected when the call is ended. The concept of a virtual circuit was first used in data communications with packet switching. A packetized data call may send packets over different physical paths through a network to its destination, but is considered to have a single virtual circuit.
Virtual Connection	A logical connection that is made to a virtual circuit.

VoIP	Voice over Internet Protocol. The technology used to transmit voice conversations over a data network using the Internet Protocol.
VPN	Virtual Private Network. A logical network overlaid on top of some existing network. For example, a company with sites around the world may build a virtual network on top of the Internet rather than lease lines between each site.
Web	An abbreviation for the Internet's [so-called] World Wide Web.
Web Browser	'A software application that is used to display web pages. The two most common web browsers are Netscape Navigator and Microsoft Internet Explorer. Both of these are capable of displaying text, graphics and multimedia information such as sound and video.'[4]
Web Hosting	A service performed by Internet Service Providers (ISPs) and Internet Access Providers (IAPs) who encourage outside companies to put their Websites on computers owned by the ISPs. These computers are attached to communications links to the Internet – often high-speed links. For this Web hosting service, the ISPs typically charge their clients by equipment and transmission capacity used.
Web Page	An HTML [HyperText Markup Language] document on the Web, usually one of many that together make up a Website.
Web Server	A powerful computer which is connected to the Internet or an Intranet. It stores documents and files – audio, video, graphics or text – and can display them to people accessing the server via hypertext transfer protocol (http).

4 Information Technology Glossary, http://www.itglossary.net/browser.html (24.02.04).

Website	Any machine on the Internet that is running a Web Server to respond to requests from remote Web Browsers [...]. In more common usage it refers to individual sets of Web Pages that can be visited with Web Browsers.
WLAN	Wireless Local Area Network. A LAN without wires.
WWW	World Wide Web. A hypermedia information service on the Internet.

Bibliography

[1] ACCC (Australian Competition and Consumer Commission). Internet Interconnection: Factors Affecting Commercial Arrangements Between Network Operators in Australia. Discussion paper, ACCC, February 2000.

[2] Adams, W. J. and J. L. Yellen. Commodity Bundling and the Burden of Monopoly. *Quarterly Journal of Economics*, 90(3): 475–498, August 1976.

[3] Altmann, J. and K. Chu. How to Charge for Network Services – Flat-Rate or Usage-Based? *Computer Networks*, 36(5/6): 519–531, August 2001.

[4] Antoniadis, P. Pricing on the Internet. European 5th Framework Project IST-1999-11429, M3I Consortium, February 2002.

[5] Apostolopoulos, T. et al. Multiple Incentive Internet Pricing for National Academic Research Networks: A Case Study. *Telecommunications Policy*, 24(6/7): 591–611, August 2000.

[6] Armstrong, M. The Theory of Access Pricing and Interconnection. In M. E. Cave, S. K. Majumdar, and I. Vogelsang (eds), *Handbook of Telecommunications Economics*, pp. 297–384. Elsevier, Amsterdam, 2002.

[7] Baake, P. and T. Wichmann. On the Economics of Internet Peering. *Netnomics*, 1(1): 89–105, 1999.

[8] Badasyan, N. and S. Chakrabarti. Private Peering among Internet Backbone Providers. Industrial Organization 0301003, Economics Working Paper at WUSTL, January 2003.

[9] Bailey, J. P. The Economics of Internet Interconnection Agreements. In L. W. McKnight and J. P. Bailey (eds), *Internet Economics*, pp. 155–168. MIT Press, Cambridge/Mass., London/England, 1997.

[10] Bailey, J. P. and L. McKnight. Scalable Internet Interconnection Agreements and Integrated Services. In B. Kahin and J. H. Keller (eds), *Coordinating the Internet*, pp. 309–324. MIT Press, Cambridge/Mass., London/England, 1997.

[11] Bakos, Y. and E. Brynjolfsson. Bundling Information Goods: Pricing, Profits and Efficiency. *Management Science*, 45(12): 1613–1630, December 1999.

[12] Bakos, Y. and E. Brynjolfsson. Aggregation and Disaggregation of Information Goods: Implications for Bundling, Site Licensing and Micropayment Systems. In B. Kahin and H. R. Varian (eds), *Internet Publishing and Beyond: The Economics of Digital Information and Intellectual Property*, pp. 114–137. MIT Press, Cambridge/Mass., London/England, 2000.

[13] Bakos, Y. and E. Brynjolfsson. Bundling and Competition on the Internet. *Marketing Science*, 19(1): 63–82, Winter 2000.

[14] Banerjee, A. and A. Ros. The Internet: Implications for Regulation and Public Policy. 27th Annual Telecommunications Policy Research Conference, Alexandria, Virginia, September 25–27 1999.

[15] Banerjee, A. and A. Ros. Interconnection Rules and Inter-Carrier Compensation: Implications for Carrier Incentives and Economic Welfare. International Telecommunications Society (ITS) 13th Biennial Conference, Buenos Aires, Argentina, July 2–5 2000.

[16] Banerjee, A. and A. Ros. The Internet: Market and Regulatory Conundrums. In D. G. Loomis and L. D. Taylor (eds), *Forecasting the Internet: Understanding the Explosive Growth of Data Communications.* Kluwer Academic Publishers, Boston, Dordrecht, London, 2002.

[17] Bartholomew, S. The Art of Peering. *BT Technology Journal*, 18(3): 33–39, July 2000.

[18] Baumann, E. Internetanbieter möchten Gebührenzähler wieder. *tagesanzeiger.ch*, November 5 2003.

[19] Baumol, W. J. and D. F. Bradford. Optimal Departures from Marginal Cost Pricing. *American Economic Review*, 60(3): 265–283, June 1970.

[20] Becker, G. S. Good-Bye, Tollbooth and Traffic Jams? *Business Week*, p. 26, May 18 1998.

[21] Besen, S. et al. Advances in Routing Technologies and Internet Peering Agreements. *American Economic Review*, 91(2): 292–296, May 2001.

[22] Bichler, M. *The Future of e-Markets: Multidimensional Market Mechanisms.* Cambridge University Press, Cambridge, 2001.

[23] Black, F. and M. Scholes. The Pricing of Options and Corporate Liabilites. *Journal of Political Economy*, 81(3): 637–654, May/June 1973.

[24] Bleich, H. and J. Kuri. Löcher im Netz. Internet-Struktur, optische Netze und die Krise der Carrier. *c't magazin für computer technik*, (15): 72–77, 2002.

[25] Bleich, H., J. Kuri, and P. Vogt. Zwischen Boom und Baustopp. Schweinezyklus beim Ausbau der Internet-Backbones. *c't magazin für computer technik*, (21): 184–187, 2003.

[26] Bleich, H. and U. Mansmann. Breitband überall. Schnelle Zugangstechniken im Vergleich. *c't magazin für computer technik*, (7): 138–143, 2002.

[27] Bohn, R. et al. Mitigating the Coming Internet Crunch: Multiple Service Levels via Precedence. Technical report, San Diego Supercomputer Center, UCSD, San Diego, March 1994.

[28] Borchers, D. Grosse Schirme, kleine Schirme. Auf allen Kanälen der 'Me Channel'. *Neue Zürcher Zeitung*, (174): 60, July 28 2000.

[29] Braeutigam, R. R. Optimal Policies for Natural Monopolies. In R. Schmalensee and R. D. Willig (eds), *Handbook of Industrial Organization*, volume 2, chapter 23, pp. 1289–1346. Elsevier, Amsterdam, 1989.

[30] Breker, L. P. A Survey of Network Pricing Schemes. Technical report, Department of Computer Science, University of Saskatchewan, Saskatoon, Canada, 1996.

[31] British Telecommunications. BT Bundles DSL with IP VPNs. *Boardwatch*, June 16 2003.

[32] Brown, S. J. and D. S. Sibley. *The Theory of Public Utility Pricing*. Cambridge University Press, Cambridge, 1986.

[33] Brownlee, N. Internet Pricing in Practice. In L. W. McKnight and J. P. Bailey (eds), *Internet Economics*, pp. 77–90. MIT Press, Cambridge/Mass., London/England, 1997.

[34] Buisson, J., J. Sergent, and V. Frattaroli. Panorama européen des conditions d'interconnexion pour le trafic internet commuté. Technical report, ARCOME, Montrouge, France, July 2000.

[35] Bundesministerium für Wirtschaft und Technologie. Monitoring Informationswirtschaft. Faktenbericht 4, NFO WorldGroup, München, Germany, February 2002.

[36] Cao, X.-R. and H.-X. Shen. Internet Pricing: Comparison and Examples. Department of Electrical and Electronic Engineering, Hong Kong University of Science and Technology, Kowloon, Hong Kong, n.d.

[37] Carpenter, B. and K. Nichols. Differentiated Services in the Internet. *Proceedings of the IEEE*, 90(9): 1479–1494, September 2002.

[38] Cave, M. and R. Mason. The Economics and Regulation of the Internet. *Oxford Review of Economic Policy*, 17(2): 188–201, Summer 2001.

[39] Chambouleyron, A. ISP Interconnection and Flat-Rated Internet Pricing. Industrial Organization 0207002, Economics Working Paper Archive at WUSTL, August 5 2002.

[40] Champsaur, P. and J.-C. Rochet. Multiproduct Duopolists. *Econometrica*, 57(3): 533–557, May 1989.

[41] Chiang, A. C. *Fundamental Methods of Mathematical Economics*. Economics Series. McGraw-Hill, Singapore, 3rd edition, 1984.

[42] Choi, S.-Y., D. O. Stahl, and A. B. Whinston. *The Economics of Electronic Commerce: The Essential Economics of Doing Business in the Electronic Marketplace*. Macmillan Technical Publishing, Indianapolis/IN, 1997.

[43] Chuang, J. C. and M. A. Sirbu. Network Delivery of Information Goods: Optimal Pricing of Articles and Subscriptions. In B. Kahin and H. R. Varian (eds), *Internet Publishing and Beyond: The Economics of Digital Information and Intellectual Property*, pp. 138–166. MIT Press, Cambridge/Mass., London/England, 2000.

[44] Clark, D. D. Adding Service Discrimination to the Internet. *Telecommunications Policy*, 20(3): 169–181, April 1996.

[45] Clark, D. D. Combining Sender and Receiver Payments in the Internet. In G. L. Rosston and D. Waterman (eds), *Interconnection and the Internet*, pp. 95–112. Lawrence Erlbaum Associates, Mahwah, New Jersey, 1997.

[46] Clark, D. D. Internet Cost Allocation and Pricing. In L. W. McKnight and J. P. Bailey (eds), *Internet Economics*, pp. 215–252. MIT Press, Cambridge/Mass., London/England, 1997.

[47] Clark, D. D., W. Lehr, and I. Liu. Provisioning for Bursty Internet Traffic: Implications for Industry and Internet Structure. MIT ITC Workshop on Internet Quality of Service, November 1999.

[48] Coase, R. The Marginal Cost Controversy. *Economica*, 13(51): 169–182, August 1946.

[49] Cocchi, R. et al. Pricing in Computer Networks: Motivation, Formulation, and Example. *IEEE/ACM Transactions on Networking*, 1(6): 614–627, December 1993.

[50] Coffman, K. G. and A. M. Odlyzko. Growth of the Internet. In I. P. Kaminow and T. Li (eds), *Optical Fiber Telecommunications IV B: Systems and Impairments*, pp. 17–56. Academic Press, San Diego, 2002.

[51] Courcoubetis, C. et al. A Study of Simple Usage-Based Charging Schemes for Broadband Networks. *Telecommunication Systems*, 15(3/4): 323–343, 2000.

[52] Courcoubetis, C., F. Kelly, and R. Weber. Measurement-Based Usage Charges in Communications Networks. *Operations Research*, 48(4): 535–548, July/August 2000.

[53] Courcoubetis, C., V. A. Siris, and G. D. Stamoulis. Application of the Many Sources Asymptotic and Effective Bandwidths to Traffic Engineering. *Telecommunication Systems*, 12(2/3): 167–191, 1999.

[54] Crémer, J. and C. Hariton. The Pricing of Critical Applications in the Internet. *Journal of Japanese and International Economies*, 13(4): 281–310, December 1999.

[55] Crémer, J., P. Rey, and J. Tirole. Connectivity in the Commercial Internet. *Journal of Industrial Economics*, 48(4): 433–472, December 2000.

[56] c't magazin für computer technik. WLAN-Preise geraten ins Rutschen. *c't magazin für computer technik*, (15): 33, July 2003.

[57] Dahl, D. S. Primer on Congestion Pricing. *Fedgazette*, pp. 3–4, April 1996.

[58] Danielsen, K. and J. Molka-Danielsen. Admissions and Preemption in Auction-Based Reservation Networks. MIT Workshop on Internet Service Quality Economics, Cambridge/Mass., December 1999.

[59] DaSilva, L. A., D. W. Petr, and N. Akar. Static Pricing and Quality of Service in Multiple-Service Networks. In *Proc. 5th Joint Conf. Information Sciences*, volume 1, pp. 355–358, Atlantic City, New Jersey, February 27–March 3 2000.

[60] Datta, B. and H. Dixon. Free Internet Access and Regulation: A Note. Discussion paper in Economics 2003/03, Department of Economics and Related Studies, University of York, York, UK, 2003.

[61] DeGraba, P. Bill and Keep at the Central Office as the Efficient Interconnection Regime. OPP Working Paper No. 33, December 2000.

[62] Dewan, R., M. Freimer, and P. Gundepudi. Interconnection Agreements between Competing Internet Service Providers. In *IEEE Proceedings of the 33rd Hawaii International Conference on System Sciences*, volume 6, p. 6014, Electronic Edition, Maui, Hawaii, January 4–7 2000.

[63] Dolan, T. Internet Pricing. Is the End of the World Wide Wait in View? *Communications & Strategies*, (37): 15–46, 1st quarter 2000.

[64] Edell, R. and P. Varaiya. Providing Internet Access: What we Learn from INDEX. *IEEE Network*, 13(5): 18–25, September/October 1999.

[65] Ermert, M. Wie viele IP-Adressen braucht der Mensch? IPv6-Fachkongress in Zürich. *Neue Zürcher Zeitung*, (100): 71, May 5 2003.

[66] Fankhauser, G. *A Network Architecture Based on Market Principles*. Phd thesis no. 13750, Swiss Federal Institute of Technology, Zurich, Switzerland, Shaker Verlag, Aachen, October 2000.

[67] Fankhauser, G. et al. Reservation-Based Charging in an Integrated Services Network. 4th INFORMS Telecommunications Conference, Boca Raton, Florida, March 1998.

[68] Fankhauser, G. and B. Plattner. Diffserv Bandwidth Brokers As Mini-Markets. International Workshop on Internet Service Quality Economics, MIT, Cambridge/Mass., December 2–3 1999.

[69] Fankhauser, G., D. Schweikert, and B. Plattner. Service Level Agreement Trading for the Differentiated Services Architecture. TIK-Report 59, Computer Engineering and Networks Laboratory, Swiss Federal Institute of Technology, Zurich, Switzerland, January 1999.

[70] Fankhauser, G., B. Stiller, and B. Plattner. Arrow: A Flexible Architecture for an Accounting and Charging Infrastructure in the Next Generation Internet. *Netnomics*, 1(2): 201–223, 1999.

[71] Farnon, M. and S. Huddle. Settlement Systems for the Internet. In B. Kahin and J. H. Keller (eds), *Coordinating the Internet*, pp. 377–403. MIT Press, Cambridge/Mass., London/England, 1997.

[72] Faulhaber, G. R. and J. L. Panzar. Optimal Two-Part Tariffs with Self-Selection. Bell Laboratories Economic Discussion Paper No. 74, 1977.

[73] FCC (Federal Communications Commission). Federal Communications Commission Resolves Carrier Compensation Rules for Internet Traffic. Order 01-131, FCC, Washington D.C., April 19 2001.

[74] Ferrari, D. and D. C. Verma. A Scheme for Real-Time Channel Establishment in Wide-Area Networks. *IEEE Journal on Selected Areas in Communication*, 8(3): 368–379, April 1990.

[75] Fischer, A., S. Nicolet, and P. Sciarini. Marschhalt auf der letzten Meile? Schwindender Liberalisierungswillen in der Schweiz. *Neue Zürcher Zeitung*, (120): B9, May 2002.

[76] Fishburn, P. C., A. M. Odlyzko, and R. C. Siders. Fixed Fee versus Unit Pricing for Information Goods: Competition, Equilibria, and Price Wars. In B. Kahin and H. R. Varian (eds), *Internet Publishing and Beyond: The Economics of Digital Information and Intellectual Property*, pp. 167–189. MIT Press, Cambridge/Mass., London/England, 2000.

[77] Flury, P. et al. Charging Considerations for Virtual Private DiffServ Networks. TIK-Report 94, Computer Engineering and Networks Laboratory, Swiss Federal Institute of Technology, Zurich, Switzerland, August 2000.

[78] Foukia, N. et al. User Behavior for a Pricing Scheme in a Multi-Provider Scenario. Workshop on Internet Service Quality Economics, Cambridge/Mass., December 1999.

[79] Friedman, D. On the Efficiency of Experimental Double Auction Markets. *American Economic Review*, 74(1): 60–72, March 1984.

[80] Friedman, D. and J. Rust (eds). *The Double Auction Market: Institutions, Theories, and Evidence.* Proceedings of the Workshop on Double Auction Markets, June, 1991 in Santa Fe, New Mexico. Addison-Wesley, Reading/Mass., 1993.

[81] Fudenberg, D. and J. Tirole. *Game Theory.* MIT Press, Cambridge/Mass., London/England, 1991.

[82] Gale, W. A. and R. Koenker. Pricing Interactive Computer Services. *The Computer Journal*, 27(1): 8–17, 1984.

[83] George, N. et al. High Expectations, Low Profitability. Perspectives from Arthur D. Little's Global Broadband Report. Technical report, Arthur D. Little, October 2003.

[84] Gerpott, T. J. and S. Böhm. Ansätze zur Preisbildung für Internet-Transportdienste. *Wirtschaftsinformatik*, 42(3): 233–243, 2000.

[85] Gerpott, T. J. and S. W. Massengeil. Electronic Markets for Telecommunications Transport Capacities. *Telecommunications Policy*, 25(8/9): 587–610, September 2001.

[86] Gibbens, R. and F. Kelly. Resource Pricing and the Evolution of Congestion Control. *Automatica*, 35(12): 1969–1985, December 1999.

[87] Gibbens, R., R. Mason, and R. Steinberg. Internet Service Classes under Competition. *IEEE Journal on Selected Areas in Communications*, 18(12): 2490–2498, December 2000.

[88] Gibson, H. R. and B. Com. *Easing the Internet Traffic Jam: A Comparison of Capacity Expansion and Congestion Tolls as Competing Alternatives for Reducing Internet Congestion.* Honours thesis for the degree of Bachelor of Economics, University of Newcastle, Australia, 1998.

[89] Gjerstad, S. and J. Dickhaut. Price Formation in Double Auctions. *Games and Economic Behavior*, 22(1): 1–29, 1998.

[90] Goldman, M. B., H. E. Leland, and D. S. Sibley. Optimal Nonuniform Prices. *Review of Economic Studies*, 51(165): 305–319, April 1984.

[91] Grigonis, R. Bandwidth for the Buck. *Network Magazine*, February 5 2001.

[92] Gupta, A. et al. Streamlining the Digital Economy: How to Avert the Tragedy of the Commons. *IEEE Internet Computing*, 1(6): 38–46, December 1997.

[93] Gupta, A. et al. Extracting Consumer's Private Information for Implementing Incentive Compatible Internet Traffic Pricing. *Journal of Management Information Systems*, 17(1): 9–29, Summer 2000.

[94] Gupta, A. et al. An Analysis of Incentives for Network Infrastructure Investment under Different Pricing Strategies. Working Paper 01-15, Management Information Systems Research Center MISRC, University of Minnesota, Minneapolis, Minnesota, April 2001.

[95] Gupta, A. et al. Estimating Internet Users' Demand Characteristics. *Journal of Management Information Systems*, 17(2/3): 203–218, June 2001.

[96] Gupta, A., D. O. Stahl, and A. B. Whinston. An Economic Approach to Networked Computing with Priority Classes. *Journal of Organizational Computing and Electronic Commerce*, 6(1): 71–95, 1996.

[97] Gupta, A., D. O. Stahl, and A. B. Whinston. Economic Issues in Electronic Commerce. In R. Kalakota and A. B. Whinston (eds), *Readings in Electronic Commerce*, pp. 197–227. Addison-Wesley, Reading/Mass., 1997.

[98] Gupta, A., D. O. Stahl, and A. B. Whinston. Priority Pricing of Integrated Services Networks. In L. W. McKnight and J. P. Bailey (eds), *Internet Economics*, pp. 323–352. MIT Press, Cambridge/Mass., London/England, 1997.

[99] Gupta, A., D. O. Stahl, and A. B. Whinston. A Stochastic Equilibrium Model of Internet Pricing. *Journal of Economic Dynamics and Control*, 21(4/5): 697–722, May 1997.

[100] Gupta, A., D. O. Stahl, and A. B. Whinston. The Economics of Network Management. *Communications of the ACM*, 42(9): 57–63, September 1999.

[101] Gut, A. *An Intermediate Course in Probability.* Springer, New York, 1995.

[102] Haan, M. The Economics of Free Internet Access. *Journal of Institutional and Theoretical Economics*, 175(3): 359–379, September 2001.

[103] Hagen, S. Die Rückkehr zur Einfachheit. Wer braucht IPv6? *Neue Zürcher Zeitung*, (221): B23, September 24 2002.

[104] Halabi, S. *Internet Routing Architectures*. Cisco Press, Indianapolis/IN, 2nd edition, 2000.

[105] Hardin, G. The Tragedy of the Commons. *Science*, 162(3859): 1243–1248, December 1968.

[106] Harsanyi, J. C. *Rational Behavior and Bargaining Equilibrium in Games and Social Situations*. Cambridge University Press, Cambridge, 1986.

[107] Hazlett, D. An Interim Solution to Internet Congestion. *Social Science Computer Review*, 15(2): 181–189, Summer 1997.

[108] Holzer, G. Handy am Breitband. Erste Praxiserfahrungen mit UMTS. *c't magazin für computer technik*, (13): 102–104, 2003.

[109] Hotelling, H. Stability in Competition. *Economic Journal*, 39(153): 41–57, March 1929.

[110] Huerlimann, A. Viel Bandbreite – wenig Inhalte. Schwierigkeiten der Telekom-Industrie, an attraktive Breitbandinhalte zu gelangen. *Neue Zürcher Zeitung*, (120): B7, May 28 2002.

[111] Hui, J. Y. Resource Allocation for Broadband Networks. *IEEE Journal of Selected Areas in Communication*, 6(9): 1598–1608, December 1988.

[112] Hui, J. Y. *Switching and Traffic Theory for Integrated Broadband Networks*. Kluwer Academic Publishers, Boston, Dordrecht, London, 1990.

[113] Huston, G. Interconnection, Peering and Settlements – Part II. *The Internet Protocol Journal*, 2(2): 2–23, June 1999.

[114] Huston, G. *ISP Survival Guide*. John Wiley & Sons, New York, 1999.

[115] Hwang, J. *A Market-Based Model for the Bandwidth Management of IntServ-DiffServ QoS Interconnection: A Network Economic Approach*. Phd thesis, School of Information Sciences, University of Pittsburgh, Pittsburgh, Pennsylvania, 2000.

[116] Hwang, J. and M. B. Weiss. On the Economics of Interconnection among Hybrid QoS Networks in the Next Generation Internet. In *Proceedings of the International Telecommunications Society*, Buenos Aires, Argentina, July 2–5 2000.

[117] IEEE Internet Computing. Bob Metcalfe on What's Wrong with the Internet: It's the Economy, Stupid. *IEEE Internet Computing*, 1(2): 6–17, March/April 1997.

[118] InvisibleHand Networks. Merkato Overview. A Platform for Real-Time Market-Based Network Resource Allocation. Technical report, InvisibleHand Networks Inc., 2002.

[119] Ismail, S. and I. Wu. Broadband Internet Access in OECD Countries: A Comparative Analysis. Staff report, Office of Strategic Planning and Policy Analysis and International Bureau, FCC, October 2003.

[120] Jehle, G. A. and P. J. Reny. *Advanced Microeconomic Theory*. Addison-Wesley, Boston, 2nd edition, 2001.

[121] Jianhua, W. *The Theory of Games*. Clarendon Press, Oxford, 1988.

[122] Jordan, S. and H. Jiang. Connection Establishment in High-Speed Networks. *IEEE Journal on Selected Areas in Communications*, 13(7): 1150–1161, September 1995.

[123] Kahin, B. and H. R. Varian. *Internet Publishing and Beyond: The Economics of Digital Information and Intellectual Property*. MIT Press, Cambridge/Mass., London/England, 2000.

[124] Kamien, M. I. and N. L. Schwartz. *Dynamic Optimization: The Calculus of Variations and Optimal Control in Economics and Management*, volume 4 of *Dynamic Economics: Theory and Applications*. North-Holland, New York, Amsterdam, Oxford, 1981.

[125] Katz, M. L. and C. Shapiro. Network Externalities, Competition, and Compatibility. *American Economic Review*, 75(3): 424–441, June 1985.

[126] Kausar, N., B. Briscoe, and J. Crowcroft. A Charging Model for Sessions on the Internet. In *Proc. 4th IEEE Symposium on Computers and Communications (ISCC' 99)*, pp. 32–38, Sharm El Sheiks, Egypt, July 6–8 1999.

[127] Kelly, F. On Tariffs, Policing and Admission Control for Multiservice Networks. *Operations Research Letters*, 15: 1–9, February 1994.

[128] Kelly, F. Notes on Effective Bandwidths. In F. Kelly, S. Zachary, and I. Ziedins (eds), *Stochastic Networks: Theory and Applications*, pp. 141–168. Oxford University Press, Oxford, 1996.

[129] Kelly, F. Charging and Accounting for Bursty Connections. In L. W. McKnight and J. P. Bailey (eds), *Internet Economics*, pp. 253–278. MIT Press, Cambridge/Mass., London/England, 1997.

[130] Kelly, F. et al. Pricing for Guaranteed Services. In D. J. Songhurst (ed), *Charging Communication Networks*, appendix A, pp. 167–192. Elsevier, Amsterdam, 1999.

[131] Kende, K. The Digital Handshake: Connecting Internet Backbones. OPP Working Paper 32, Office of Plans and Policy, FCC, Washington D.C., September 2000.

[132] Kilkki, K., M. Kalervo, and J. Ruutu. Internet Charging Reconsidered. 5th Annual Networld and Interop Engineers Conference (Interop' 98), Las Vegas, Nevada, May 1998.

[133] Kridel, D., P. Rappoport, and L. Taylor. The Demand for High-Speed Access to the Internet. In D. G. Loomis and L. D. Taylor (eds), *Forecasting the Internet – Understanding the Explosive Growth of Data Communications*, pp. 11–22. Kluwer Academic Publishers, Boston, Dordrecht, London, 2002.

[134] Laffont, J.-J. et al. Internet Interconnection and the Off-Net-Cost Pricing Principle. IDEI Conference on the Economics of the Software and Internet Industries, Toulouse, France, January 18–20 2001.

[135] Laffont, J.-J. et al. Internet Peering. *American Economic Review*, 91(2): 287–291, May 2001.

[136] Laffont, J.-J., P. Rey, and J. Tirole. Network Competition: I. Overview and Nondiscriminatory Pricing. *RAND Journal of Economics*, 29(1): 1–37, Spring 1998.

[137] Laffont, J.-J. and J. Tirole. *Competition in Telecommunications.* MIT Press, Cambridge/Mass., London/England, 2000.

[138] Lazar, A. A. and N. Semret. Auctions for Network Resource Sharing. Technical Report CU/CTR/TR 468-97-02, Center for Telecommunications Research, Columbia University, New York, New York, February 1997.

[139] Lazar, A. A. and N. Semret. Design, Analysis and Simulation of the Progressive Second Price Auction for Network Bandwidth Sharing. Game Theory and Information 9809001, Economics Working Paper Archive at WUSTL, 1998.

[140] Leber, M. Re: Bandwidth Pricing Issue. ISP-LISTs, isp-colo@isp-colo.com, April 22 2001.

[141] Lehr, W. and L. W. McKnight. Show me the Money: Contracts and Agents in Service Level Agreement Markets, 2002.

[142] Lehr, W. and M. B. Weiss. The Political Economy of Congestion Charges and Settlements in Packet Networks. *Telecommunications Policy*, 20(3): 219–231, April 1996.

[143] Little, I. and J. Wright. Peering and Settlement in the Internet: An Economic Analysis. *Journal of Regulatory Economics*, 18(2): 151–173, September 2000.

[144] MacKie-Mason, J. K. A Smart Market for Resource Reservation in a Multiple Quality of Service Information Network. Technical report, University of Michigan, Ann Arbor, Michigan, September 1997.

[145] MacKie-Mason, J. K. and J. F. Riveros. Economics and Electronic Access to Scholarly Information. In B. Kahin and H. R. Varian (eds), *Internet Publishing and Beyond: The Economics of Digital Information and Intellectual Property*, pp. 203–229. MIT Press, Cambridge/Mass., London/England, 2000.

[146] MacKie-Mason, J. K. and H. R. Varian. Generalized Vickrey Auctions. Technical report, Department of Economics, University of Michigan, Ann Arbor, Michigan, July 1994.

[147] MacKie-Mason, J. K. and H. R. Varian. Some FAQs about Usage-Based Pricing. Technical report, University of Michigan, Ann Arbor, Michigan, September 1994.

[148] MacKie-Mason, J. K. and H. R. Varian. Pricing Congestible Network Resources. *IEEE Journal of Selected Areas in Communications*, 13(7): 1141–1149, September 1995.

[149] MacKie-Mason, J. K. and H. R. Varian. Some Economics of the Internet. In W. Sichel and D. L. Alexander (eds), *Networks, Infrastructure and the New Task for Regulation*, pp. 107–136. University of Michigan Press, Ann Arbor, 1996.

[150] MacKie-Mason, J. K. and H. R. Varian. Economic FAQs about the Internet. In L. W. McKnight and J. P. Bailey (eds), *Internet Economics*, pp. 27–62. MIT Press, Cambridge/Mass., London/England, 1997.

[151] MacKieMason, J. K. and H. R. Varian. Pricing the Internet. In B. Kahin and J. H. Keller (eds), *Public Access to the Internet*, pp. 269–314. MIT Press, Cambridge/Mass., London/England, 1995.

[152] Maistre, Le, R. DSL Breaks Growth Record. *Boardwatch*, June 12 2003.

[153] Maistre, Le, R. DSL Growth Explodes in 2003. *Boardwatch*, September 12 2003.

[154] Maitland, J. Peer-to-Peer Pressure. *Boardwatch*, April 30 2003.

[155] Maitland, J. Time Warner Whacks Wi-Fi Users. *Boardwatch*, September 18 2003.

[156] Manenti, F. M. Congestion, Private Peering and Capacity Investment on the Internet. Industrial Organization 0212003, Economics Working Paper at WUSTL, December 2002.

[157] Mansmann, U. Gebremster Schaum. ADSL ist noch ausbaufähig. *c't magazin für computer technik*, (21): 156–158, 2002.

[158] Mansmann, U. and J. Endres. Himmlisches Vergnügen. Internet per Satellit soll Downloads beschleunigen. *c't magazin für computer technik*, (15): 106–111, 2002.

[159] Mansmann, U. and R. Hüskes. DSL mit Turbolader. Schnell und günstig ins Internet. *c't magazin für computer technik*, (16): 116–221, 2003.

[160] Mas-Colell, A., M. D. Whinston, and J. R. Green. *Microeconomic Theory*. Oxford University Press, Oxford, 1995.

[161] Mason, R. and T. M. Valletti. Competition in Communication Networks: Pricing and Regulation. *Oxford Review of Economic Policy*, 17(3): 389–415, 2001.

[162] Massey, M. Usage-Based Pricing. *Telephony Online*, May 28 2002.

[163] Matsumoto, C. Cable Still Rules US Broadband. *Boardwatch*, June 12 2003.

[164] Matutes, C. and P. Regibeau. Compatibility and Bundling of Complementary Goods in a Duopoly. *Journal of Industrial Economics*, 40(1): 37–54, March 1992.

[165] May, R. J. The Storm over Broadband Bundling. *CNET News.com*, April 17 2003.

[166] McAfee, R. P., J. McMillan, and M. D. Whinston. Multiproduct Monopoly, Commodity Bundling, and Correlation of Values. *Quarterly Journal of Economics*, 104(2): 371–383, May 1989.

[167] McIntosh, N. Heavy Surfers Pay the Price. *The Guardian*, England, UK, August 3 2000.

[168] Milgrom, P., B. Mitchell, and P. Srinagesh. Competitive Effects of Internet Peering Policies. In I. Vogelsang and B. M. Compaine (eds), *The Internet Upheaval*, pp. 175–195. MIT Press, Cambridge/Mass., London/England, 2000.

[169] Müller, M. Analyse und Entwurf von Tarifierungsmodellen für Kommunikationsdienste. Institut für Technische Informatik und Kommunikationsnetze TIK, ETH Zurich, Switzerland, Juni 1997.

[170] Murphy, J., L. Murphy, and E. C. Posner. Distributed Pricing for Embedded ATM Networks. In J. Labetoulle and J. W. Roberts (eds), *Proceedings of the 14th International Teletraffic Congress (ITC-14)*, pp. 1053–1063, Elsevier, Antibes, France, June 6–10 1994.

[171] Nagel, J. M. An Internet Ex-Post Pricing Scheme Based on the Effective Bandwidth Theory. M. S. in Telecommunications Program, University of Maryland, College Park, Maryland, August 10 1999.

[172] Nash, J. F. The Bargaining Problem. *Econometrica*, 18(2): 155–162, April 1950.

[173] Nash, J. F. Two-Person Cooperative Games. *Econometrica*, 21(1): 128–140, January 1953.

[174] Nelson, S. Internet Congestion and Pricing: A Preliminary Study. In *1998 Communications Research Forum*, pp. 446–483, 1998.

[175] Newton, H. *Newton's Telecom Dictionary*. CMP Books, San Francisco, 19th edition, March 2003.

[176] Nichols, K., V. Jacobson, and L. Zhang. A Two-Bit Differentiated Services Architecture for the Internet. Internet RFC 2638, IETF, 1999.

[177] NZZ. Local Area ist überall. Swisscom Mobile installiert PWLAN-Basisstationen. *Neue Zürcher Zeitung*, (90): 81, April 19 2002.

[178] NZZ. Viele offene Fragen vor dem UMTS-Start. Verhaltener Netzaufbau auf dem Testmarkt Zürich. *Neue Zürcher Zeitung*, (118): 45, May 25/26 2002.

[179] NZZ. Jeder Zweite surft noch mit analogem Modem. *Neue Zürcher Zeitung*, (43): 77, February 21 2003.

[180] NZZ. UMTS-Dienste für Private noch viele Monate entfernt. *Neue Zürcher Zeitung*, (113): 25, May 17/18 2003.

[181] Odlyzko, A. A Modest Proposal for Preventing Internet Congestion. Technical Report 97.35.1, AT&T Research Labs, Florham Park, New Jersey, September 1997.

[182] Odlyzko, A. The Economics of the Internet: Utility, Utilization, Pricing, and Quality of Service. Technical report, AT&T Research Labs, Florham Park, New Jersey, 1998.

[183] Odlyzko, A. Paris Metro Pricing for the Internet. In *Proceedings of the ACM Conference on Electronic Commerce (EC'99)*, pp. 140–147, ACM Press, Denver, Colorado, November 3–5 1999.

[184] Odlyzko, A. Paris Metro Pricing: The Minimalist Differentiated Services Solution. In *Proceeings of the 7th International Workshop on Quality of Service (IWQoS'99)*, pp. 159–161, IEEE Computer Society Press, London, UK, May 31–June 4 1999.

[185] Odlyzko, A. The Internet and Other Networks: Utilization Rates and their Implications. *Information Economics Policy*, 12(4): 341–365, December 2000.

[186] Odlyzko, A. Internet Pricing and the History of Communications. *Computer Networks*, 36(5/6): 493–518, August 2001.

[187] Oftel (Office of Telecommunications). Consultation on Future Interconnection Arrangements for Dial-Up Internet in the United Kingdom. Technical report, Oftel, London, November 2000.

[188] Orda, A. and N. Shimkin. Incentive Pricing in Multi-Class Systems. *Telecommunication Systems*, 13(2-4): 241–267, 2000.

[189] Owen, G. *Game Theory*. Academic Press, San Diego, 3rd edition, 1995.

[190] Parameswaran, M., J. Stallaert, and A. B. Whinston. A Market-Based Allocation Mechanism for the DiffServ Framework. *Decision Support Systems*, 31(3): 351–361, August 2001.

[191] Parris, C. and D. Ferrari. A Resource Based Pricing Policy for Real-time Channels in a Packet-Switching Network. Technical report, University of California, Berkeley, California, 1992.

[192] Peterson, L. L. and B. S. Davie. *Computer Networks: A Systems Approach*. Morgan Kaufmann Publishers, San Francisco, 3rd edition, 2003.

[193] Pigou, A. C. *The Economics of Welfare*. Macmillan, London, 1920.

[194] Ramsey, F. A Contribution to the Theory of Taxation. *Economic Journal*, 37(145): 47–61, March 1927.

[195] Rassenti, S. J., V. L. Smith, and R. L. Bulfin. A Combinatorial Auction Mechanism for Airport Time Slot Allocation. *Bell Journal of Economics*, 13(2): 402–417, Autumn 1982.

[196] Reardon, M. Ipv6 Coming to America. *Boardwatch*, June 26 2003.

[197] Reichl, P., G. Fankhauser, and B. Stiller. Auction Models for Multi-Provider Internet Connections. In *Proc. Messung, Modellierung und Bewertung MMB'99*, pp. 71–75, Trier, Germany, September 21–24 1999.

[198] Rogerson, R. Usage-Related Charges for the JANET Network. JISC (Joint Information Systems Committee) Circular 3/98, March 1998.

[199] Rothkopf, M. H., A. Pekeč, and R. M. Harstad. Computationally Manageable Combinational Auctions. *Management Science*, 44(8): 1131–1147, August 1998.

[200] Rubner, D. Internet Flat Rate: Fluch oder Segen? *Neue Zürcher Zeitung*, (30): B32, February 6 2001.

[201] Rupp, H. B. Ein Preissystem für das Internet. Diskussionsbeitrag 164, Wissenschaftliches Institut für Kommunikationsdienste, Bad Honnef, Germany, August 1996.

[202] Rupp, H. B. *The Economics of an Integrated Services Internet*. Phd thesis, Humboldt-Universität zu Berlin, Germany, Shaker Verlag Aachen, 2001.

[203] Sagawa, P. I. The Balkanization of the Internet. *The McKinsey Quarterly*, (1): 126–139, 1997.

[204] Sandholm, T. Approaches to Winner Determination in Combinatorial Auctions. *Decision Support Systems*, 28(1/2): 165–76, March 2000.

[205] Sandvine. Peer-to-Peer File Sharing. Industry white paper, Sandvine Inc., Waterloo, Canada, December 2002.

[206] Schmalensee, R. Gaussian Demand and Commodity Bundling. *Journal of Business*, 57(1(2)): 211–230, January 1984.

[207] Schmid, P. Die Entbündelung muss vollständig sein – Bitstream Access und Linesharing genügen nicht. *Neue Zürcher Zeitung*, (287): B3, December 2002.

[208] Schnellhaaß, H.-M. Peak-Load Pricing: Allgemeine Grundsätze. *Wirtschaftswissenschaftliches Studium (WiSt)*, (10): 463–469, 1978.

[209] Semret, N. *Market Mechanisms for Network Resource Sharing*. Phd thesis, Columbia University, New York, New York, 1999.

[210] Semret, N. Inter-ISP Bandwidth Markets. Technical paper, InvisibleHand Networks Inc., 2002.

[211] Semret, N. Internet Server Farms as Bandwidth Markets. Technical paper, InvisibleHand Networks Inc., 2002.

[212] Semret, N. et al. Market Pricing of Differentiated Internet Services. 6th IEEE/IFIP International Workshop on Quality of Service (IWQoS'98) Napa, California, May 1998.

[213] Semret, N. et al. Peering and Provisioning of Differentiated Internet Services. In *Proceedings of IEEE INFOCOM*, volume 2, pp. 414–420, Tel Aviv, Israel, March 26–30 2000.

[214] Semret, N. et al. Pricing, Provisioning and Peering: Dynamic Markets for Differentiated Internet Services and Implications for Network Interconnections. *IEEE Journal on Selected Areas in Communications*, 18(12): 2499–2513, December 2000.

[215] Settele, C. Ohne Kabel und Strippe. *NZZ am Sonntag*, p. 87, July 6 2003.

[216] Settele, C. Epidemie im Paradies. *NZZ Folio – Die Zeitschrift der Neuen Zürcher Zeitung*, (2): 25–28, February 2004.

[217] Shaked, A. and J. Sutton. Multiproduct Firms and Market Structure. *RAND Journal of Economics*, 21(1): 45–62, Spring 1990.

[218] Shapiro, C. and H. R. Varian. *Information Rules: A Strategic Guide to the Network Economy.* Harvard Business School Press, Boston/Mass., 1999.

[219] Shenker, S. et al. Pricing in Computer Networks: Reshaping the Research Agenda. *Telecommunications Policy*, 20(3): 183–201, April 1996.

[220] Shy, O. *The Economics of Network Industries.* Cambridge University Press, Cambridge, 2001.

[221] Sidak, J. G. and D. F. Spulber. Cyberjam: The Law and Economics of Internet Congestion of the Telephone Network. *Harvard Journal of Law and Public Policy*, 21(2): 329–394, Spring 1998.

[222] Singh, R. et al. A Comparative Evaluation of Internet Pricing Models: Smart Markets and Dynamic Capacity Contracting. In *Proceedings of the 10th Annual Workshop on Information Technologies and Systems (WITS)*, Brisbane, Australia, December 9–10 2000.

[223] Siris, V. et al. Charging in Communication Networks. In D. J. Songhurst (ed), *Charging Communication Networks*, chapter 1, pp. 1–22. Elsevier, Amsterdam, 1999.

[224] Songhurst, D. J. et al. Open Issues. In D. J. Songhurst (ed), *Charging Communication Networks*, chapter 6, pp. 149–166. Elsevier, Amsterdam, 1999.

[225] Songhurst, D. J. and F. Kelly. The abc Scheme. In *Charging Communication Networks*, chapter 2, pp. 23–36. Elsevier, Amsterdam, 1999.

[226] Stahl, D. O. Congestion Pricing More Profitable than AOL Pricing. Center for Research in Electronic Commerce, University of Texas, Austin, Texas, 1997.

[227] Stahl, D. O. A Critical Survey of Internet Pricing Proposals. In A. Dumont and J. Dryden (eds), *The Economics of the Information Society*, pp. 142–154. Office for Official Publications of the European Communities, Luxembourg, 1997.

[228] Stahl, D. O. The Inefficiency of First and Second Price Auctions in Dynamic Stochastic Environments. *Netnomics*, 4(1): 1–18, March 2002.

[229] Staubli, R. Gute Chancen für den Erfolg von Richtfunk. Die WLL-Technologie als Alternative zu Mietleitungen. *Neue Zürcher Zeitung*, (122): B25, May 21 2001.

[230] Steiner, P. O. Peak Loads and Efficient Pricing. *Quarterly Journal of Economics*, 71(4): 585–610, November 1957.

[231] Stiller, B. et al. The Cumulus Pricing Scheme and its Integration into a Generic and Modular Internet Charging System for Differentiated Services. TIK-Report 96, Swiss Federal Institute of Technology, Zurich, Switzerland, September 2000.

[232] Stiller, B., G. Fankhauser, and B. Plattner. Charging of Multimedia Flows in an Integrated Services Network. 8th International Workshop on Network and Operating Systems Support for Digital Audio and Video (NOSSDAV'98), Cambridge, England, July 1998.

[233] Stiller, B., P. Reichl, and S. Leinen. Pricing and Cost Recovery for Internet Services: Practical Review, Classification, and Application of Relevant Models. *Netnomics*, 3(1): 149–171, March 2001.

[234] Stremersch, S. and G. J. Tellis. Strategic Bundling of Products and Prices: A New Synthesis for Marketing. *Journal of Marketing*, 66(1): 55–72, January 2002.

[235] Takahashi, E. and Y. Tanaka. Bandwidth Allocation by Using Generalized Vickrey Auction. In *4th Asia-Pacific Symposium on Information and Telecommunication Technologies (APSITT 2001)*, pp. 233–237, Kathmandu/Nepal, Atami/Japan, November 5–8 2001.

[236] Tektronix. QoS in the IP Network: Definitions, Processes and Initiatives. White paper, Tektronix, 2001.

[237] TeleGeography. *Hubs and Spokes: A Telegeography Internet Reader*. Washington D.C., 2000.

[238] Thomas, R. Phone Bundling: Why the Buzz? *ACA (A Current Affair) Online Stories*, May 23 2003.

[239] Tirole, J. *The Theory of Industrial Organization*. MIT Press, Cambridge/Mass., London/England, 12th edition, 2001.

[240] Toutain, F. and O. Huber. A General Preemption-Based Admission Policy Using a Smart Market Approach. In *Proceedings of IEEE INFOCOM'96*, volume 2, pp. 794–801, IEEE Computer Society Press, San Francisco, California, March 24–28 1996.

[241] Tuffin, B. Revisited Progressive Second Price Auction for Charging Telecommunication Networks. *Telecommunication Systems*, 20(3-4): 255–263, 2002.

[242] Vahldiek, A. Highspeed für alle. Alternativen zu T-DSL. *c't magazin für computer technik*, (13): 110–115, 2001.

[243] Varian, H. R. Price Discrimination. In R. Schmalensee and R. D. Willig (eds), *Handbook of Industrial Organization*, volume 1, chapter 10, pp. 597–654. Elsevier, Amsterdam, 1989.

[244] Varian, H. R. Economic Mechanism Design for Computerized Agents. In *First USENIX Workshop on Electronic Commerce*, pp. 13–21, New York, New York, July 11–12 1995.

[245] Varian, H. R. Pricing Information Goods. In Research Libraries Group (ed), *Proceedings of the Symposium on Scholarship of the New Information Environment*, Harvard Law School, Cambridge/Mass., 1995.

[246] Varian, H. R. Estimating the Demand for Bandwidth. Technical report, University of California, Berkeley, California, August 1999, revised August 2000.

[247] Vickrey, W. Counterspeculation, Auctions, and Competitive Sealed Tenders. *Journal of Finance*, 16(1): 8–37, March 1961.

[248] Villasis, S. J. An Optimal Pricing Mechanism for Internet's End-Users. M. S. in Economics, University of Idaho, Moscow, Idaho, May 1996.

[249] Wang, Q., J. M. Peha, and M. A. Sirbu. Optimal Pricing for Integrated Services Networks. In L. W. McKnight and J. P. Bailey (eds), *Internet Economics*, pp. 353–376. MIT Press, Cambridge/Mass., London/England, 1997.

[250] Wang, X. and H. Schulzrinne. RNAP: A Resource Negotiation and Pricing Protocol. In *International Workshop on Network and Operating Systems Support for Digital Audio and Video (NOSSDAV'99)*, pp. 77–93, Basking Ridge, New Jersey, June 23–25 1999.

[251] Wang, X. and H. Schulzrinne. Performance Study of Congestion Price Based Adaptive Service. In *Proceedings of International Workshop on Network and Operation System Support for Digital Audio and Video (NOSSDAV'00)*, pp. 1–10, Chapel Hill, North Carolina, June 26–28 2000.

[252] Wang, X. and H. Schulzrinne. Pricing Network Resources for Adaptive Applications in a Differentiated Services Network. In *Proceedings of IEEE INFOCOM' 2001*, pp. 943–952, Anchorage, Alaska, April 22–26 2001.

[253] Weinberg, N. Backbone Bullies. *Forbes.com*, June 12 2000.

[254] Weiss, M. and S. Shin. Internet Interconnection Economic Model and its Analysis: Peering and Settlement. 17th World Computer Congress, Montreal, Canada, August 2002.

[255] Willig, R. D. Pareto-Superior Nonlinear Outlay Schedules. *Bell Journal of Economics*, 9(1): 56–69, Spring 1978.

[256] Wilson, R. *Nonlinear Pricing.* Oxford University Press, New York, Oxford, 1993.

[257] Wolfstetter, E. *Topics in Microeconomics – Industrial Organization, Auctions, and Incentives.* Cambridge University Press, Cambridge, 1999.

[258] Wright, J. Terminating Calls to Internet Service Providers. Department of Economics, University of Auckland, New Zealand, June 2001.

[259] Wurman, P. R., W. E. Walsh, and M. P. Wellman. Flexible Double Auctions for Electronic Commerce: Theory and Implementation. *Decision Support Systems*, 24(1): 17–27, November 1998.

URLs (Universal Resource Locators)

ACA Online Stories
http://aca.ninemsn.com.au/stories/default.asp (26.11.03)

Boardwatch
http://www.boardwatch.com (26.11.03)

CIENA Corporation Glossary
http://www.ciena.com/resources/resources_glossary.htm (26.11.03)

CNET News.com
http://news.com.com/ (26.11.03)

e-paranoids.com
www.e-paranoids.com/b/bi/binary_prefix.html (15.01.05)

Fedgazette
http://minneapolisfed.org/pubs/fedgaz/ (26.11.03)

Forbes.com
http://www.forbes.com (26.11.03)

Information Technology Glossary
http://www.itglossary.net/browser.html (24.02.04)

Internet Architecture Board
http://www.iab.org/iab/ (26.11.03)

ISP-LISTS
http://isp-lists.isp-planet.com (26.11.03)

M3I Market Managed Multiservice Internet
http://www.m3i.org (26.11.03)

Network Magazine
http://www.networkmagazine.com (26.11.03)

Swisscom Mobile GPRS
http://www.swisscom-mobile.ch/gprs (26.11.03)

Tagesanzeiger.ch
http://www.tages-anzeiger.ch (26.11.03)

Telephony Online
http://www.telephonyonline.com (26.11.03)

Index

www.ingramcontent.com/pod-product-compliance
Ingram Content Group UK Ltd.
Pitfield, Milton Keynes, MK11 3LW, UK
UKHW021012120926
8556IPUK00039B/1073